ROMEO AND JULIET

ADAPTED BY
RICHARD APPIGNANESI

ILLUSTRATED BY
SONIA LEONG

SELF
MADE
HERO

Published by
SelfMadeHero
139–141 Pancras Road
London NW1 1UN
www.selfmadehero.com

This edition printed in 2014

First published in 2007

Illustrator: Sonia Leong
Text Adaptor: Richard Appignanesi
Designer: Andy Huckle
Textual Consultant: Nick de Somogyi
Publisher: Emma Hayley

ISBN-13: 978-0-9552856-0-8

10 11 12 13 14 15 16 17 18 19 20
Printed and bound in China

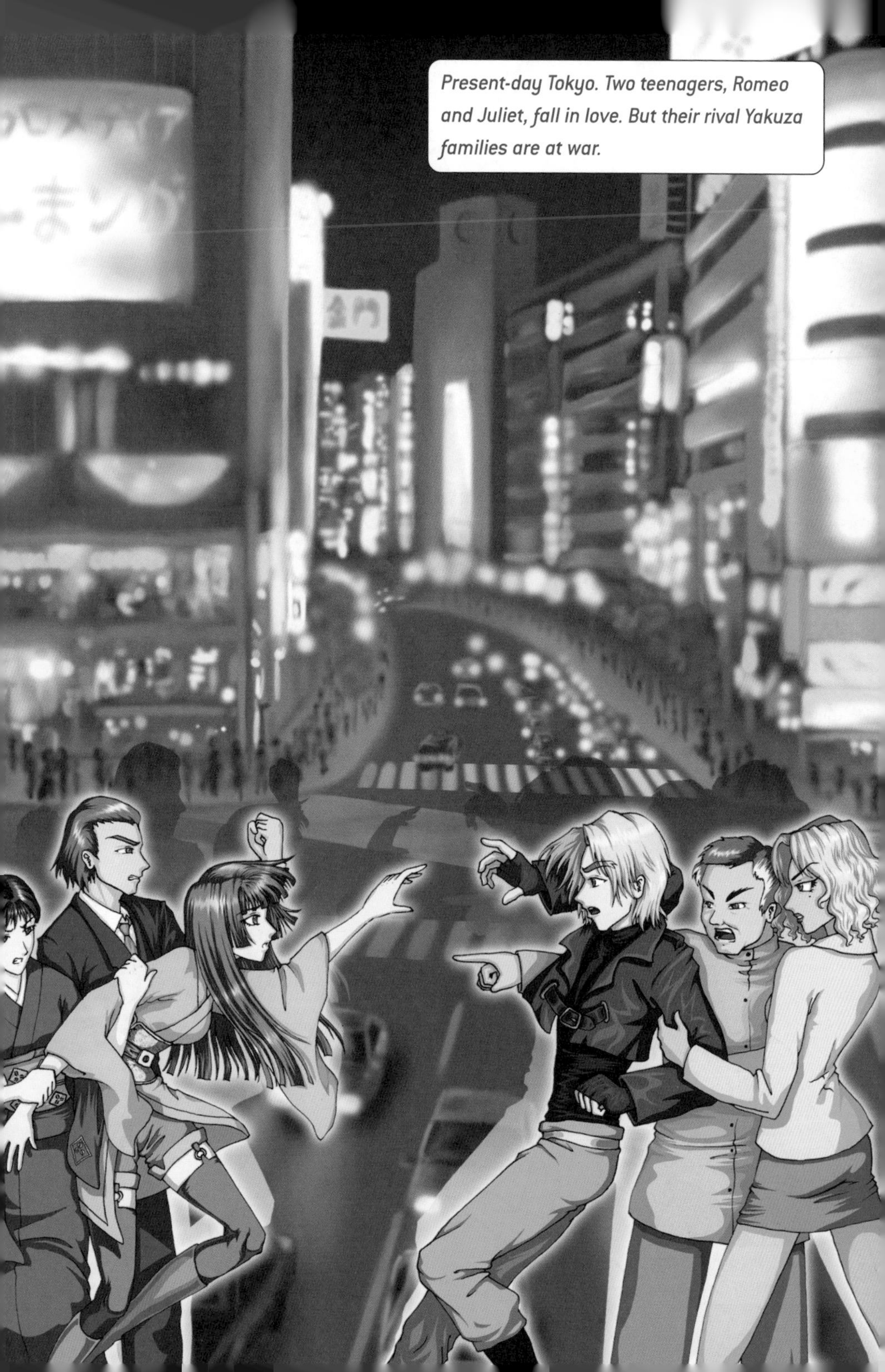
Present-day Tokyo. Two teenagers, Romeo and Juliet, fall in love. But their rival Yakuza families are at war.

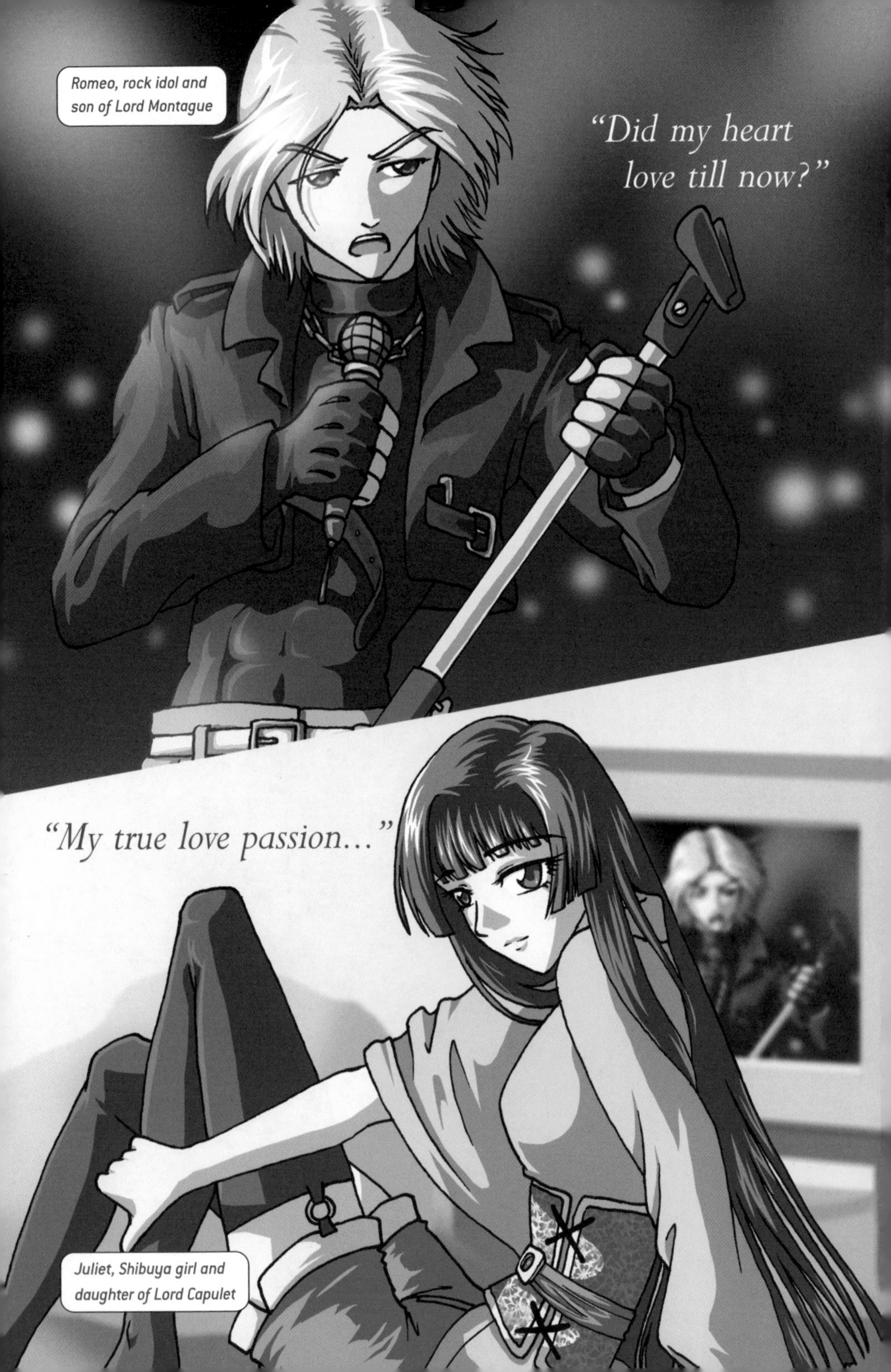
Romeo, rock idol and son of Lord Montague
"Did my heart love till now?"
"My true love passion..."
Juliet, Shibuya girl and daughter of Lord Capulet

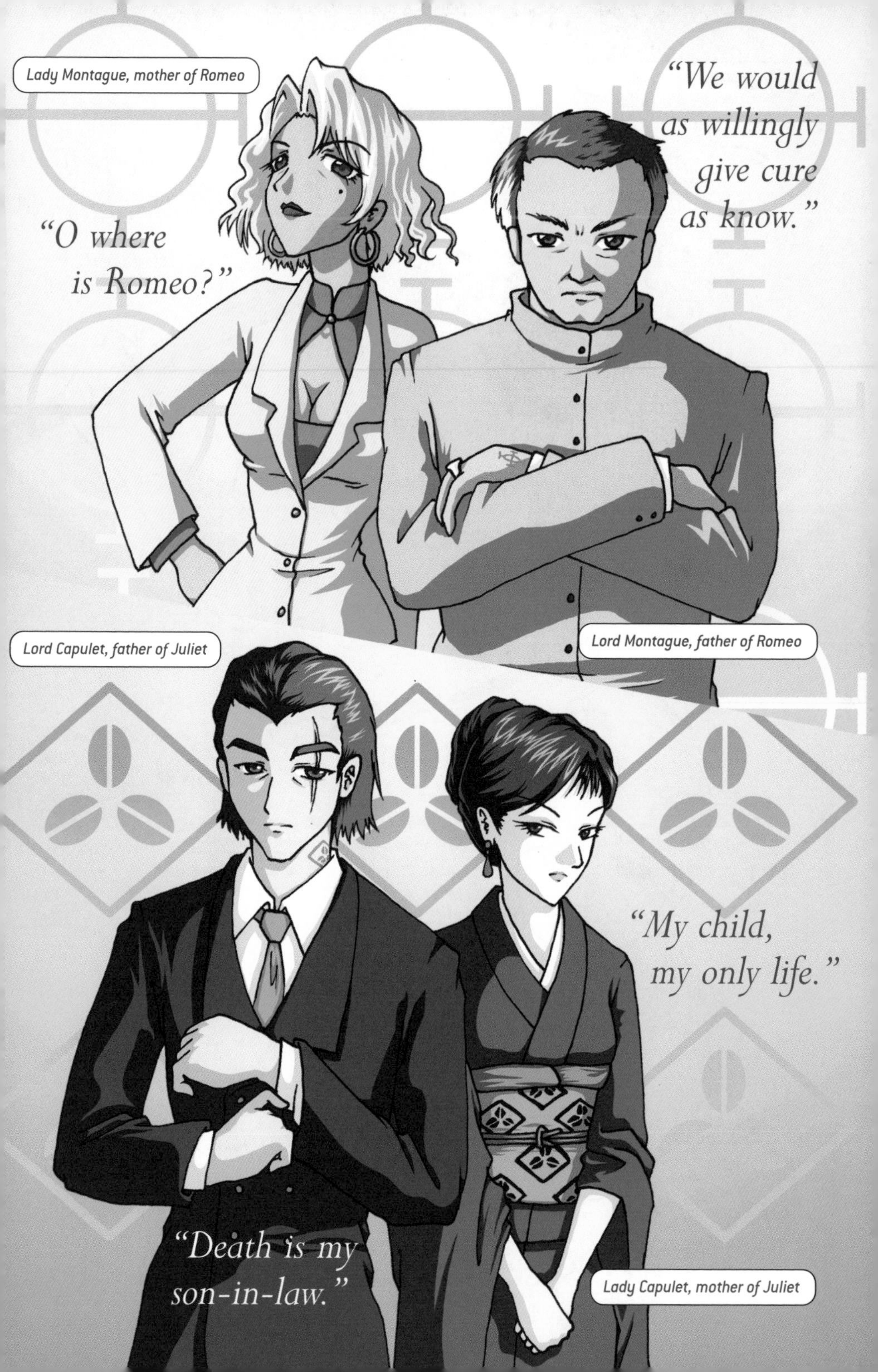
Lady Montague, mother of Romeo
"O where is Romeo?"
"We would as willingly give cure as know."
Lord Montague, father of Romeo
Lord Capulet, father of Juliet
"Death is my son-in-law."
"My child, my only life."
Lady Capulet, mother of Juliet

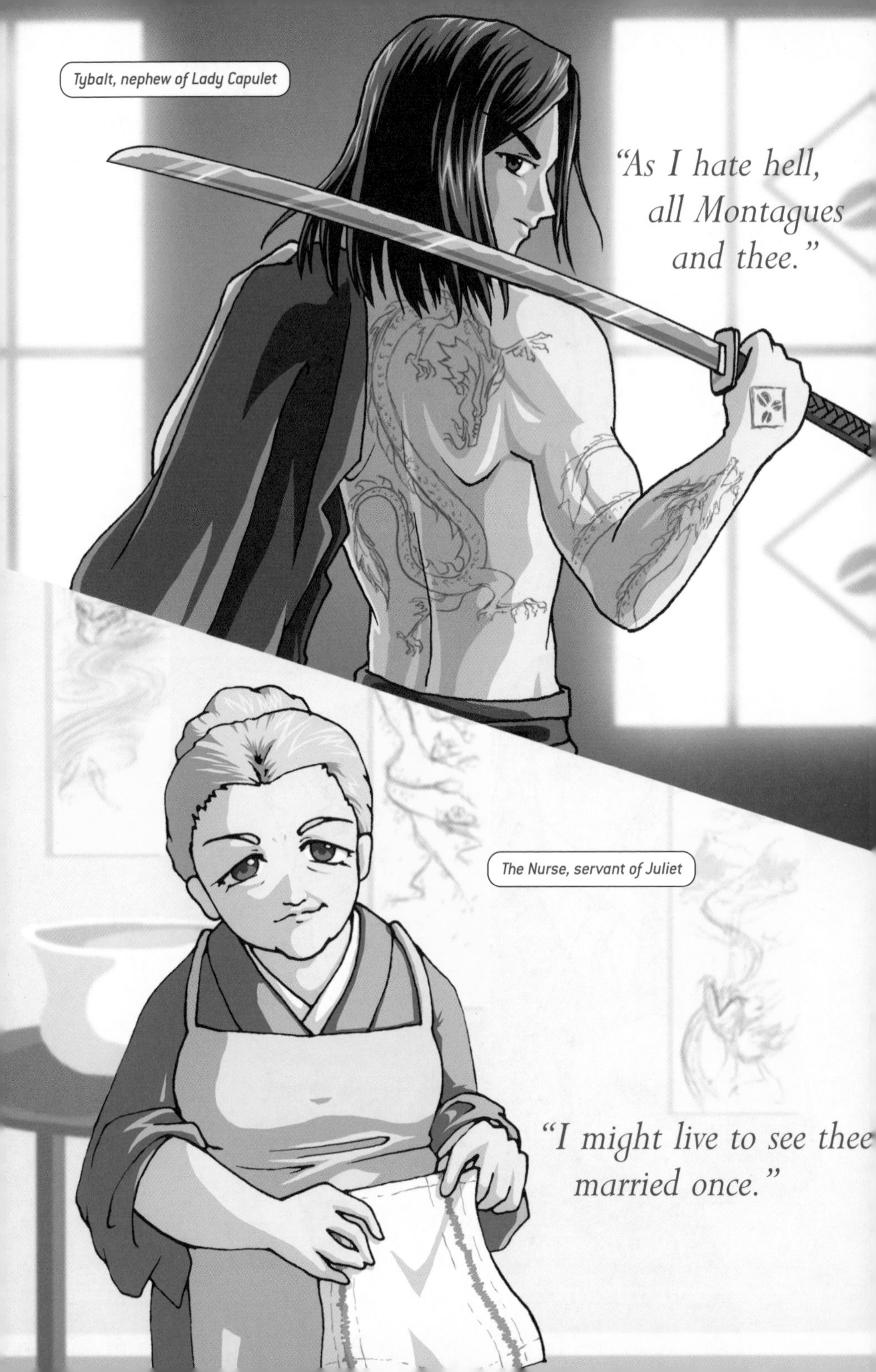
Tybalt, nephew of Lady Capulet
"As I hate hell, all Montagues and thee."
The Nurse, servant of Juliet
"I might live to see thee married once."

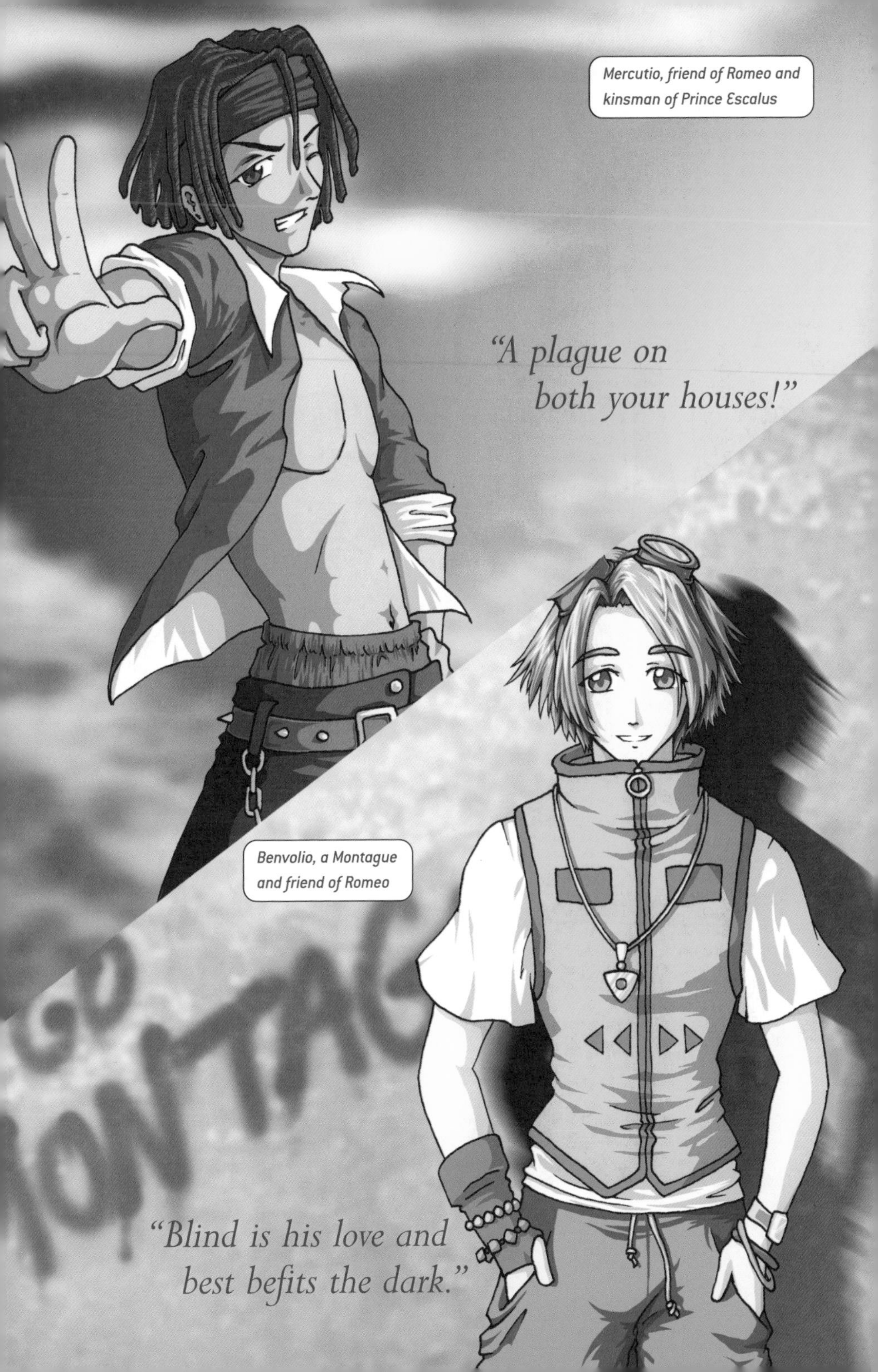
Mercutio, friend of Romeo and kinsman of Prince Escalus
"A plague on both your houses!"
Benvolio, a Montague and friend of Romeo
"Blind is his love and best befits the dark."

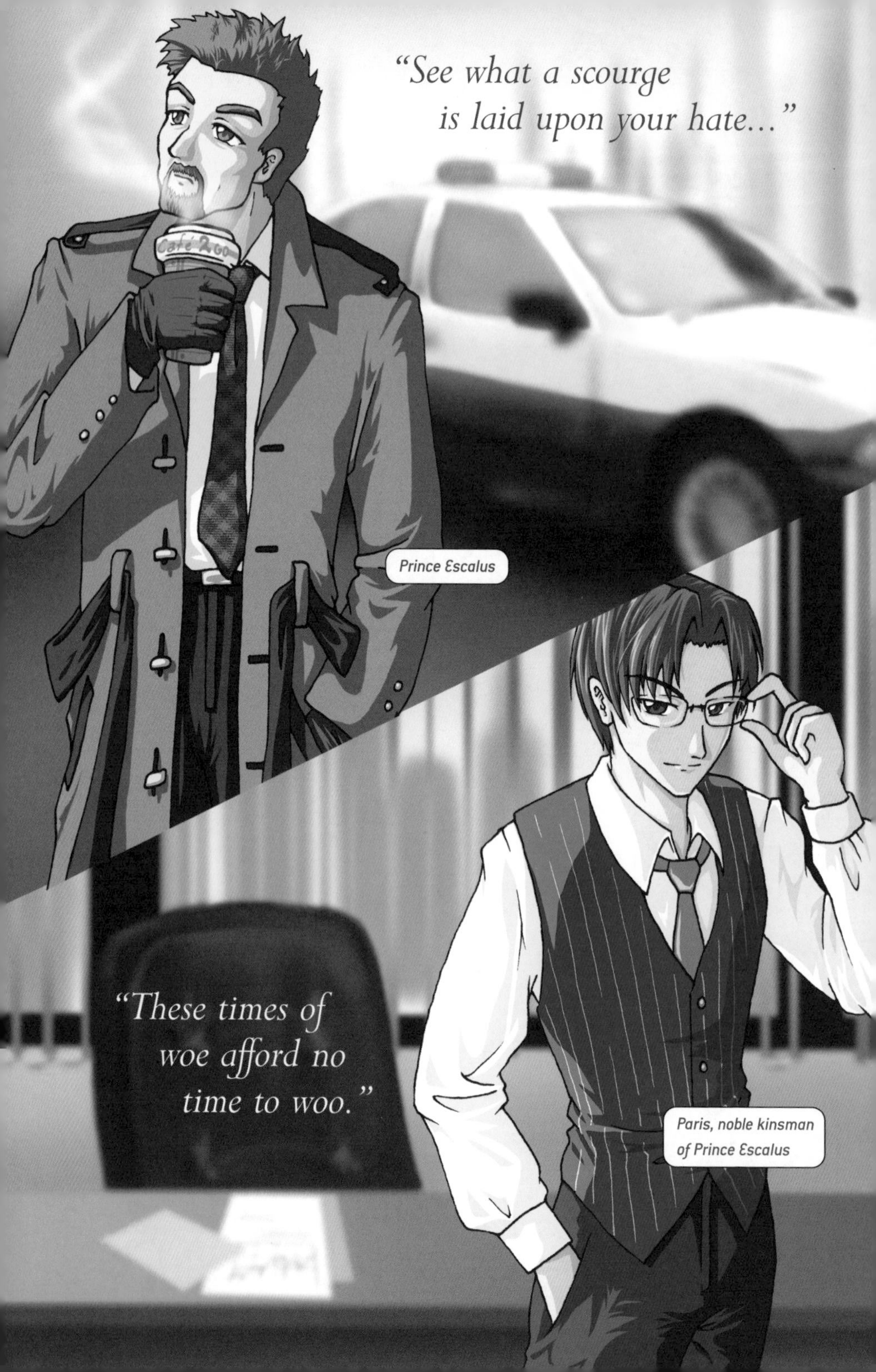
"See what a scourge is laid upon your hate..."
Cafe 2go
Prince Escalus
"These times of woe afford no time to woo."
Paris, noble kinsman of Prince Escalus

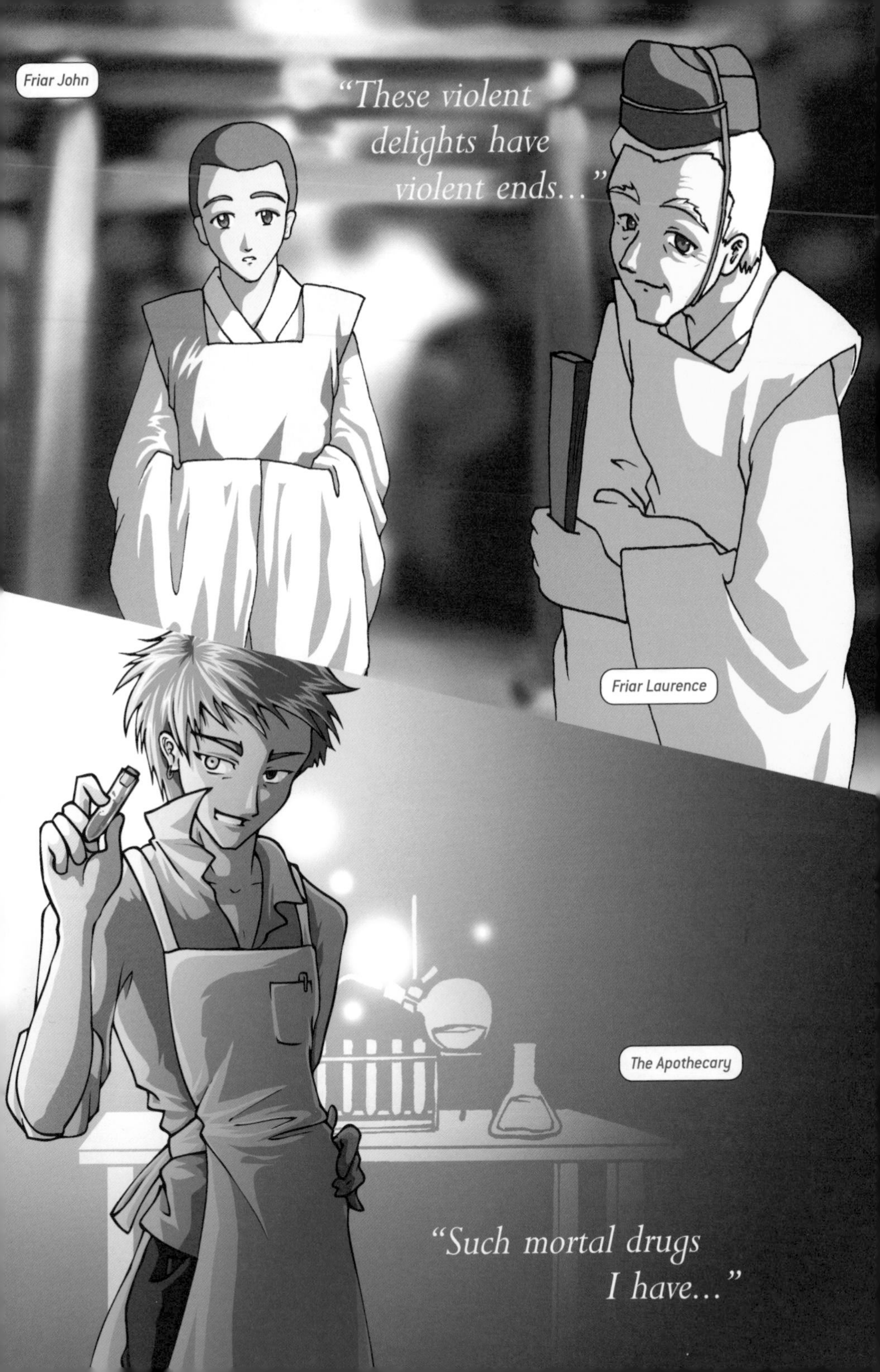
Friar John
"These violent delights have violent ends..."
Friar Laurence
The Apothecary
"Such mortal drugs I have..."

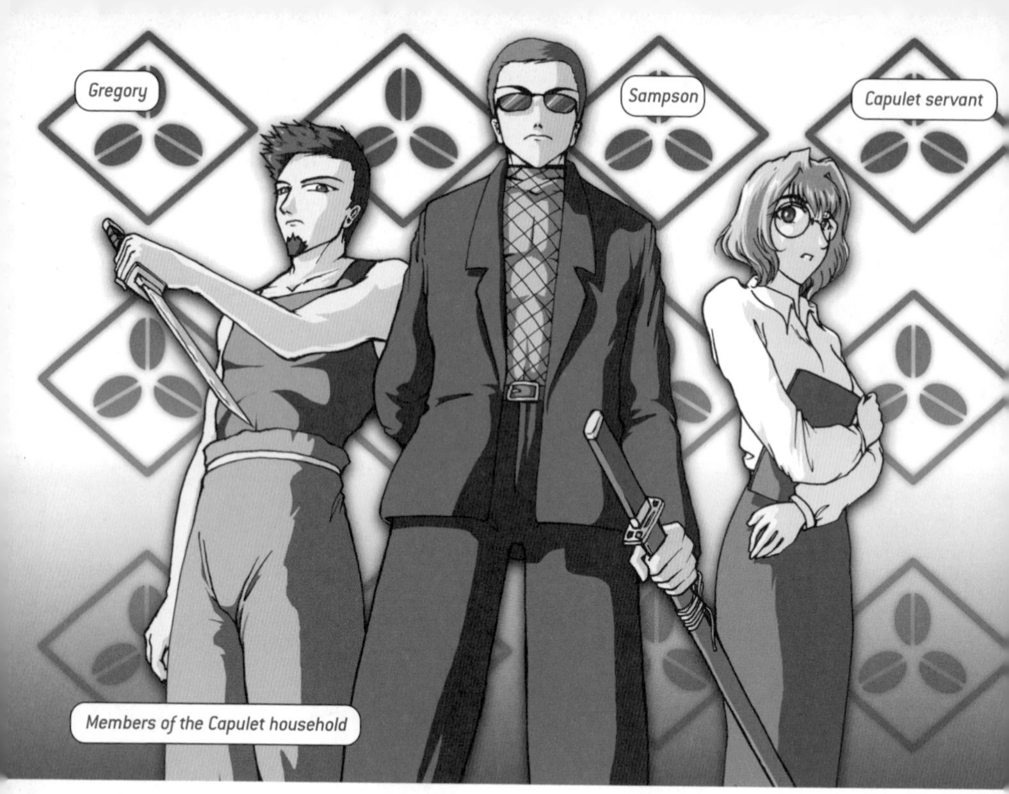
Gregory
Sampson
Capulet servant
Members of the Capulet household

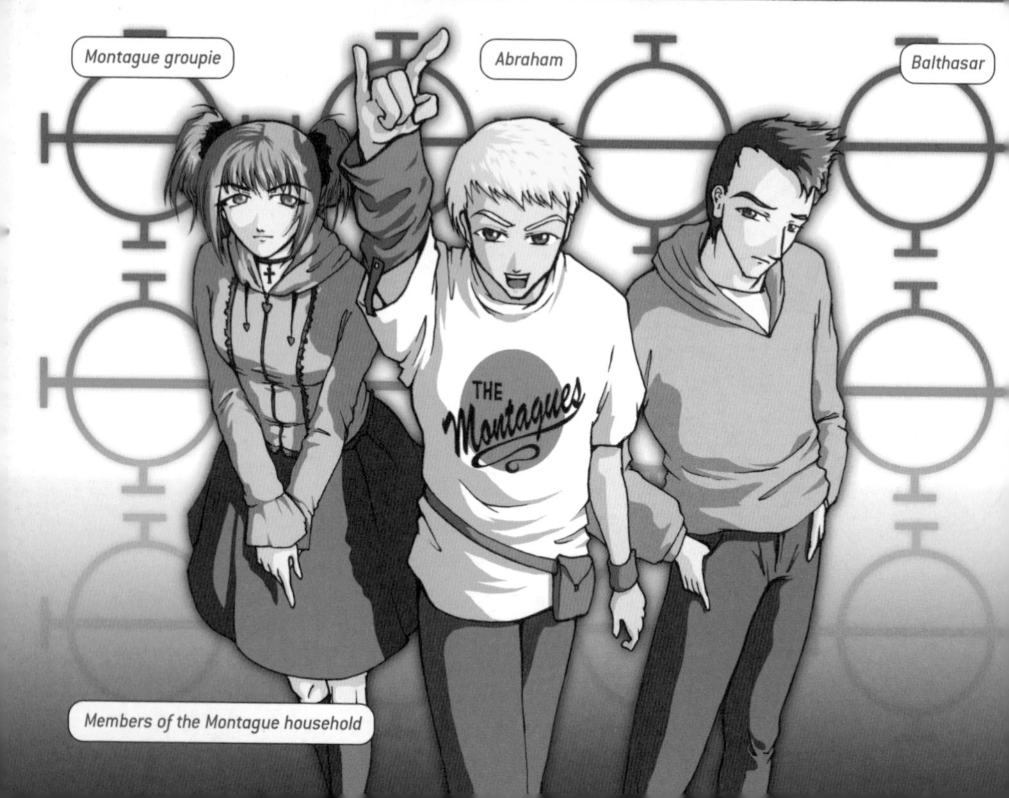
Montague groupie
Abraham
Balthasar
THE Montagues
Members of the Montague household

The Most Excellent and Lamentable Tragedy of

ROMEO AND JULIET

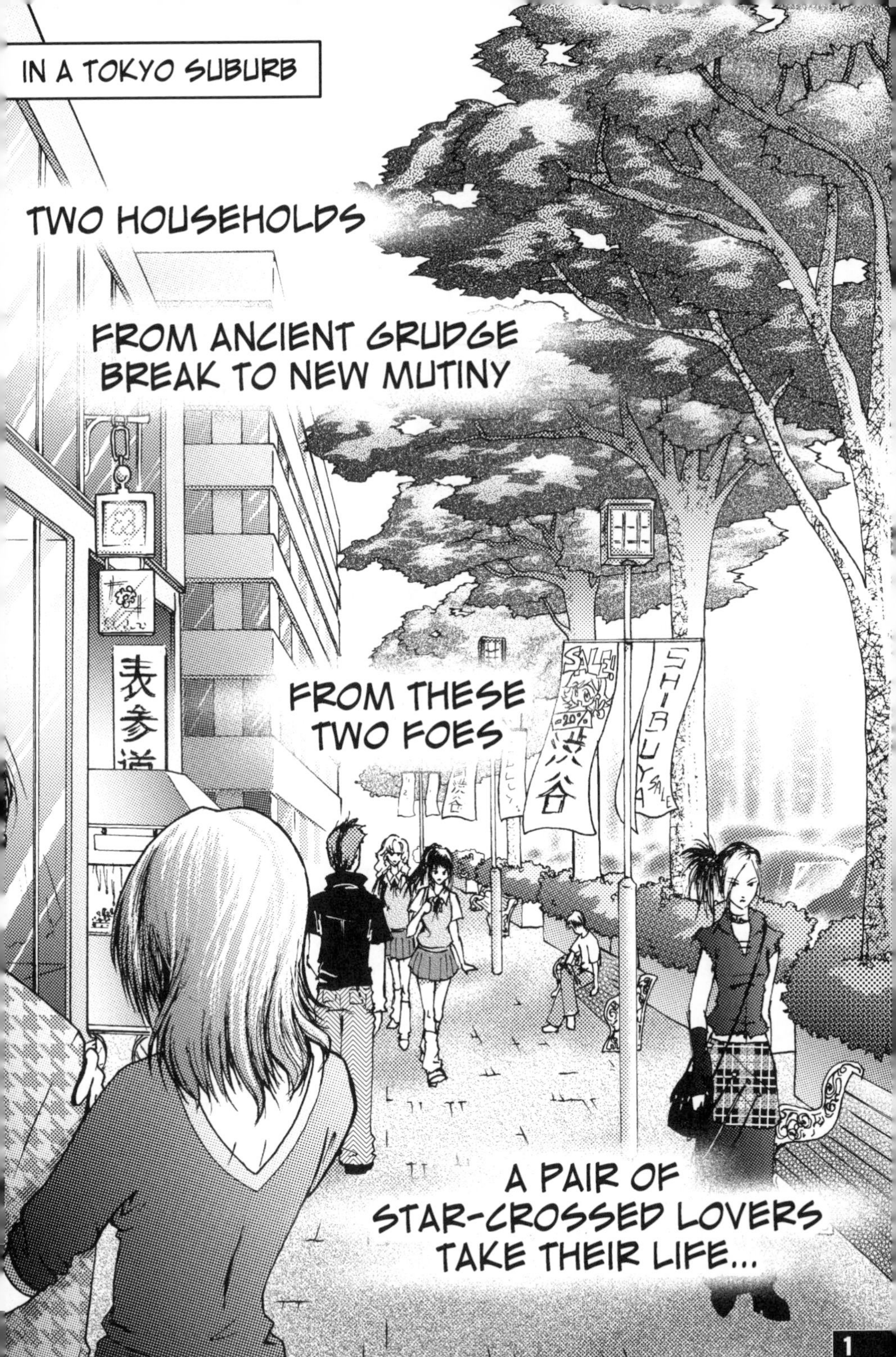
IN A TOKYO SUBURB
TWO HOUSEHOLDS
FROM ANCIENT GRUDGE BREAK TO NEW MUTINY
表参道
SALE!
-20%
渋谷
SHIBUYA
SALE
FROM THESE TWO FOES
A PAIR OF STAR-CROSSED LOVERS TAKE THEIR LIFE...

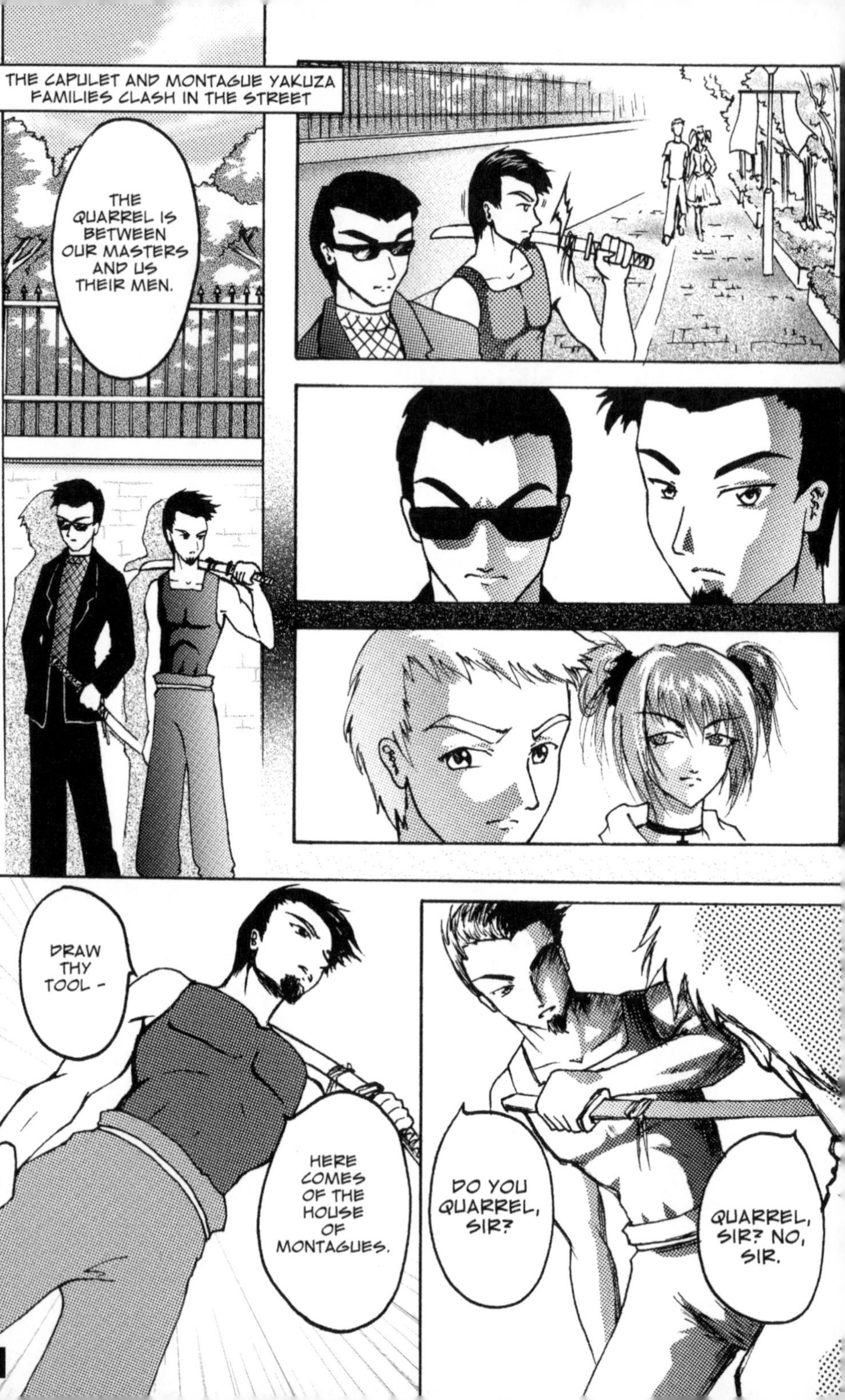
THE CAPULET AND MONTAGUE YAKUZA FAMILIES CLASH IN THE STREET
THE QUARREL IS BETWEEN OUR MASTERS AND US THEIR MEN.
DRAW THY TOOL -
HERE COMES OF THE HOUSE OF MONTAGUES.
DO YOU QUARREL, SIR?
QUARREL, SIR? NO, SIR.

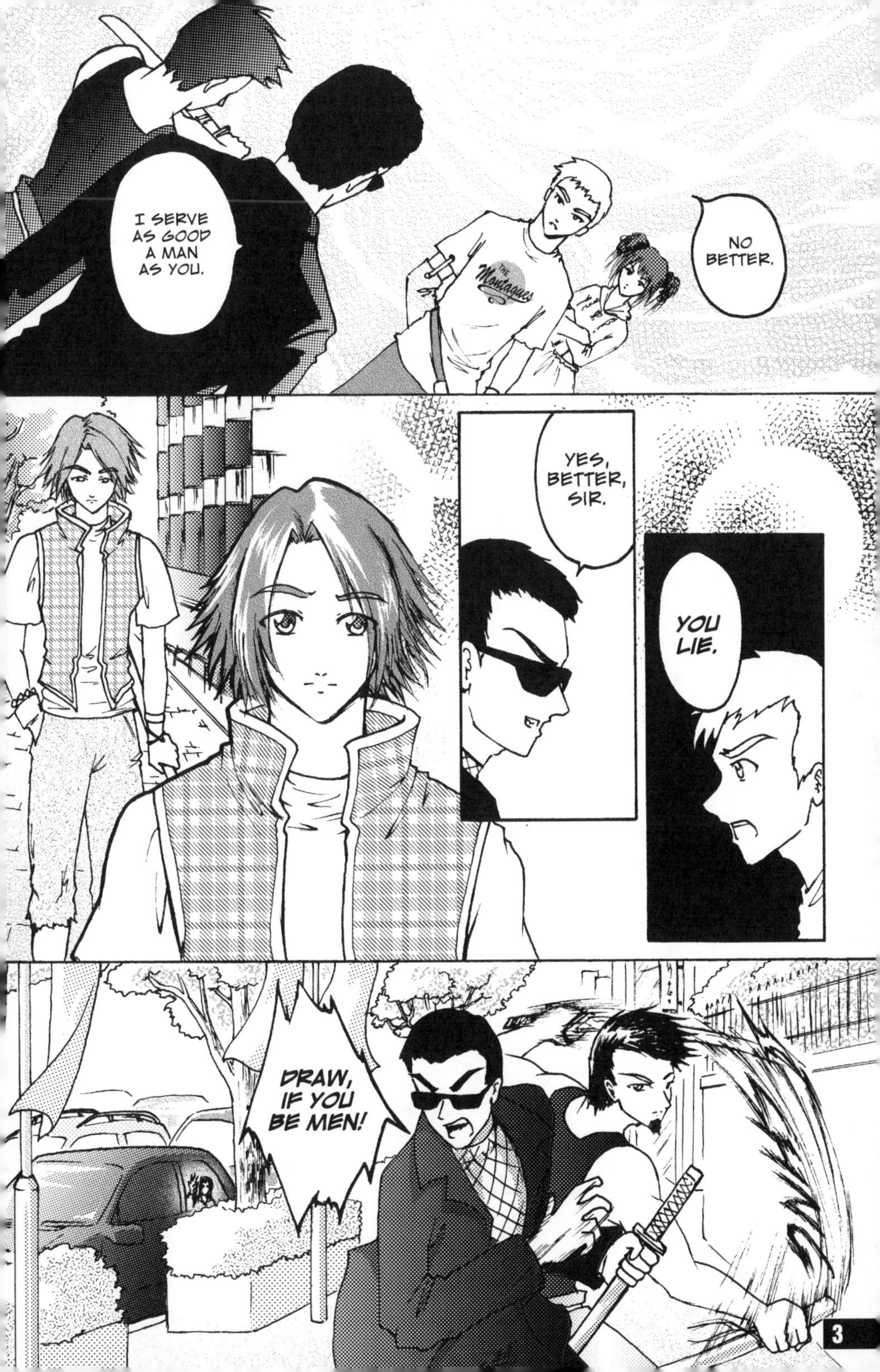
I SERVE AS GOOD A MAN AS YOU.
NO BETTER.
YES, BETTER, SIR.
YOU LIE.
DRAW, IF YOU BE MEN!
THE Montagues

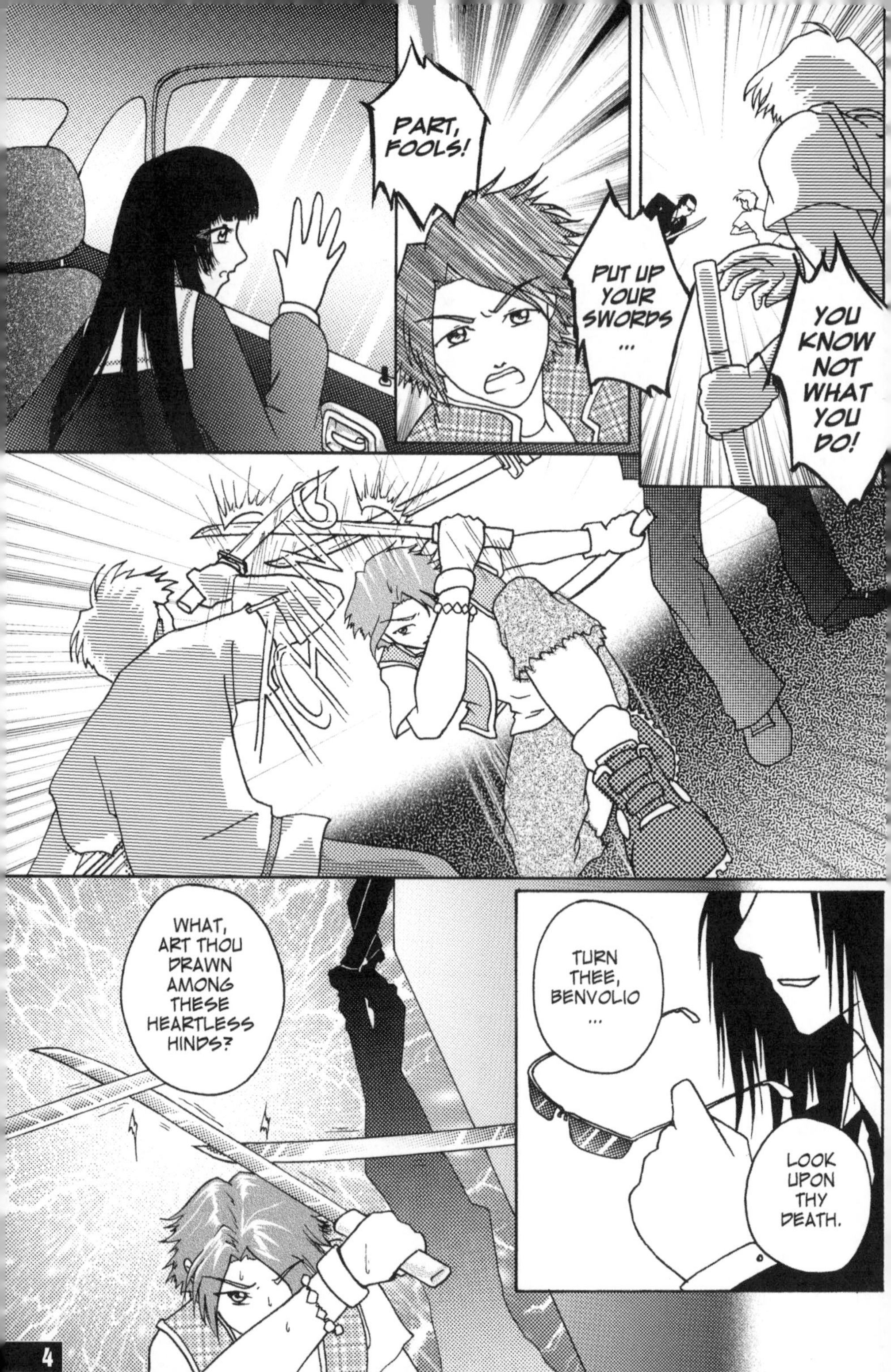
PART, FOOLS!
PUT UP YOUR SWORDS ...
YOU KNOW NOT WHAT YOU DO!
WHAT, ART THOU DRAWN AMONG THESE HEARTLESS HINDS?
TURN THEE, BENVOLIO ...
LOOK UPON THY DEATH.

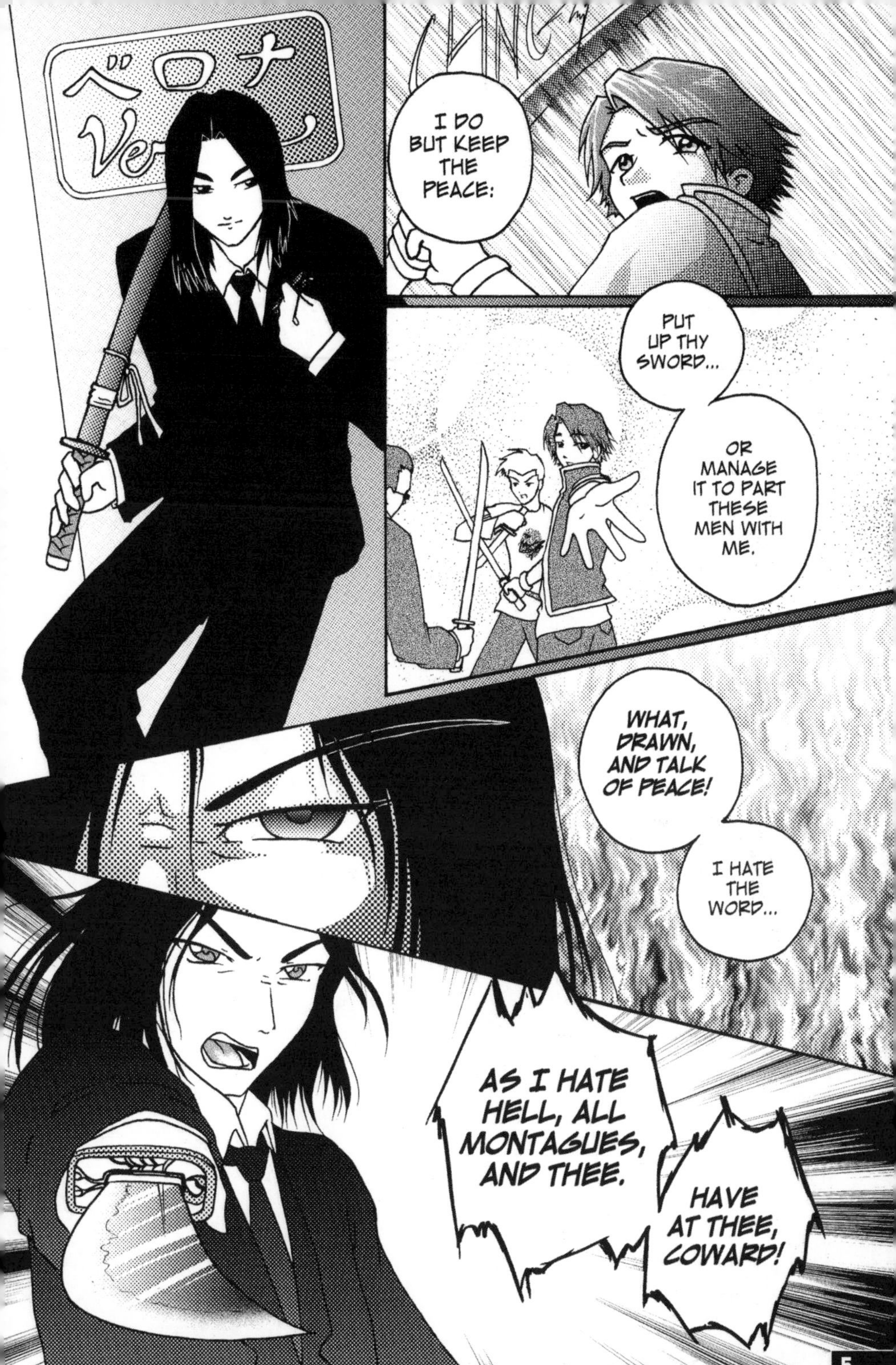

ベロナ
I DO BUT KEEP THE PEACE:
PUT UP THY SWORD...
OR MANAGE IT TO PART THESE MEN WITH ME.
WHAT, DRAWN, AND TALK OF PEACE!
I HATE THE WORD...
AS I HATE HELL, ALL MONTAGUES, AND THEE.
HAVE AT THEE, COWARD!

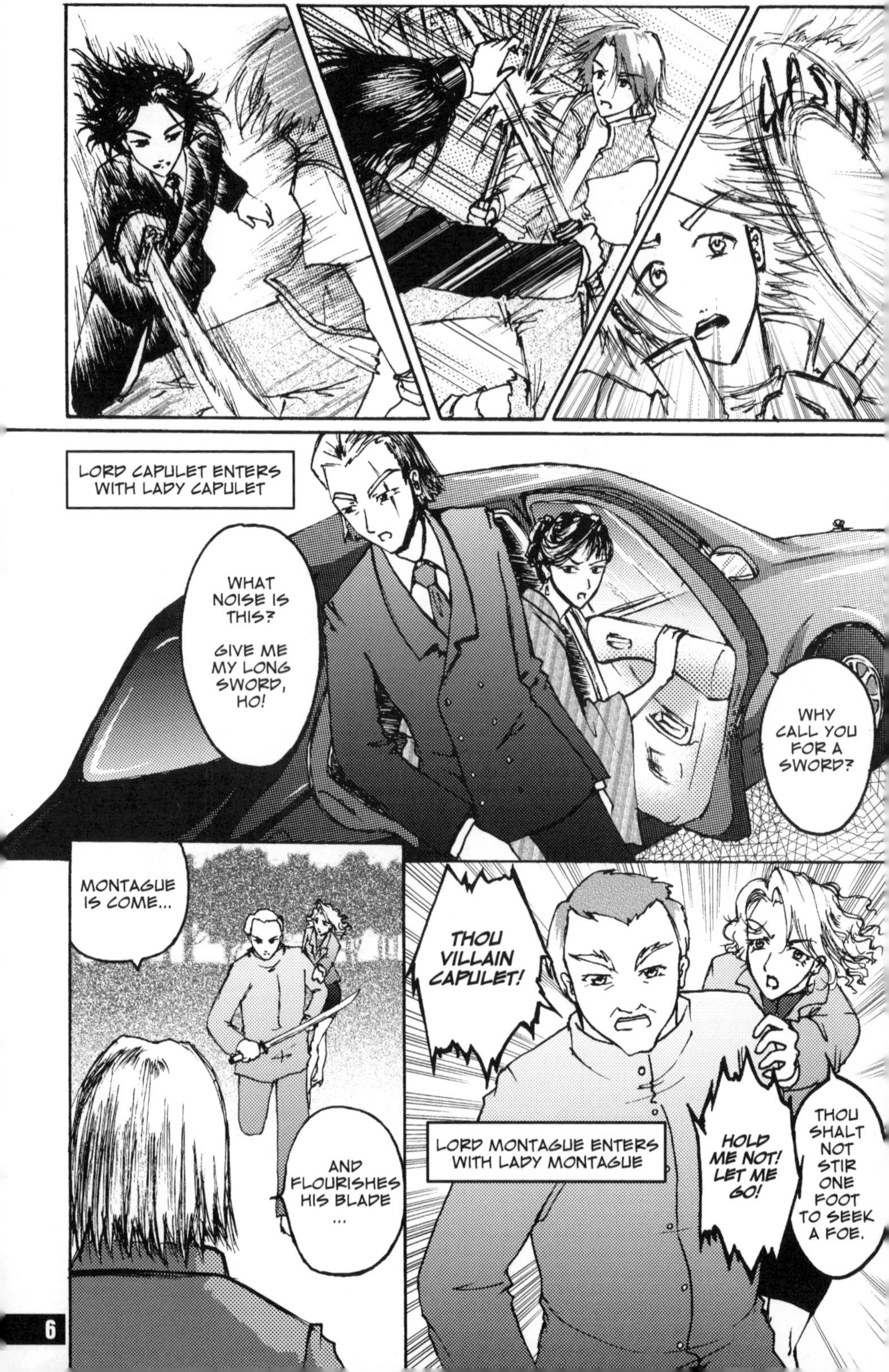

WASH!
LORD CAPULET ENTERS WITH LADY CAPULET
WHAT NOISE IS THIS? GIVE ME MY LONG SWORD, HO!
WHY CALL YOU FOR A SWORD?
MONTAGUE IS COME...
AND FLOURISHES HIS BLADE ...
THOU VILLAIN CAPULET!
LORD MONTAGUE ENTERS WITH LADY MONTAGUE
HOLD ME NOT! LET ME GO!
THOU SHALT NOT STIR ONE FOOT TO SEEK A FOE.

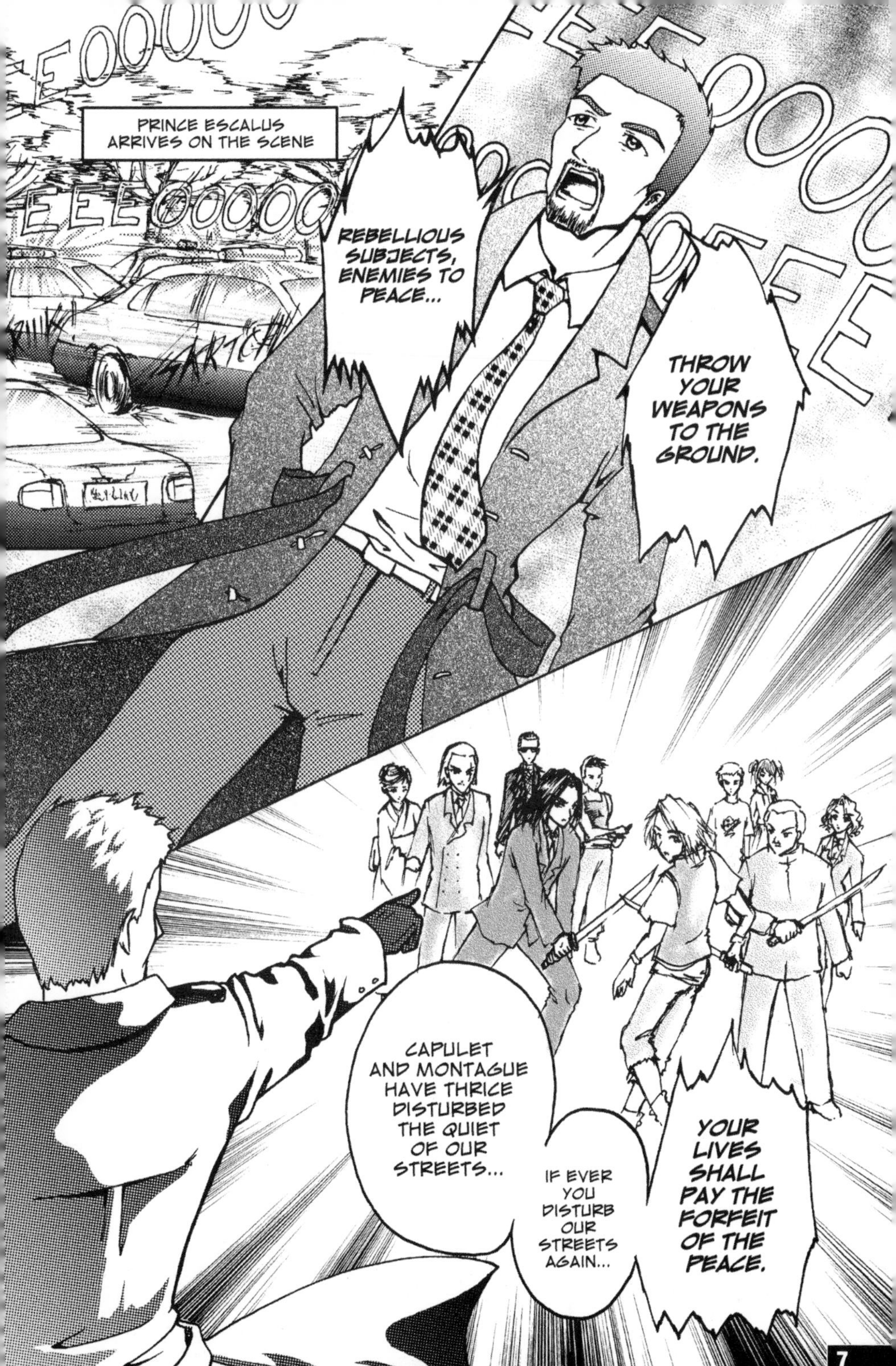
EEEOOOOO
PRINCE ESCALUS ARRIVES ON THE SCENE
EEEOOOOO
REBELLIOUS SUBJECTS, ENEMIES TO PEACE...
THROW YOUR WEAPONS TO THE GROUND.
CAPULET AND MONTAGUE HAVE THRICE DISTURBED THE QUIET OF OUR STREETS...
IF EVER YOU DISTURB OUR STREETS AGAIN...
YOUR LIVES SHALL PAY THE FORFEIT OF THE PEACE.

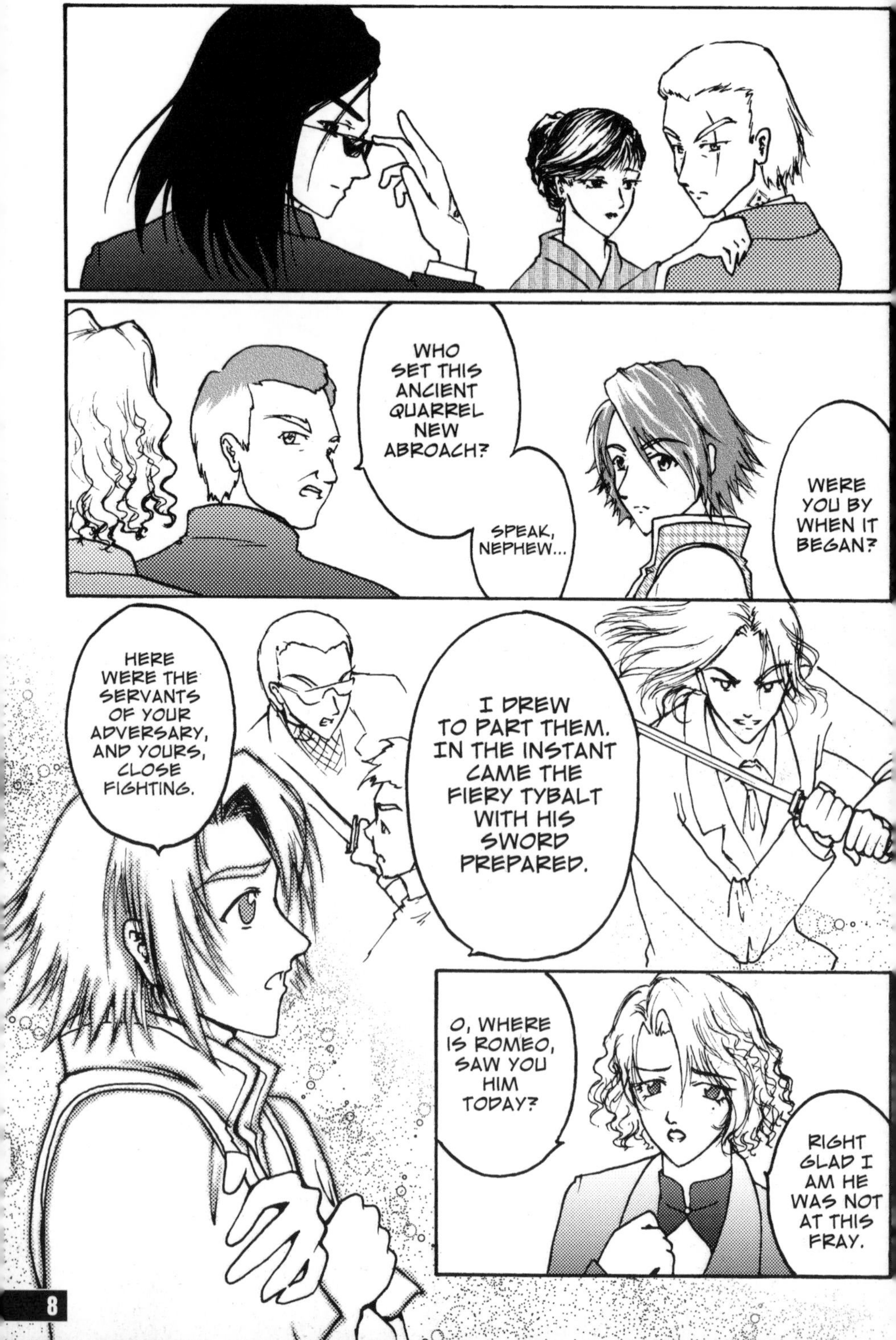
WHO SET THIS ANCIENT QUARREL NEW ABROACH?
SPEAK, NEPHEW...
WERE YOU BY WHEN IT BEGAN?
HERE WERE THE SERVANTS OF YOUR ADVERSARY, AND YOURS, CLOSE FIGHTING.
I DREW TO PART THEM. IN THE INSTANT CAME THE FIERY TYBALT WITH HIS SWORD PREPARED.
O, WHERE IS ROMEO, SAW YOU HIM TODAY?
RIGHT GLAD I AM HE WAS NOT AT THIS FRAY.

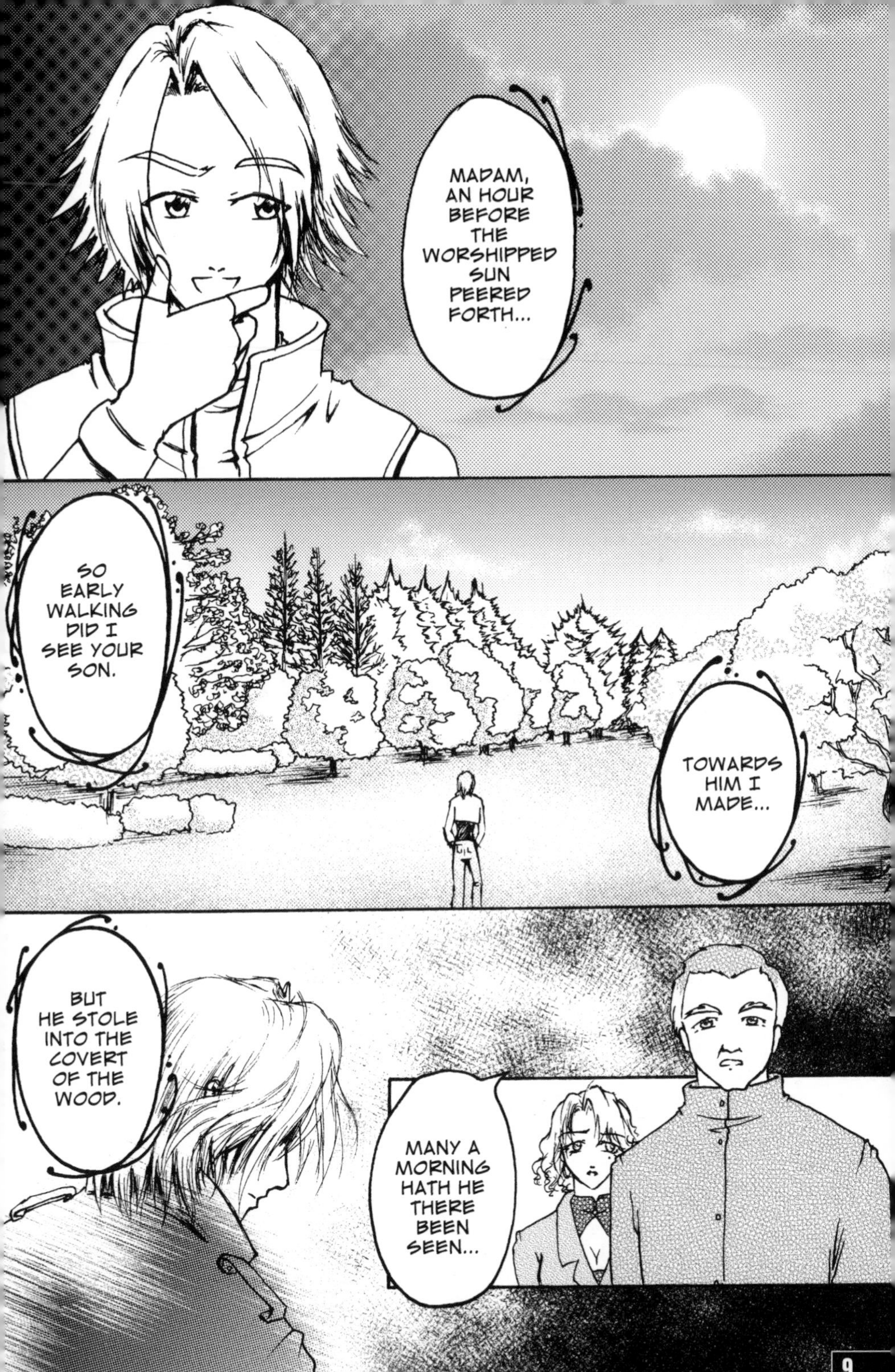
MADAM, AN HOUR BEFORE THE WORSHIPPED SUN PEERED FORTH...
SO EARLY WALKING DID I SEE YOUR SON.
TOWARDS HIM I MADE...
BUT HE STOLE INTO THE COVERT OF THE WOOD.
MANY A MORNING HATH HE THERE BEEN SEEN...

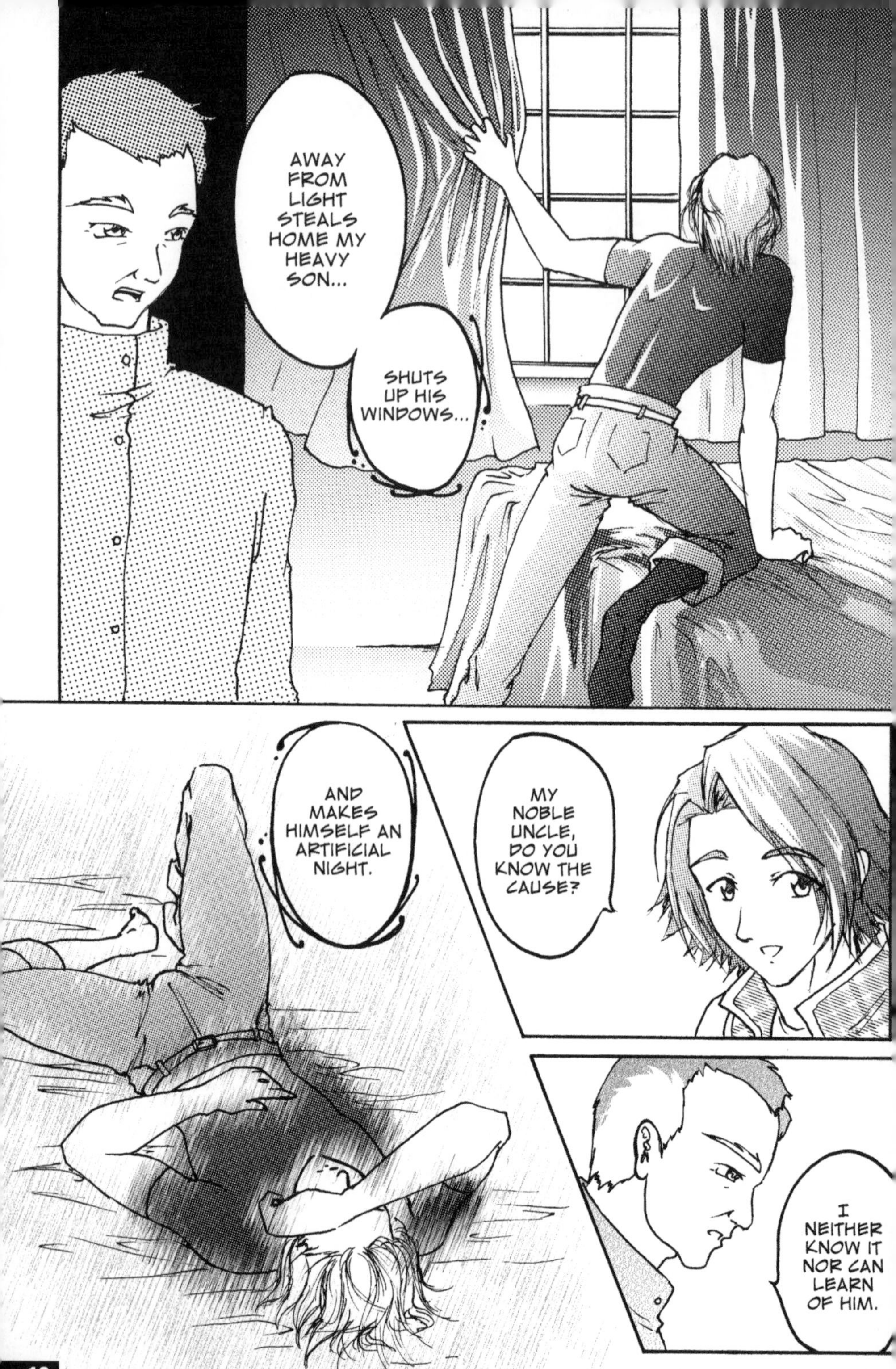
AWAY FROM LIGHT STEALS HOME MY HEAVY SON...
SHUTS UP HIS WINDOWS...
AND MAKES HIMSELF AN ARTIFICIAL NIGHT.
MY NOBLE UNCLE, DO YOU KNOW THE CAUSE?
I NEITHER KNOW IT NOR CAN LEARN OF HIM.

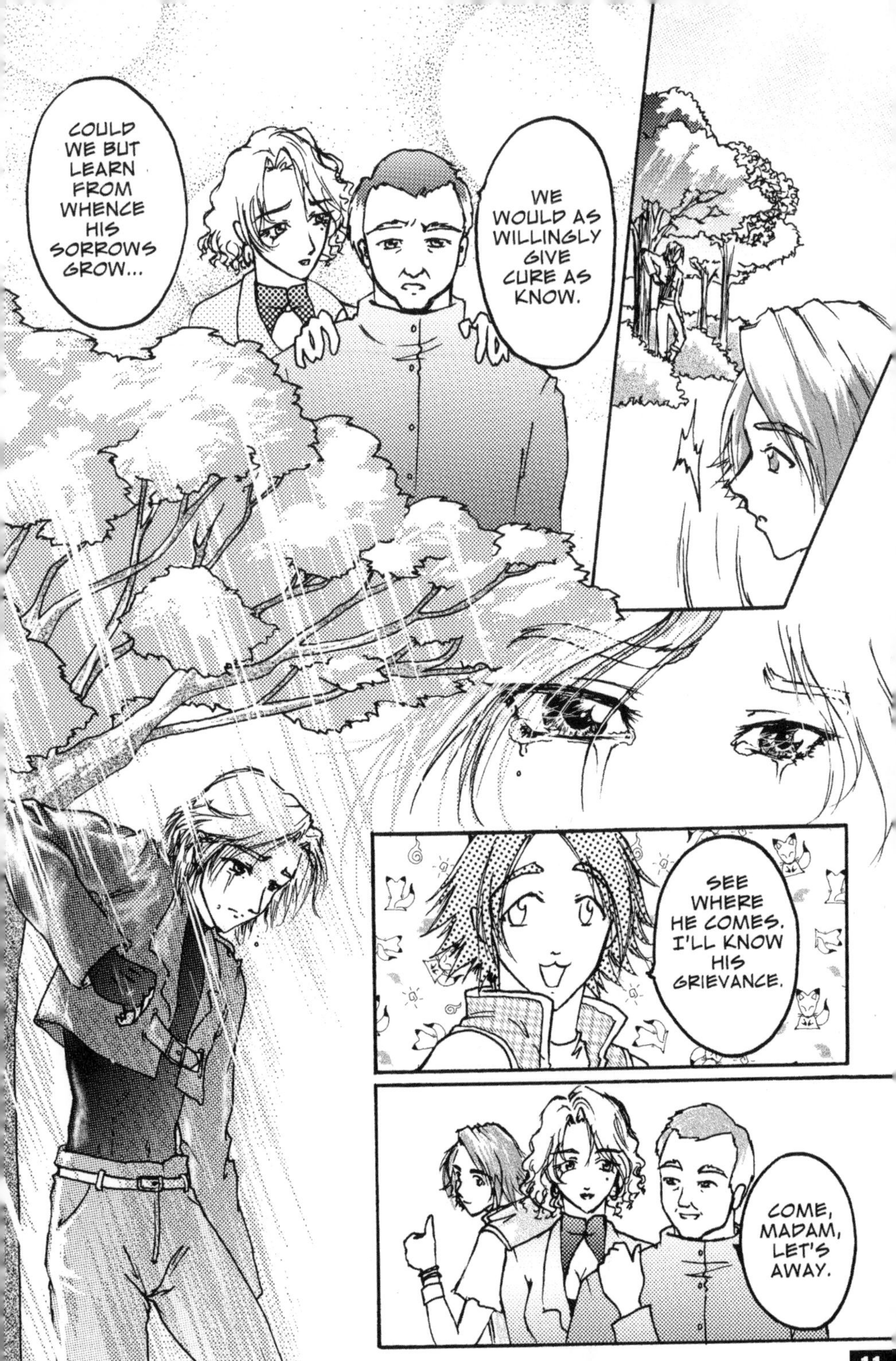

COULD WE BUT LEARN FROM WHENCE HIS SORROWS GROW...
WE WOULD AS WILLINGLY GIVE CURE AS KNOW.
SEE WHERE HE COMES. I'LL KNOW HIS GRIEVANCE.
COME, MADAM, LET'S AWAY.

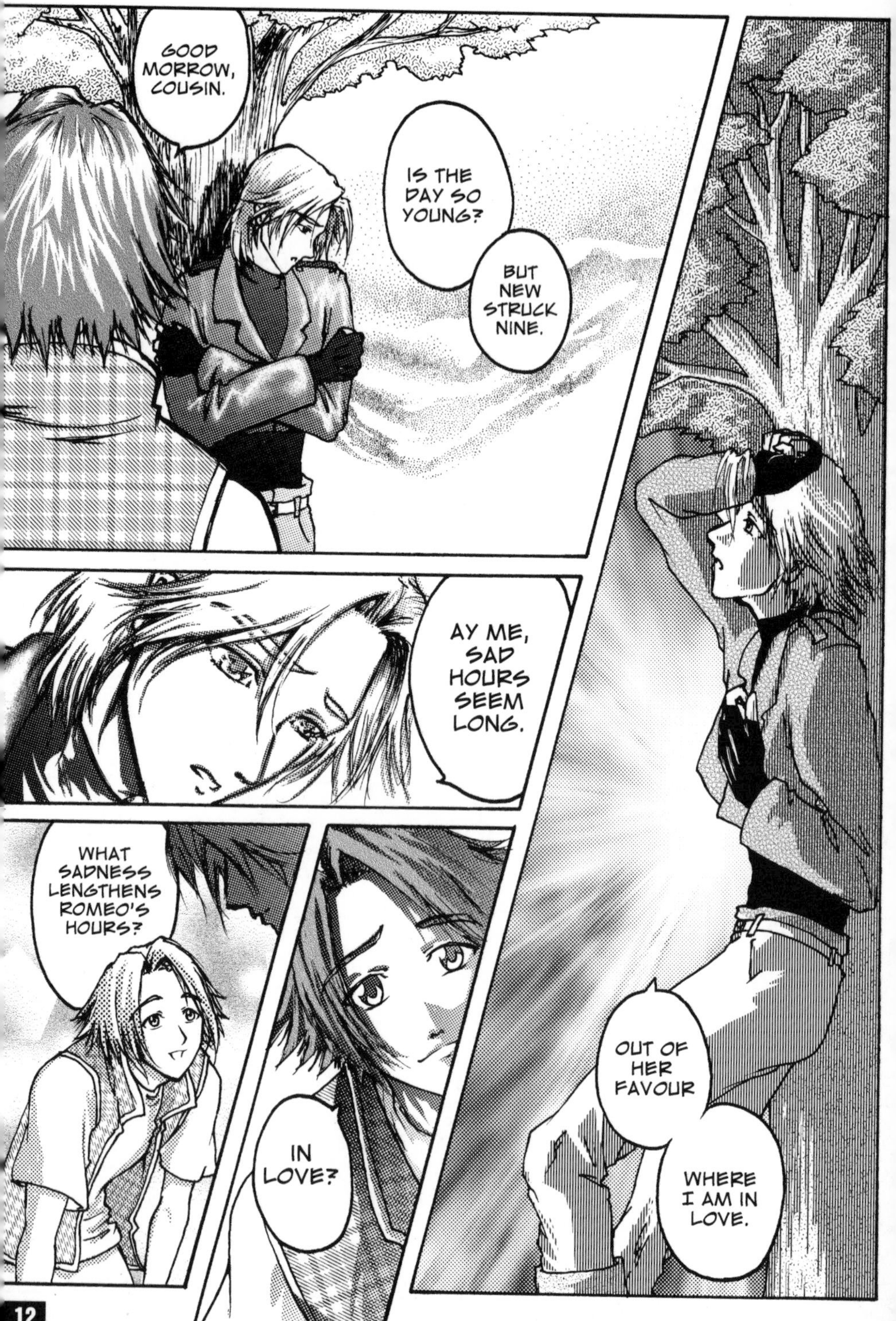

GOOD MORROW, COUSIN.
IS THE DAY SO YOUNG?
BUT NEW STRUCK NINE.
AY ME, SAD HOURS SEEM LONG.
WHAT SADNESS LENGTHENS ROMEO'S HOURS?
IN LOVE?
OUT OF HER FAVOUR
WHERE I AM IN LOVE.

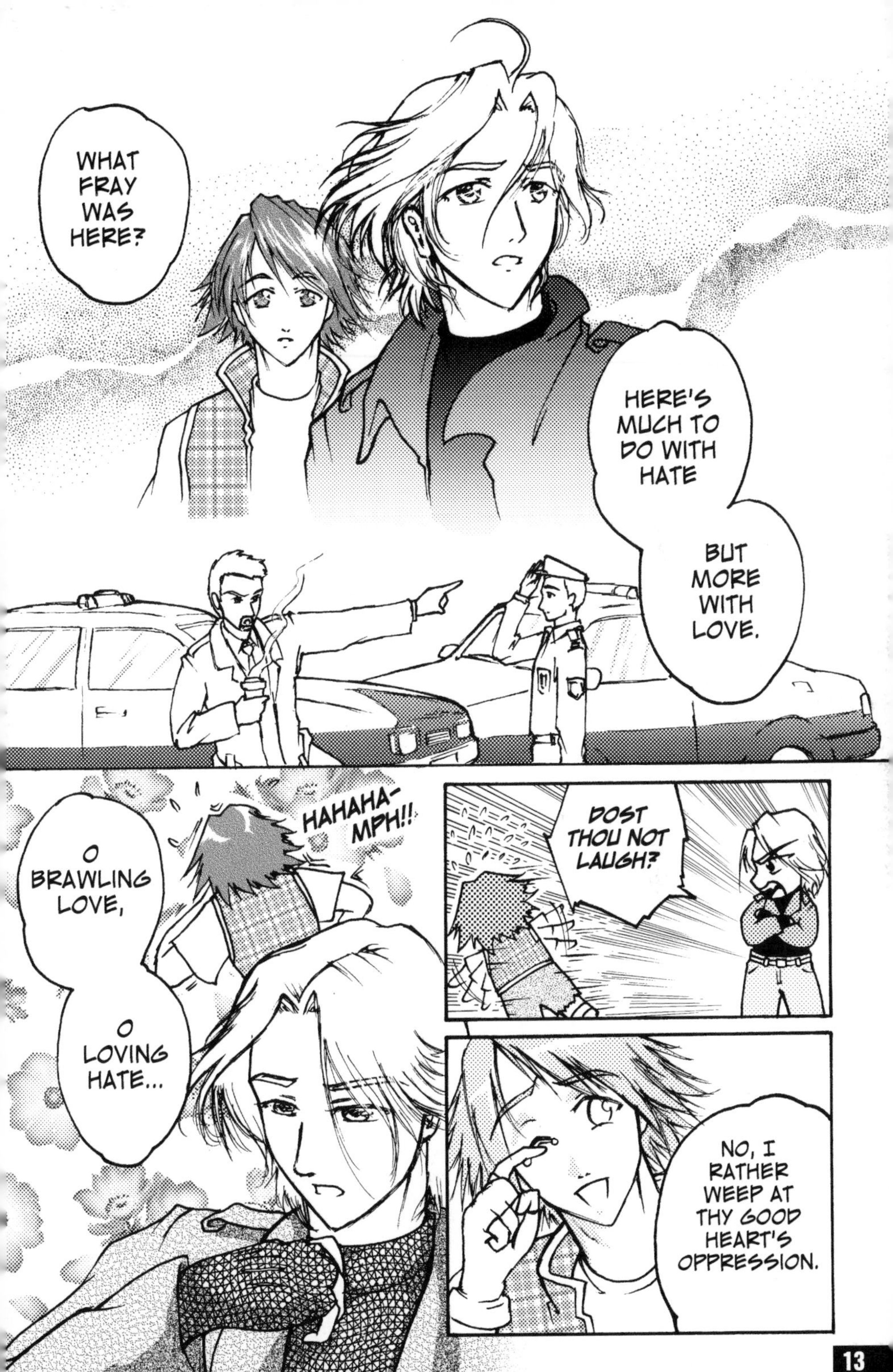
WHAT FRAY WAS HERE?
HERE'S MUCH TO DO WITH HATE
BUT MORE WITH LOVE.
O BRAWLING LOVE,
HAHAHA-MPH!!
O LOVING HATE...
DOST THOU NOT LAUGH?
NO, I RATHER WEEP AT THY GOOD HEART'S OPPRESSION.

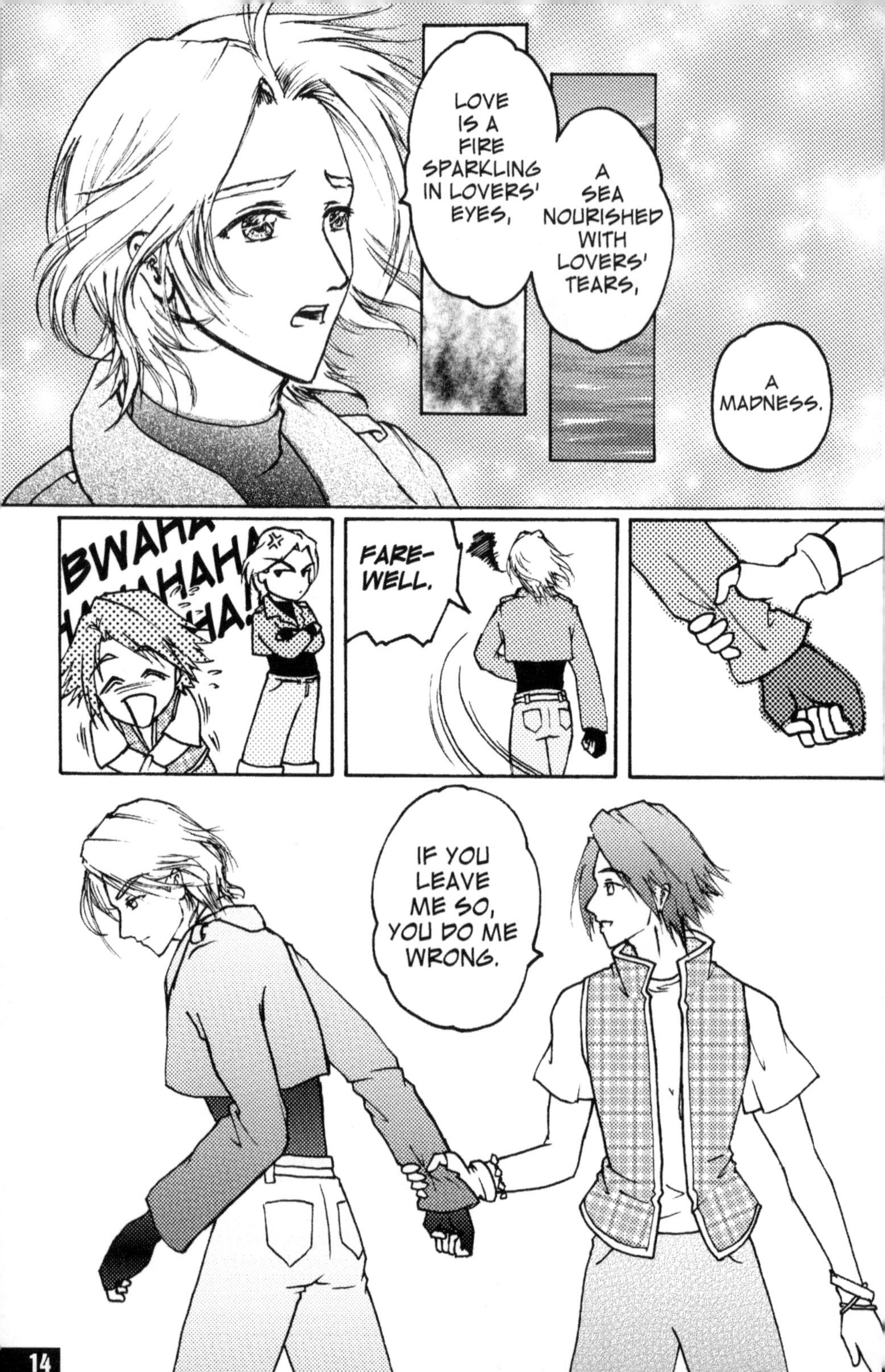
LOVE IS A FIRE SPARKLING IN LOVERS' EYES,
A SEA NOURISHED WITH LOVERS' TEARS,
A MADNESS.
BWAHAHAHAHAHAHA!
FARE-WELL.
IF YOU LEAVE ME SO, YOU DO ME WRONG.

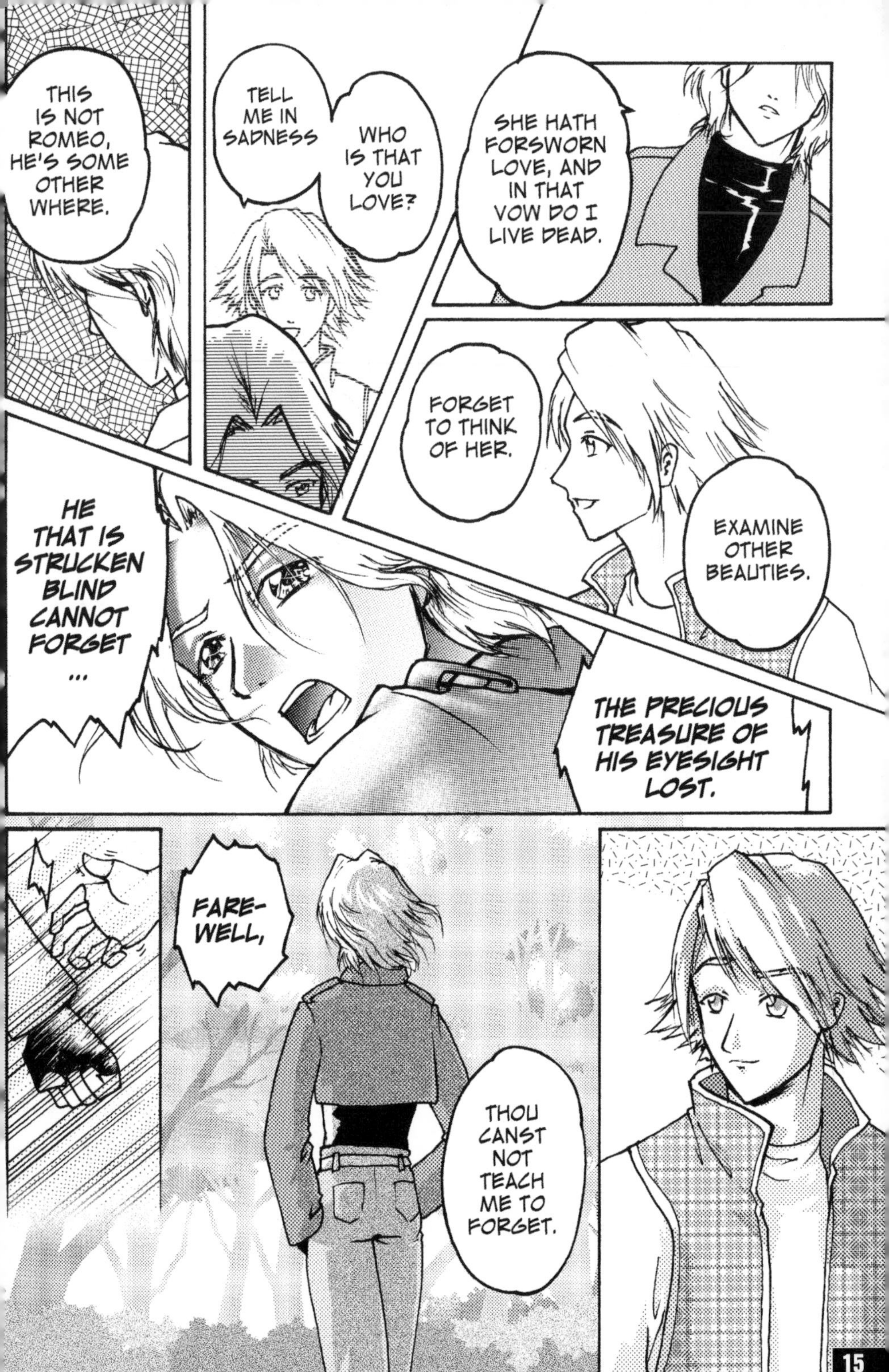
THIS IS NOT ROMEO, HE'S SOME OTHER WHERE.
TELL ME IN SADNESS
WHO IS THAT YOU LOVE?
SHE HATH FORSWORN LOVE, AND IN THAT VOW DO I LIVE DEAD.
FORGET TO THINK OF HER.
EXAMINE OTHER BEAUTIES.
HE THAT IS STRUCKEN BLIND CANNOT FORGET ...
THE PRECIOUS TREASURE OF HIS EYESIGHT LOST.
FARE-WELL,
THOU CANST NOT TEACH ME TO FORGET.

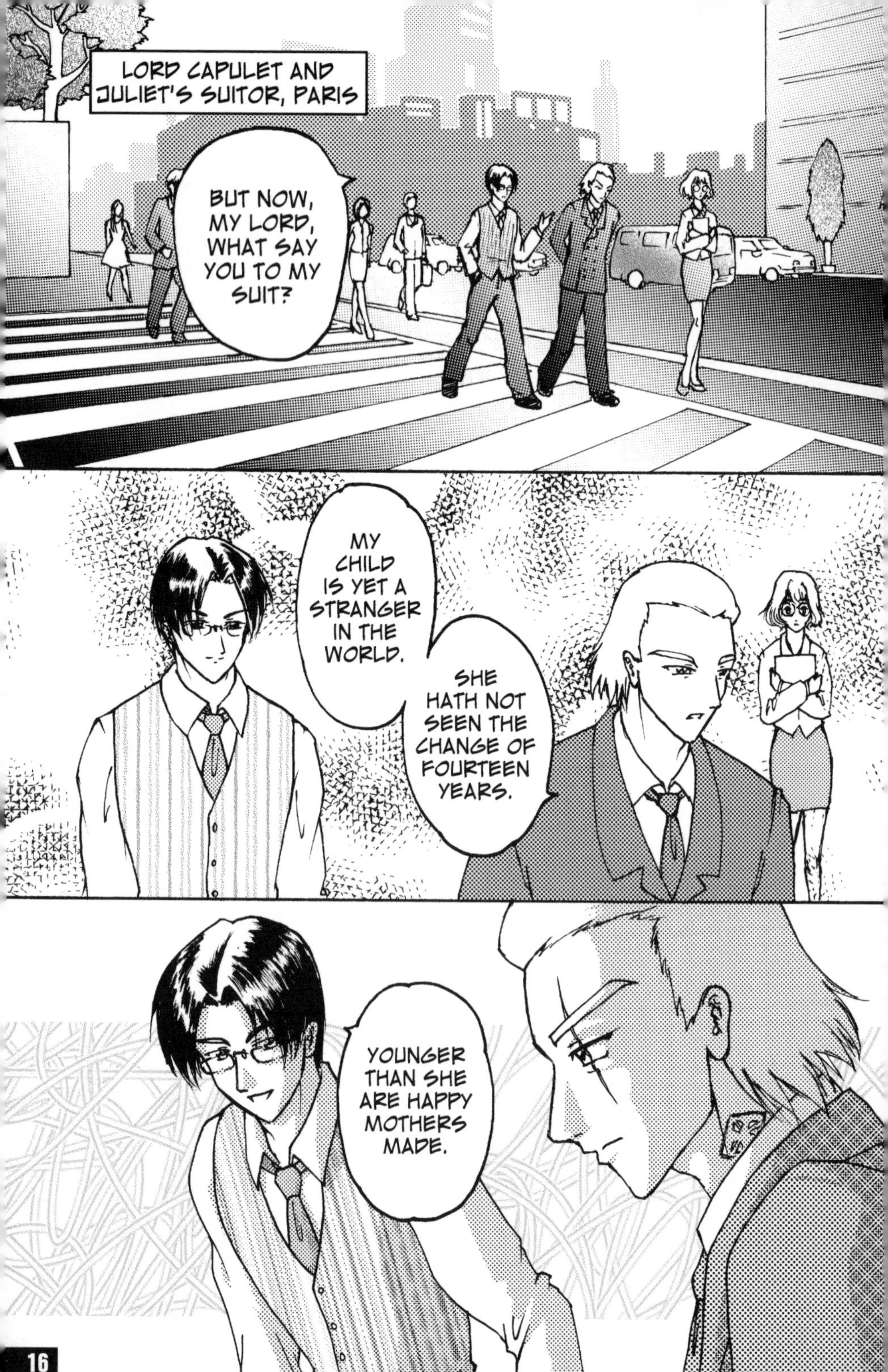
LORD CAPULET AND JULIET'S SUITOR, PARIS
BUT NOW, MY LORD, WHAT SAY YOU TO MY SUIT?
MY CHILD IS YET A STRANGER IN THE WORLD.
SHE HATH NOT SEEN THE CHANGE OF FOURTEEN YEARS.
YOUNGER THAN SHE ARE HAPPY MOTHERS MADE.

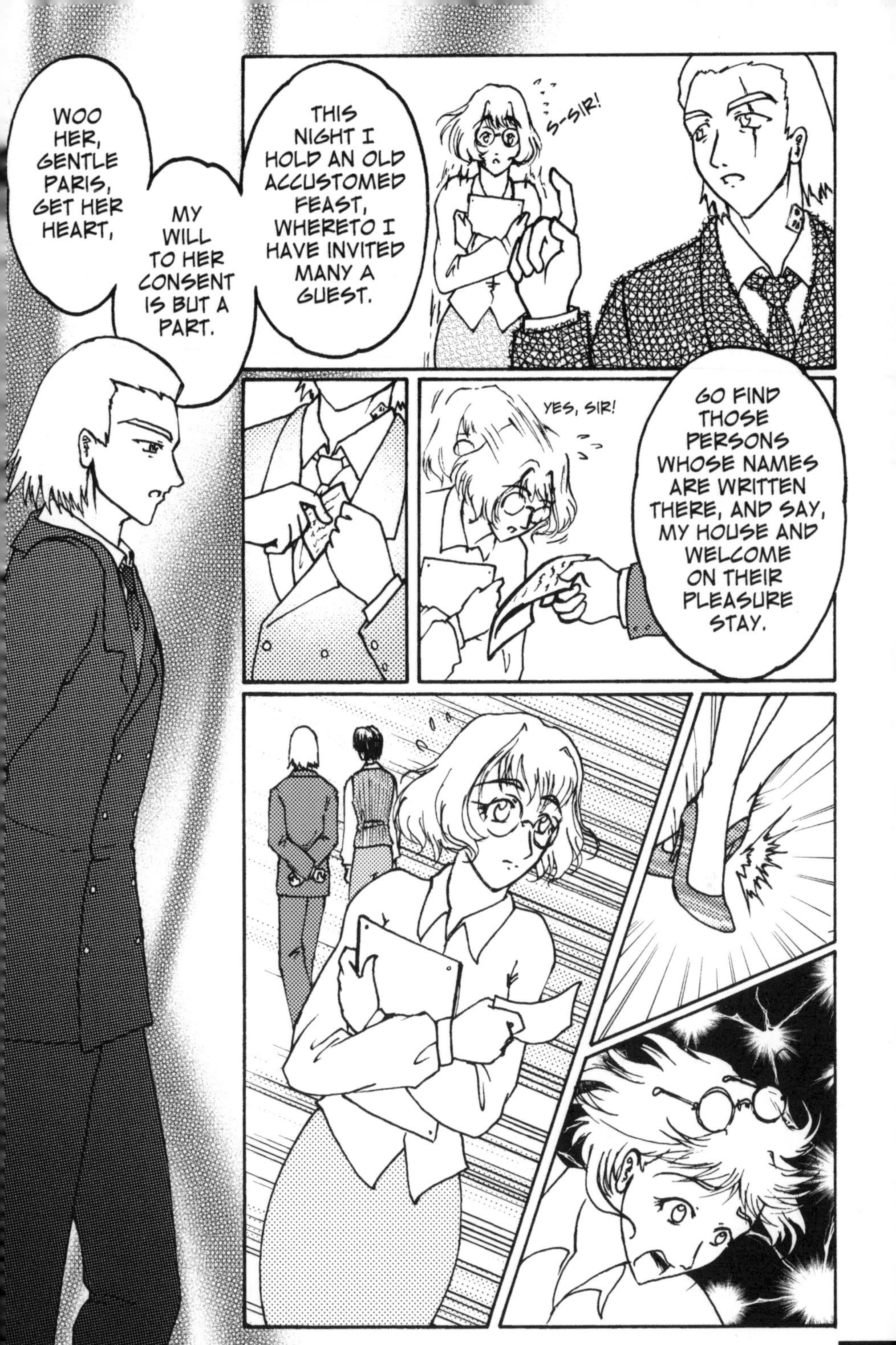
S-SIR!
THIS NIGHT I HOLD AN OLD ACCUSTOMED FEAST, WHERETO I HAVE INVITED MANY A GUEST.
MY WILL TO HER CONSENT IS BUT A PART.
WOO HER, GENTLE PARIS, GET HER HEART,
GO FIND THOSE PERSONS WHOSE NAMES ARE WRITTEN THERE, AND SAY, MY HOUSE AND WELCOME ON THEIR PLEASURE STAY.
YES, SIR!

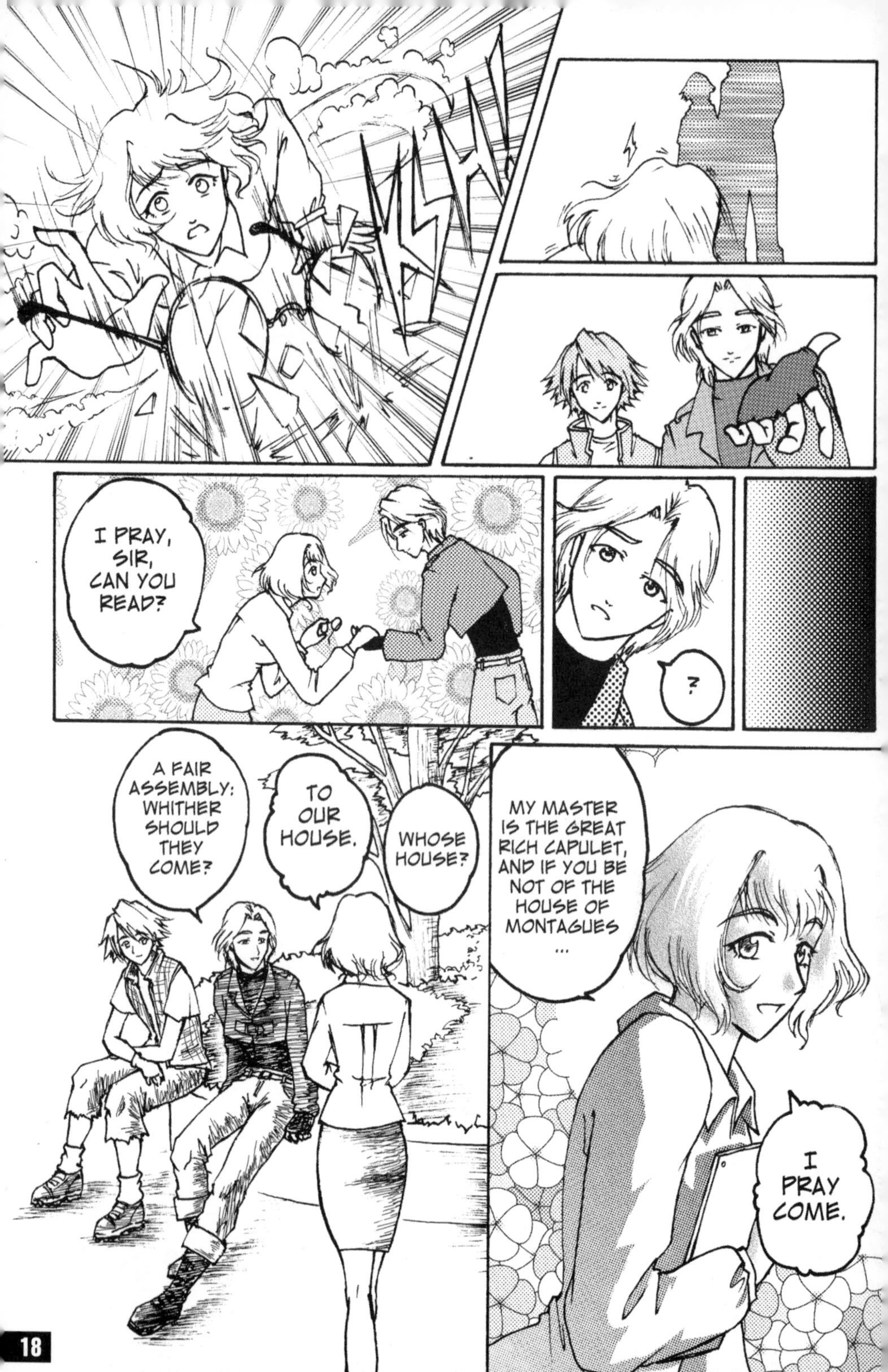
I PRAY, SIR, CAN YOU READ?
?
A FAIR ASSEMBLY: WHITHER SHOULD THEY COME?
TO OUR HOUSE.
WHOSE HOUSE?
MY MASTER IS THE GREAT RICH CAPULET, AND IF YOU BE NOT OF THE HOUSE OF MONTAGUES ...
I PRAY COME.

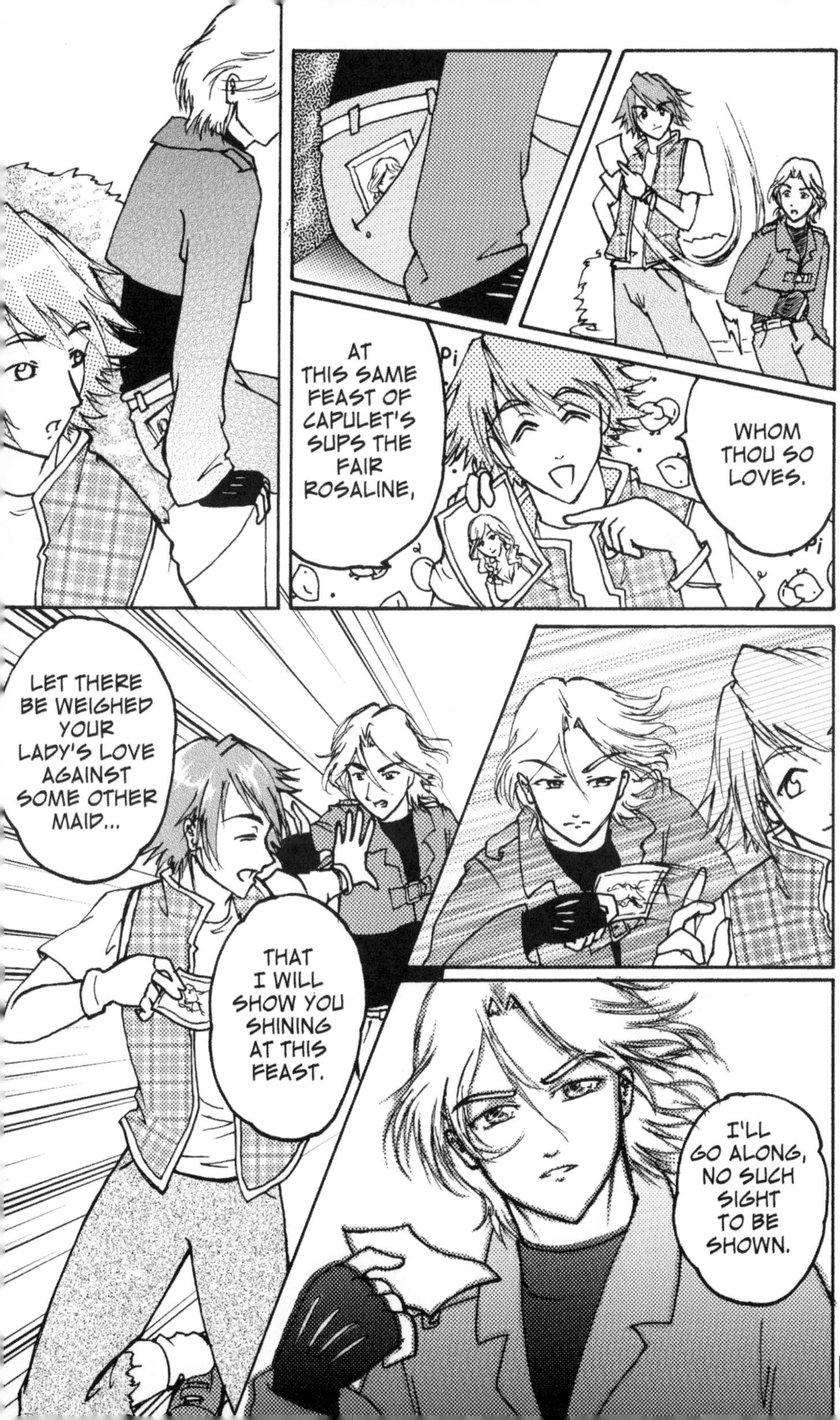
AT THIS SAME FEAST OF CAPULET'S SUPS THE FAIR ROSALINE,
WHOM THOU SO LOVES.
Pi
LET THERE BE WEIGHED YOUR LADY'S LOVE AGAINST SOME OTHER MAID...
THAT I WILL SHOW YOU SHINING AT THIS FEAST.
I'LL GO ALONG, NO SUCH SIGHT TO BE SHOWN.

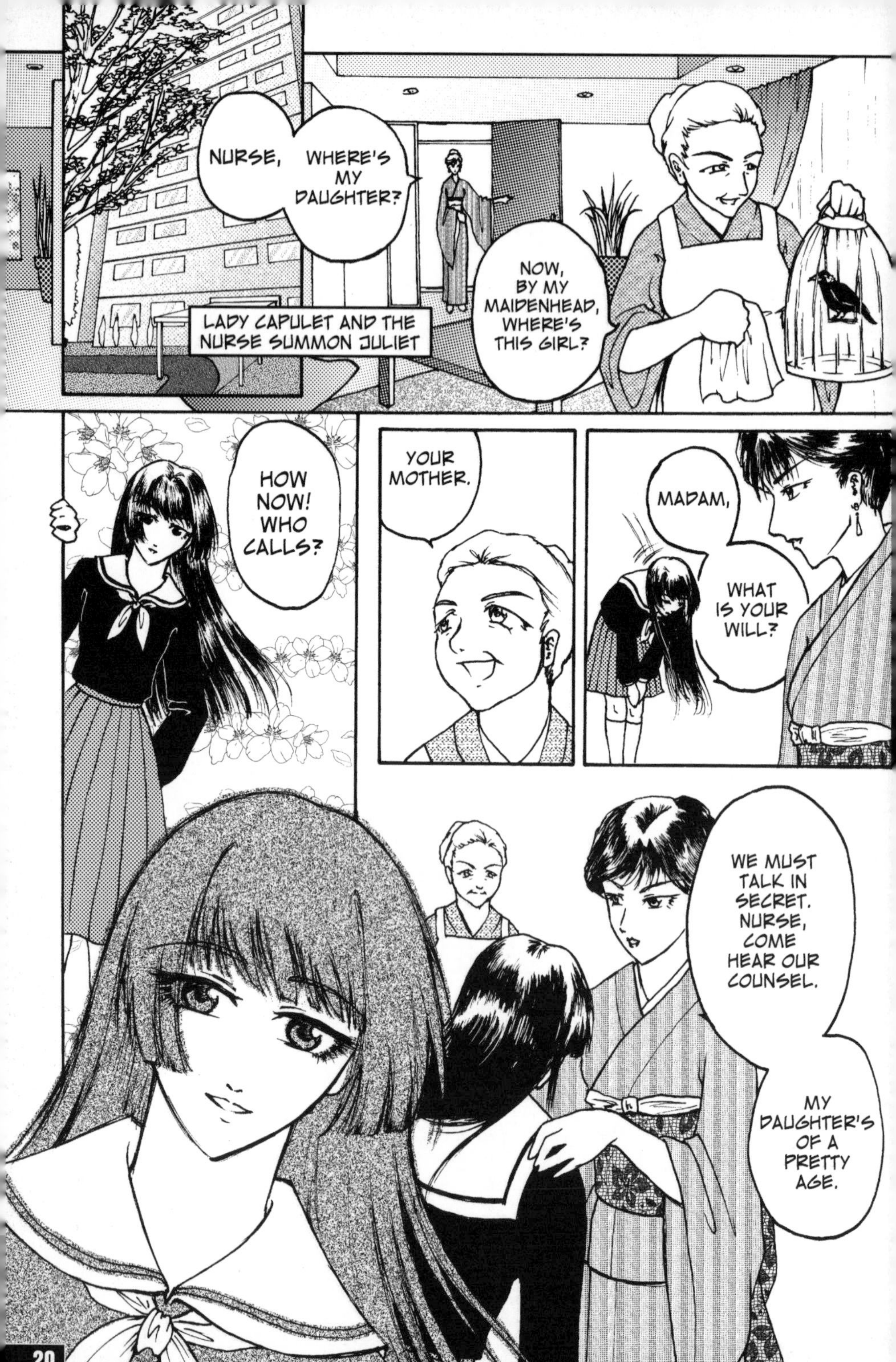

LADY CAPULET AND THE NURSE SUMMON JULIET
NURSE, WHERE'S MY DAUGHTER?
NOW, BY MY MAIDENHEAD, WHERE'S THIS GIRL?
HOW NOW! WHO CALLS?
YOUR MOTHER.
MADAM, WHAT IS YOUR WILL?
WE MUST TALK IN SECRET. NURSE, COME HEAR OUR COUNSEL.
MY DAUGHTER'S OF A PRETTY AGE.

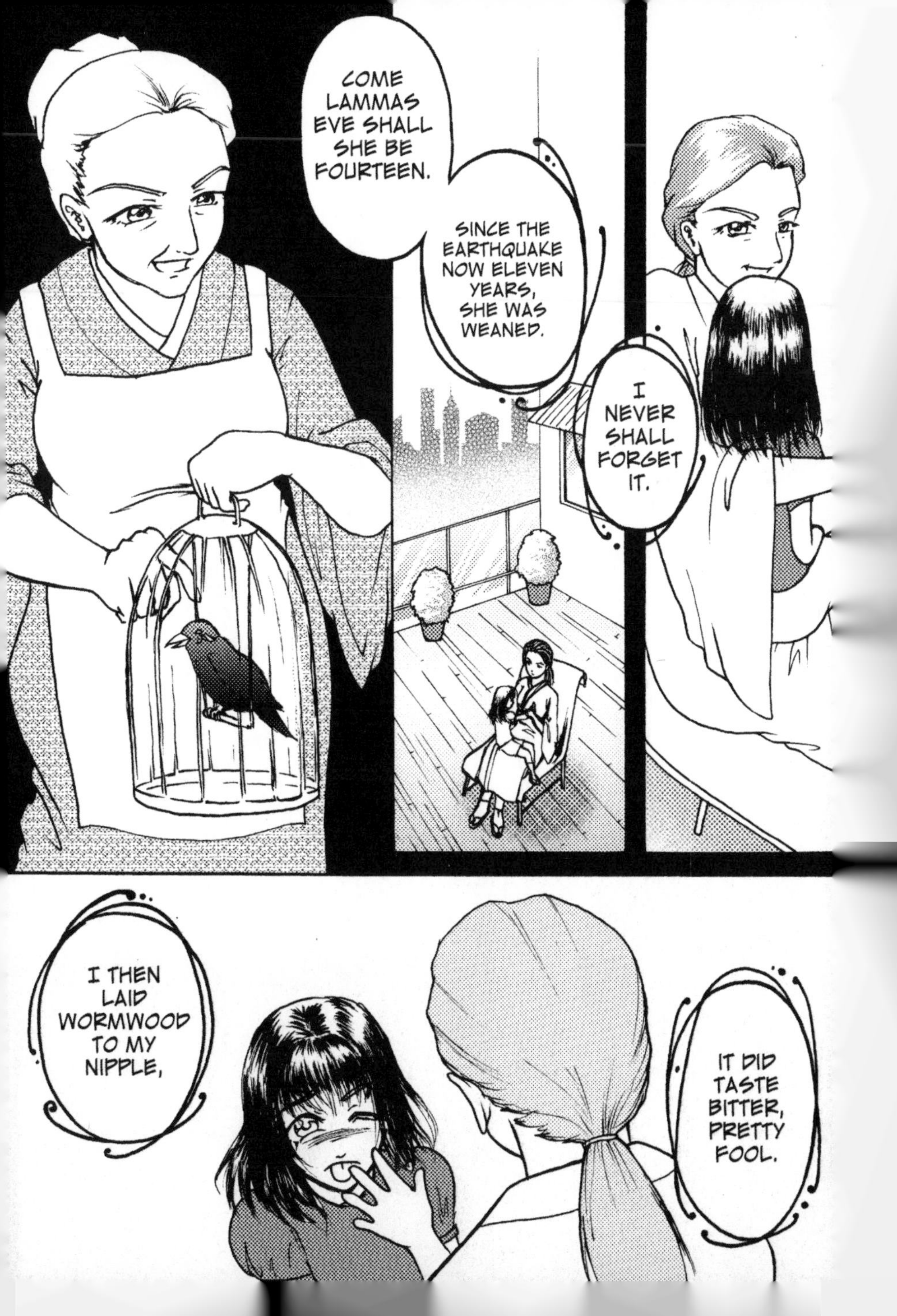
COME LAMMAS EVE SHALL SHE BE FOURTEEN.
SINCE THE EARTHQUAKE NOW ELEVEN YEARS, SHE WAS WEANED.
I NEVER SHALL FORGET IT.
I THEN LAID WORMWOOD TO MY NIPPLE,
IT DID TASTE BITTER, PRETTY FOOL.

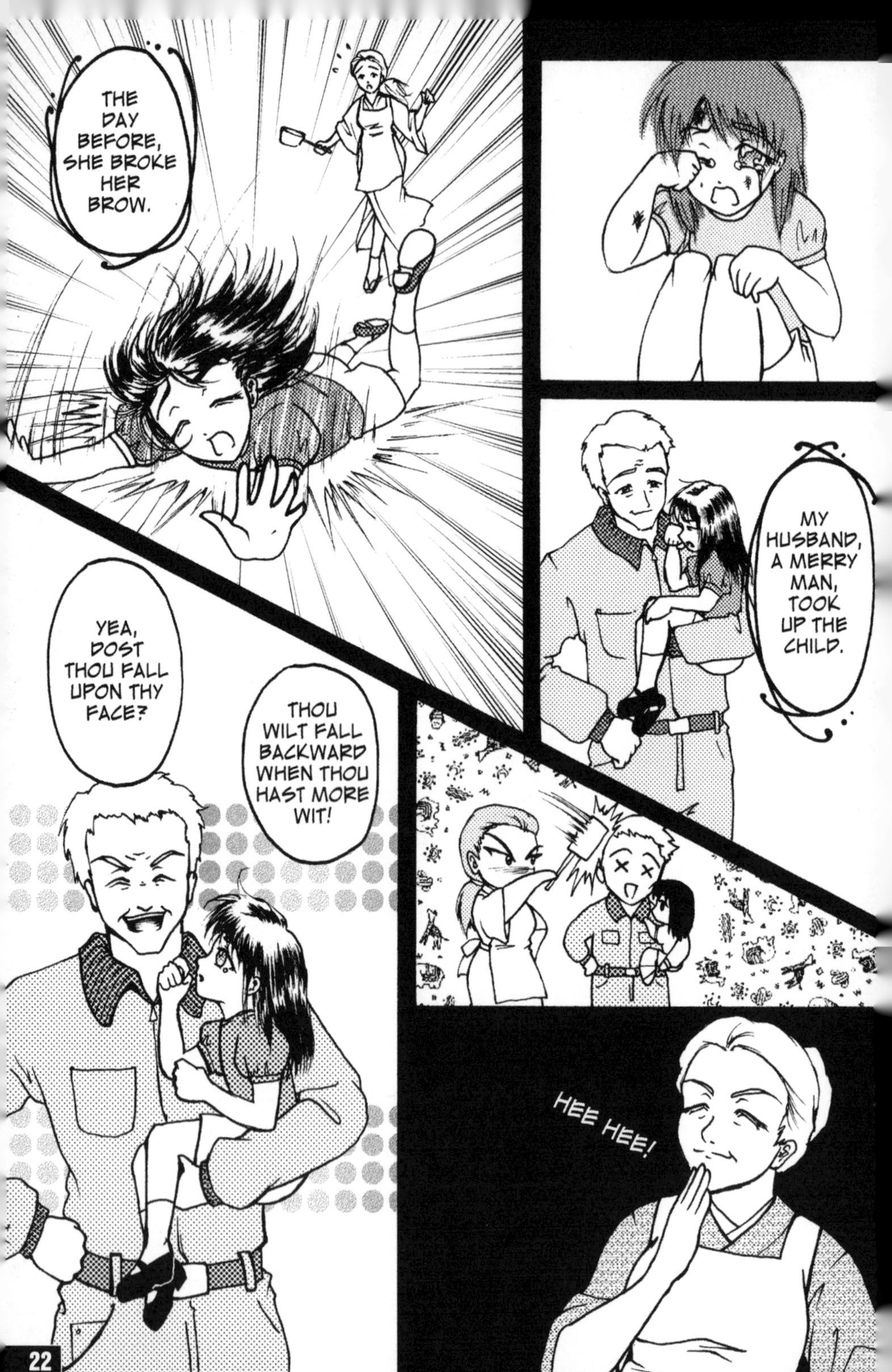
THE DAY BEFORE, SHE BROKE HER BROW.
MY HUSBAND, A MERRY MAN, TOOK UP THE CHILD.
YEA, DOST THOU FALL UPON THY FACE?
THOU WILT FALL BACKWARD WHEN THOU HAST MORE WIT!
HEE HEE!

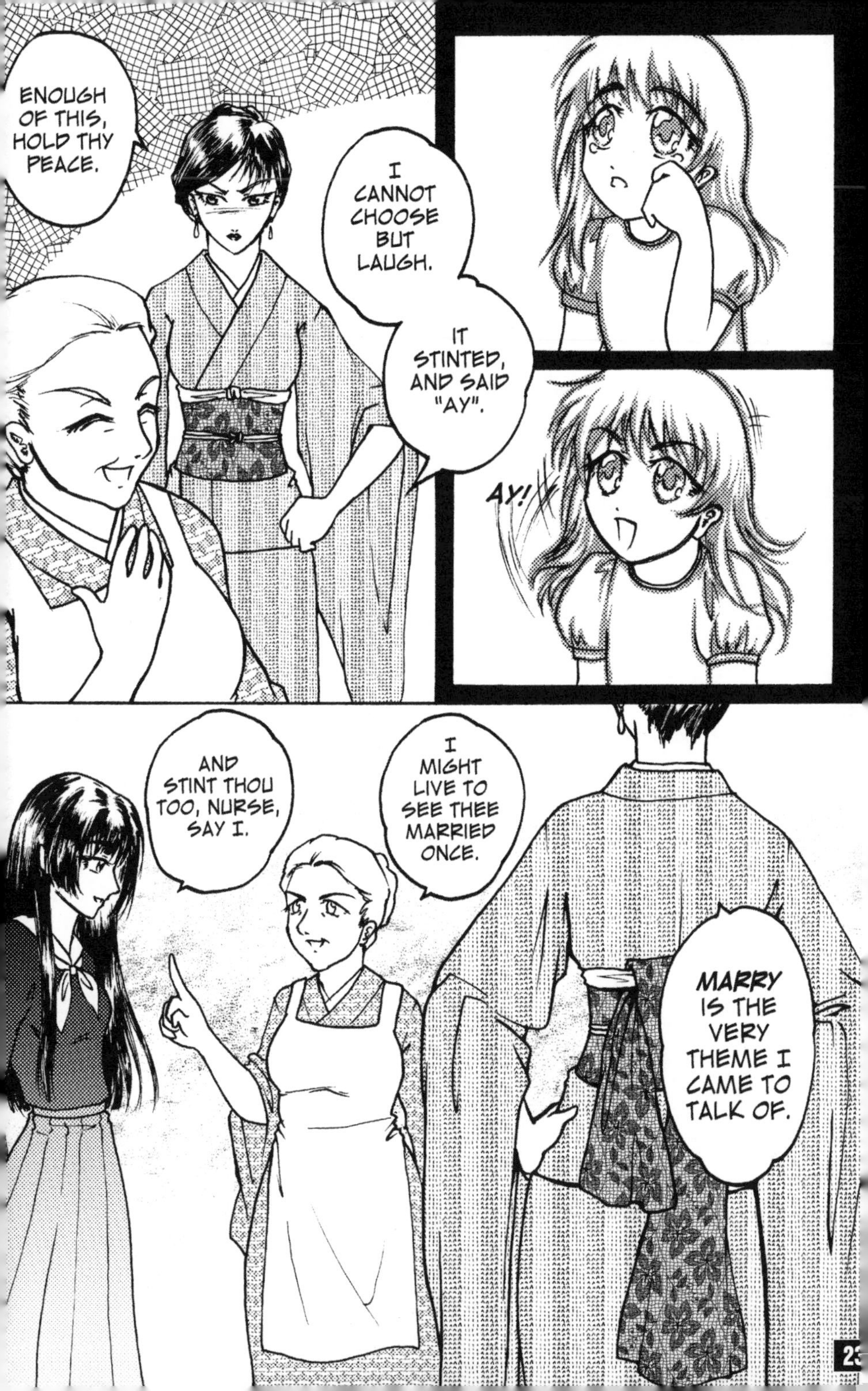
ENOUGH OF THIS, HOLD THY PEACE.
I CANNOT CHOOSE BUT LAUGH.
IT STINTED, AND SAID "AY".
AY!
AND STINT THOU TOO, NURSE, SAY I.
I MIGHT LIVE TO SEE THEE MARRIED ONCE.
MARRY IS THE VERY THEME I CAME TO TALK OF.

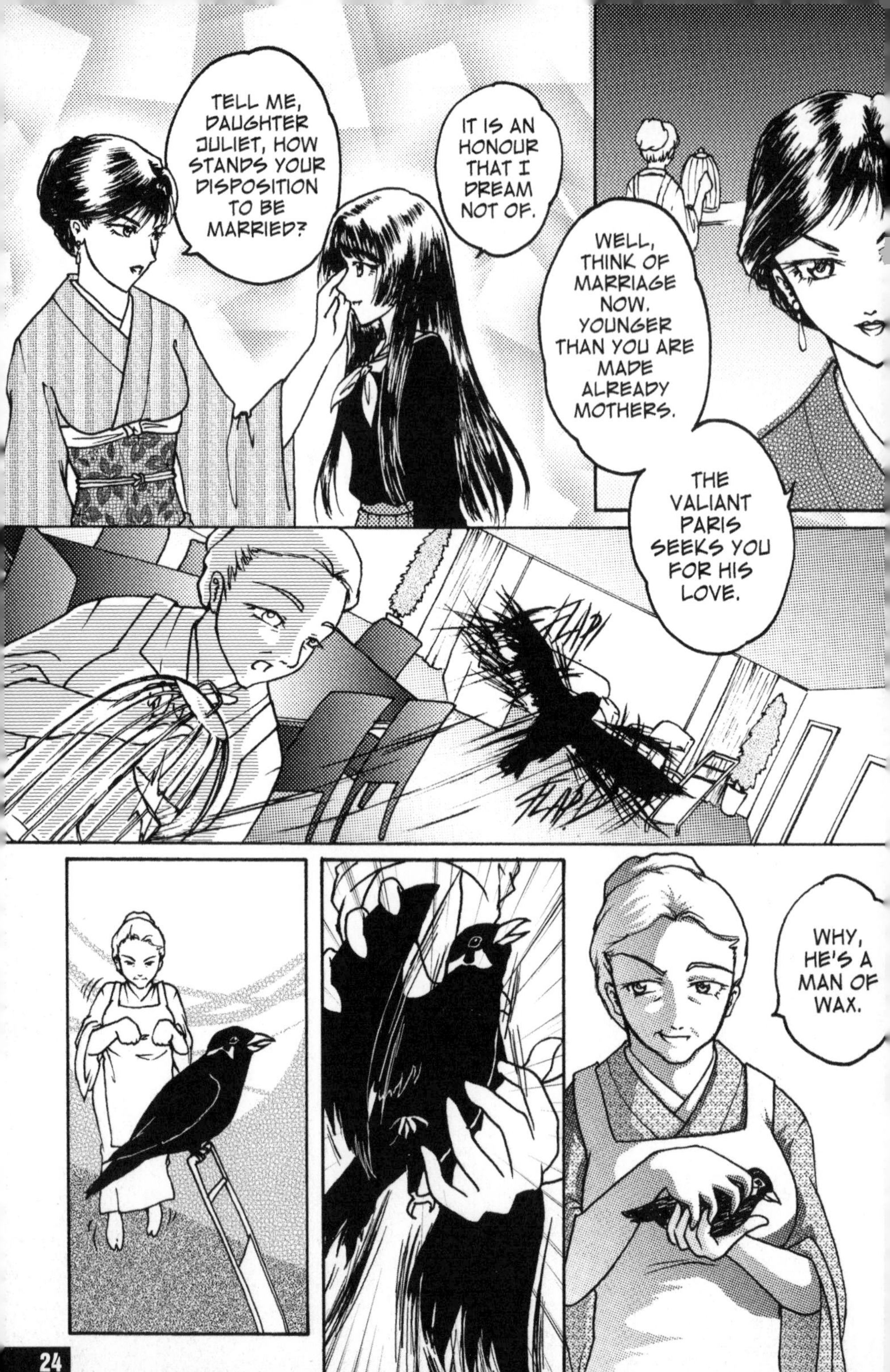

TELL ME, DAUGHTER JULIET, HOW STANDS YOUR DISPOSITION TO BE MARRIED?
IT IS AN HONOUR THAT I DREAM NOT OF.
WELL, THINK OF MARRIAGE NOW. YOUNGER THAN YOU ARE MADE ALREADY MOTHERS.
THE VALIANT PARIS SEEKS YOU FOR HIS LOVE.
FLAP!
FLAP!
WHY, HE'S A MAN OF WAX.

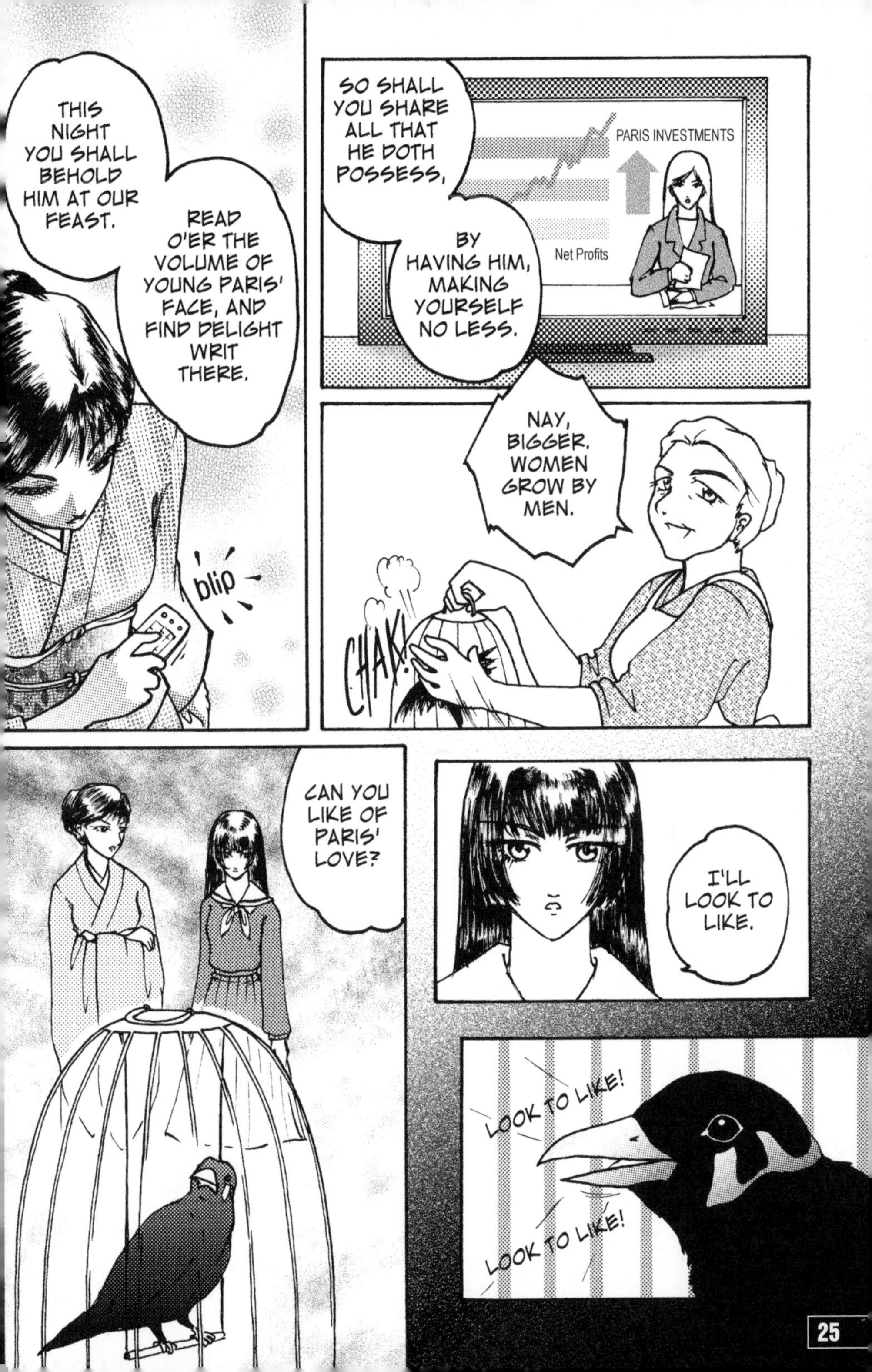
THIS NIGHT YOU SHALL BEHOLD HIM AT OUR FEAST.
READ O'ER THE VOLUME OF YOUNG PARIS' FACE, AND FIND DELIGHT WRIT THERE.
blip
SO SHALL YOU SHARE ALL THAT HE DOTH POSSESS,
PARIS INVESTMENTS
Net Profits
BY HAVING HIM, MAKING YOURSELF NO LESS.
NAY, BIGGER. WOMEN GROW BY MEN.
CHAK!
CAN YOU LIKE OF PARIS' LOVE?
I'LL LOOK TO LIKE.
LOOK TO LIKE!
LOOK TO LIKE!

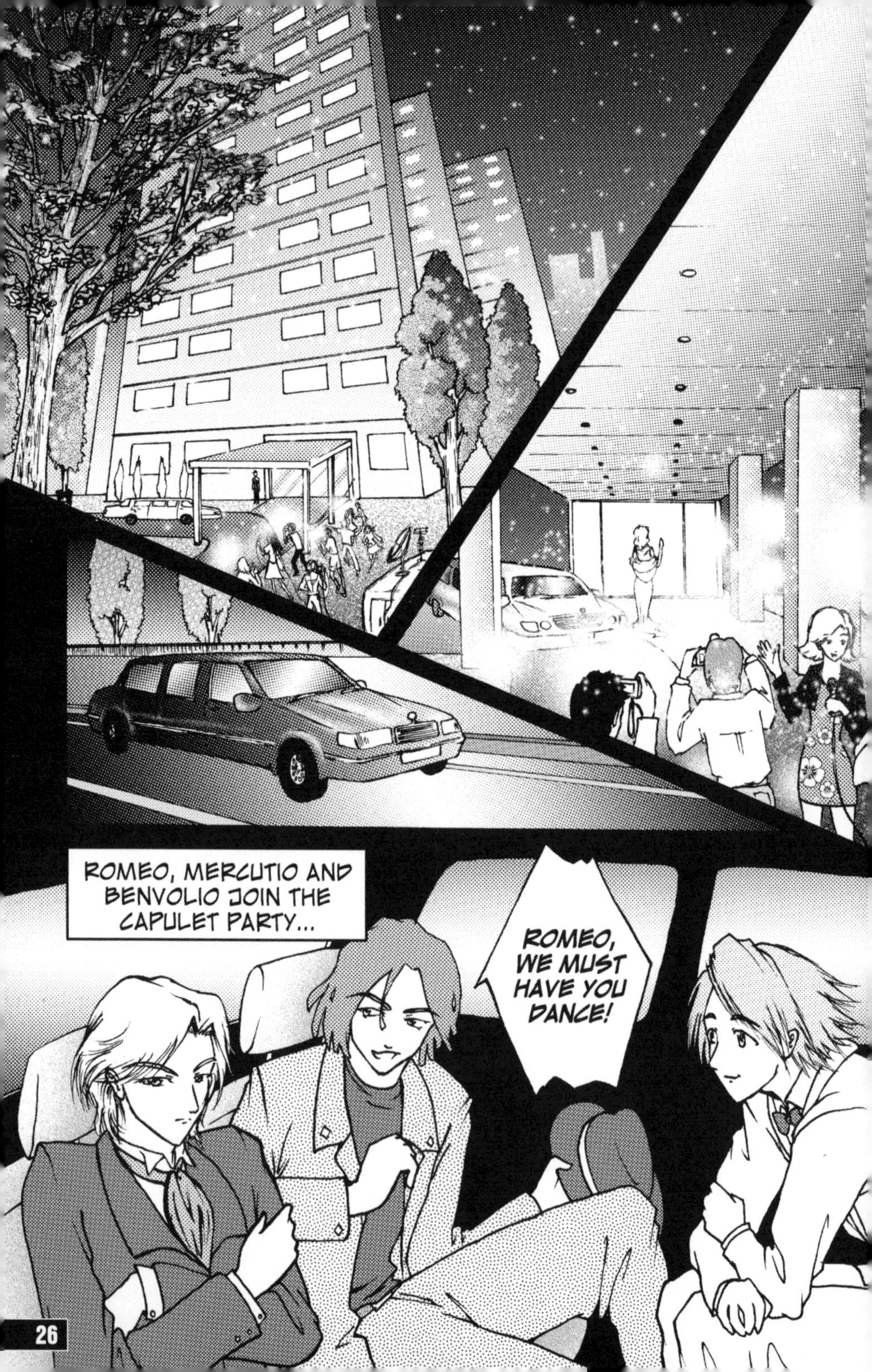
ROMEO, MERCUTIO AND BENVOLIO JOIN THE CAPULET PARTY...
ROMEO, WE MUST HAVE YOU DANCE!

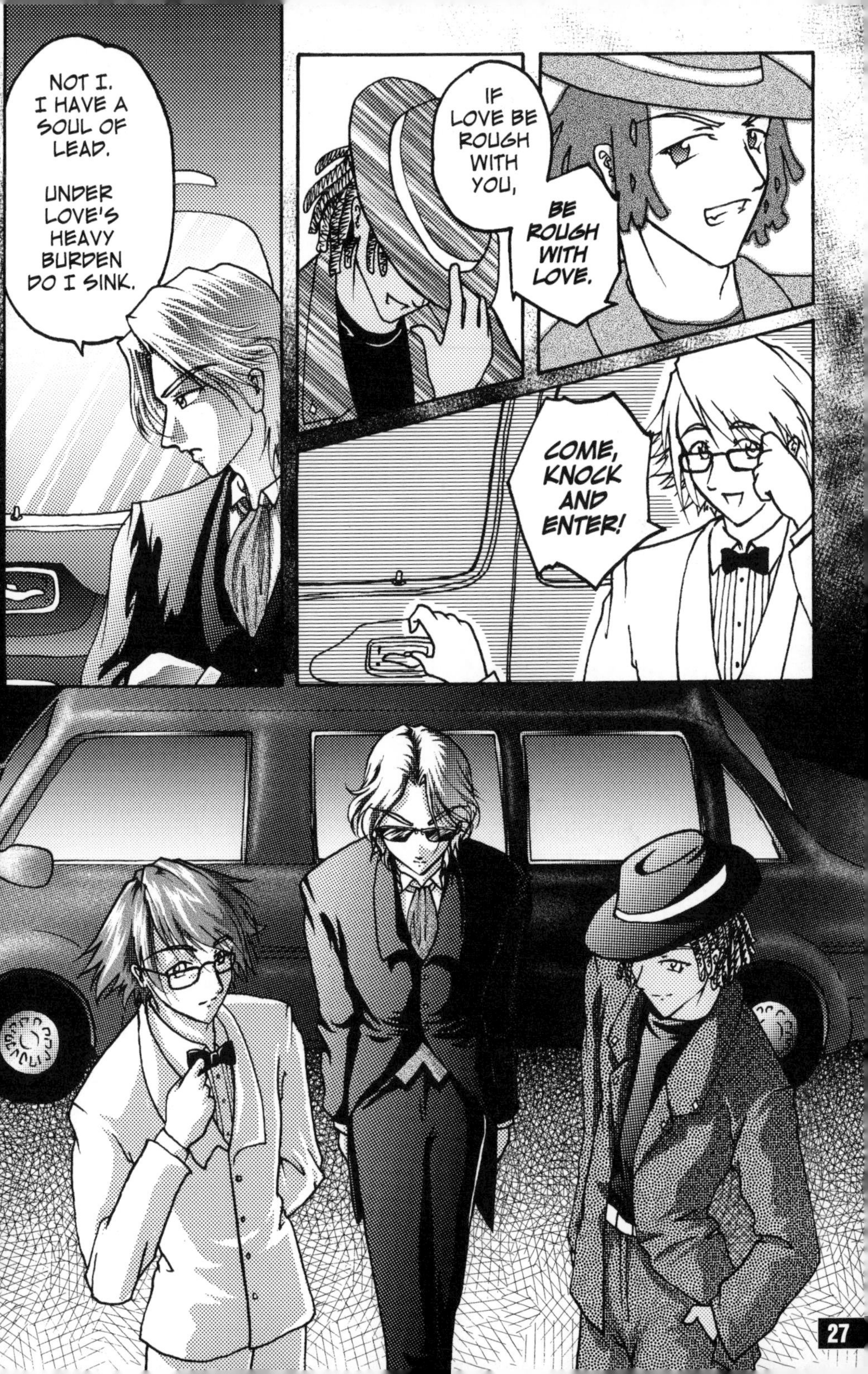
NOT I. I HAVE A SOUL OF LEAD.
UNDER LOVE'S HEAVY BURDEN DO I SINK.
IF LOVE BE ROUGH WITH YOU,
BE ROUGH WITH LOVE.
COME, KNOCK AND ENTER!

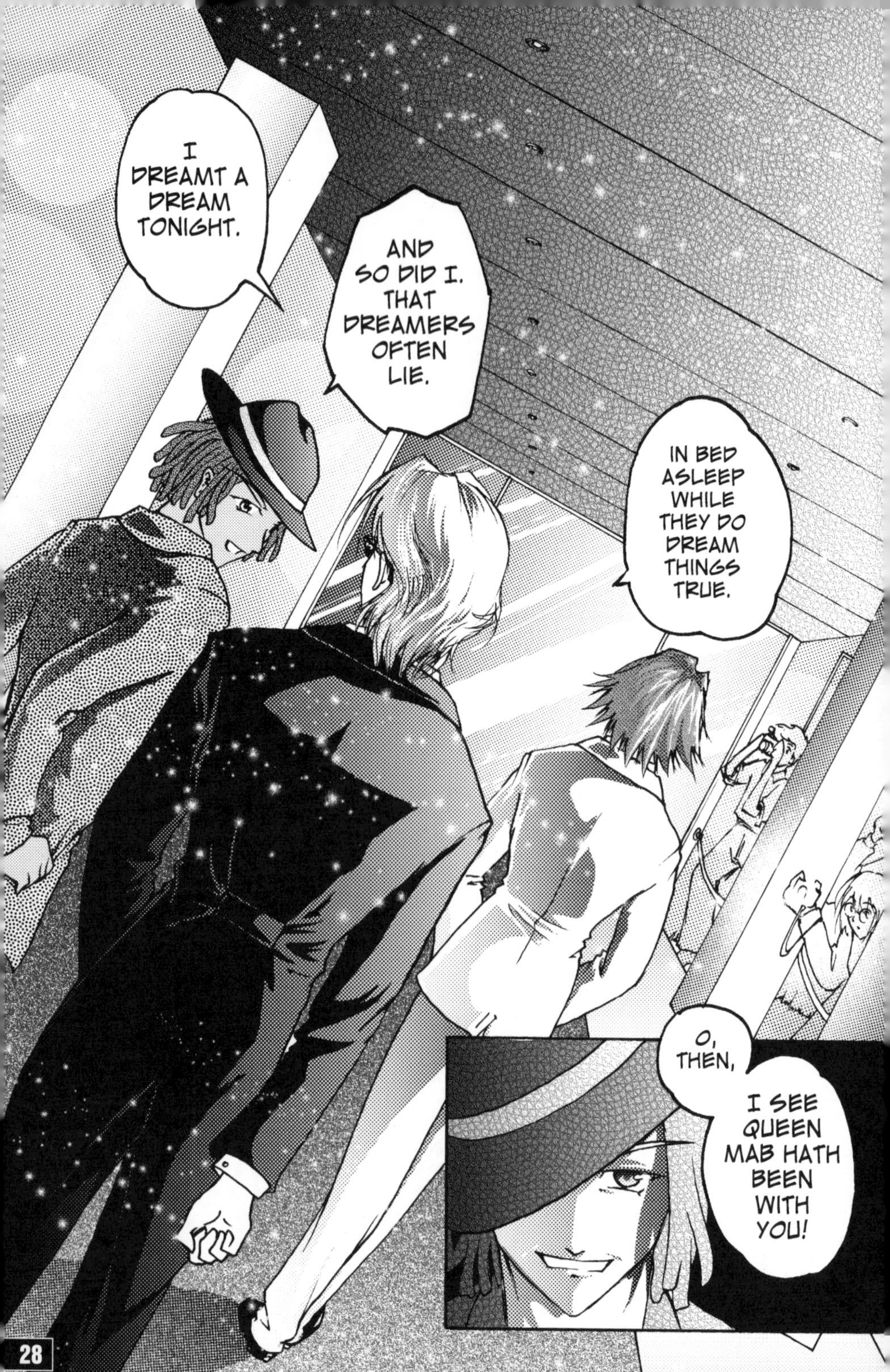
I DREAMT A DREAM TONIGHT.
AND SO DID I. THAT DREAMERS OFTEN LIE.
IN BED ASLEEP WHILE THEY DO DREAM THINGS TRUE.
O, THEN,
I SEE QUEEN MAB HATH BEEN WITH YOU!

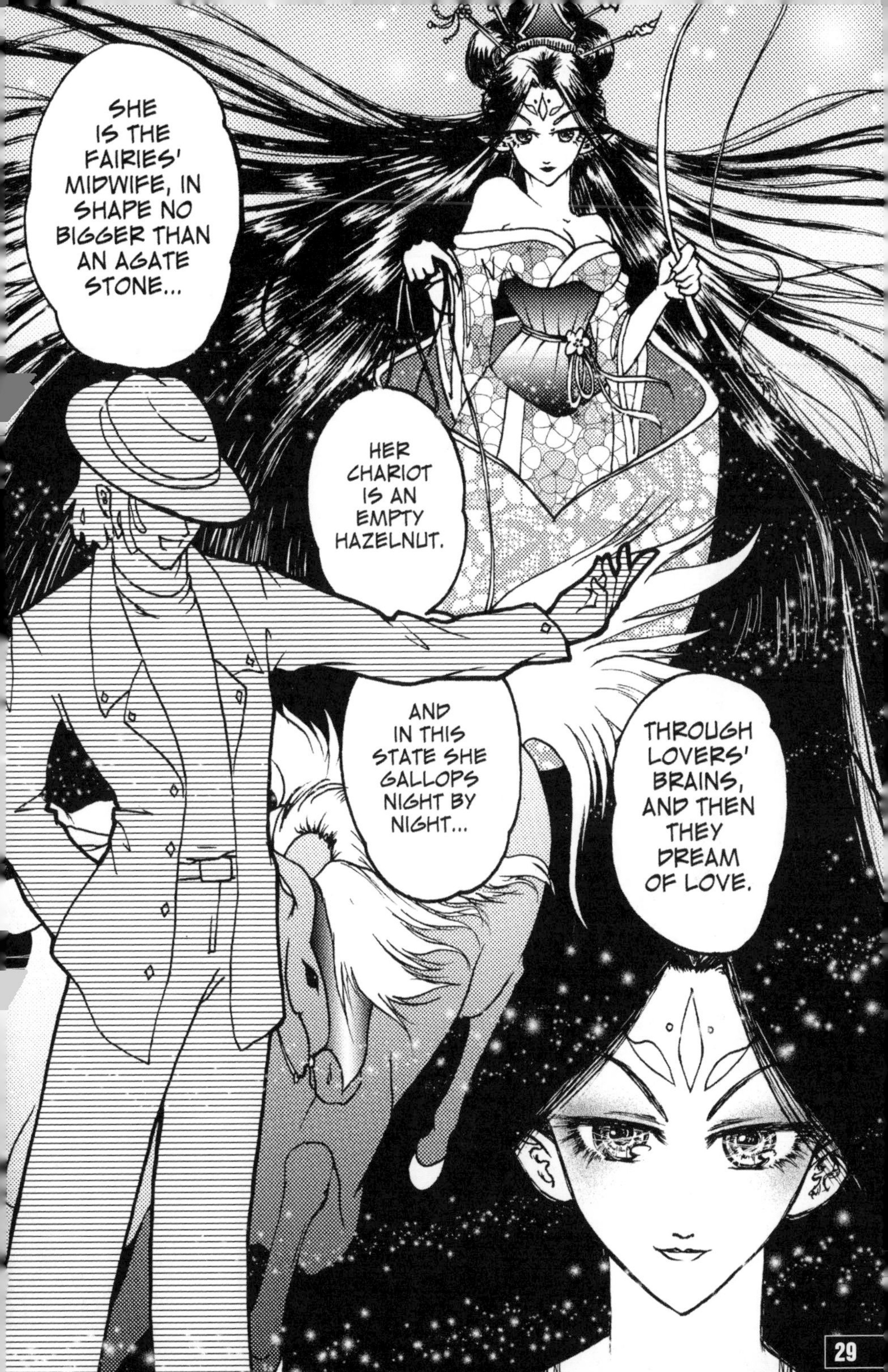
SHE IS THE FAIRIES' MIDWIFE, IN SHAPE NO BIGGER THAN AN AGATE STONE...
HER CHARIOT IS AN EMPTY HAZELNUT.
AND IN THIS STATE SHE GALLOPS NIGHT BY NIGHT...
THROUGH LOVERS' BRAINS, AND THEN THEY DREAM OF LOVE.

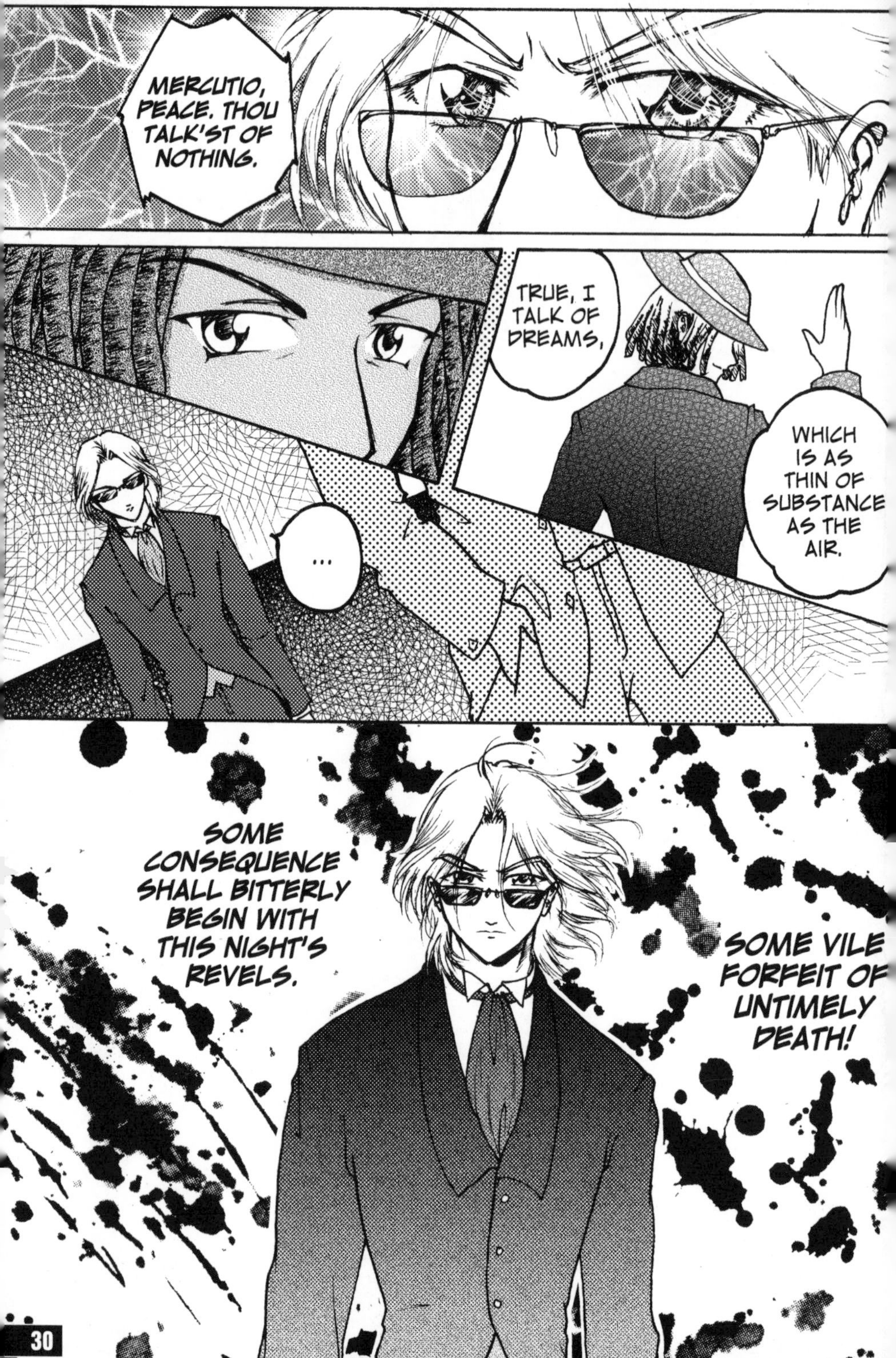
MERCUTIO, PEACE. THOU TALK'ST OF NOTHING.
TRUE, I TALK OF DREAMS,
WHICH IS AS THIN OF SUBSTANCE AS THE AIR.
...
SOME CONSEQUENCE SHALL BITTERLY BEGIN WITH THIS NIGHT'S REVELS.
SOME VILE FORFEIT OF UNTIMELY DEATH!

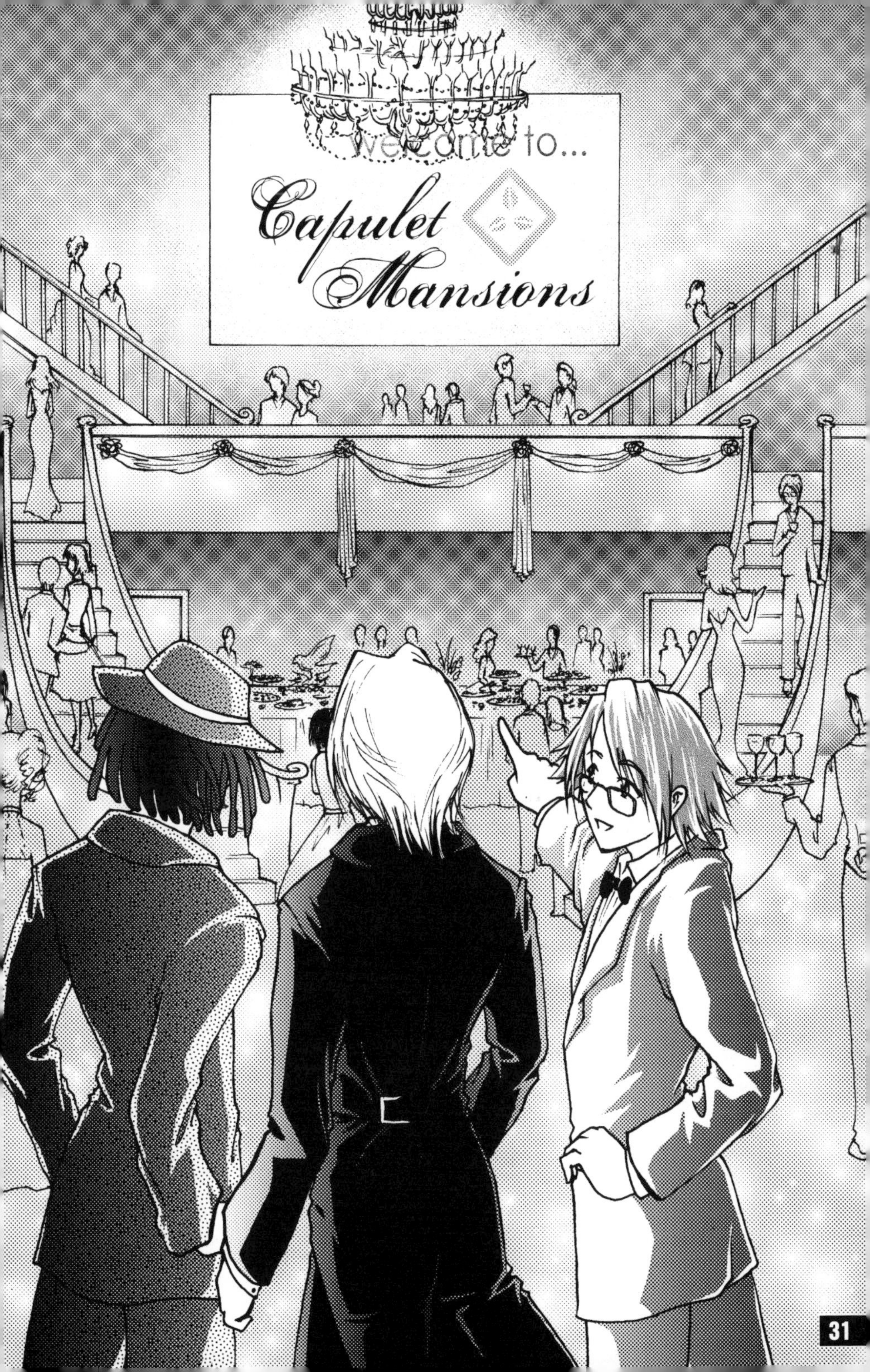
welcome to...
Capulet Mansions

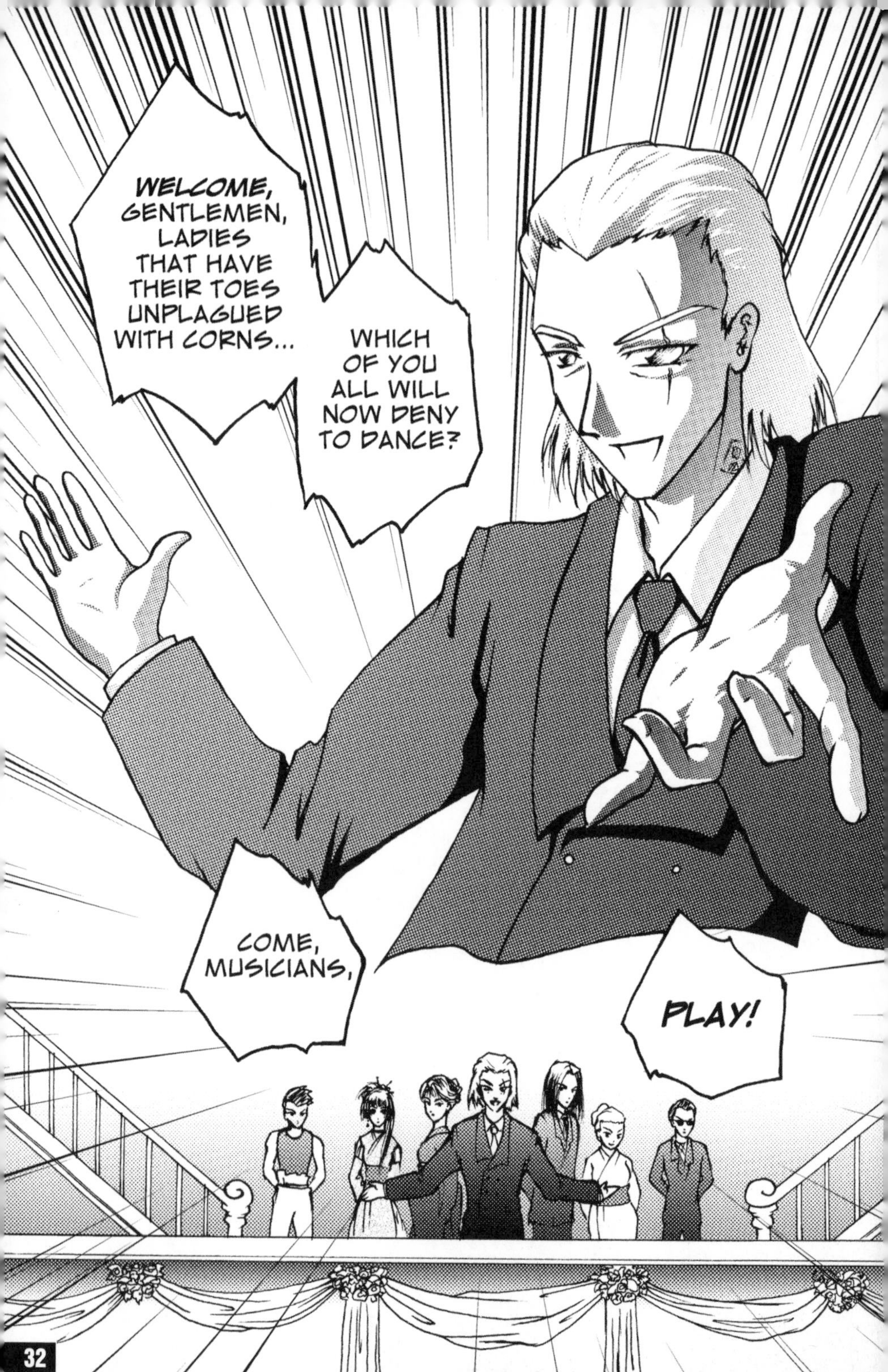
WELCOME, GENTLEMEN, LADIES THAT HAVE THEIR TOES UNPLAGUED WITH CORNS...
WHICH OF YOU ALL WILL NOW DENY TO DANCE?
COME, MUSICIANS,
PLAY!

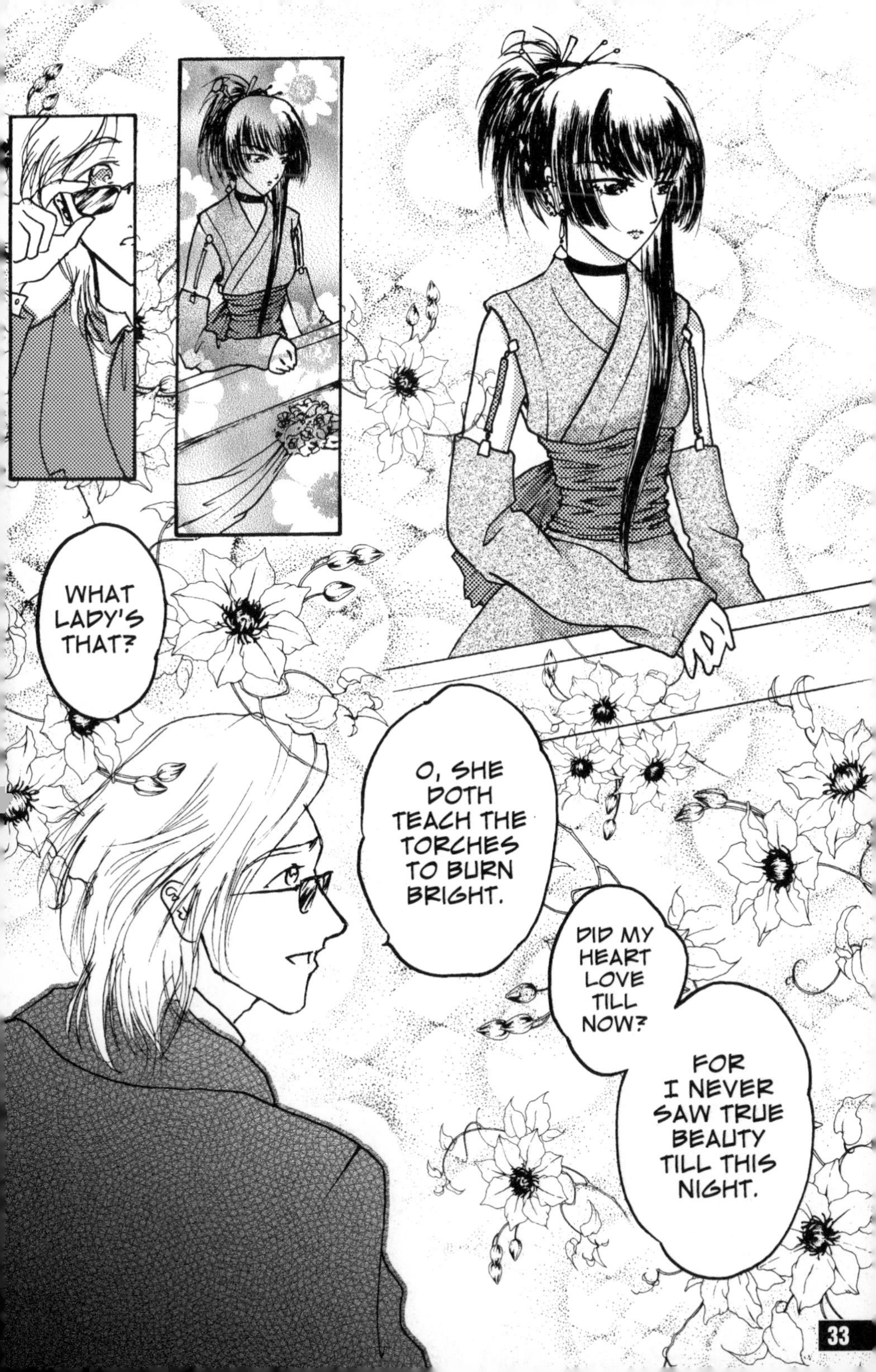
WHAT LADY'S THAT?
O, SHE DOTH TEACH THE TORCHES TO BURN BRIGHT.
DID MY HEART LOVE TILL NOW?
FOR I NEVER SAW TRUE BEAUTY TILL THIS NIGHT.

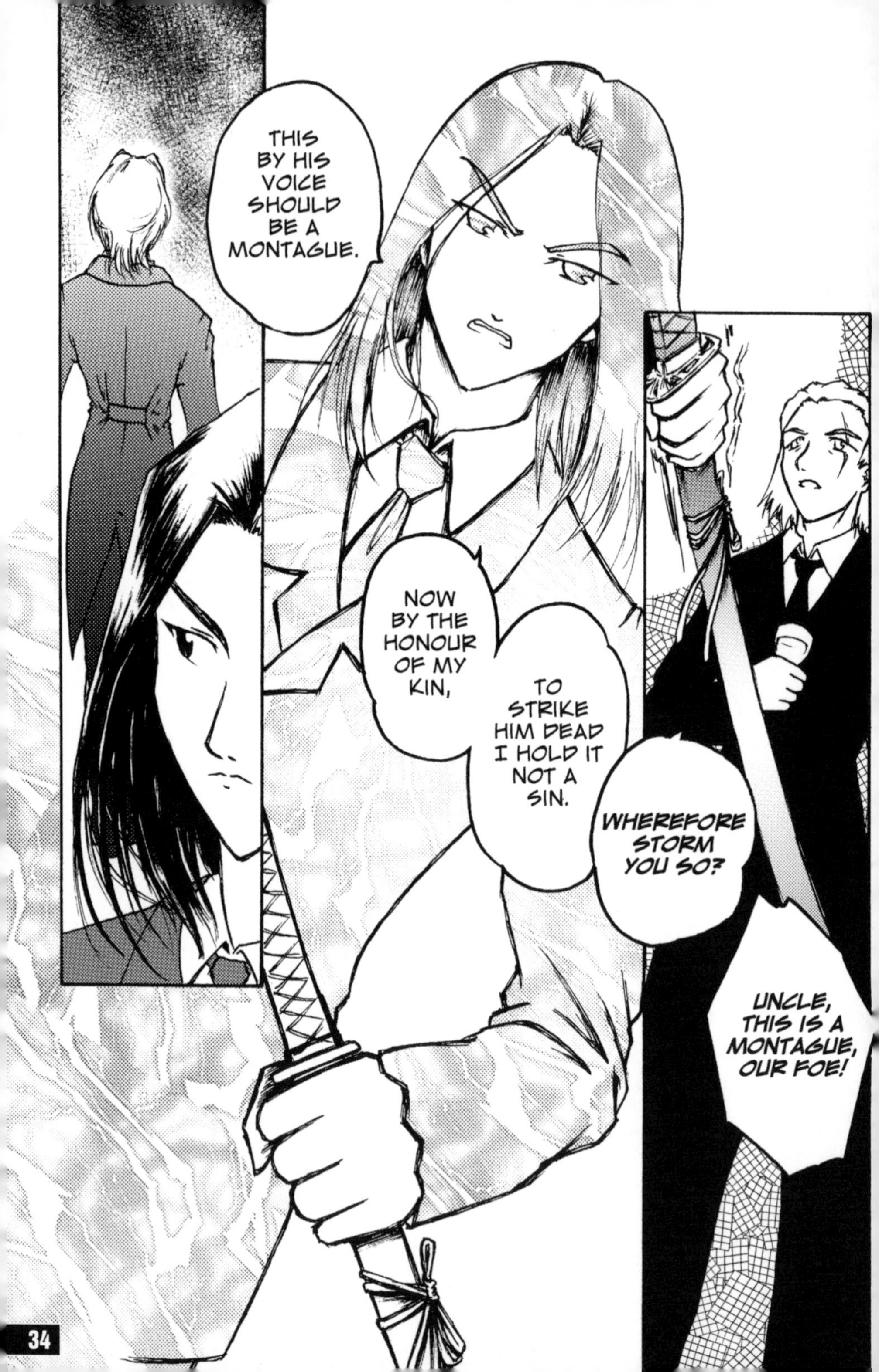
THIS BY HIS VOICE SHOULD BE A MONTAGUE.
NOW BY THE HONOUR OF MY KIN,
TO STRIKE HIM DEAD I HOLD IT NOT A SIN.
WHEREFORE STORM YOU SO?
UNCLE, THIS IS A MONTAGUE, OUR FOE!

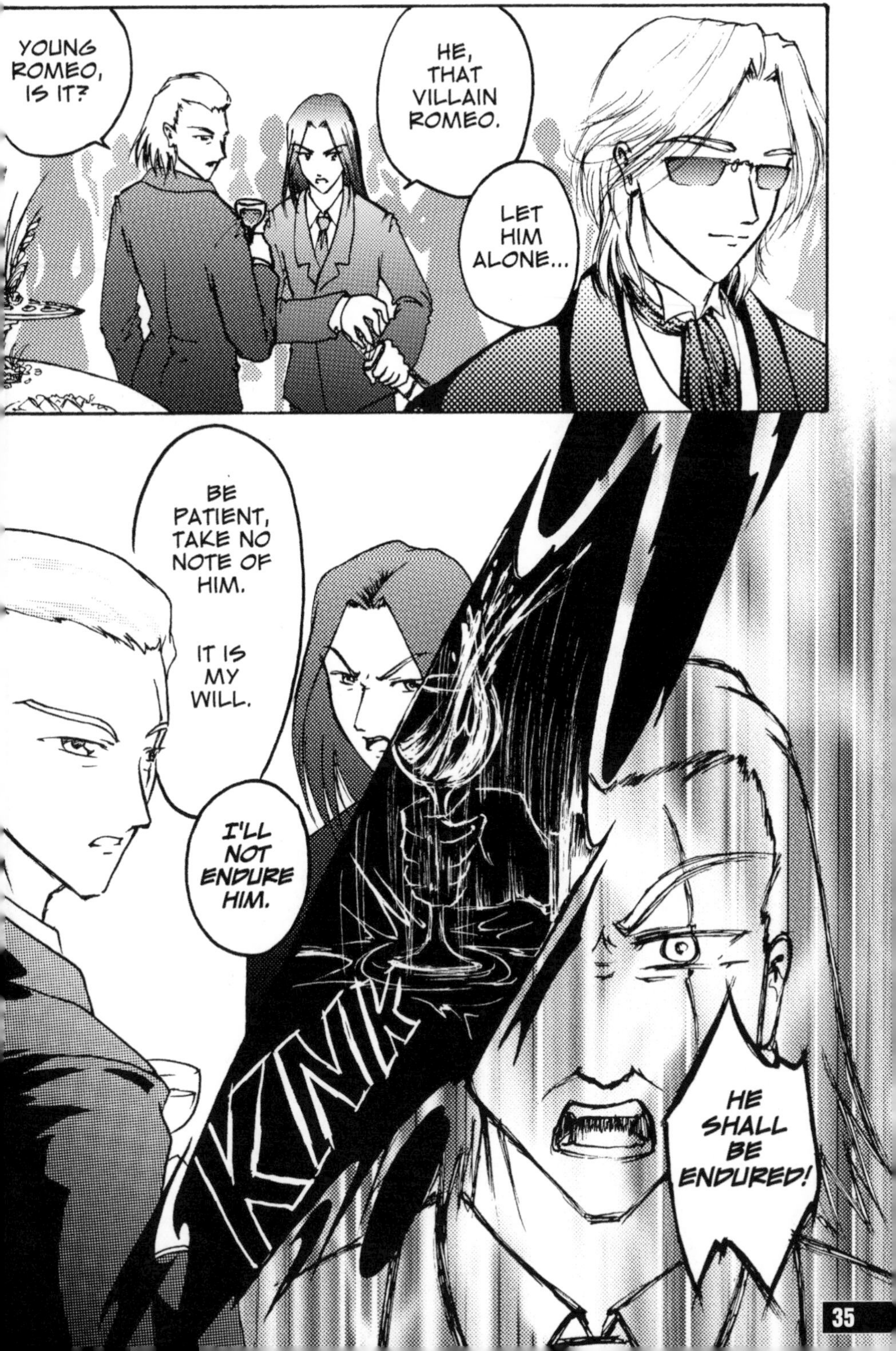
YOUNG ROMEO, IS IT?
HE, THAT VILLAIN ROMEO.
LET HIM ALONE...
BE PATIENT, TAKE NO NOTE OF HIM.
IT IS MY WILL.
I'LL NOT ENDURE HIM.
KINK
HE SHALL BE ENDURED!

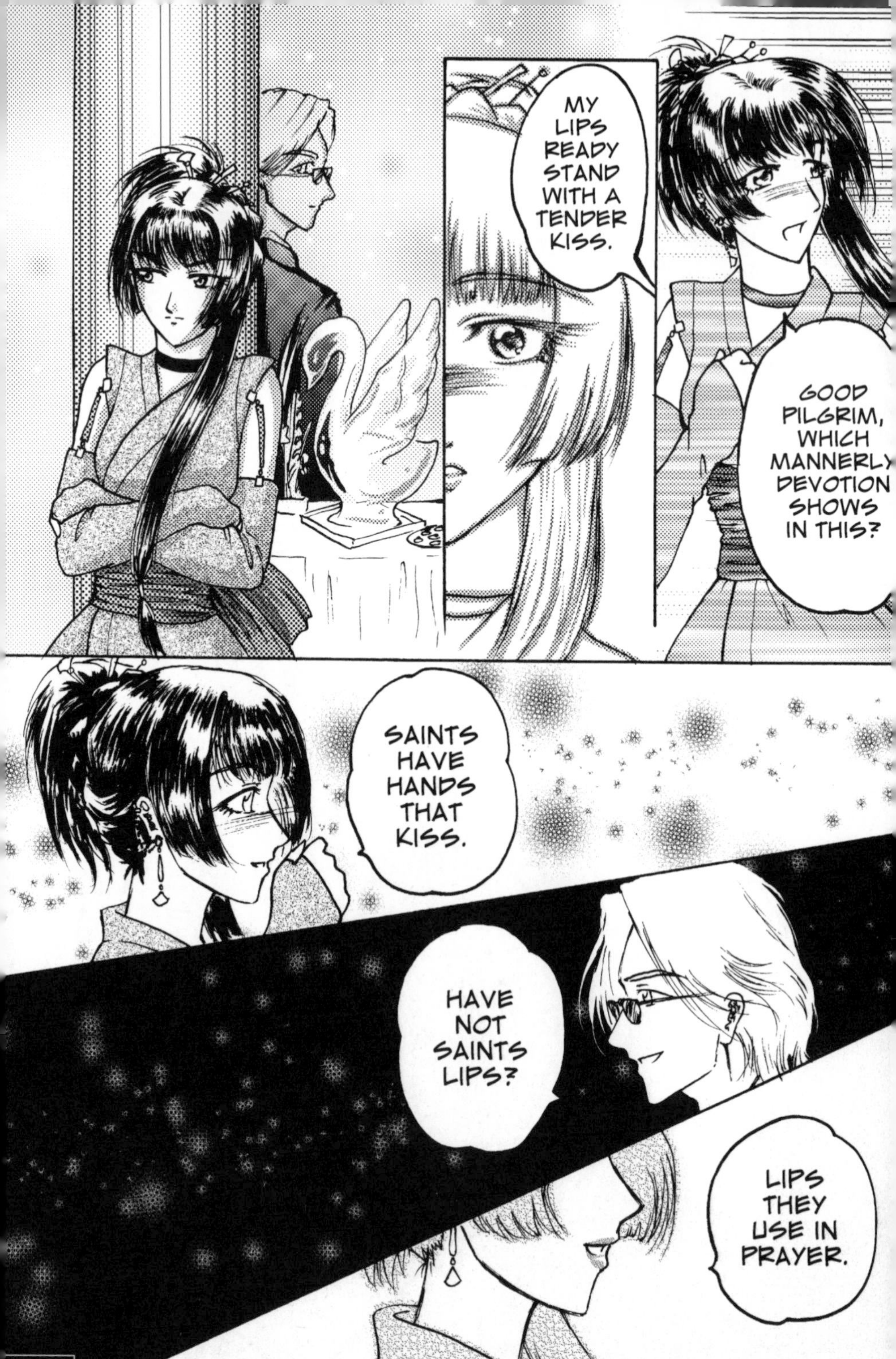

MY LIPS READY STAND WITH A TENDER KISS.
GOOD PILGRIM, WHICH MANNERLY DEVOTION SHOWS IN THIS?
SAINTS HAVE HANDS THAT KISS.
HAVE NOT SAINTS LIPS?
LIPS THEY USE IN PRAYER.

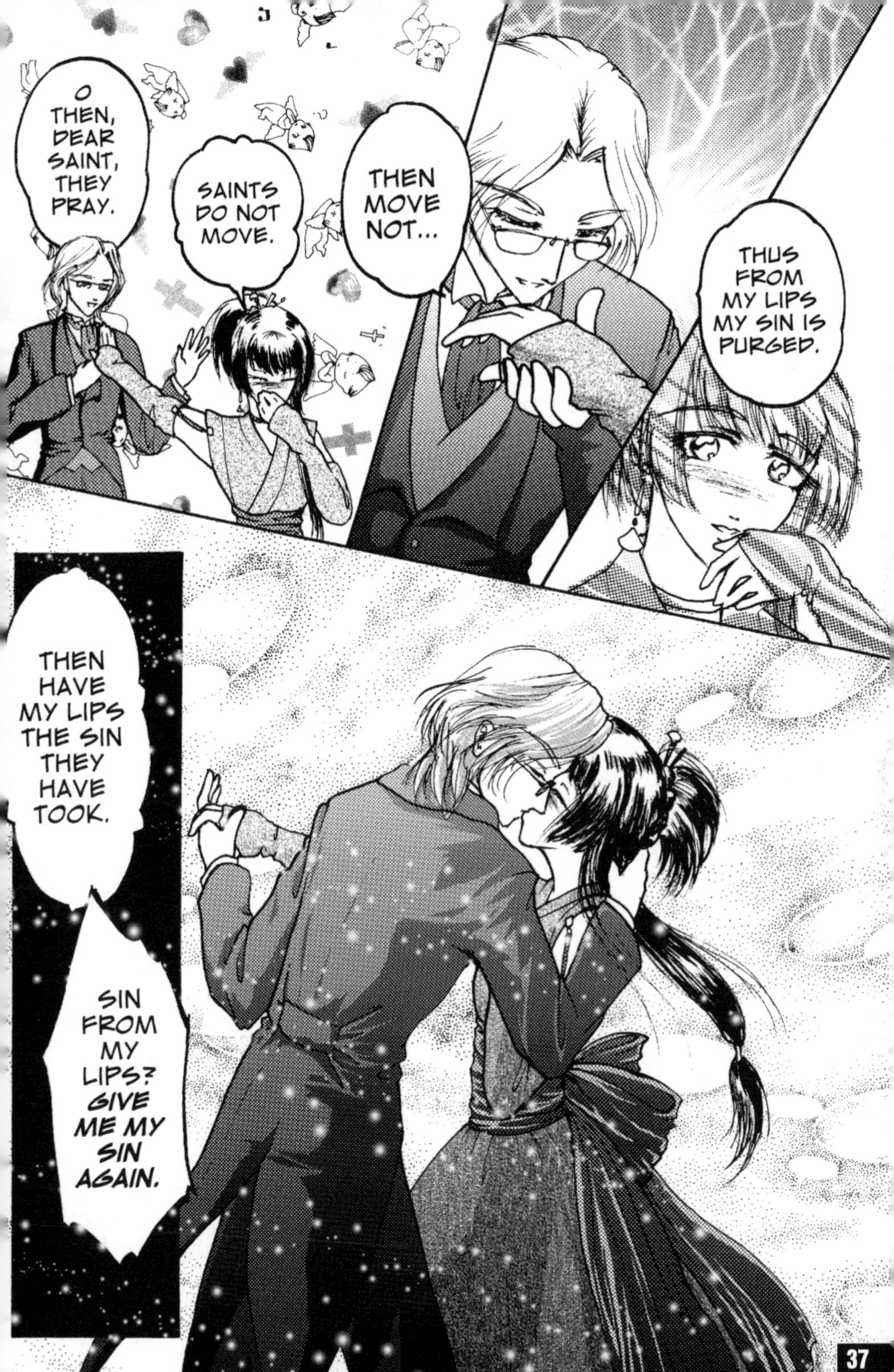
O THEN, DEAR SAINT, THEY PRAY.
SAINTS DO NOT MOVE.
THEN MOVE NOT...
THUS FROM MY LIPS MY SIN IS PURGED.
THEN HAVE MY LIPS THE SIN THEY HAVE TOOK.
SIN FROM MY LIPS? *GIVE ME MY SIN AGAIN.*

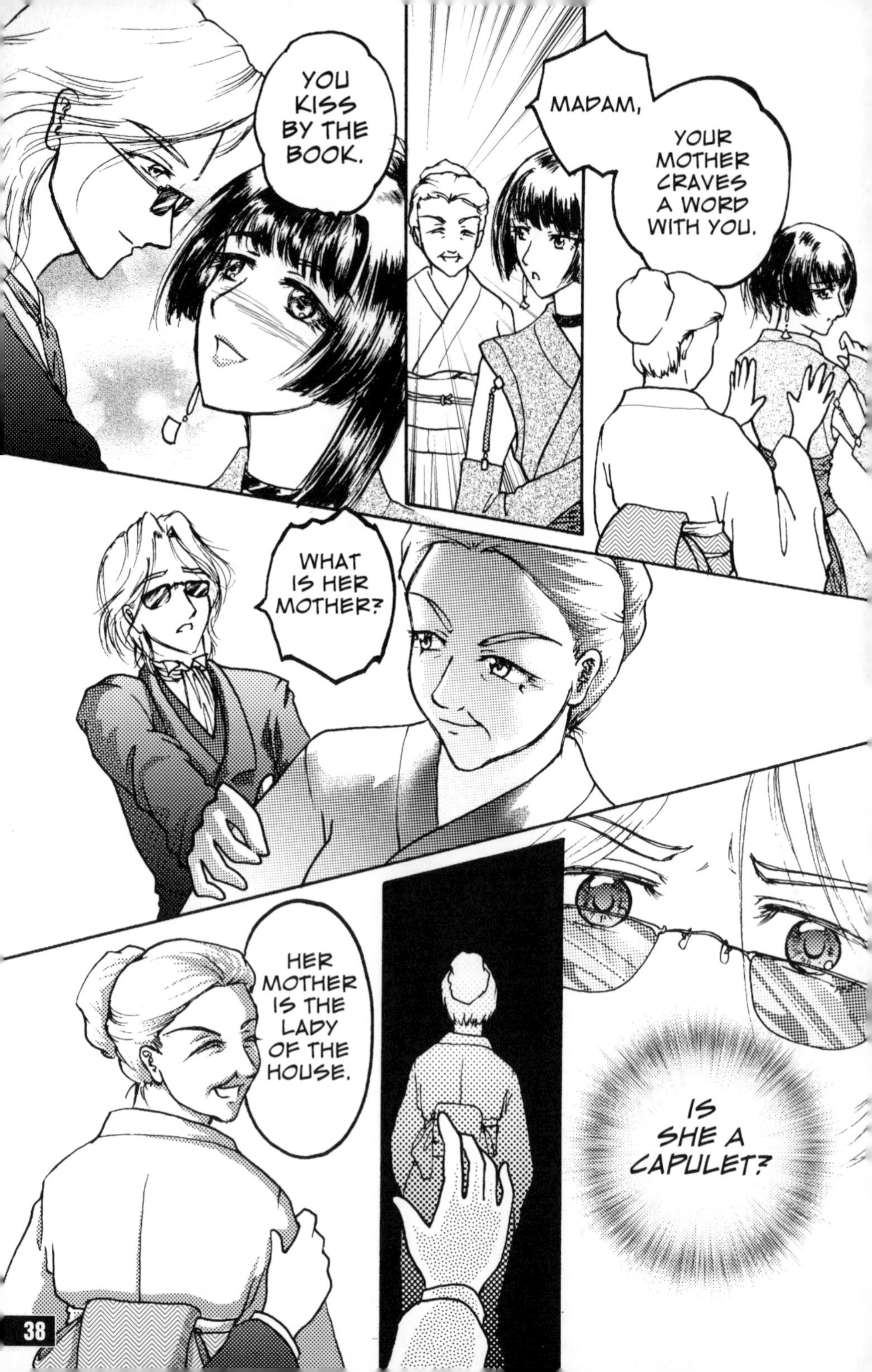
YOU KISS BY THE BOOK.
MADAM,
YOUR MOTHER CRAVES A WORD WITH YOU.
WHAT IS HER MOTHER?
HER MOTHER IS THE LADY OF THE HOUSE.
IS SHE A CAPULET?

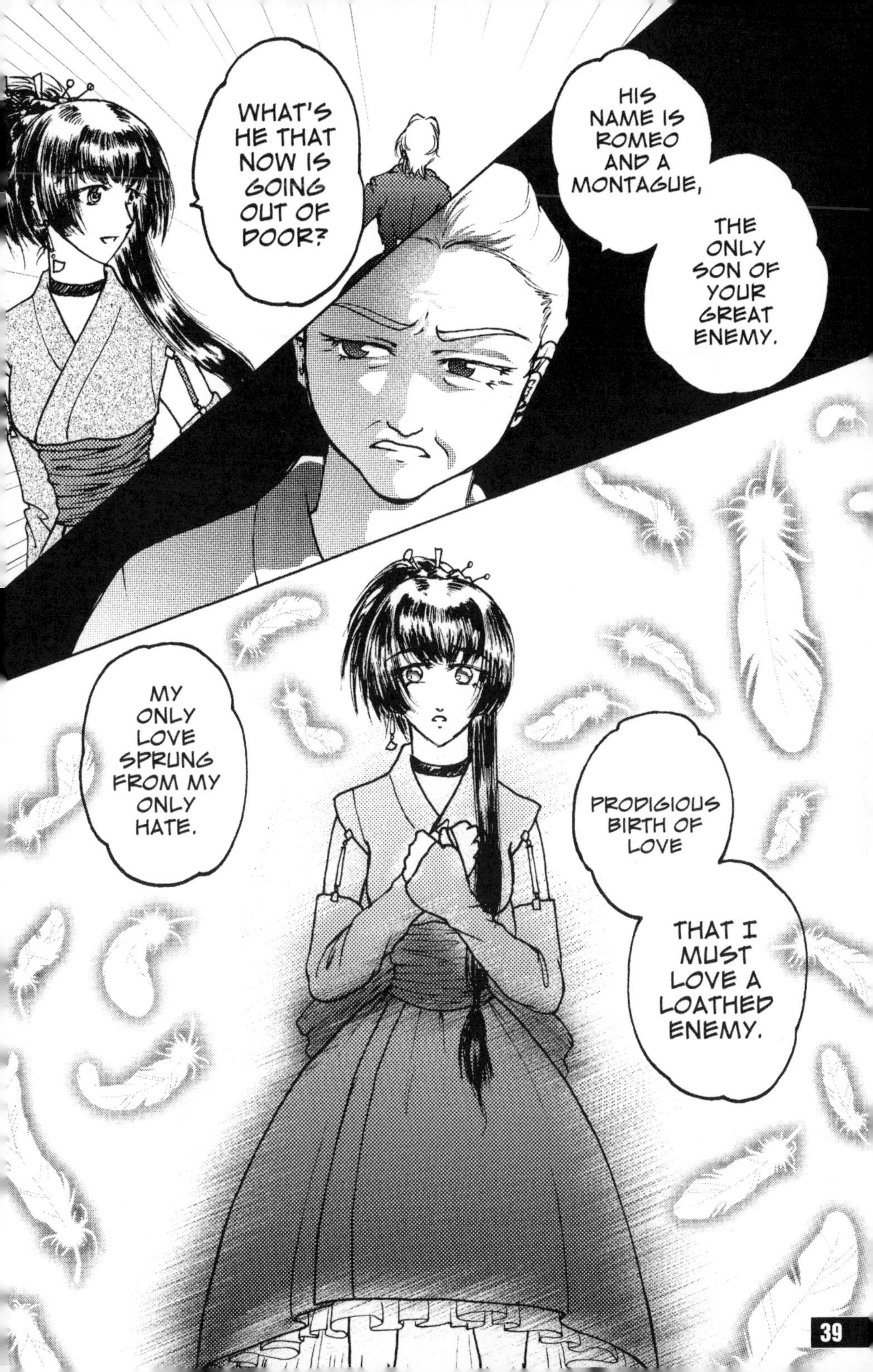
WHAT'S HE THAT NOW IS GOING OUT OF DOOR?
HIS NAME IS ROMEO AND A MONTAGUE,
THE ONLY SON OF YOUR GREAT ENEMY.
MY ONLY LOVE SPRUNG FROM MY ONLY HATE.
PRODIGIOUS BIRTH OF LOVE
THAT I MUST LOVE A LOATHED ENEMY.

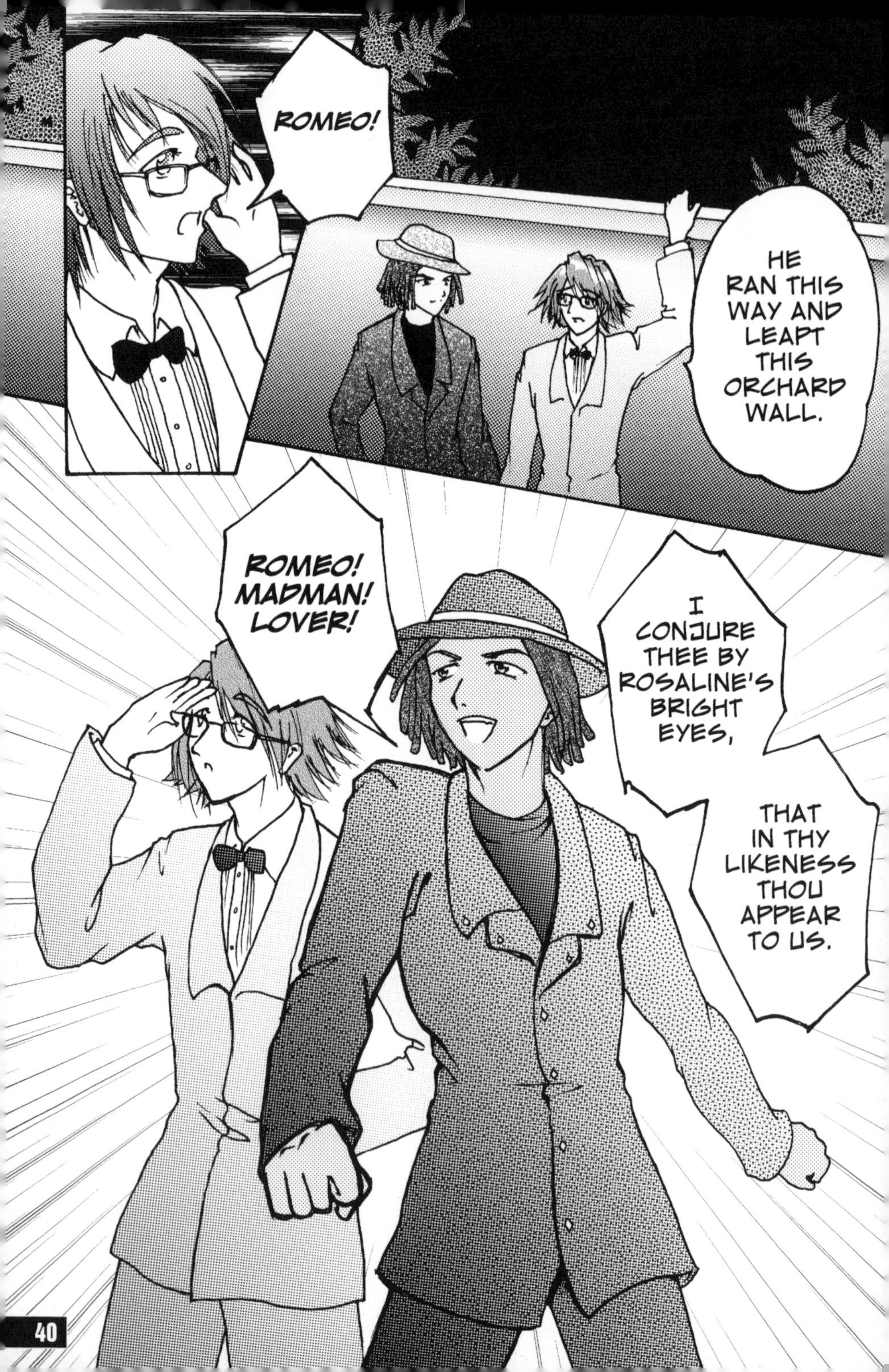
ROMEO!
HE RAN THIS WAY AND LEAPT THIS ORCHARD WALL.
ROMEO! MADMAN! LOVER!
I CONJURE THEE BY ROSALINE'S BRIGHT EYES,
THAT IN THY LIKENESS THOU APPEAR TO US.

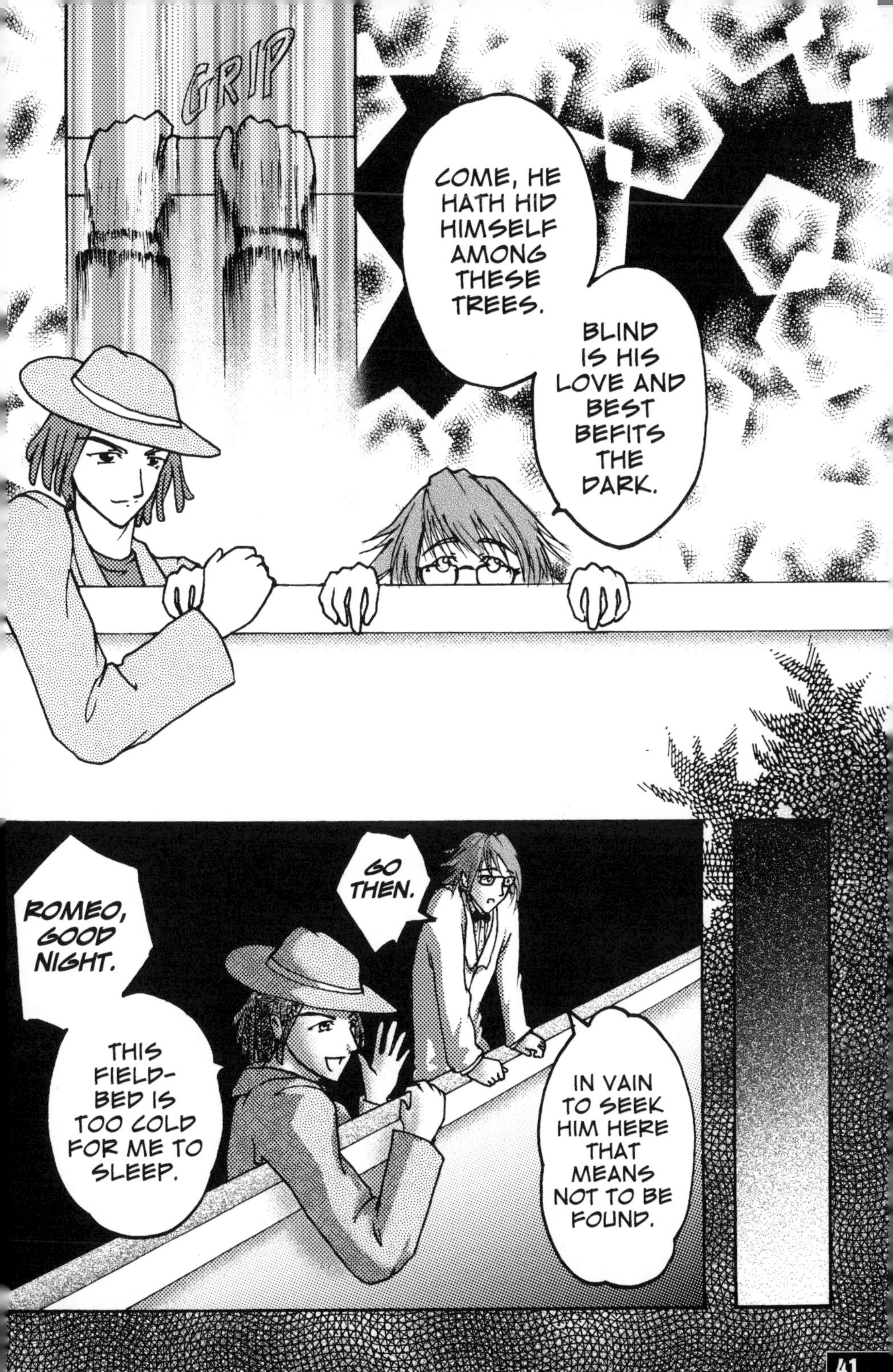
GRIP
COME, HE HATH HID HIMSELF AMONG THESE TREES.
BLIND IS HIS LOVE AND BEST BEFITS THE DARK.
GO THEN.
ROMEO, GOOD NIGHT.
THIS FIELD-BED IS TOO COLD FOR ME TO SLEEP.
IN VAIN TO SEEK HIM HERE THAT MEANS NOT TO BE FOUND.

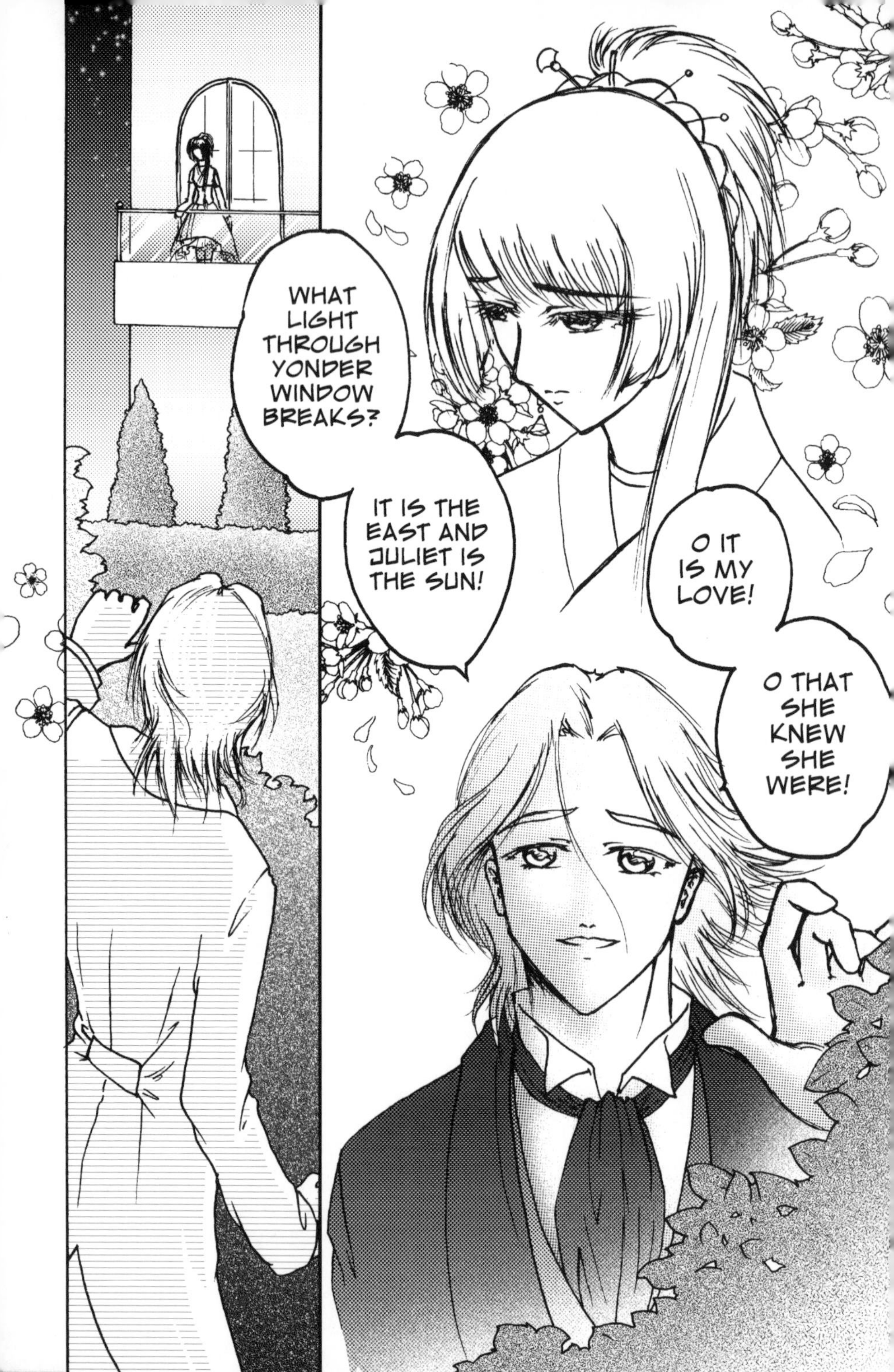
WHAT LIGHT THROUGH YONDER WINDOW BREAKS?
IT IS THE EAST AND JULIET IS THE SUN!
O IT IS MY LOVE!
O THAT SHE KNEW SHE WERE!

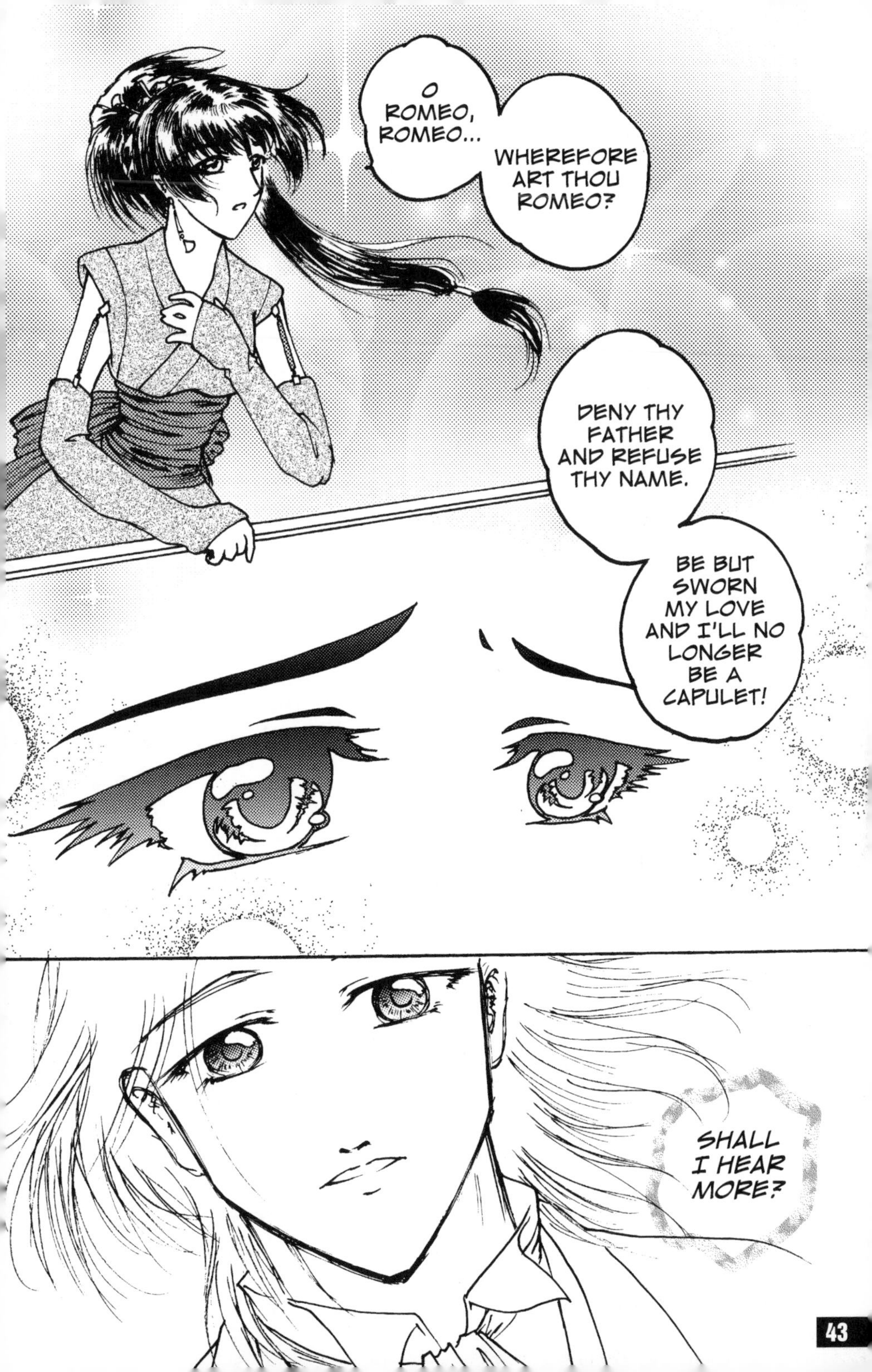
O ROMEO, ROMEO...
WHEREFORE ART THOU ROMEO?
DENY THY FATHER AND REFUSE THY NAME.
BE BUT SWORN MY LOVE AND I'LL NO LONGER BE A CAPULET!
SHALL I HEAR MORE?

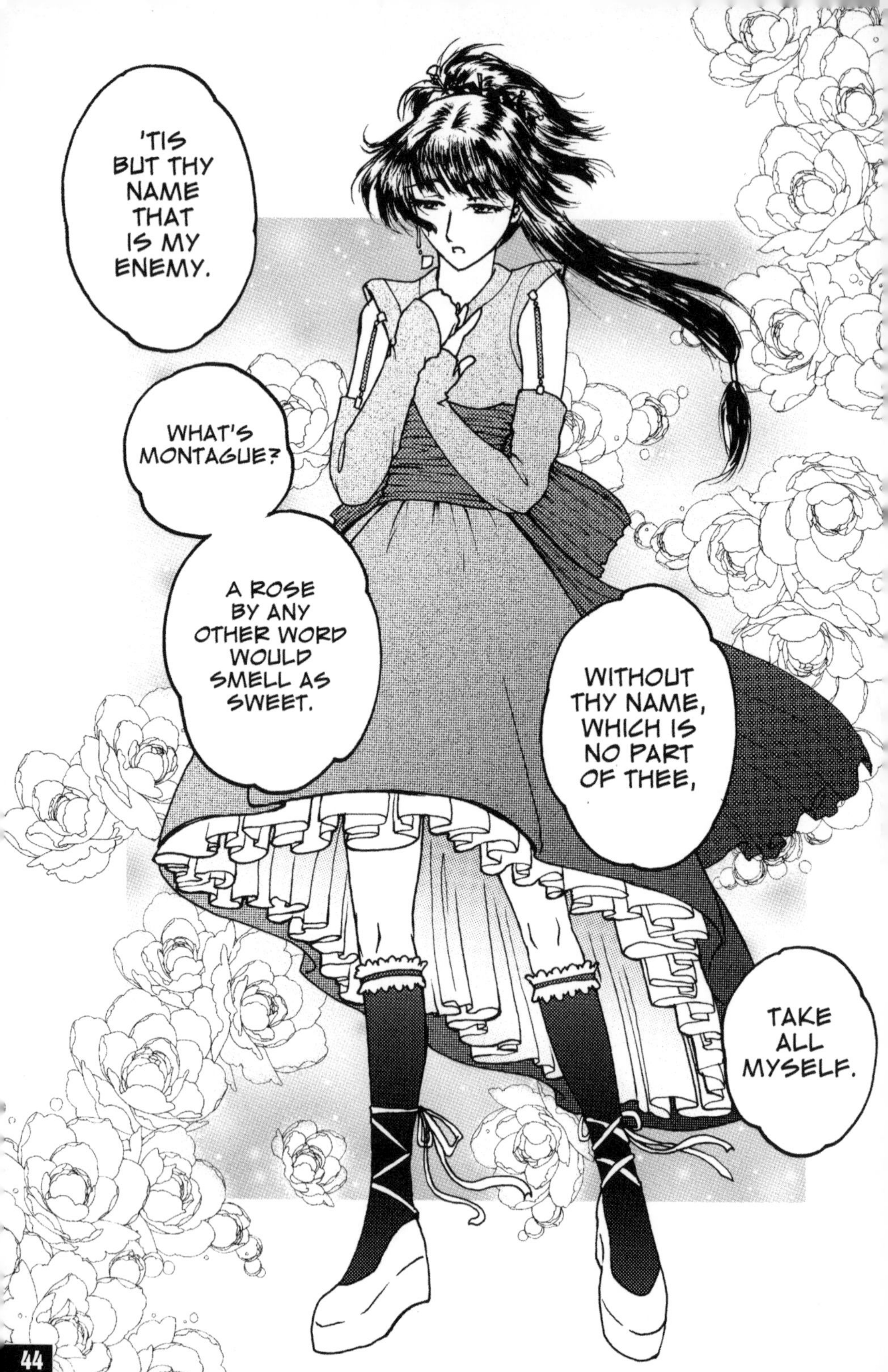
'TIS BUT THY NAME THAT IS MY ENEMY.
WHAT'S MONTAGUE?
A ROSE BY ANY OTHER WORD WOULD SMELL AS SWEET.
WITHOUT THY NAME, WHICH IS NO PART OF THEE,
TAKE ALL MYSELF.

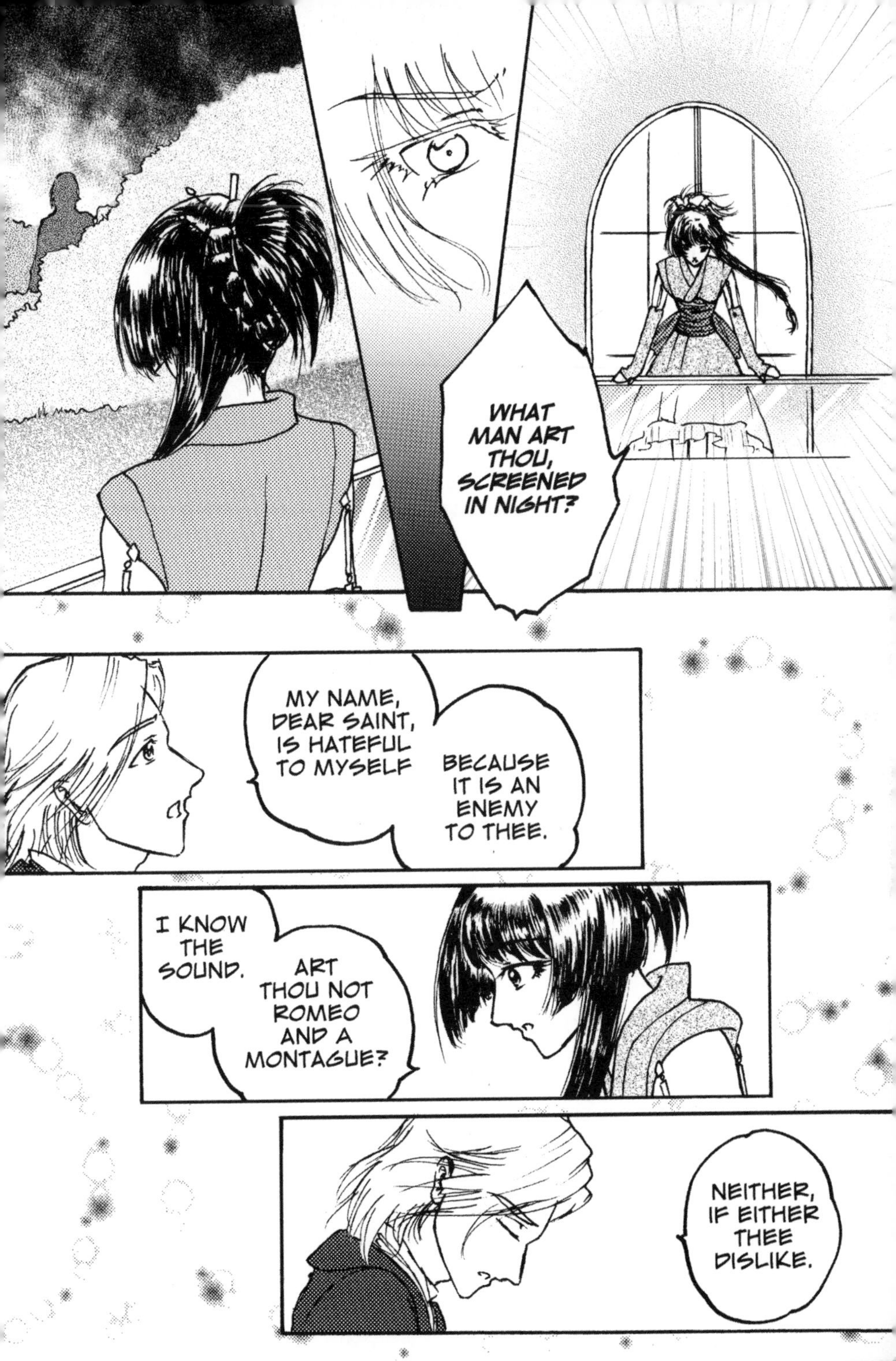
WHAT MAN ART THOU, SCREENED IN NIGHT?
MY NAME, DEAR SAINT, IS HATEFUL TO MYSELF
BECAUSE IT IS AN ENEMY TO THEE.
I KNOW THE SOUND.
ART THOU NOT ROMEO AND A MONTAGUE?
NEITHER, IF EITHER THEE DISLIKE.

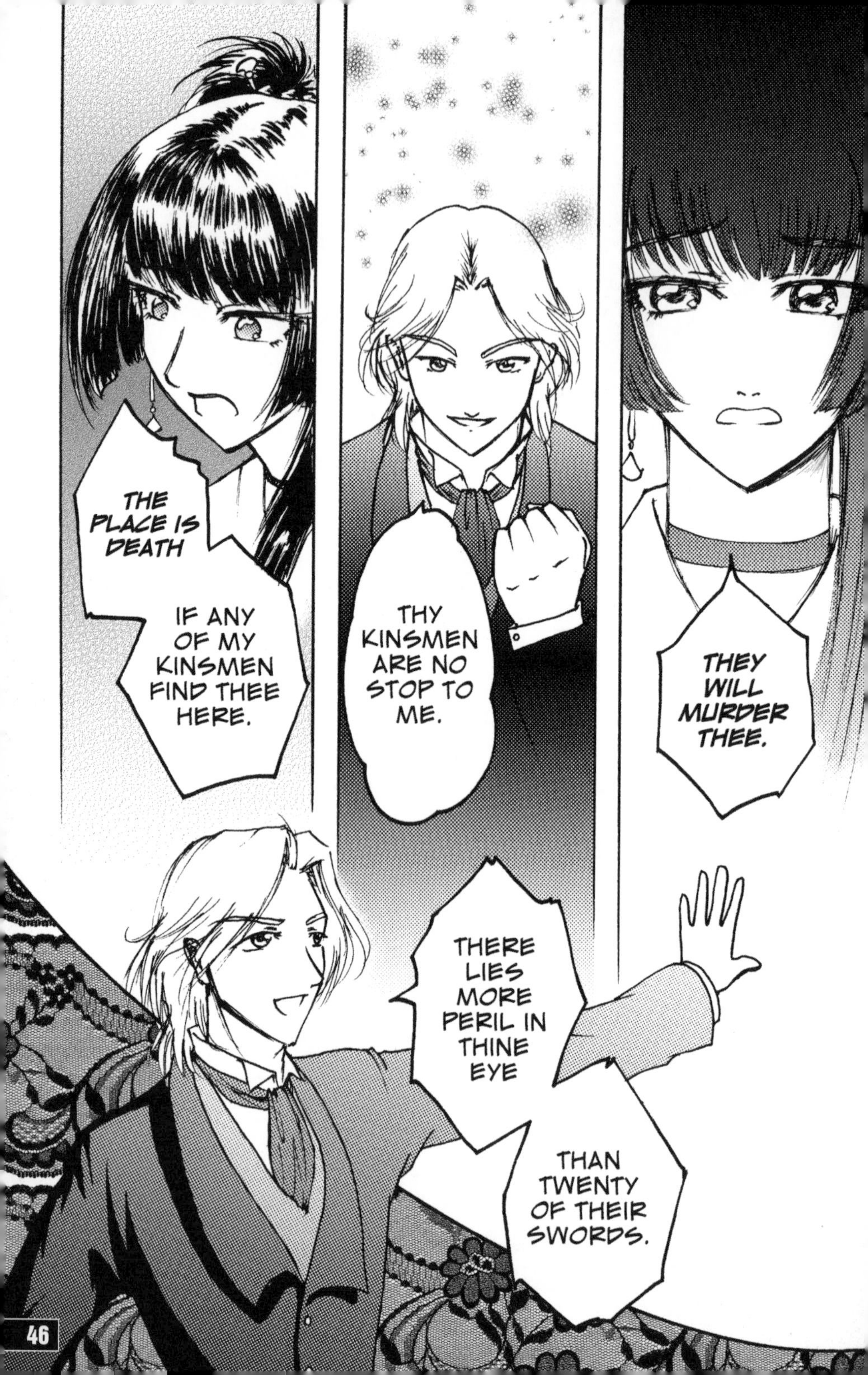
THE PLACE IS DEATH
IF ANY OF MY KINSMEN FIND THEE HERE.
THY KINSMEN ARE NO STOP TO ME.
THEY WILL MURDER THEE.
THERE LIES MORE PERIL IN THINE EYE
THAN TWENTY OF THEIR SWORDS.

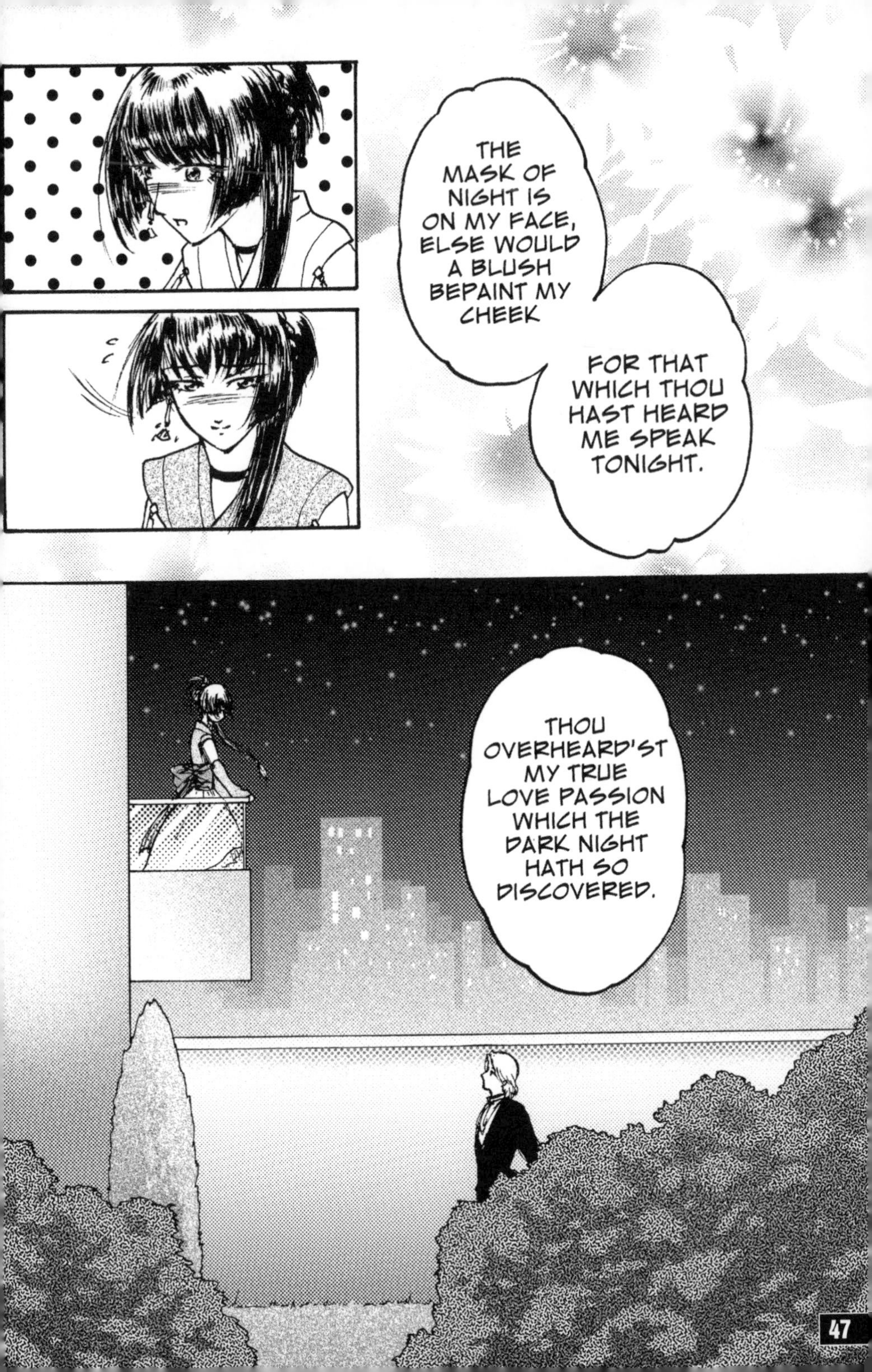
THE MASK OF NIGHT IS ON MY FACE, ELSE WOULD A BLUSH BEPAINT MY CHEEK
FOR THAT WHICH THOU HAST HEARD ME SPEAK TONIGHT.
THOU OVERHEARD'ST MY TRUE LOVE PASSION WHICH THE DARK NIGHT HATH SO DISCOVERED.

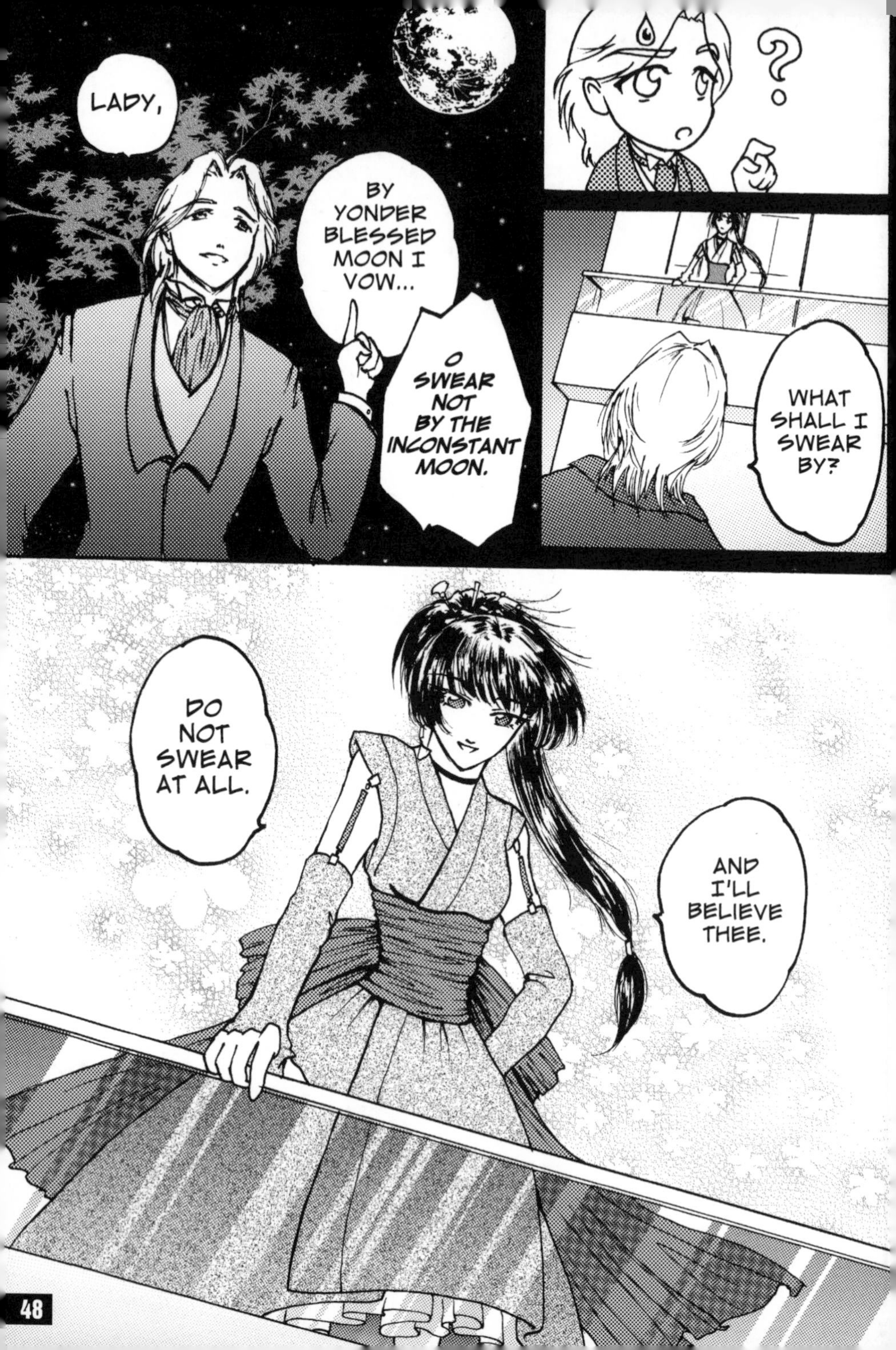
LADY,
BY YONDER BLESSED MOON I VOW...
O SWEAR NOT BY THE INCONSTANT MOON.
?
WHAT SHALL I SWEAR BY?
DO NOT SWEAR AT ALL.
AND I'LL BELIEVE THEE.

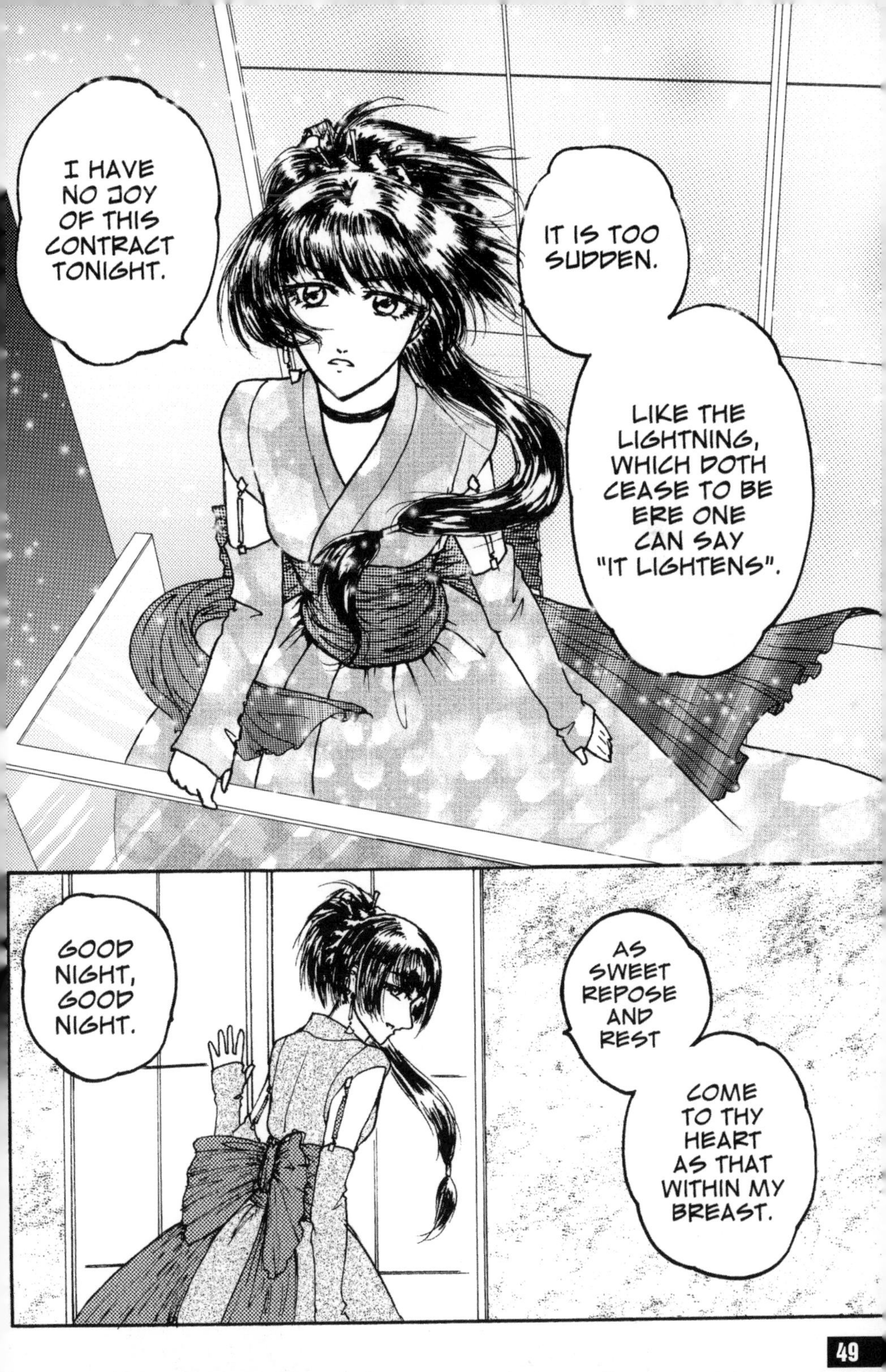
I HAVE NO JOY OF THIS CONTRACT TONIGHT.
IT IS TOO SUDDEN.
LIKE THE LIGHTNING, WHICH DOTH CEASE TO BE ERE ONE CAN SAY "IT LIGHTENS".
GOOD NIGHT, GOOD NIGHT.
AS SWEET REPOSE AND REST
COME TO THY HEART AS THAT WITHIN MY BREAST.

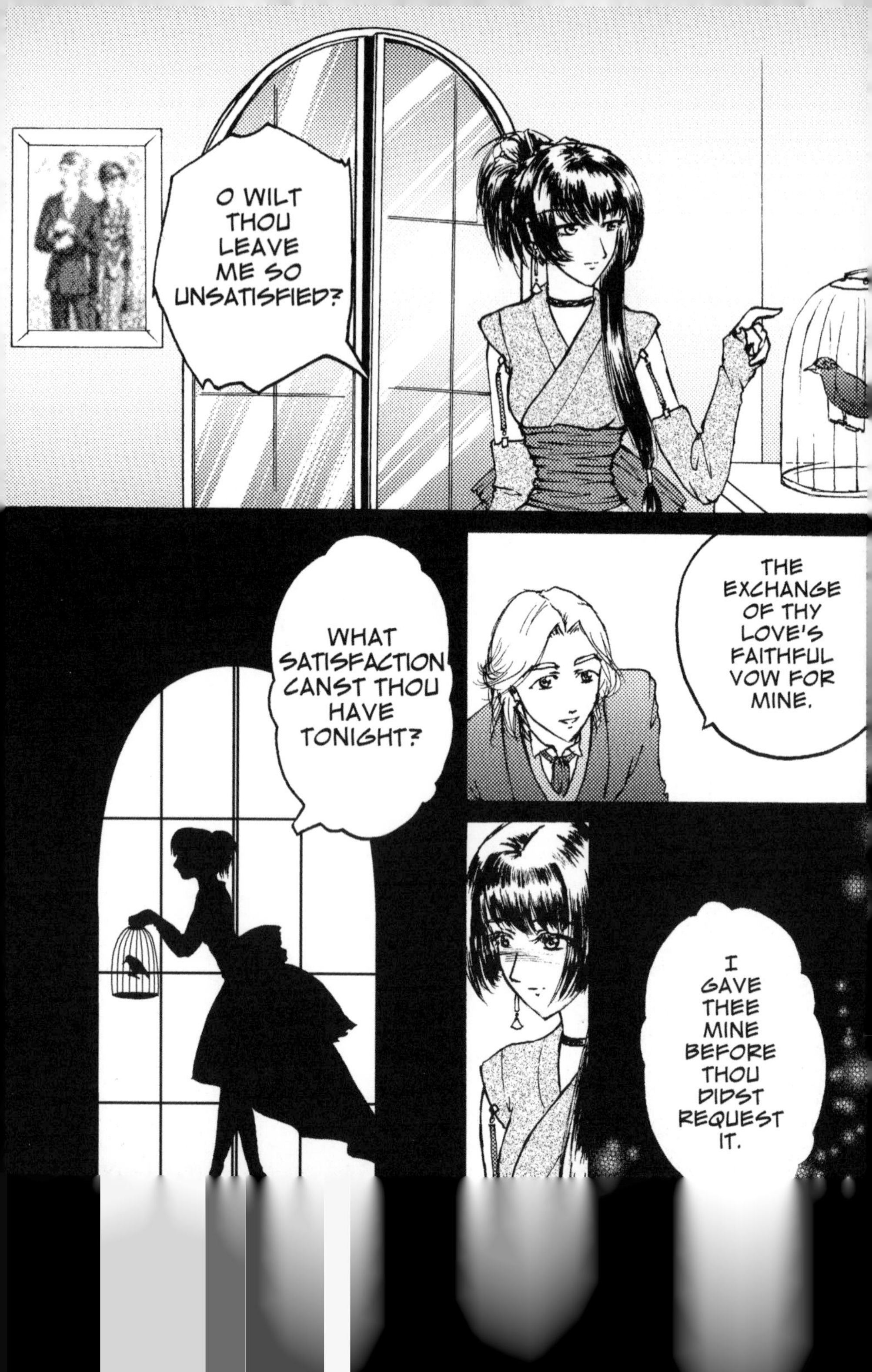
O WILT THOU LEAVE ME SO UNSATISFIED?
THE EXCHANGE OF THY LOVE'S FAITHFUL VOW FOR MINE.
WHAT SATISFACTION CANST THOU HAVE TONIGHT?
I GAVE THEE MINE BEFORE THOU DIDST REQUEST IT.

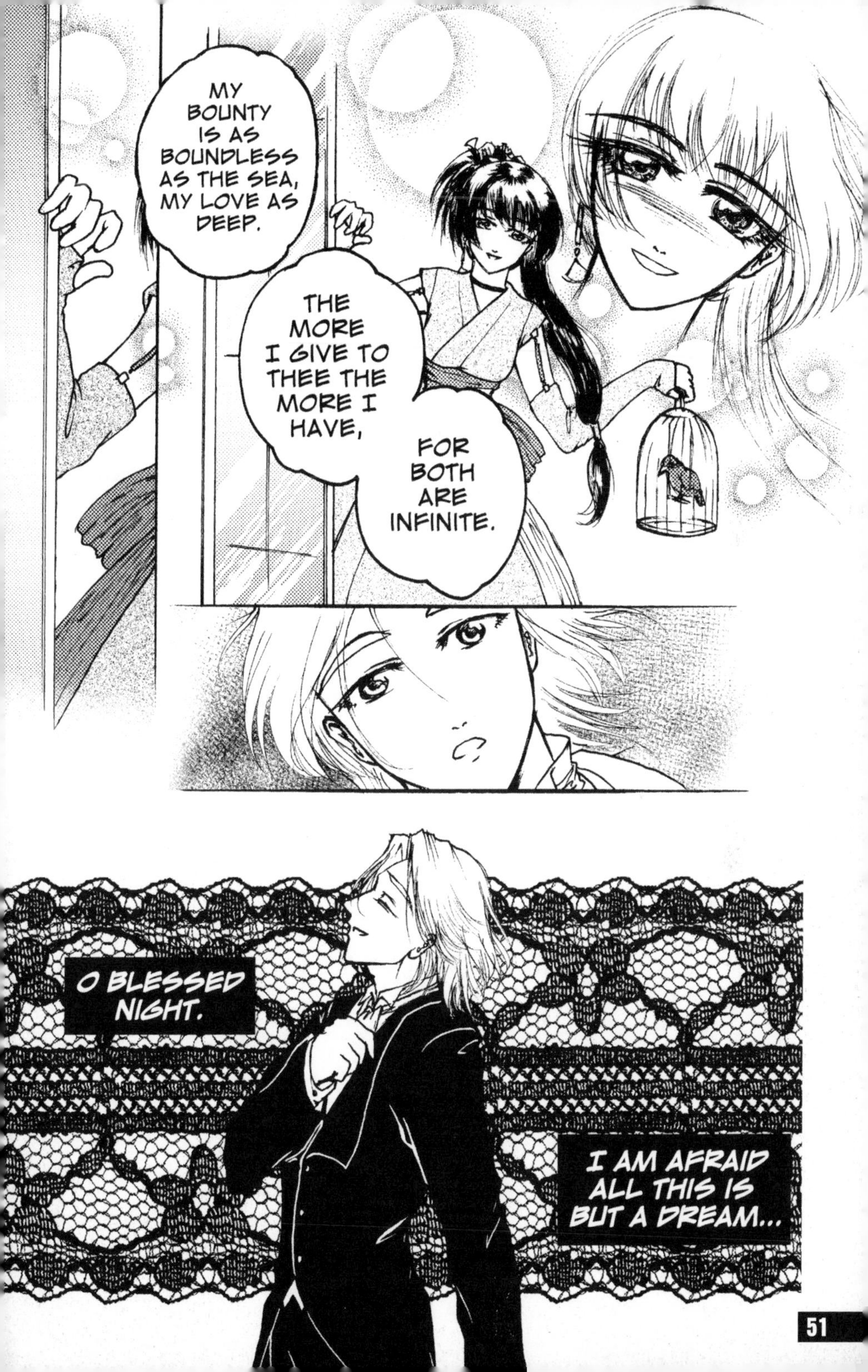
MY BOUNTY IS AS BOUNDLESS AS THE SEA, MY LOVE AS DEEP.
THE MORE I GIVE TO THEE THE MORE I HAVE,
FOR BOTH ARE INFINITE.
O BLESSED NIGHT.
I AM AFRAID ALL THIS IS BUT A DREAM...

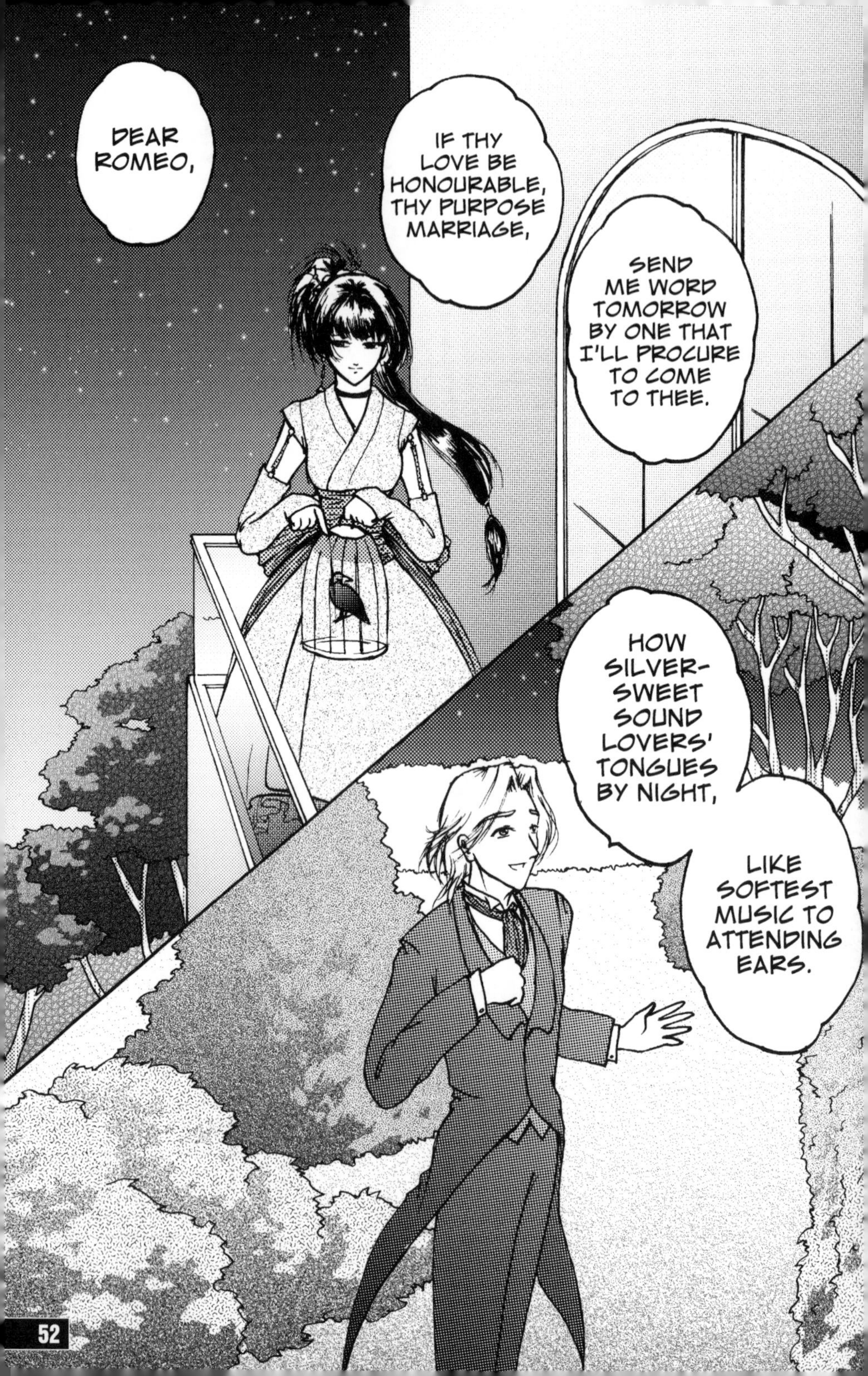
DEAR ROMEO,
IF THY LOVE BE HONOURABLE, THY PURPOSE MARRIAGE,
SEND ME WORD TOMORROW BY ONE THAT I'LL PROCURE TO COME TO THEE.
HOW SILVER-SWEET SOUND LOVERS' TONGUES BY NIGHT,
LIKE SOFTEST MUSIC TO ATTENDING EARS.

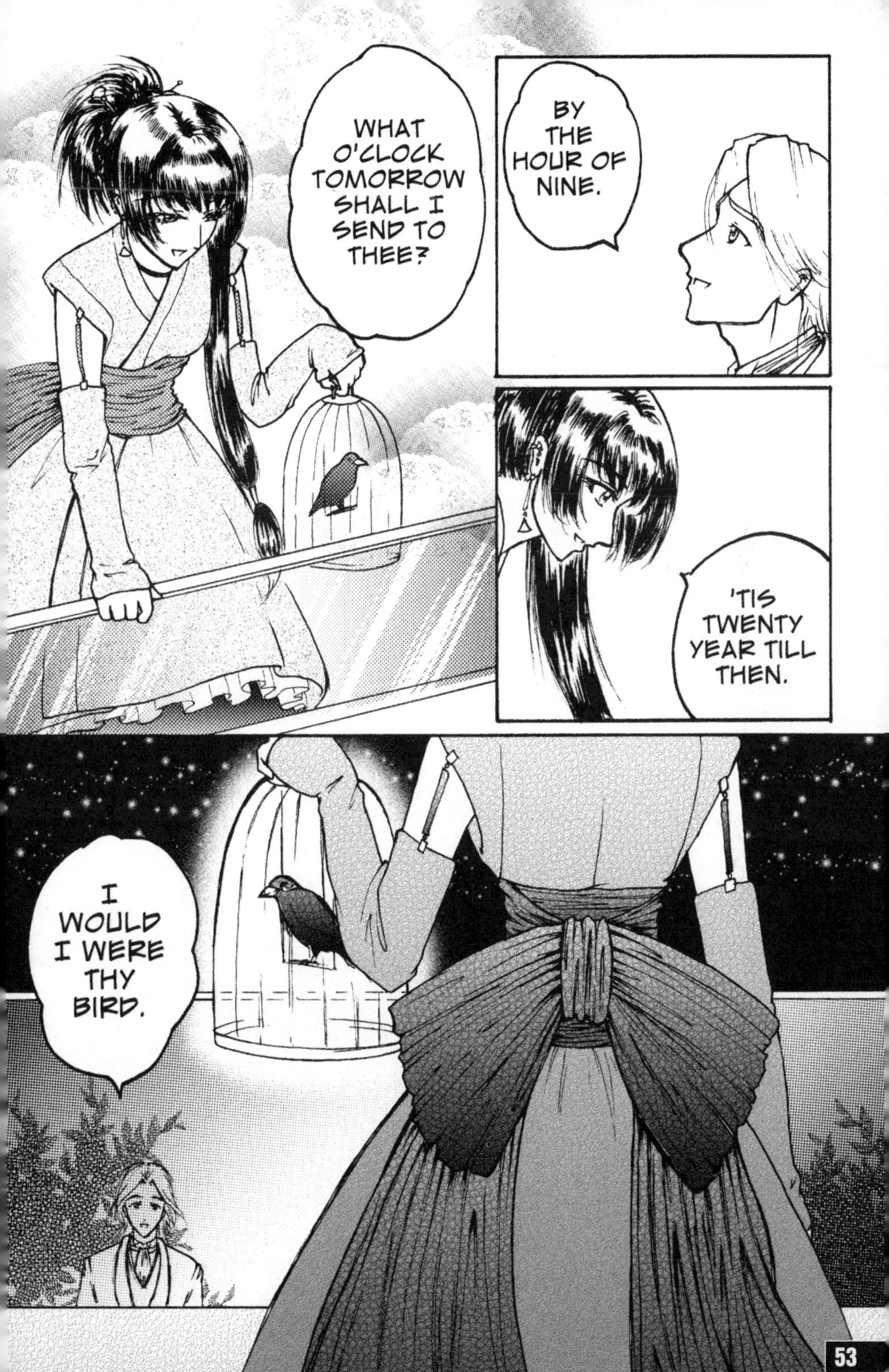
WHAT O'CLOCK TOMORROW SHALL I SEND TO THEE?
BY THE HOUR OF NINE.
'TIS TWENTY YEAR TILL THEN.
I WOULD I WERE THY BIRD.

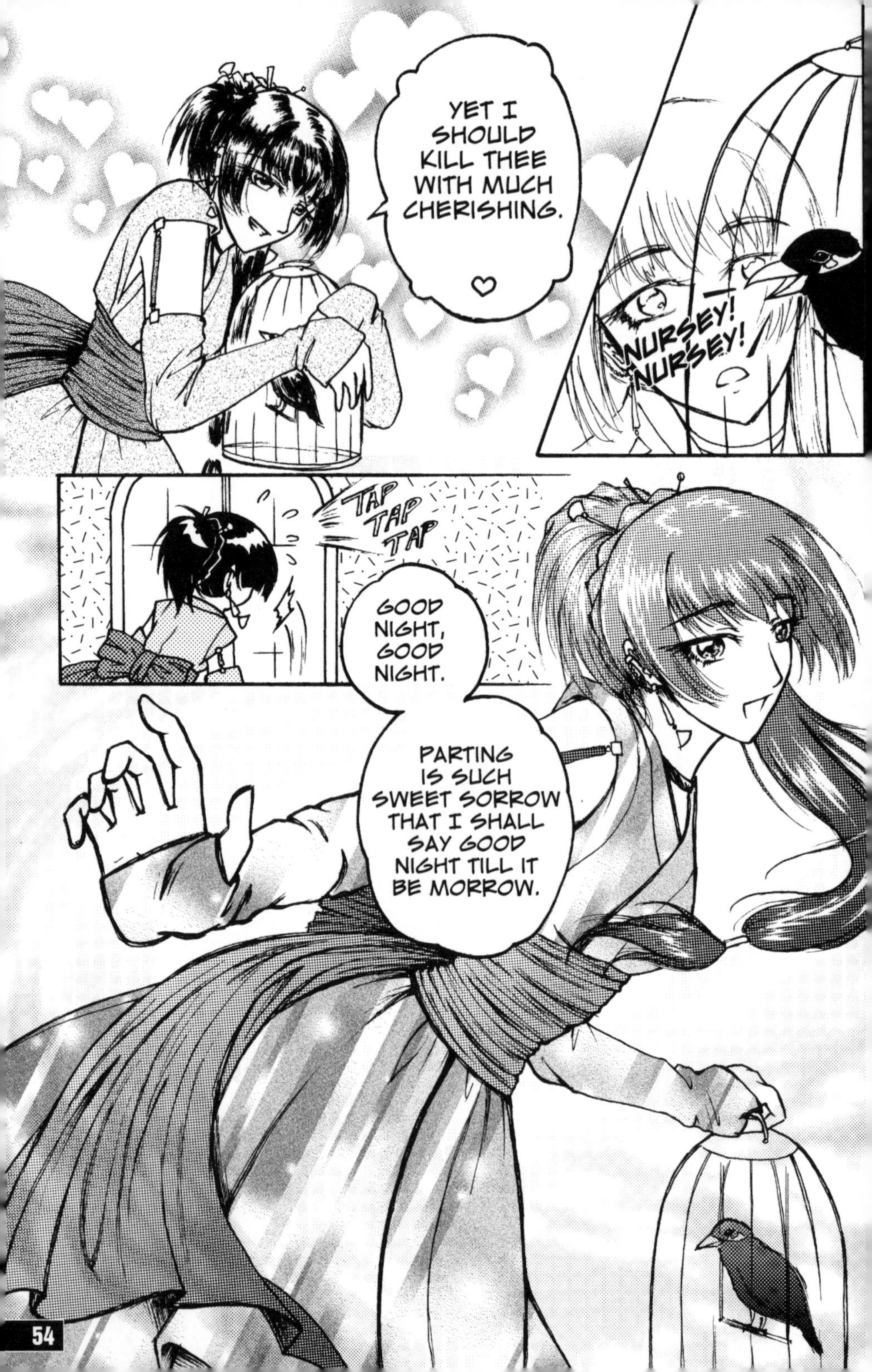
YET I SHOULD KILL THEE WITH MUCH CHERISHING. ♡
NURSEY! NURSEY!
TAP TAP TAP
GOOD NIGHT, GOOD NIGHT.
PARTING IS SUCH SWEET SORROW THAT I SHALL SAY GOOD NIGHT TILL IT BE MORROW.

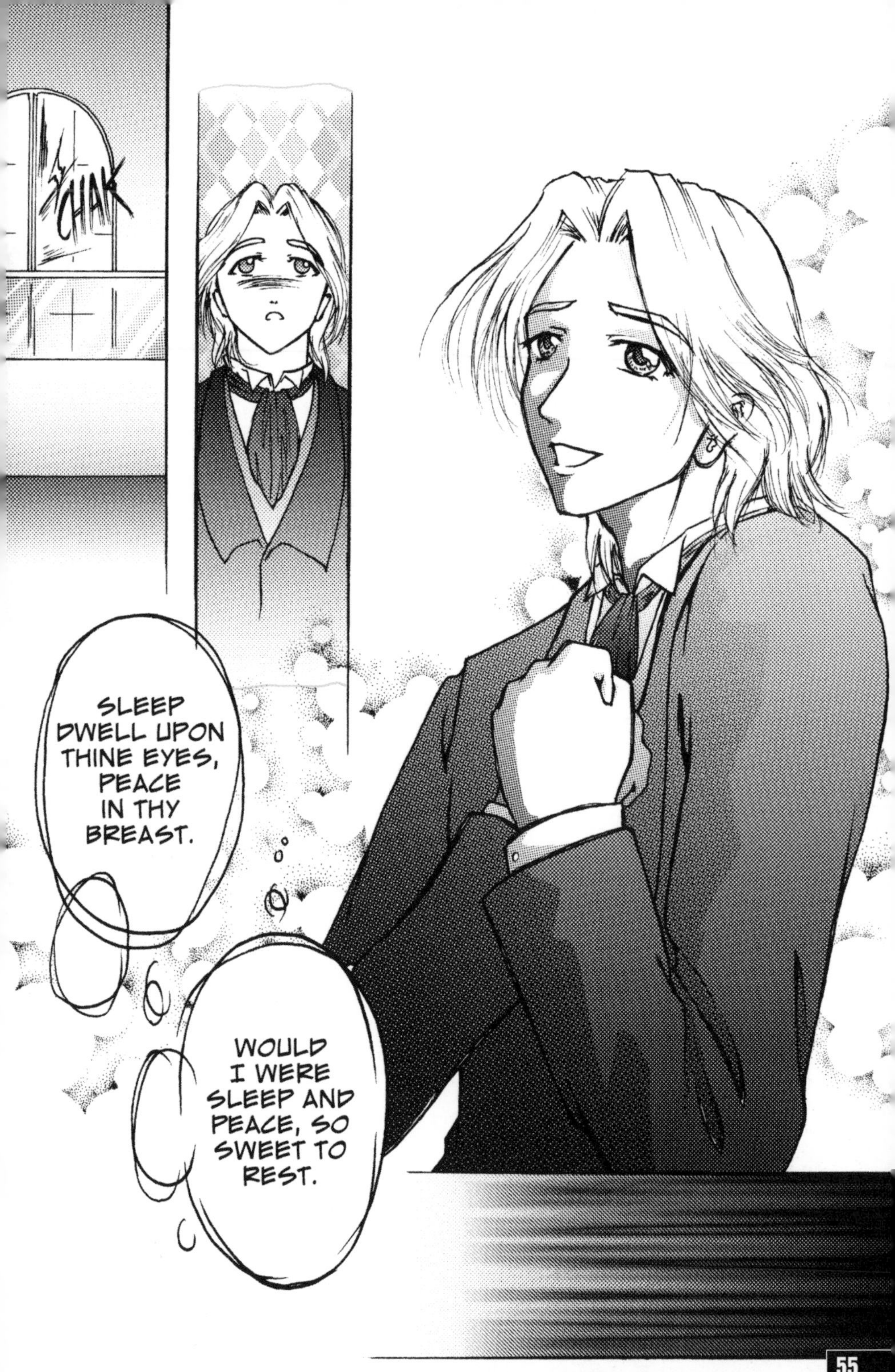
CHAK
SLEEP DWELL UPON THINE EYES, PEACE IN THY BREAST.
WOULD I WERE SLEEP AND PEACE, SO SWEET TO REST.

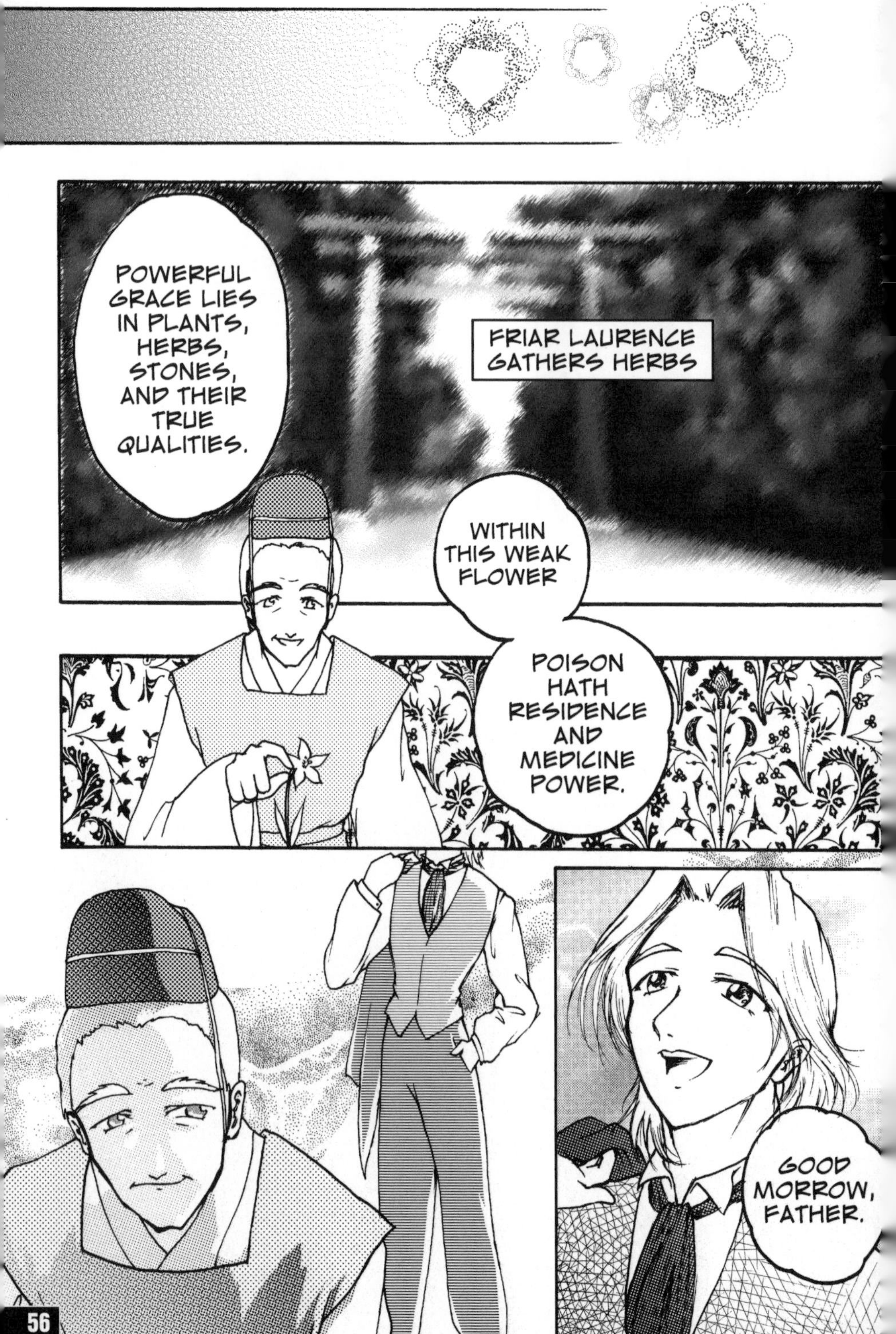
POWERFUL GRACE LIES IN PLANTS, HERBS, STONES, AND THEIR TRUE QUALITIES.
FRIAR LAURENCE GATHERS HERBS
WITHIN THIS WEAK FLOWER
POISON HATH RESIDENCE AND MEDICINE POWER.
GOOD MORROW, FATHER.

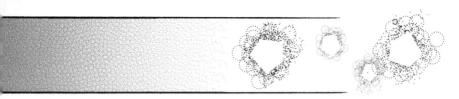

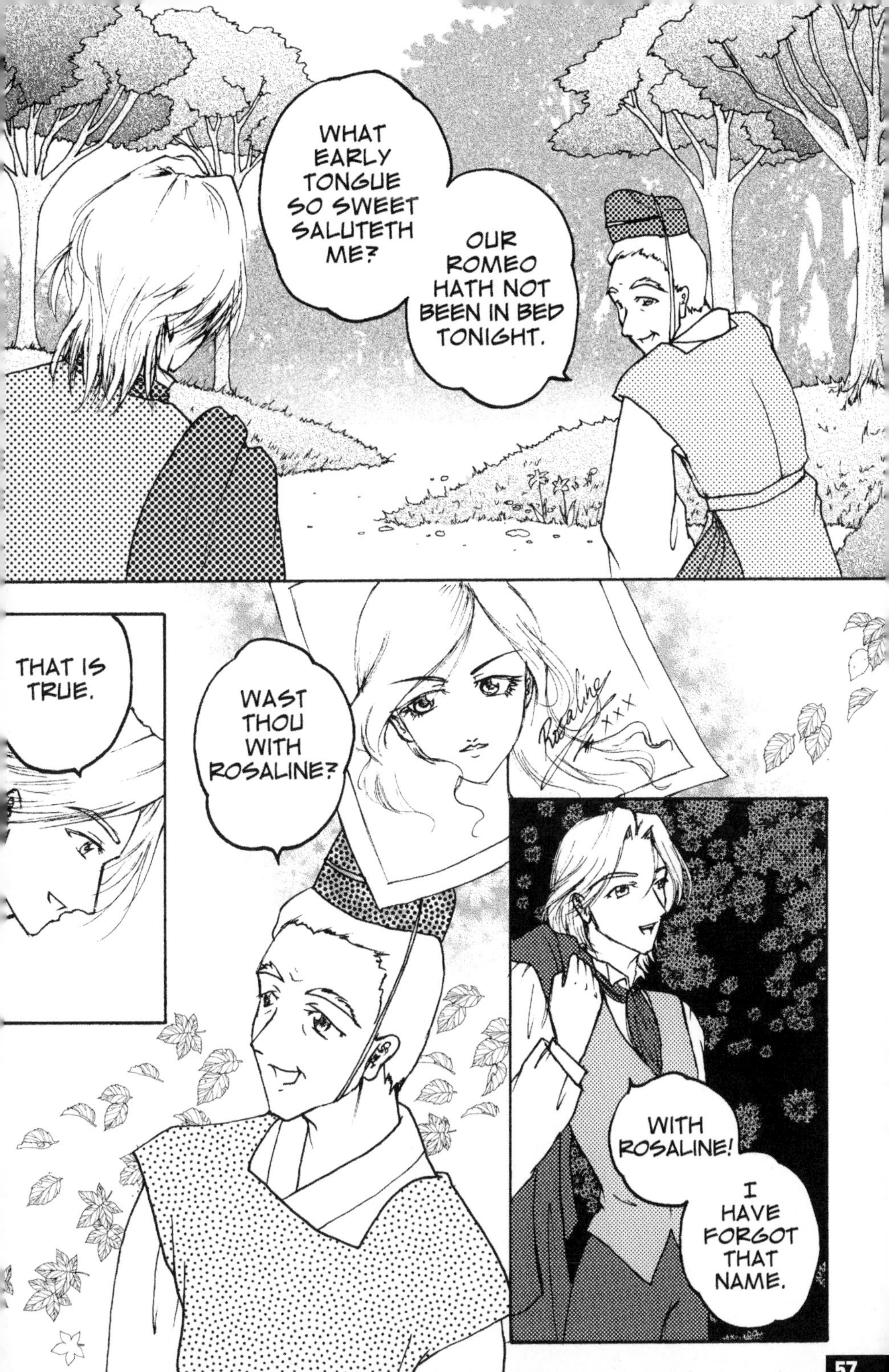
WHAT EARLY TONGUE SO SWEET SALUTETH ME?
OUR ROMEO HATH NOT BEEN IN BED TONIGHT.
THAT IS TRUE.
WAST THOU WITH ROSALINE?
Rosaline xxx
WITH ROSALINE!
I HAVE FORGOT THAT NAME.

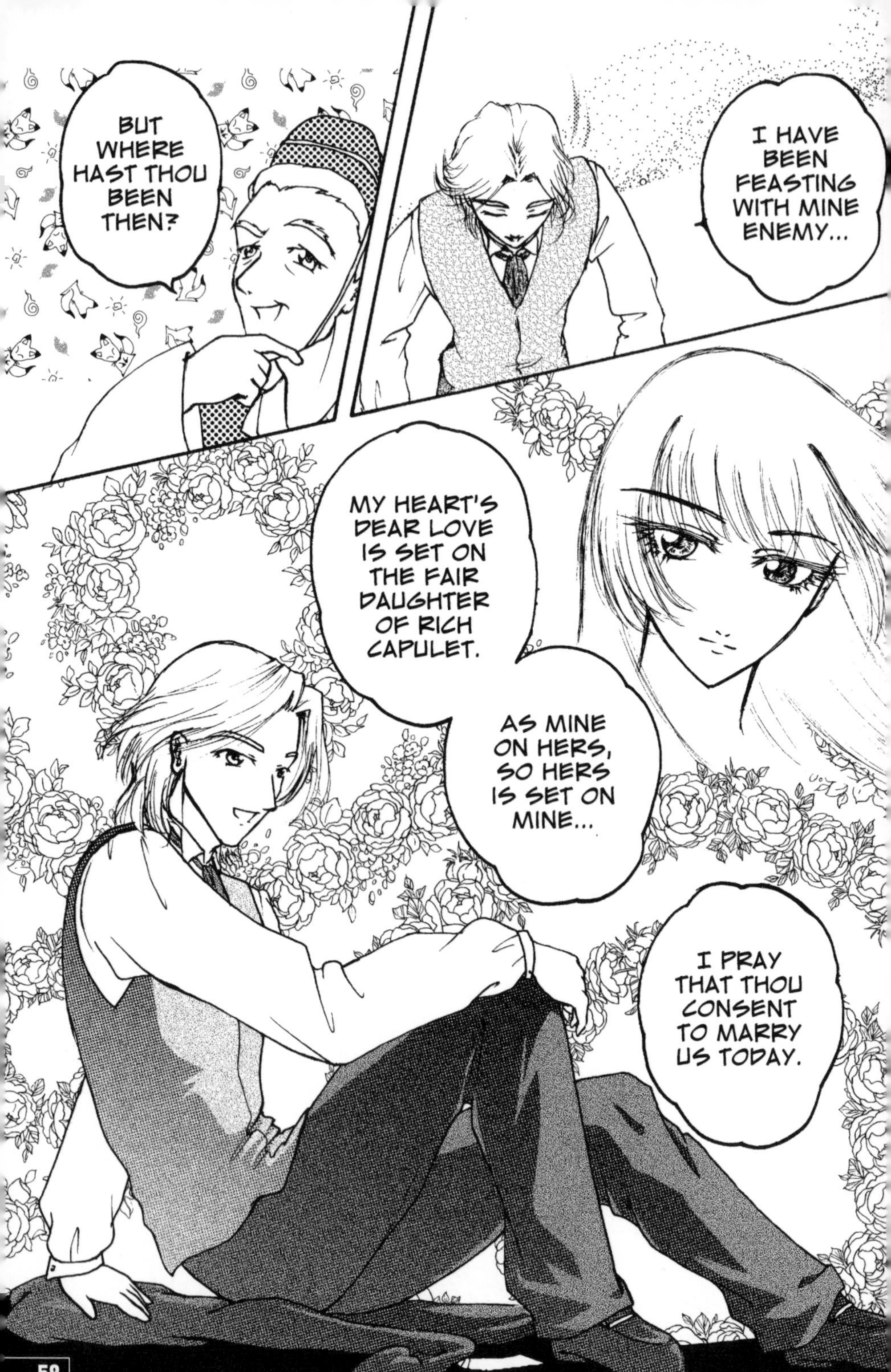
BUT WHERE HAST THOU BEEN THEN?
I HAVE BEEN FEASTING WITH MINE ENEMY...
MY HEART'S DEAR LOVE IS SET ON THE FAIR DAUGHTER OF RICH CAPULET.
AS MINE ON HERS, SO HERS IS SET ON MINE...
I PRAY THAT THOU CONSENT TO MARRY US TODAY.

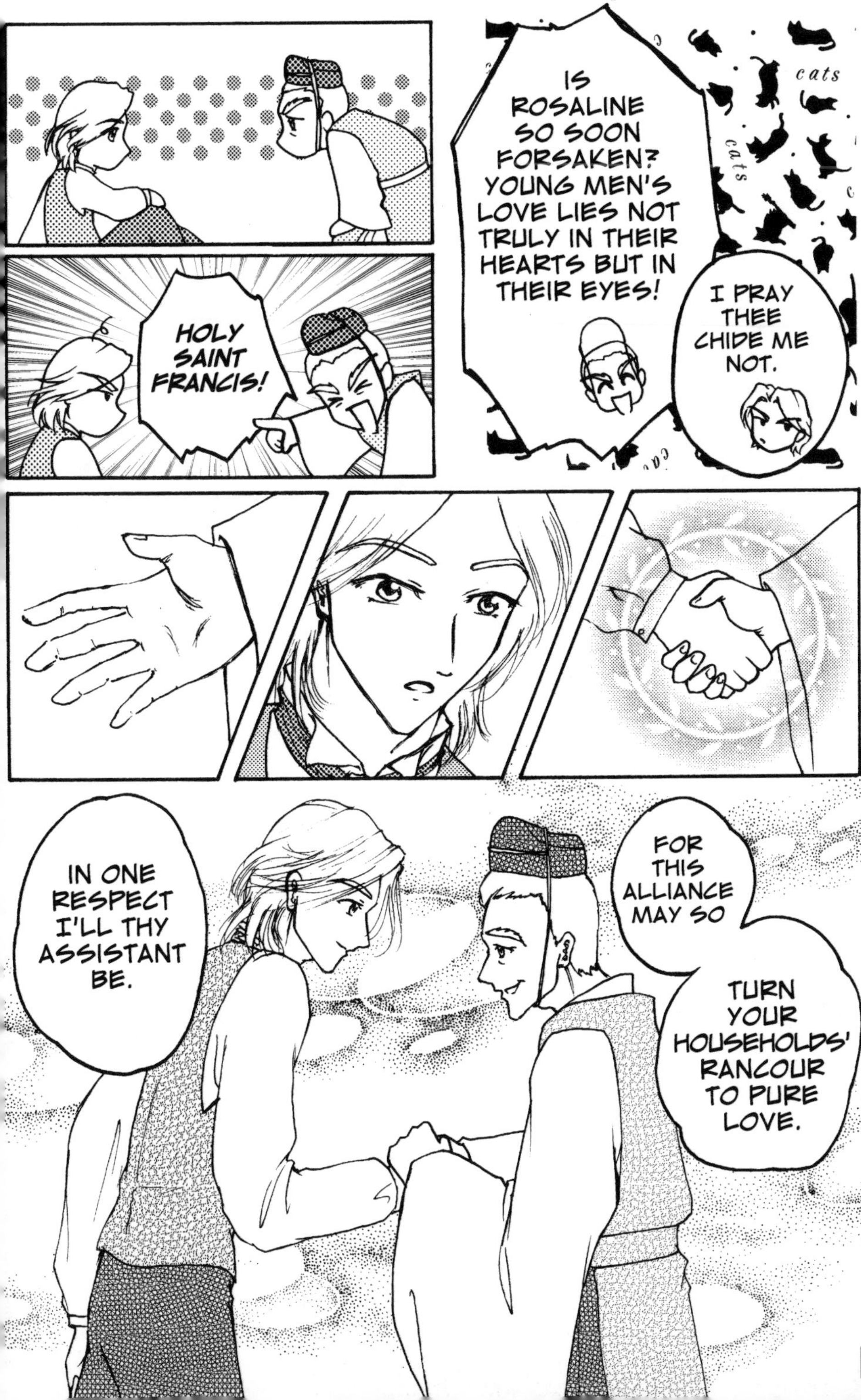
HOLY SAINT FRANCIS!
IS ROSALINE SO SOON FORSAKEN? YOUNG MEN'S LOVE LIES NOT TRULY IN THEIR HEARTS BUT IN THEIR EYES!
cats
I PRAY THEE CHIDE ME NOT.
IN ONE RESPECT I'LL THY ASSISTANT BE.
FOR THIS ALLIANCE MAY SO
TURN YOUR HOUSEHOLDS' RANCOUR TO PURE LOVE.

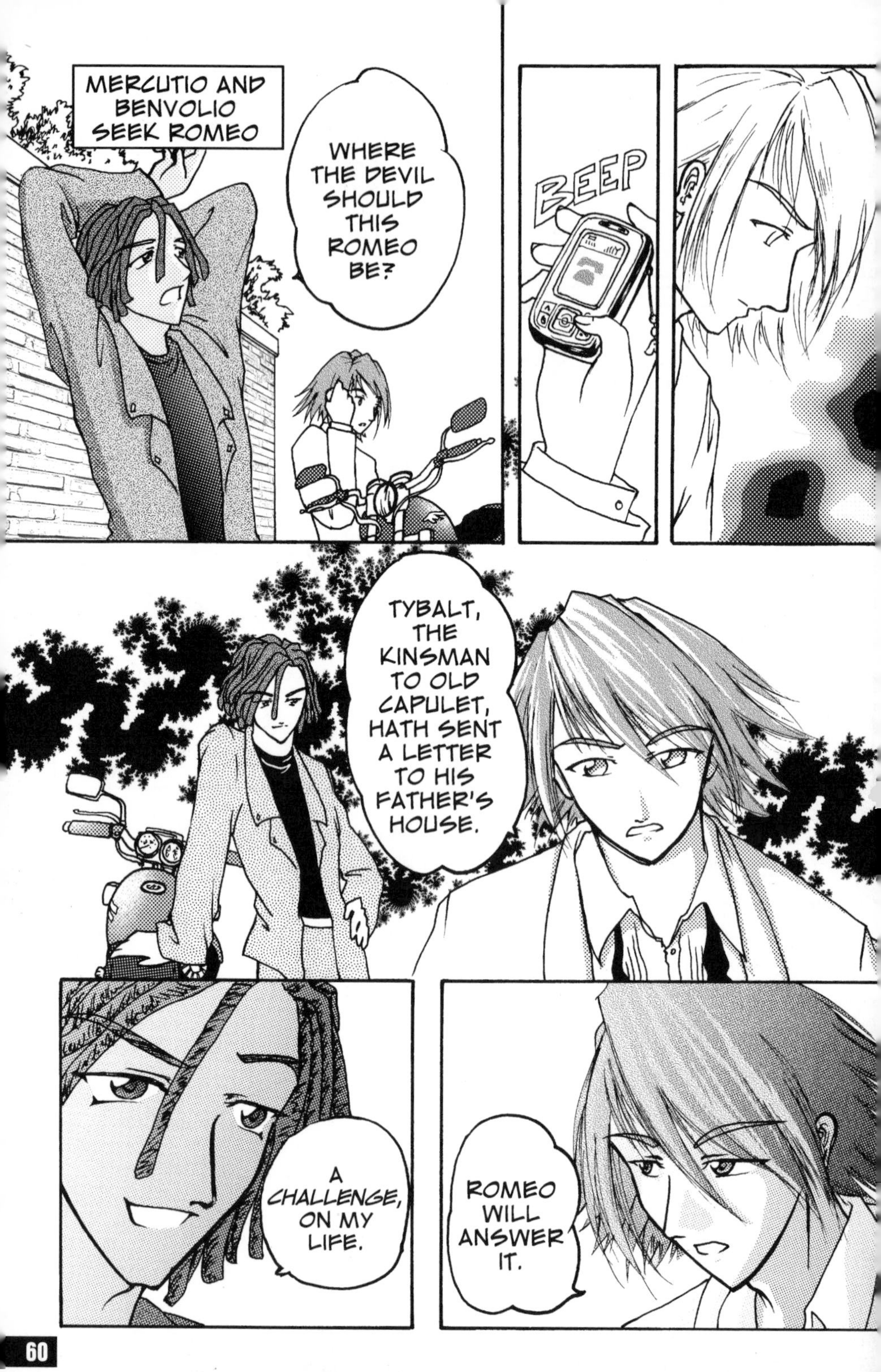
MERCUTIO AND BENVOLIO SEEK ROMEO
WHERE THE DEVIL SHOULD THIS ROMEO BE?
BEEP
TYBALT, THE KINSMAN TO OLD CAPULET, HATH SENT A LETTER TO HIS FATHER'S HOUSE.
A CHALLENGE, ON MY LIFE.
ROMEO WILL ANSWER IT.

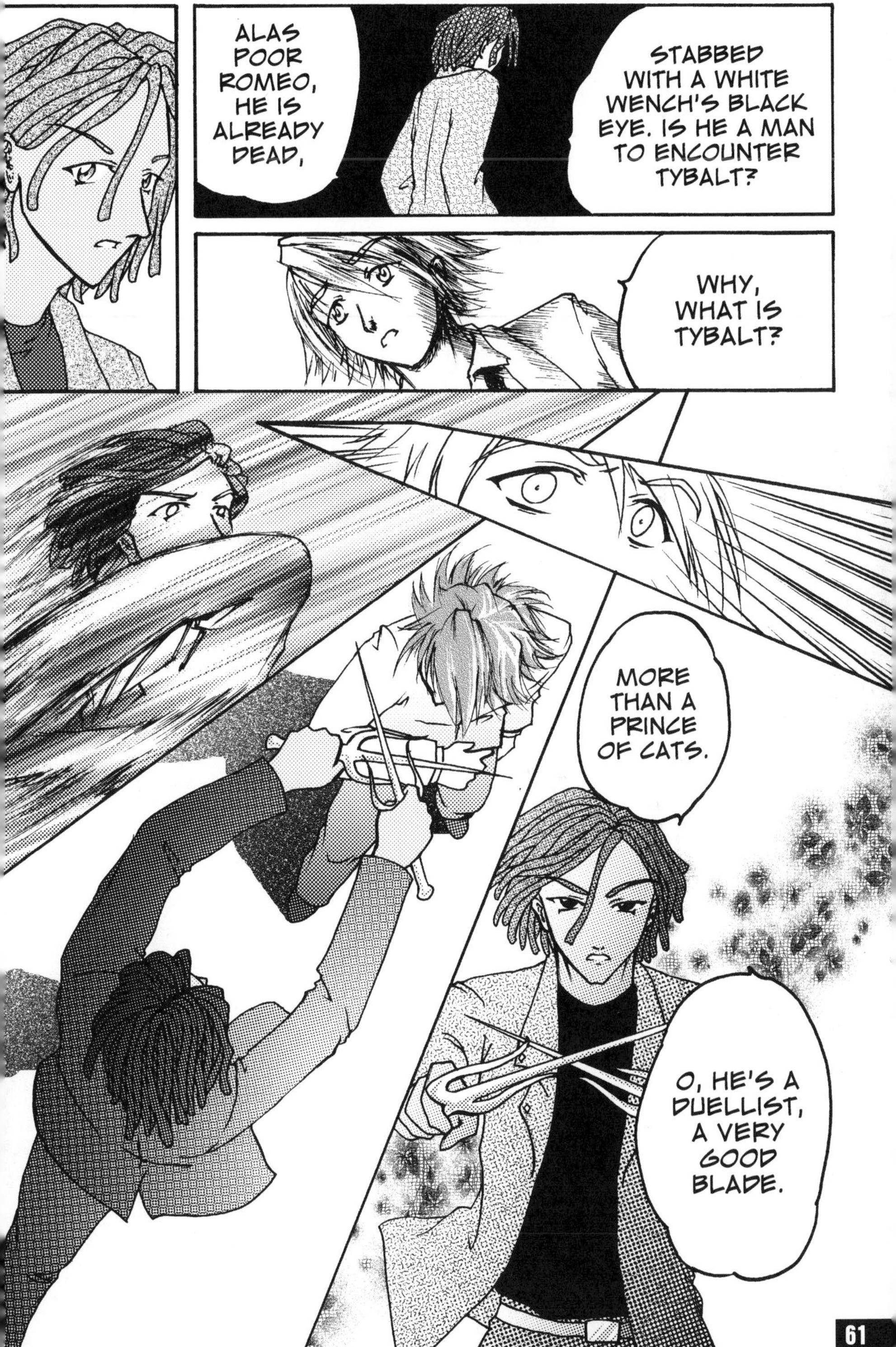
ALAS POOR ROMEO, HE IS ALREADY DEAD,
STABBED WITH A WHITE WENCH'S BLACK EYE. IS HE A MAN TO ENCOUNTER TYBALT?
WHY, WHAT IS TYBALT?
MORE THAN A PRINCE OF CATS.
O, HE'S A DUELLIST, A VERY GOOD BLADE.

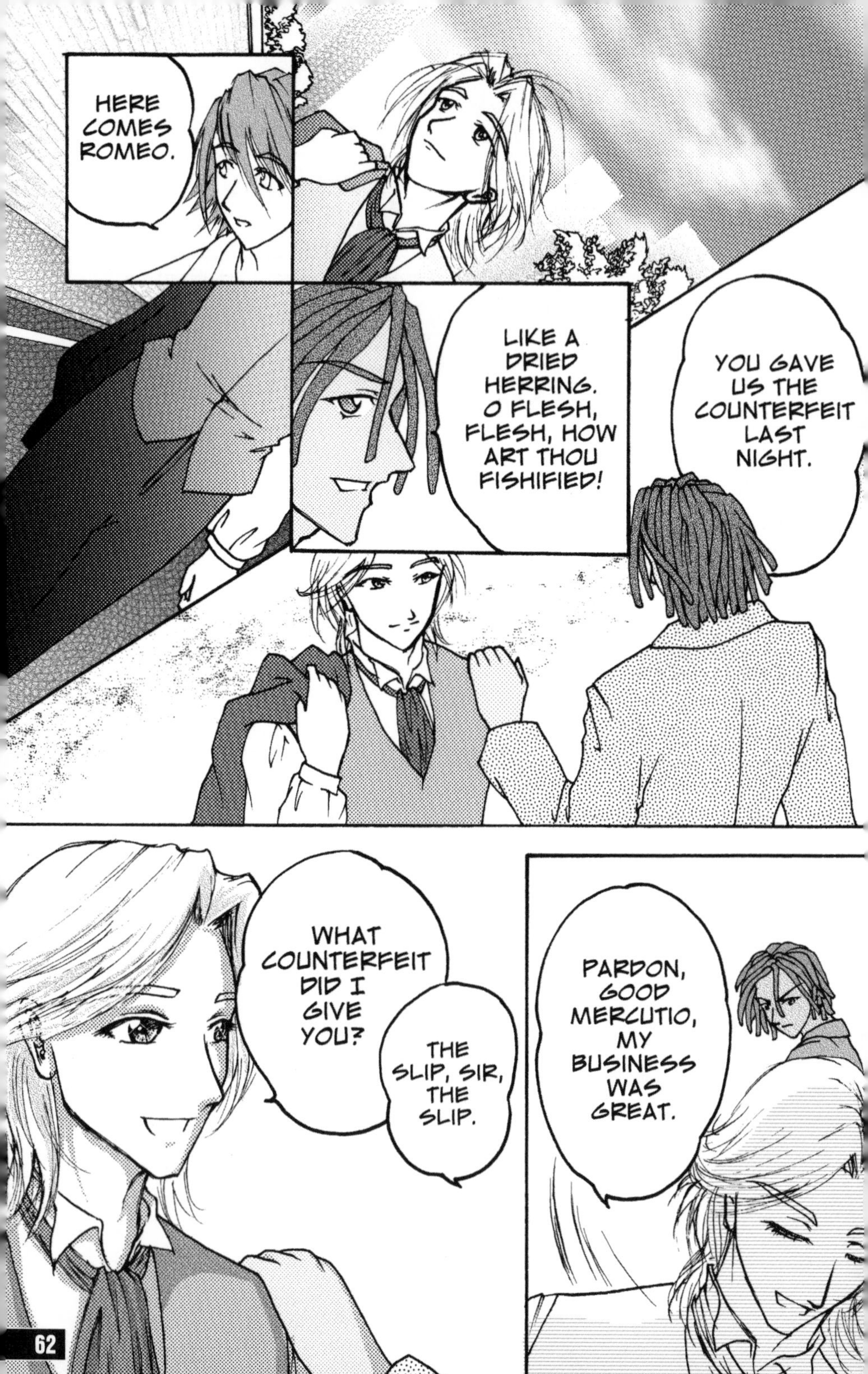
HERE COMES ROMEO.
LIKE A DRIED HERRING. O FLESH, FLESH, HOW ART THOU FISHIFIED!
YOU GAVE US THE COUNTERFEIT LAST NIGHT.
WHAT COUNTERFEIT DID I GIVE YOU?
THE SLIP, SIR, THE SLIP.
PARDON, GOOD MERCUTIO, MY BUSINESS WAS GREAT.

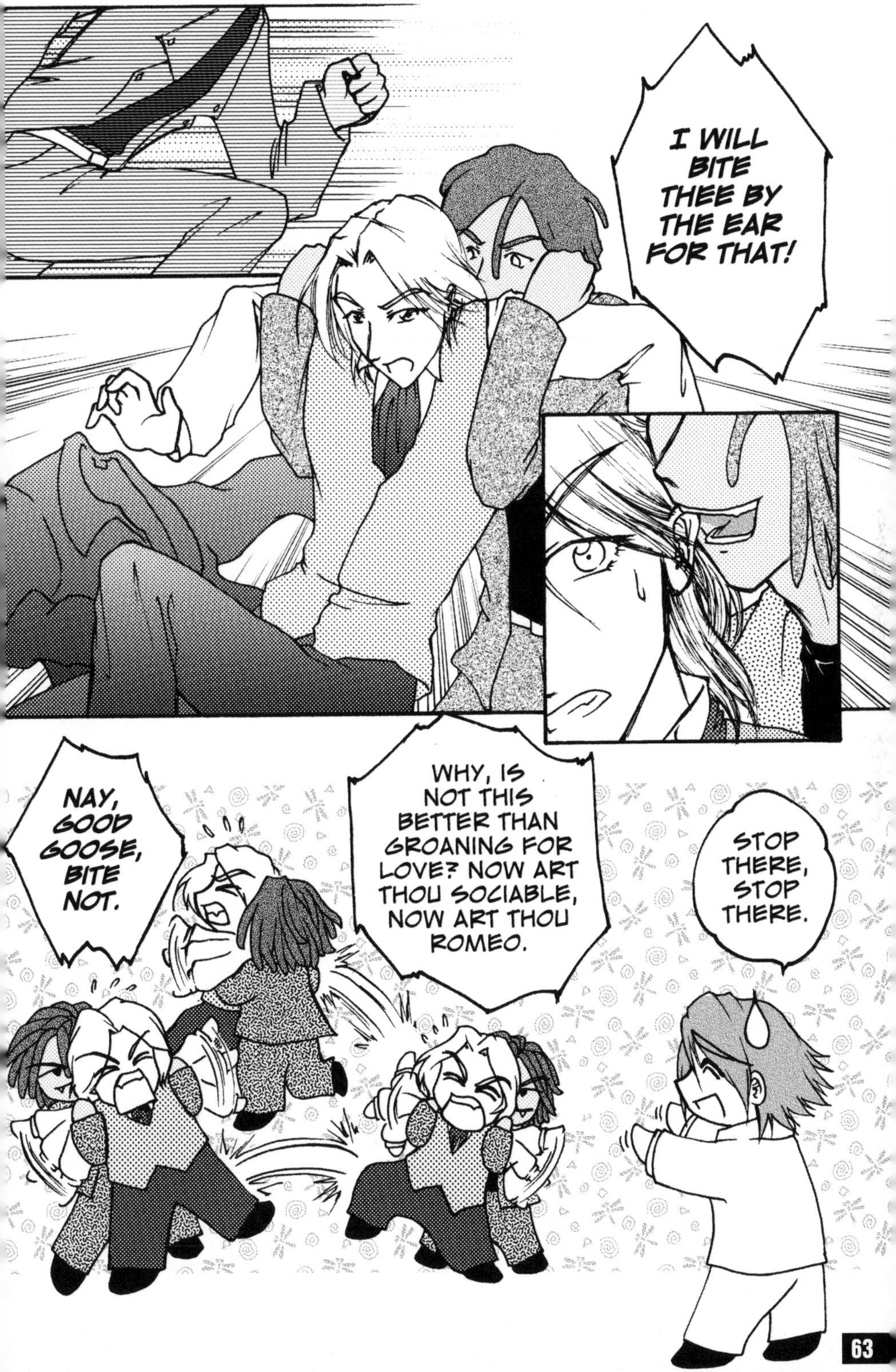
I WILL BITE THEE BY THE EAR FOR THAT!
STOP THERE, STOP THERE.
WHY, IS NOT THIS BETTER THAN GROANING FOR LOVE? NOW ART THOU SOCIABLE, NOW ART THOU ROMEO.
NAY, GOOD GOOSE, BITE NOT.

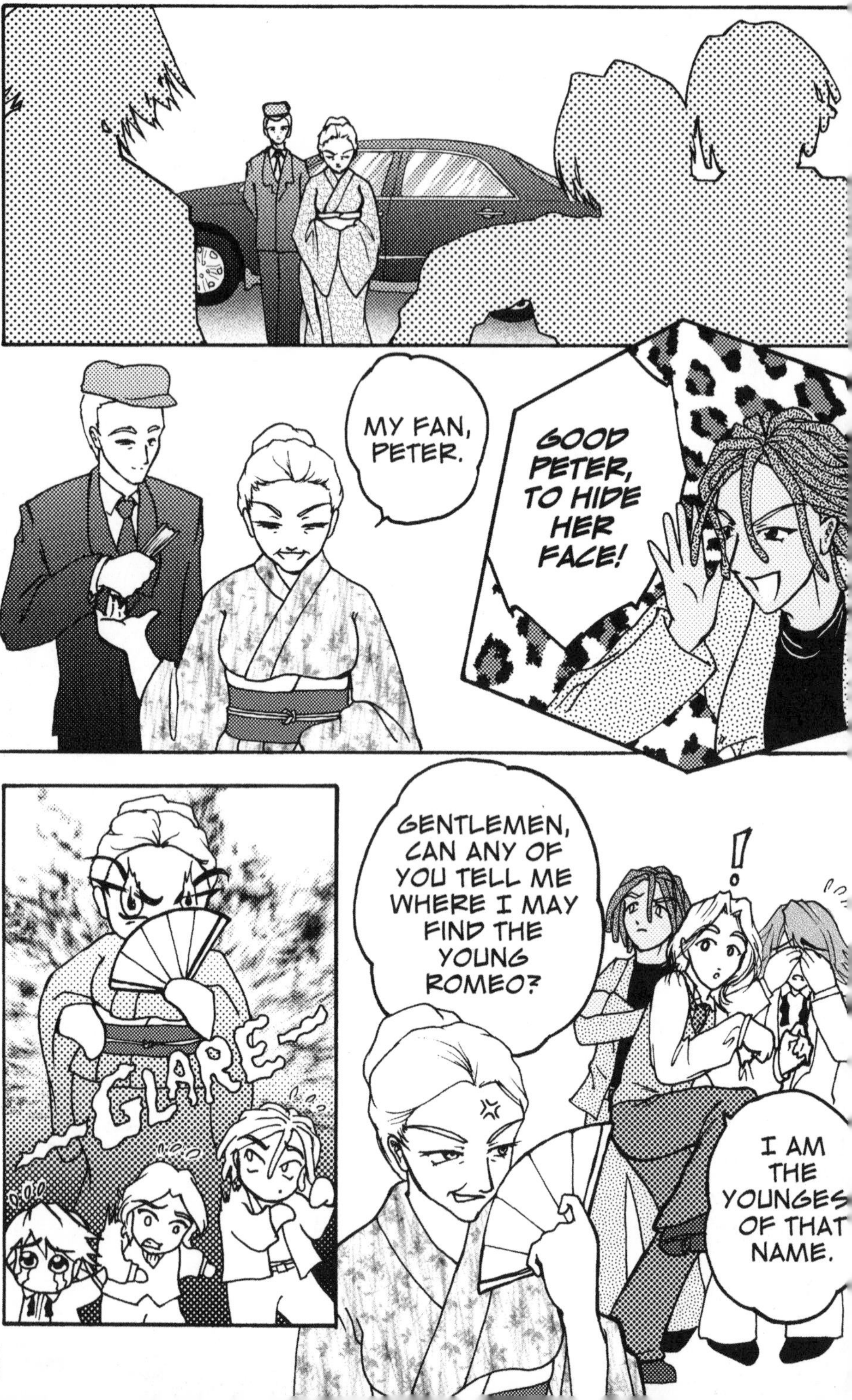
MY FAN, PETER.
GOOD PETER, TO HIDE HER FACE!
GLARE
GENTLEMEN, CAN ANY OF YOU TELL ME WHERE I MAY FIND THE YOUNG ROMEO?
!
I AM THE YOUNGES OF THAT NAME.

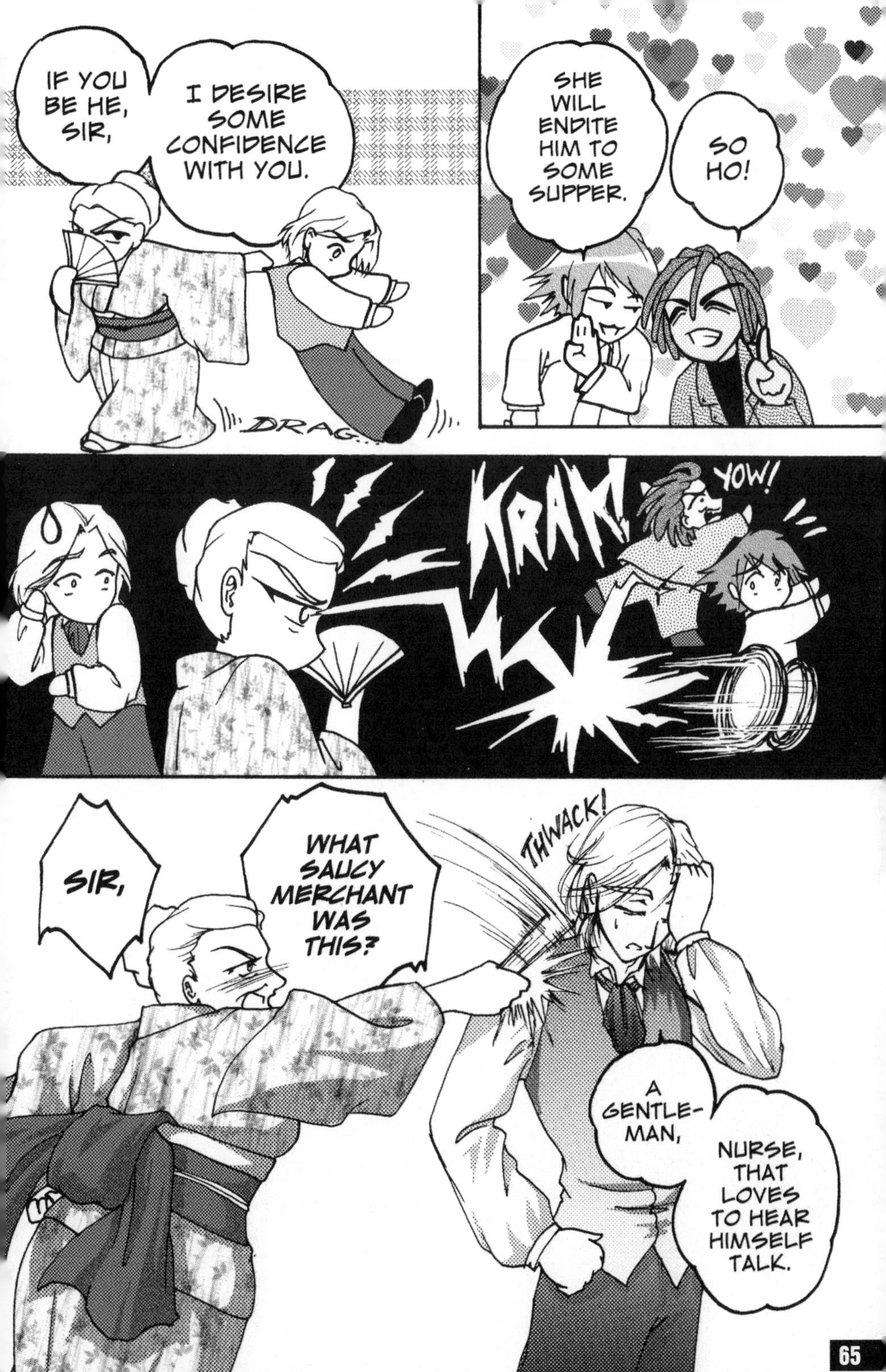
IF YOU BE HE, SIR,
I DESIRE SOME CONFIDENCE WITH YOU.
DRAG...
SHE WILL ENDITE HIM TO SOME SUPPER.
SO HO!
KRAM!
YOW!
SIR,
WHAT SAUCY MERCHANT WAS THIS?
THWACK!
A GENTLE-MAN,
NURSE, THAT LOVES TO HEAR HIMSELF TALK.

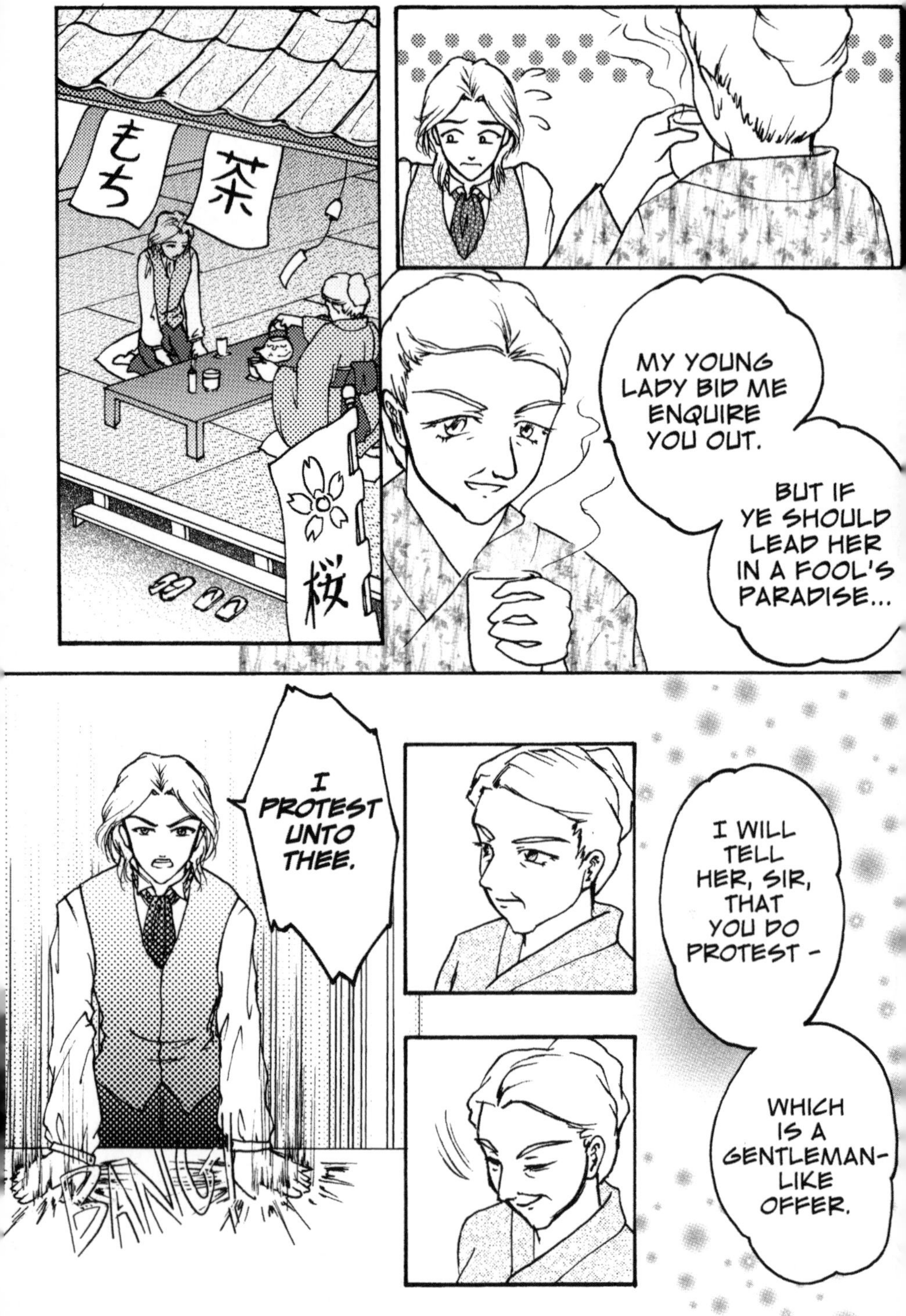
もち
茶
桜
MY YOUNG LADY BID ME ENQUIRE YOU OUT.
BUT IF YE SHOULD LEAD HER IN A FOOL'S PARADISE...
I PROTEST UNTO THEE.
BANG!
I WILL TELL HER, SIR, THAT YOU DO PROTEST -
WHICH IS A GENTLEMAN-LIKE OFFER.

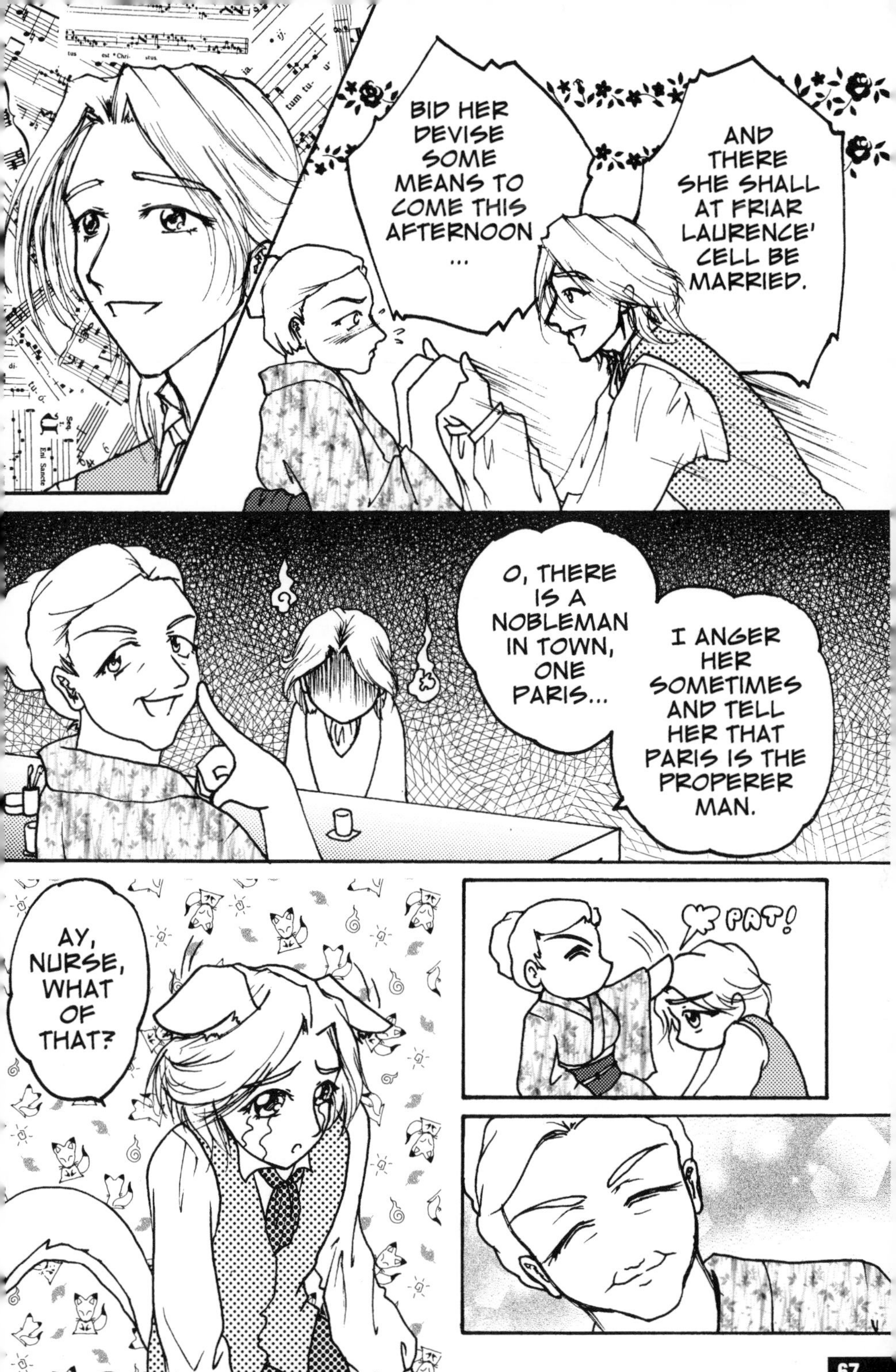
BID HER DEVISE SOME MEANS TO COME THIS AFTERNOON ...
AND THERE SHE SHALL AT FRIAR LAURENCE' CELL BE MARRIED.
O, THERE IS A NOBLEMAN IN TOWN, ONE PARIS...
I ANGER HER SOMETIMES AND TELL HER THAT PARIS IS THE PROPERER MAN.
AY, NURSE, WHAT OF THAT?
PAT!

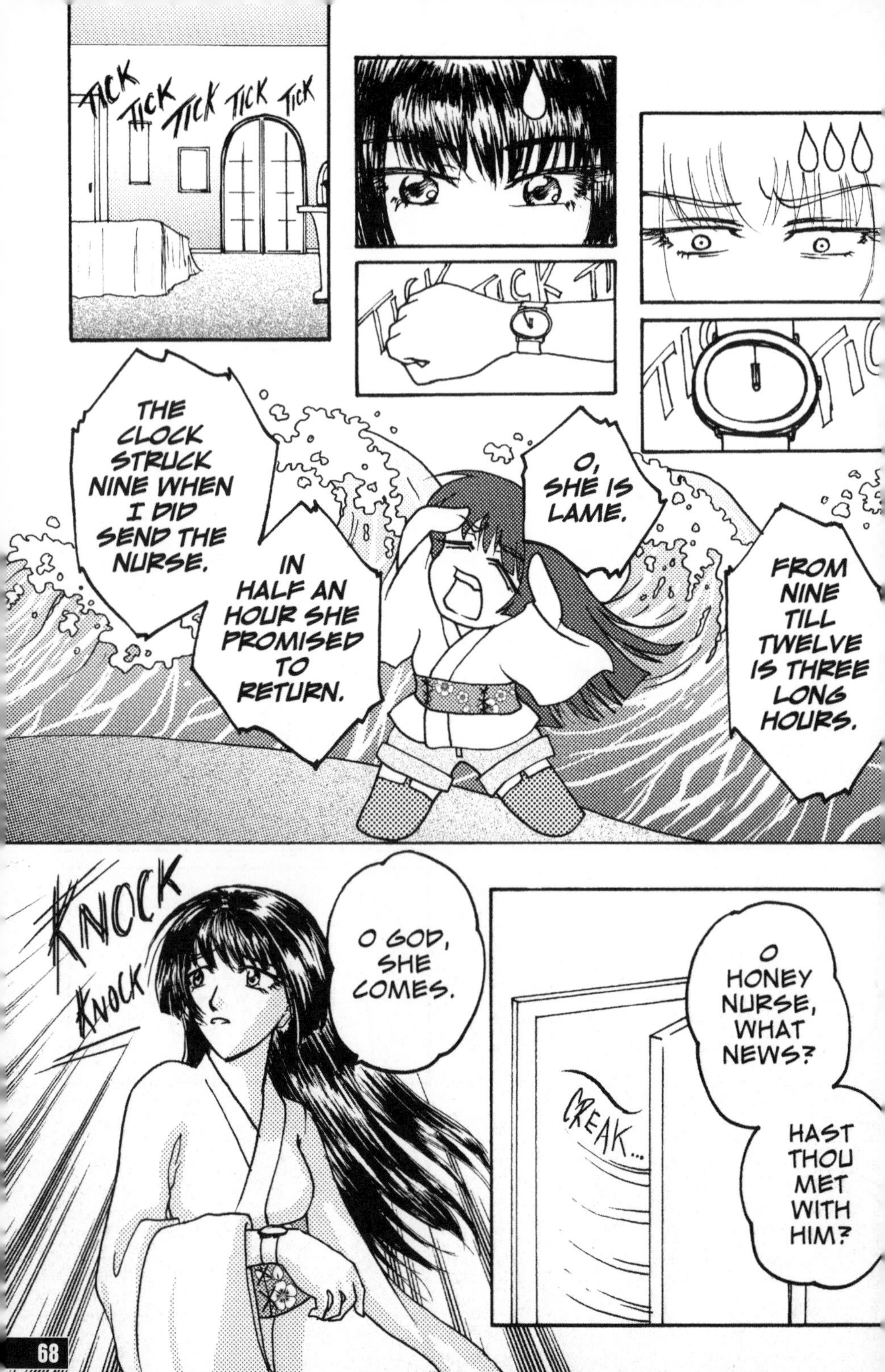
TICK TICK TICK TICK TICK
THE CLOCK STRUCK NINE WHEN I DID SEND THE NURSE.
IN HALF AN HOUR SHE PROMISED TO RETURN.
O, SHE IS LAME.
FROM NINE TILL TWELVE IS THREE LONG HOURS.
KNOCK KNOCK
O GOD, SHE COMES.
CREAK...
O HONEY NURSE, WHAT NEWS?
HAST THOU MET WITH HIM?

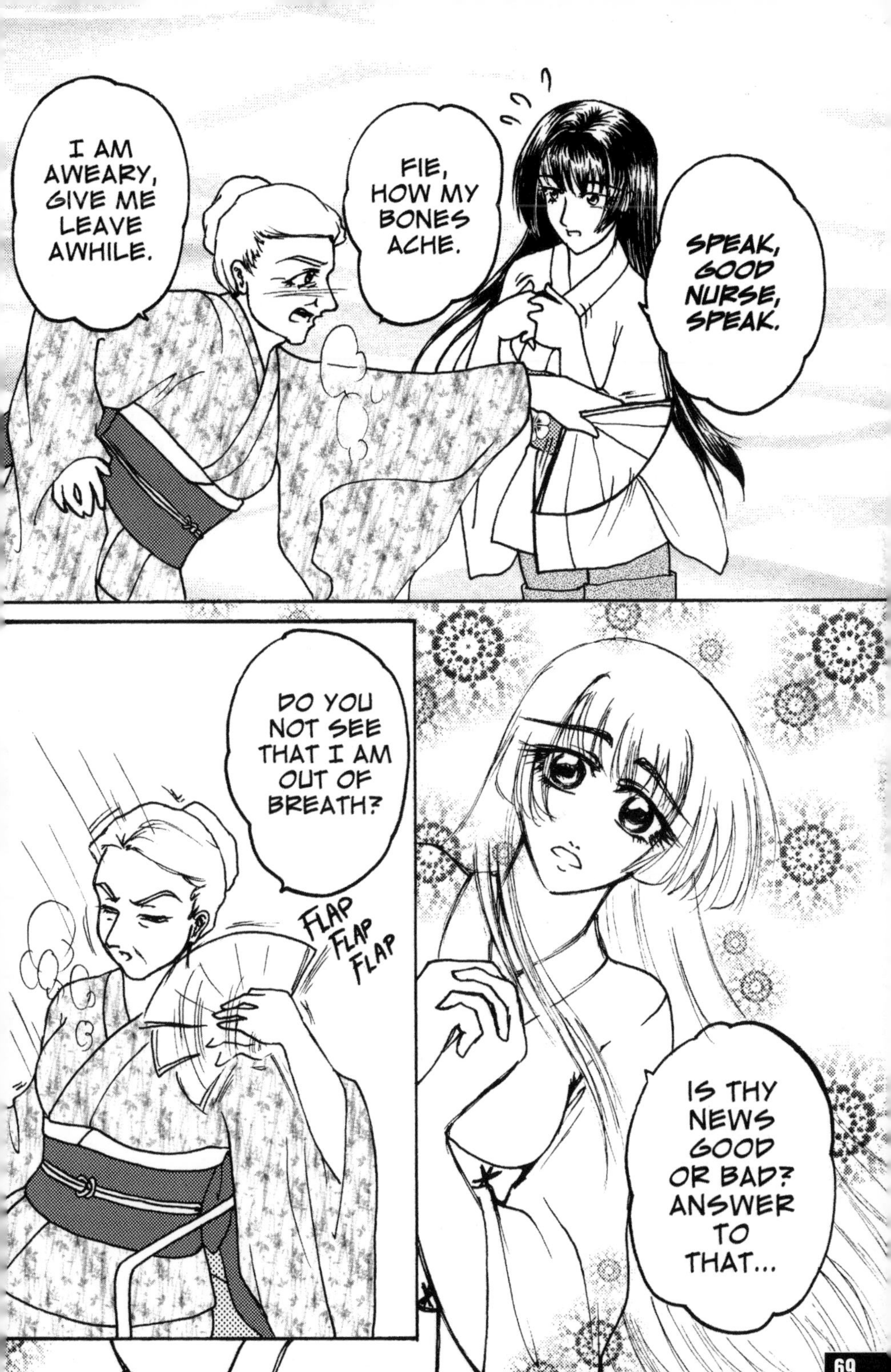
I AM AWEARY, GIVE ME LEAVE AWHILE.
FIE, HOW MY BONES ACHE.
SPEAK, GOOD NURSE, SPEAK.
DO YOU NOT SEE THAT I AM OUT OF BREATH?
FLAP FLAP FLAP
IS THY NEWS GOOD OR BAD? ANSWER TO THAT...

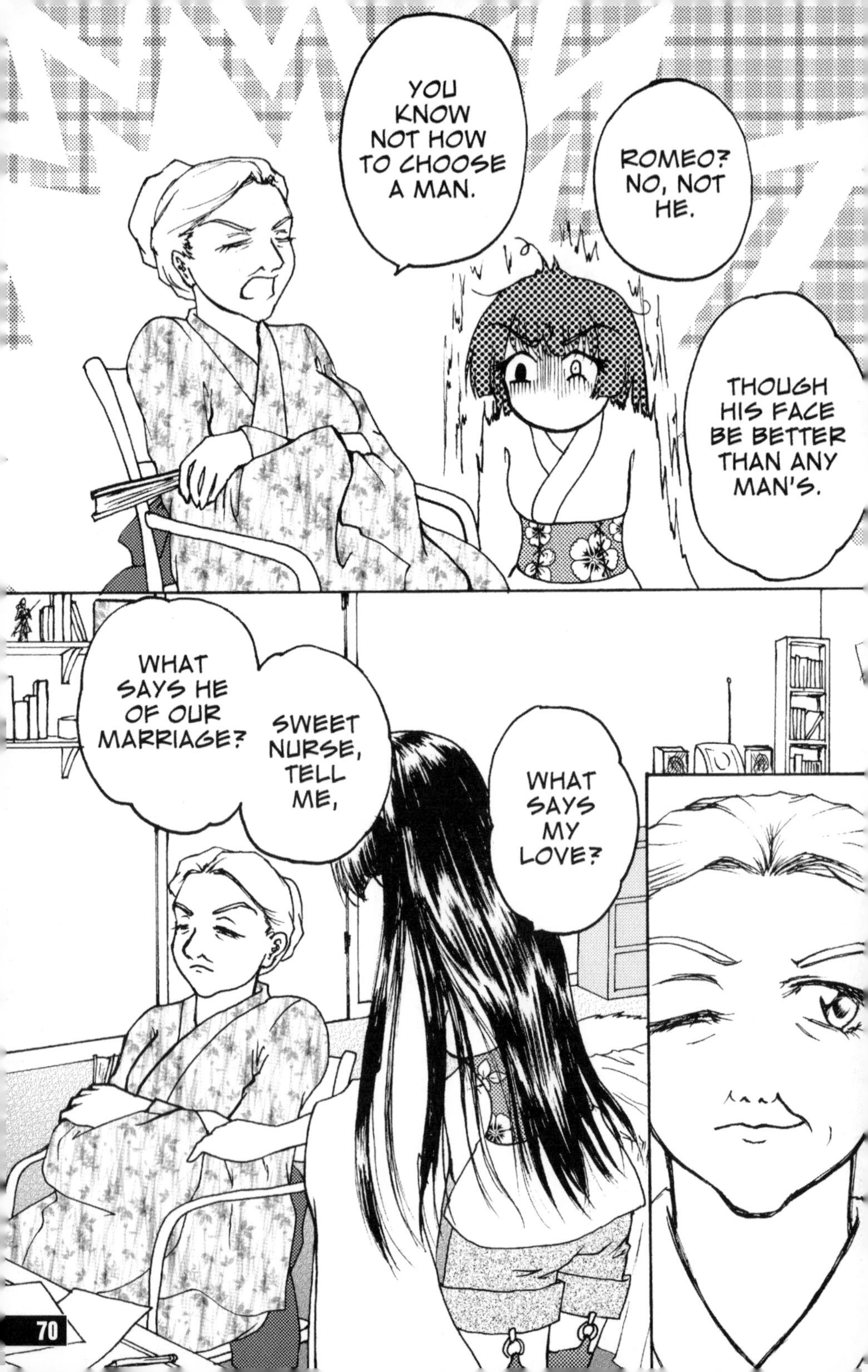
YOU KNOW NOT HOW TO CHOOSE A MAN.
ROMEO? NO, NOT HE.
THOUGH HIS FACE BE BETTER THAN ANY MAN'S.
SWEET NURSE, TELL ME,
WHAT SAYS HE OF OUR MARRIAGE?
WHAT SAYS MY LOVE?

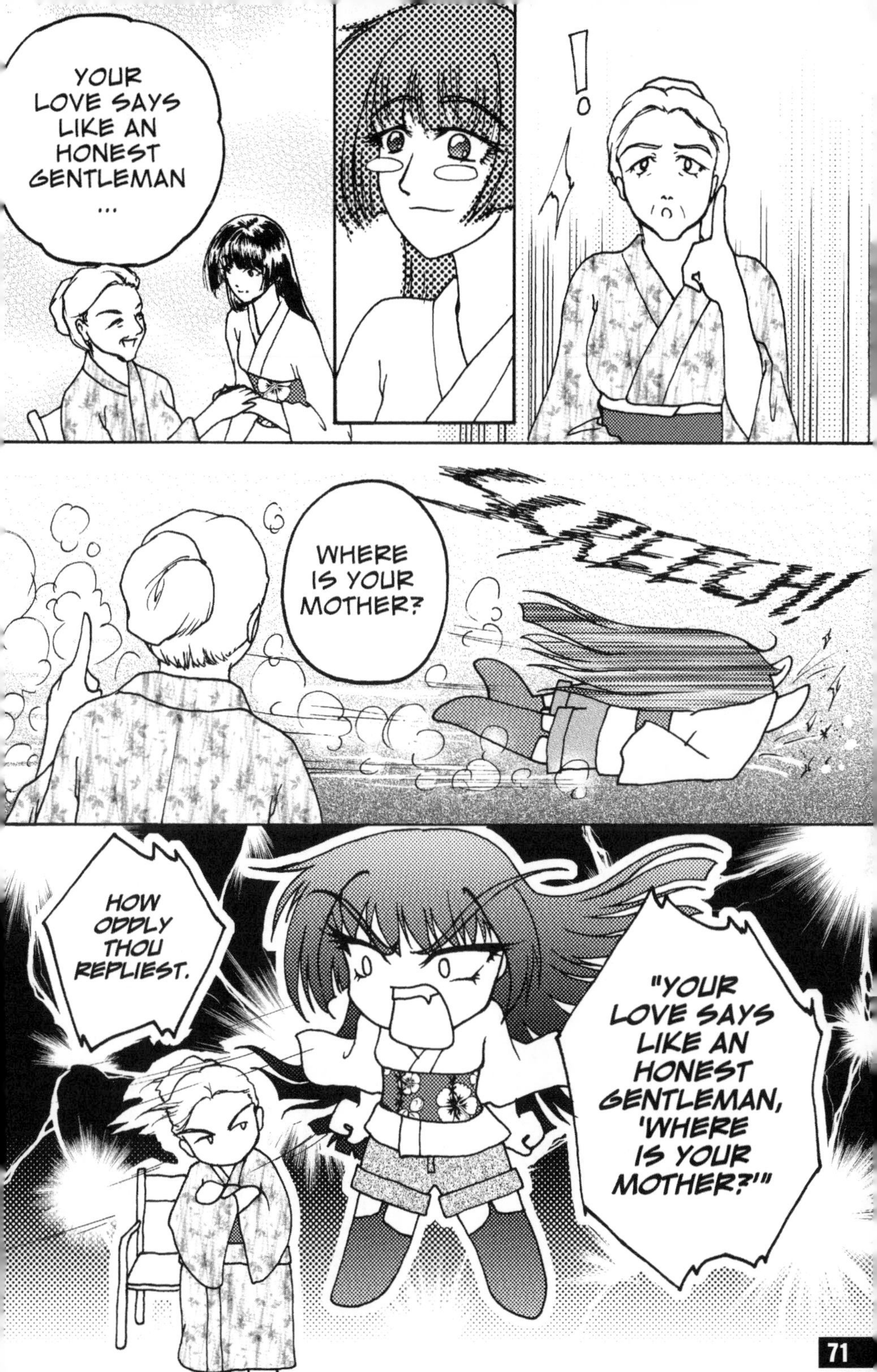
YOUR LOVE SAYS LIKE AN HONEST GENTLEMAN ...
!
WHERE IS YOUR MOTHER?
SKEECH!!
HOW ODDLY THOU REPLIEST.
"YOUR LOVE SAYS LIKE AN HONEST GENTLEMAN, 'WHERE IS YOUR MOTHER?'"

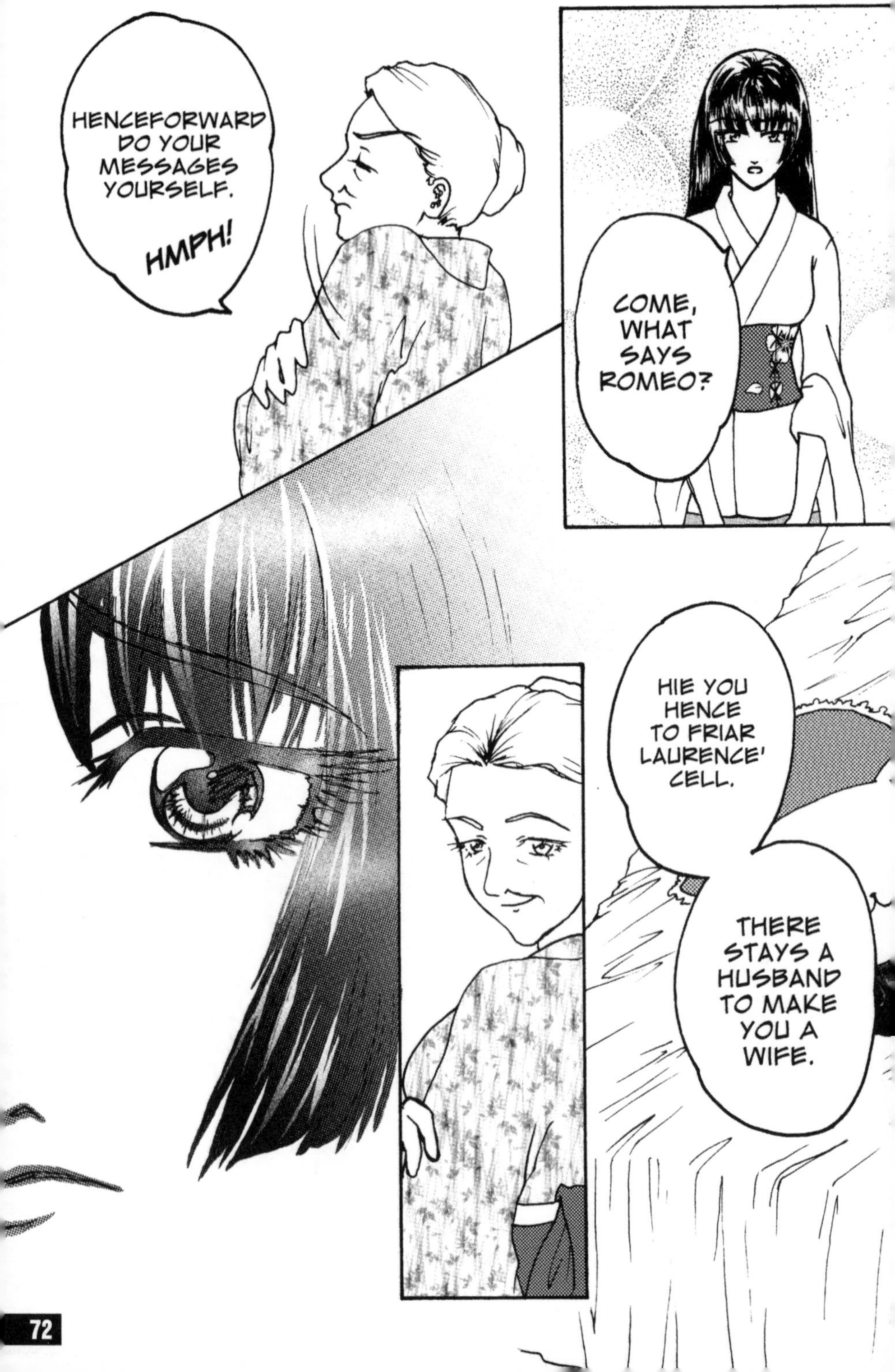
HENCEFORWARD DO YOUR MESSAGES YOURSELF.
HMPH!
COME, WHAT SAYS ROMEO?
HIE YOU HENCE TO FRIAR LAURENCE' CELL.
THERE STAYS A HUSBAND TO MAKE YOU A WIFE.

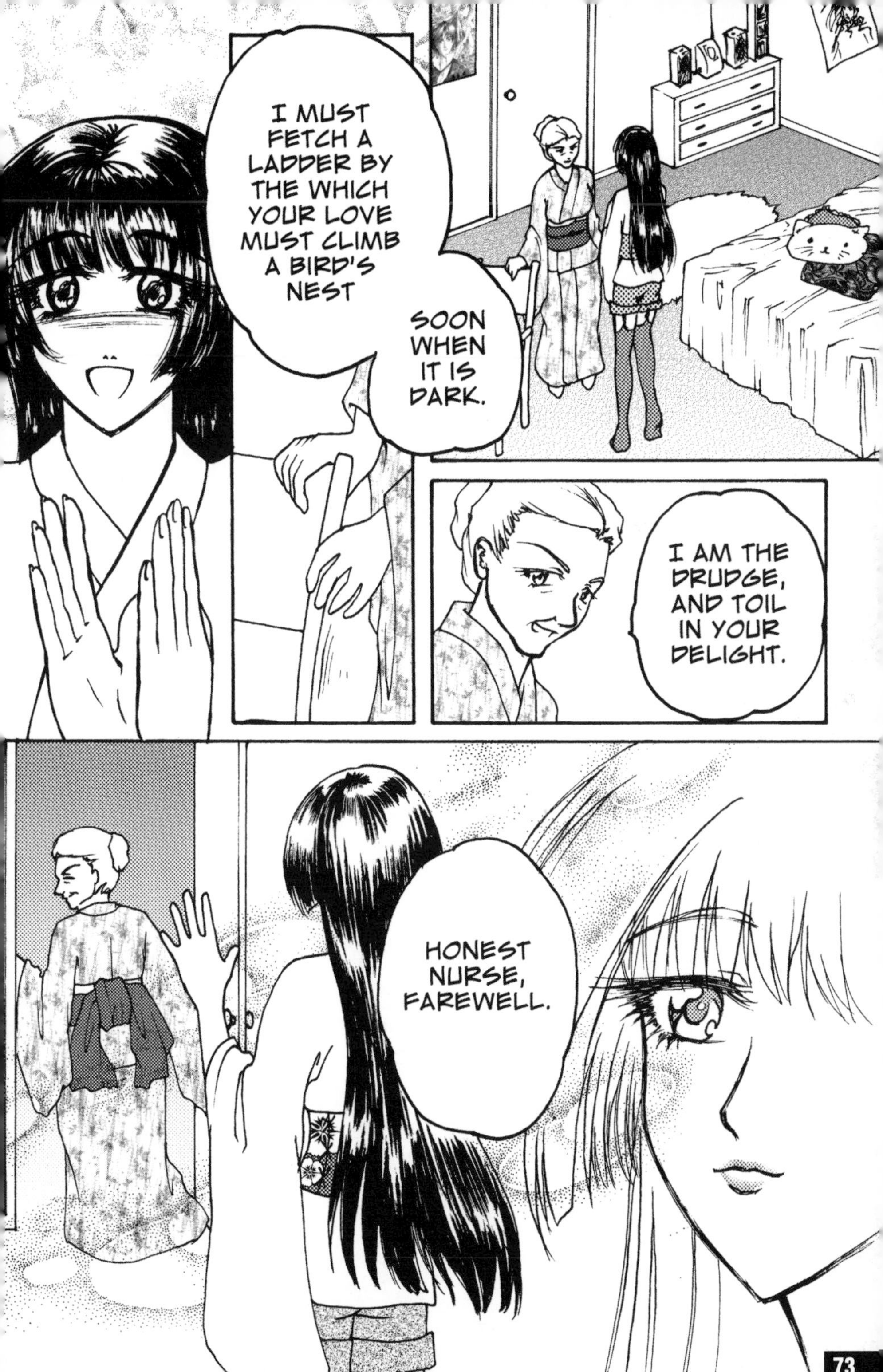
I MUST FETCH A LADDER BY THE WHICH YOUR LOVE MUST CLIMB A BIRD'S NEST
SOON WHEN IT IS DARK.
I AM THE DRUDGE, AND TOIL IN YOUR DELIGHT.
HONEST NURSE, FAREWELL.

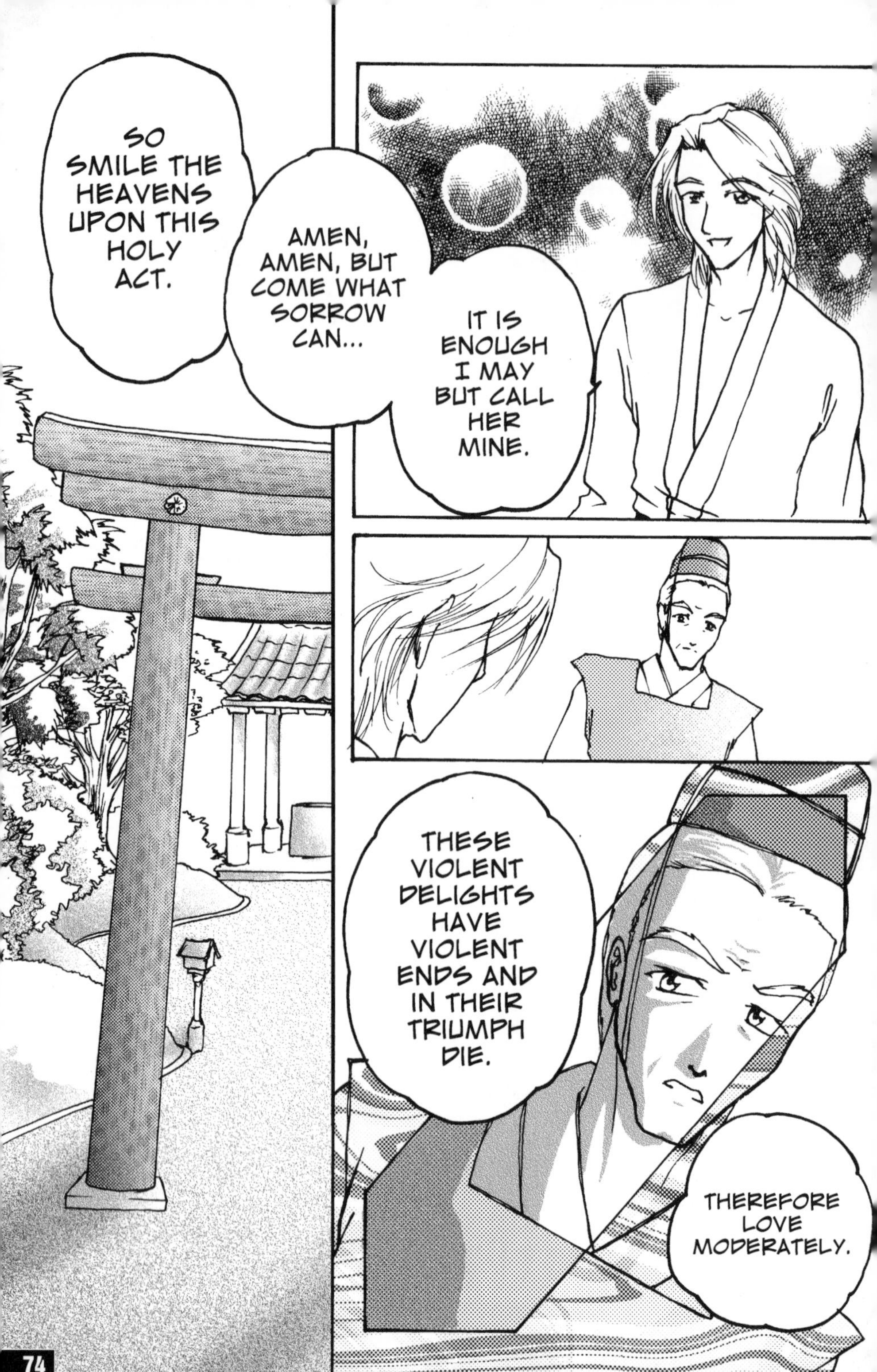
SO SMILE THE HEAVENS UPON THIS HOLY ACT.
AMEN, AMEN, BUT COME WHAT SORROW CAN...
IT IS ENOUGH I MAY BUT CALL HER MINE.
THESE VIOLENT DELIGHTS HAVE VIOLENT ENDS AND IN THEIR TRIUMPH DIE.
THEREFORE LOVE MODERATELY.

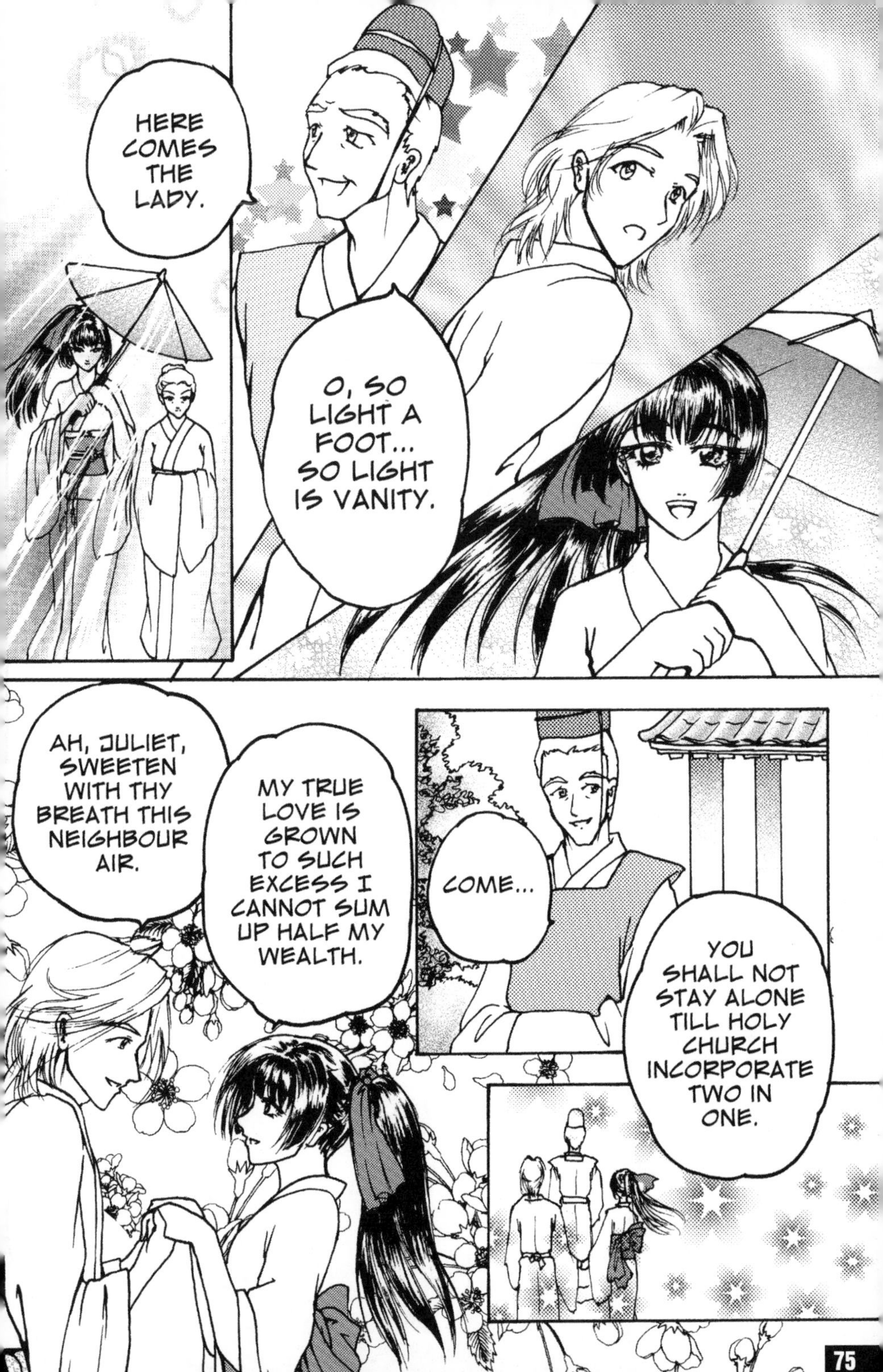
HERE COMES THE LADY.
O, SO LIGHT A FOOT... SO LIGHT IS VANITY.
AH, JULIET, SWEETEN WITH THY BREATH THIS NEIGHBOUR AIR.
MY TRUE LOVE IS GROWN TO SUCH EXCESS I CANNOT SUM UP HALF MY WEALTH.
COME...
YOU SHALL NOT STAY ALONE TILL HOLY CHURCH INCORPORATE TWO IN ONE.

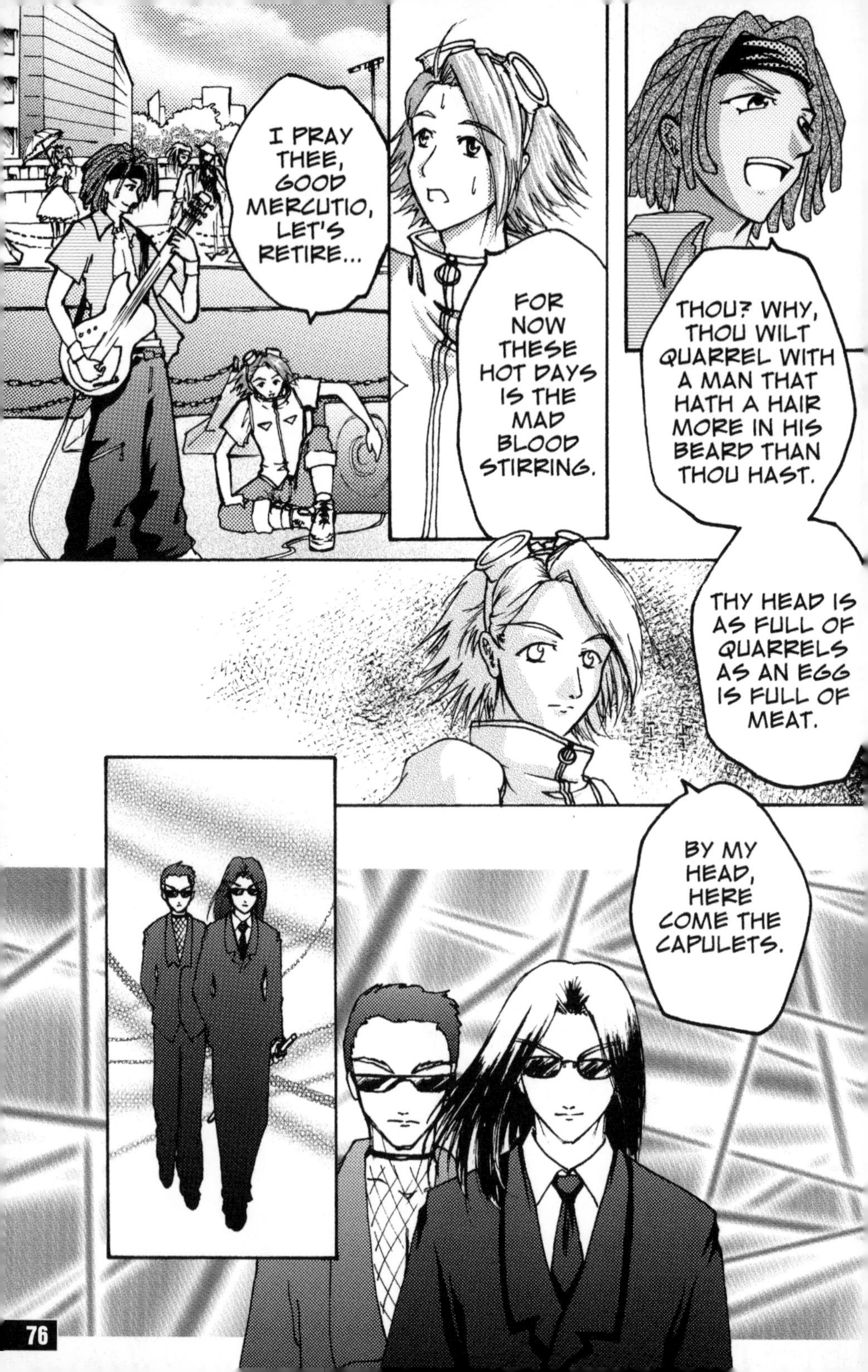
I PRAY THEE, GOOD MERCUTIO, LET'S RETIRE...
FOR NOW THESE HOT DAYS IS THE MAD BLOOD STIRRING.
THOU? WHY, THOU WILT QUARREL WITH A MAN THAT HATH A HAIR MORE IN HIS BEARD THAN THOU HAST.
THY HEAD IS AS FULL OF QUARRELS AS AN EGG IS FULL OF MEAT.
BY MY HEAD, HERE COME THE CAPULETS.

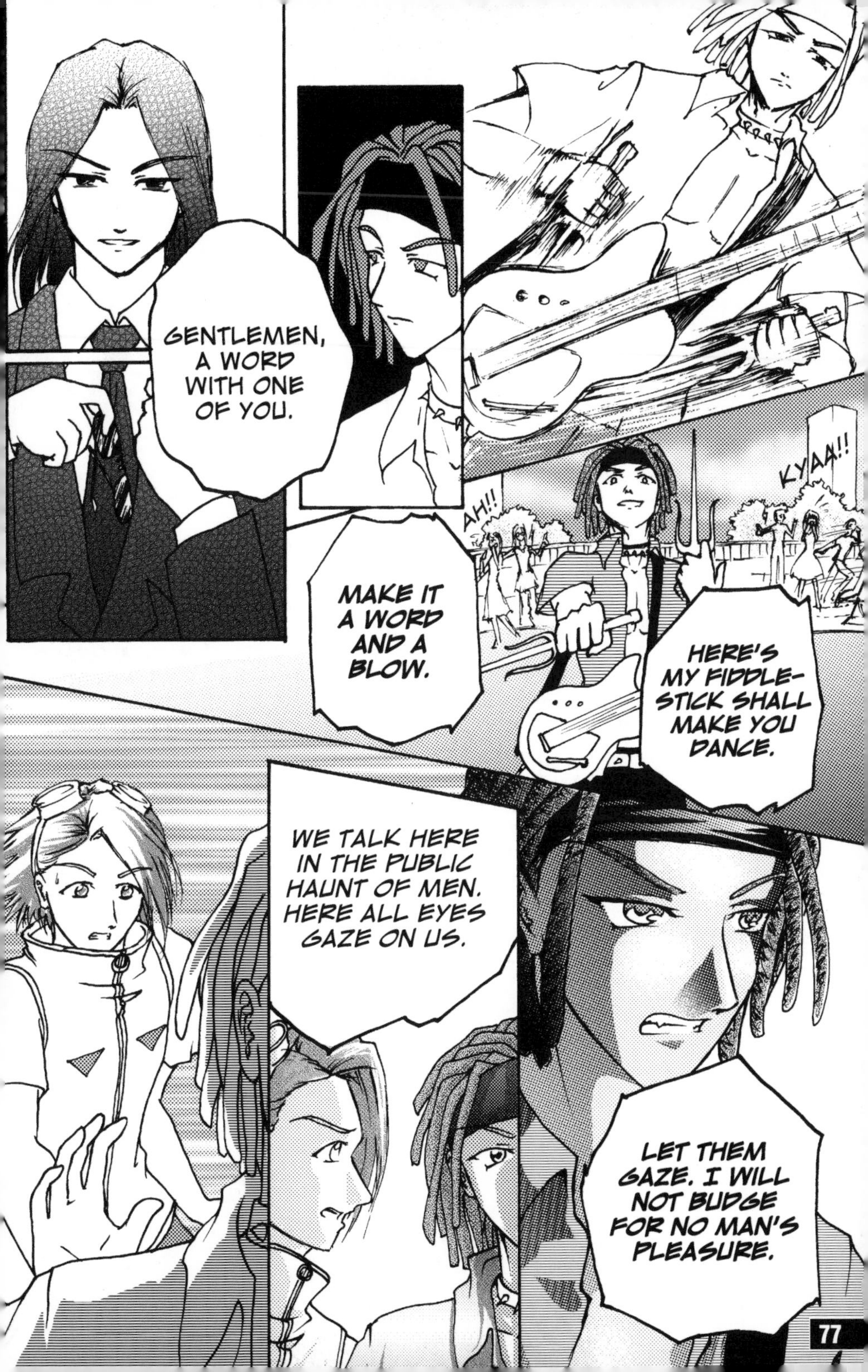
GENTLEMEN, A WORD WITH ONE OF YOU.
MAKE IT A WORD AND A BLOW.
AH!!
KYAA!!
HERE'S MY FIDDLE-STICK SHALL MAKE YOU DANCE.
WE TALK HERE IN THE PUBLIC HAUNT OF MEN. HERE ALL EYES GAZE ON US.
LET THEM GAZE. I WILL NOT BUDGE FOR NO MAN'S PLEASURE.

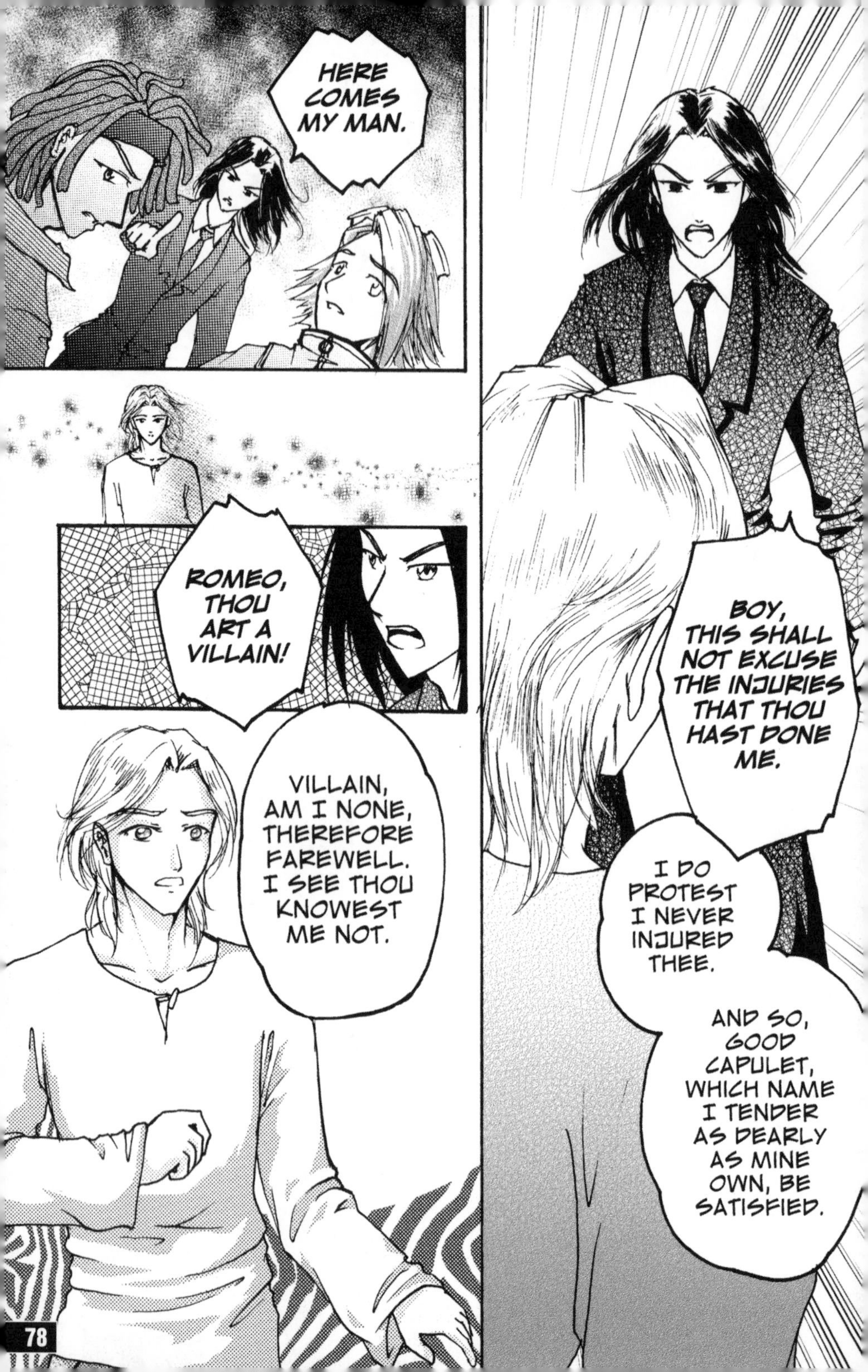
HERE COMES MY MAN.
ROMEO, THOU ART A VILLAIN!
VILLAIN, AM I NONE, THEREFORE FAREWELL. I SEE THOU KNOWEST ME NOT.
BOY, THIS SHALL NOT EXCUSE THE INJURIES THAT THOU HAST DONE ME.
I DO PROTEST I NEVER INJURED THEE.
AND SO, GOOD CAPULET, WHICH NAME I TENDER AS DEARLY AS MINE OWN, BE SATISFIED.

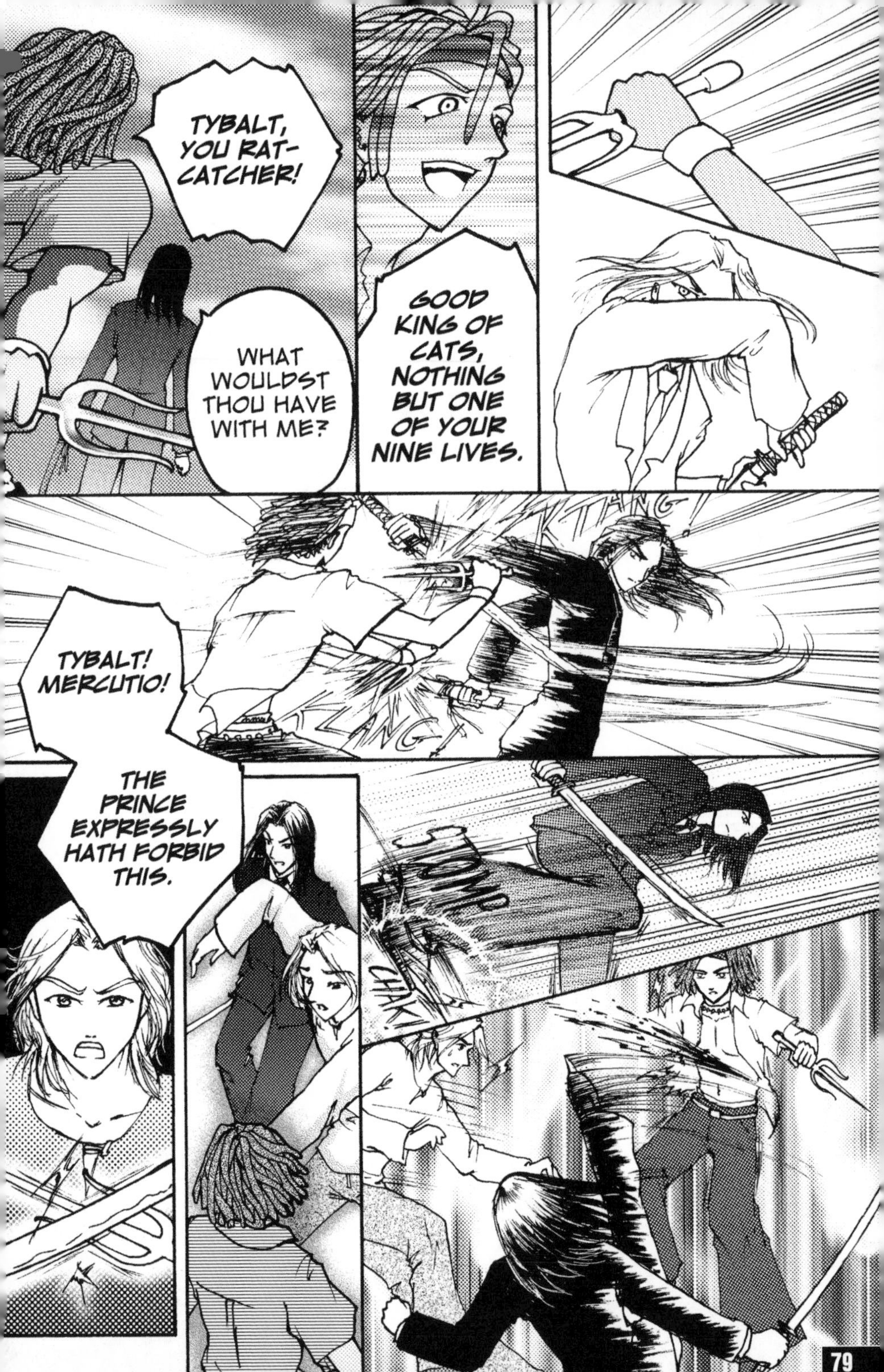
TYBALT, YOU RAT-CATCHER!
WHAT WOULDST THOU HAVE WITH ME?
GOOD KING OF CATS, NOTHING BUT ONE OF YOUR NINE LIVES.
KTANG!
TYBALT! MERCUTIO!
KLANG!
THE PRINCE EXPRESSLY HATH FORBID THIS.
STOMP
CHAK!

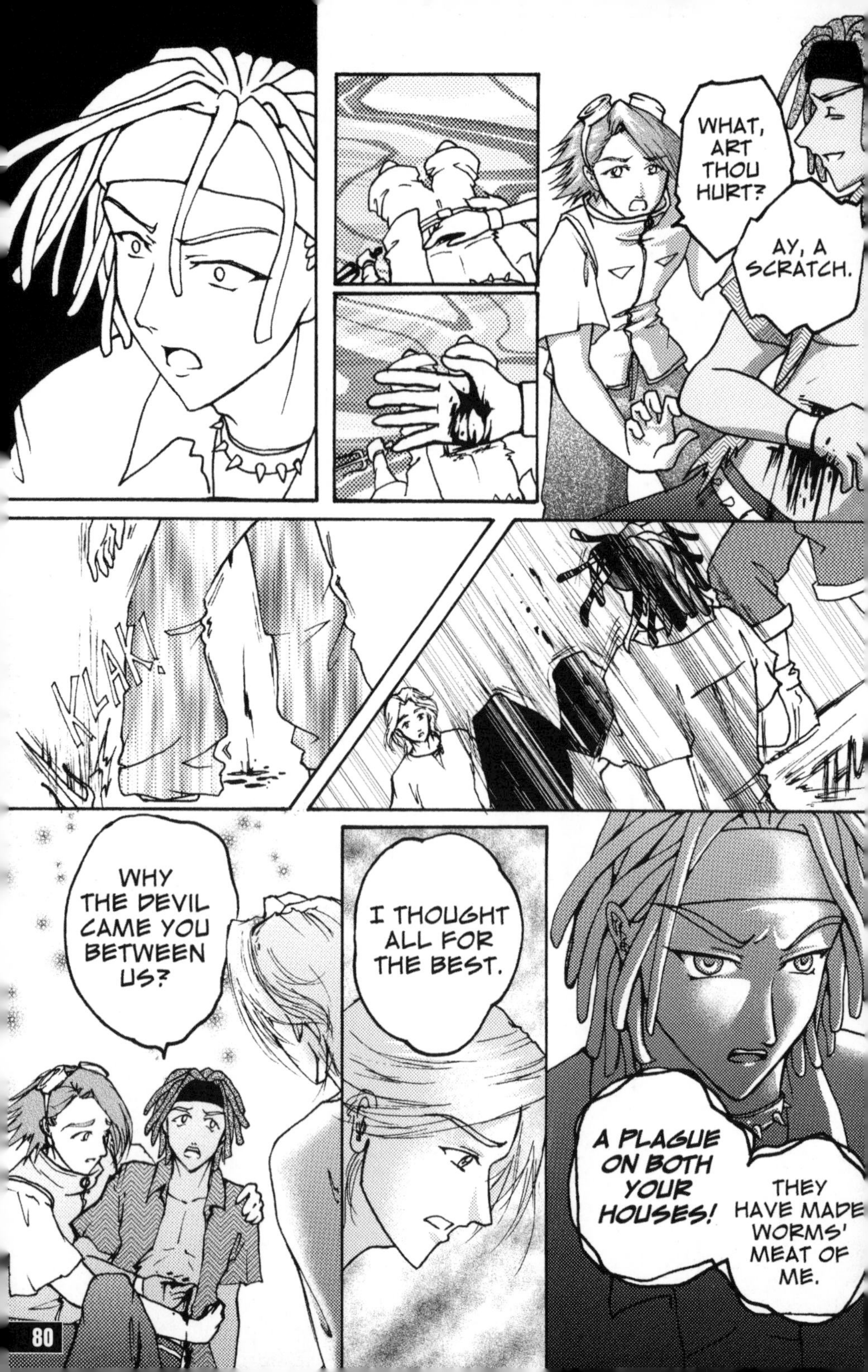
WHAT, ART THOU HURT?
AY, A SCRATCH.
KLAK!
THU
WHY THE DEVIL CAME YOU BETWEEN US?
I THOUGHT ALL FOR THE BEST.
A PLAGUE ON BOTH YOUR HOUSES!
THEY HAVE MADE WORMS' MEAT OF ME.

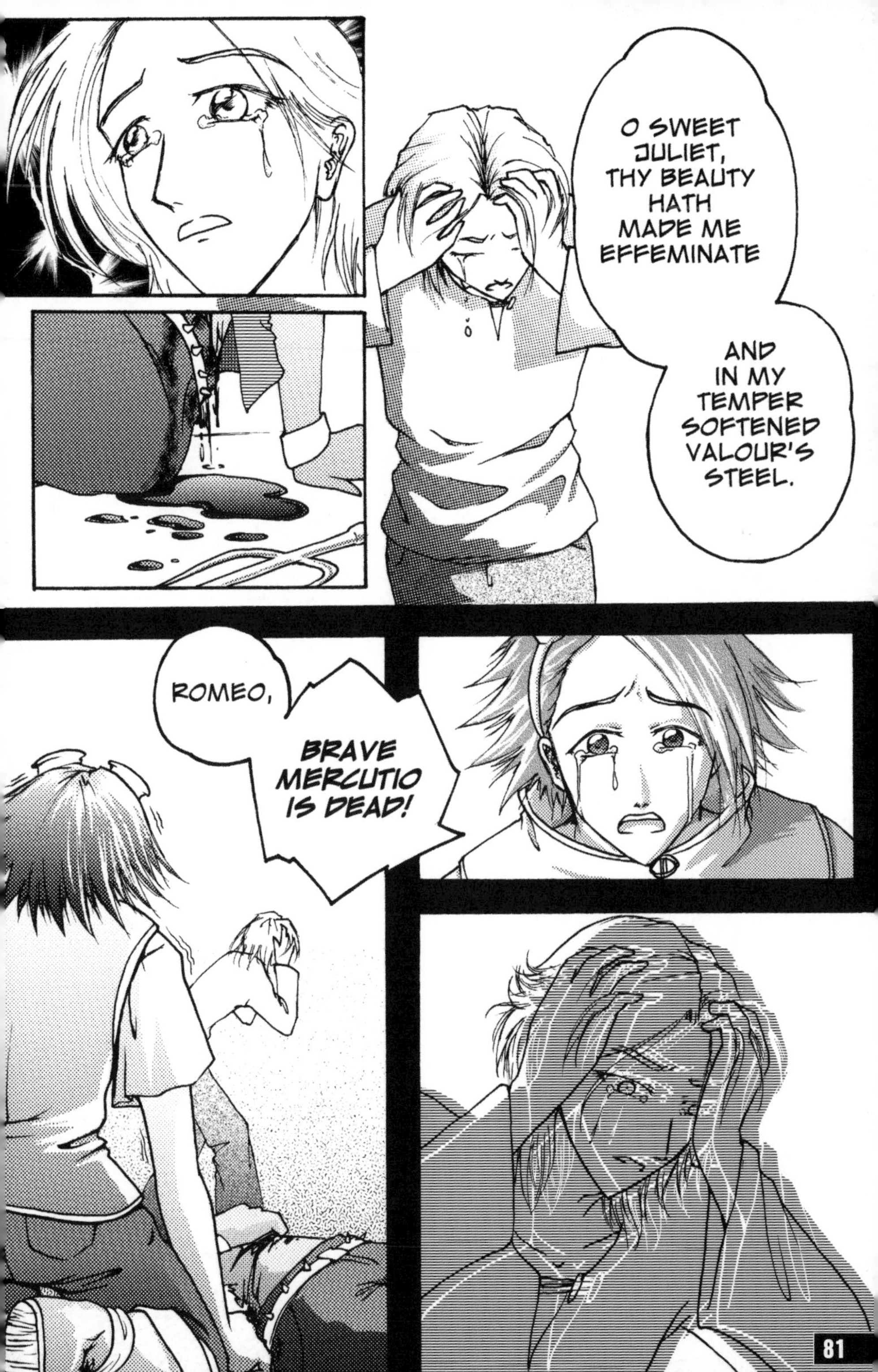
O SWEET JULIET, THY BEAUTY HATH MADE ME EFFEMINATE
AND IN MY TEMPER SOFTENED VALOUR'S STEEL.
ROMEO,
BRAVE MERCUTIO IS DEAD!

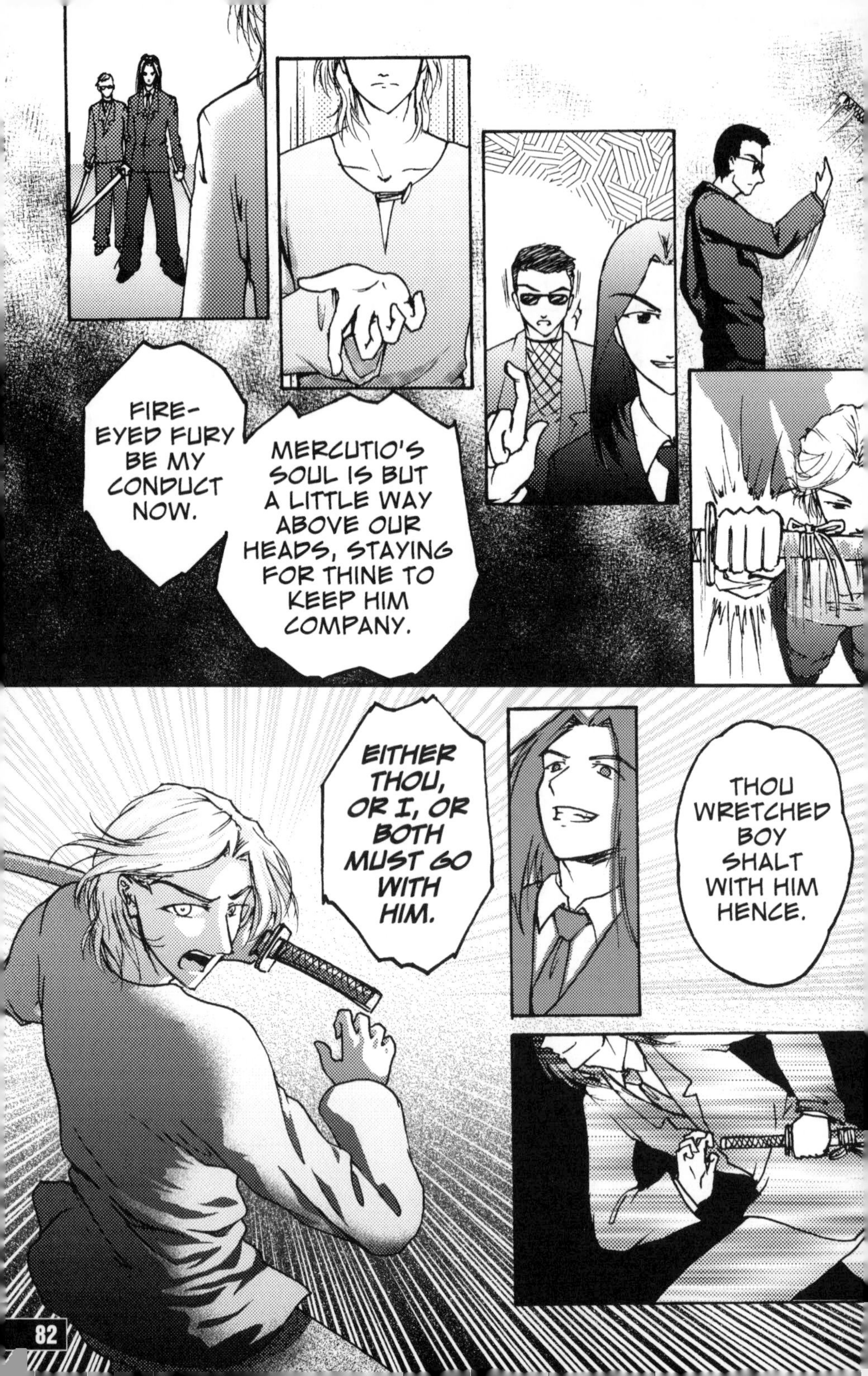

FIRE-EYED FURY BE MY CONDUCT NOW.
MERCUTIO'S SOUL IS BUT A LITTLE WAY ABOVE OUR HEADS, STAYING FOR THINE TO KEEP HIM COMPANY.
EITHER THOU, OR I, OR BOTH MUST GO WITH HIM.
THOU WRETCHED BOY SHALT WITH HIM HENCE.

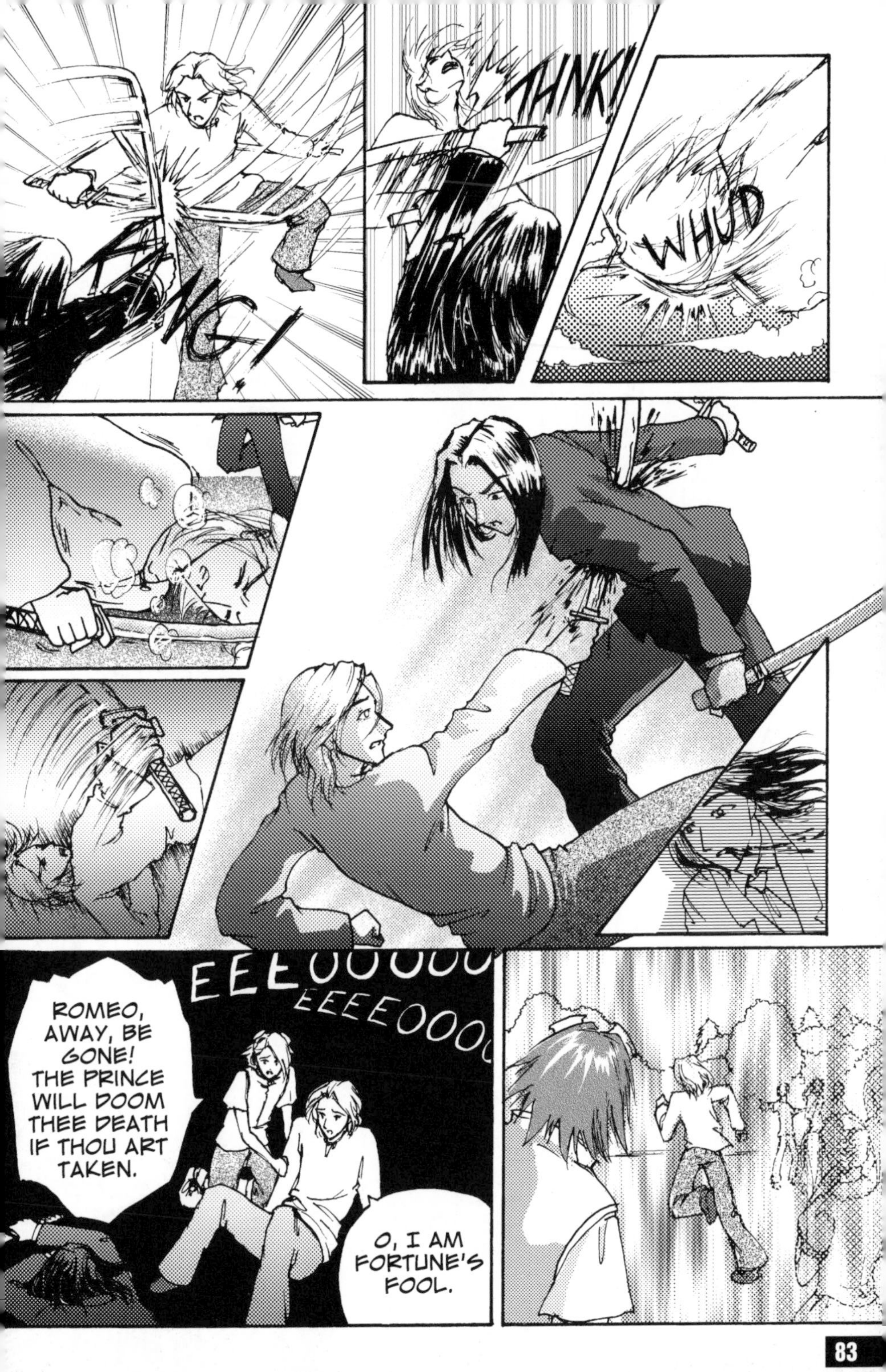
KANG!
THNK!
WHUD
EEEOOOOO
EEEEOOOO
ROMEO, AWAY, BE GONE! THE PRINCE WILL DOOM THEE DEATH IF THOU ART TAKEN.
O, I AM FORTUNE'S FOOL.

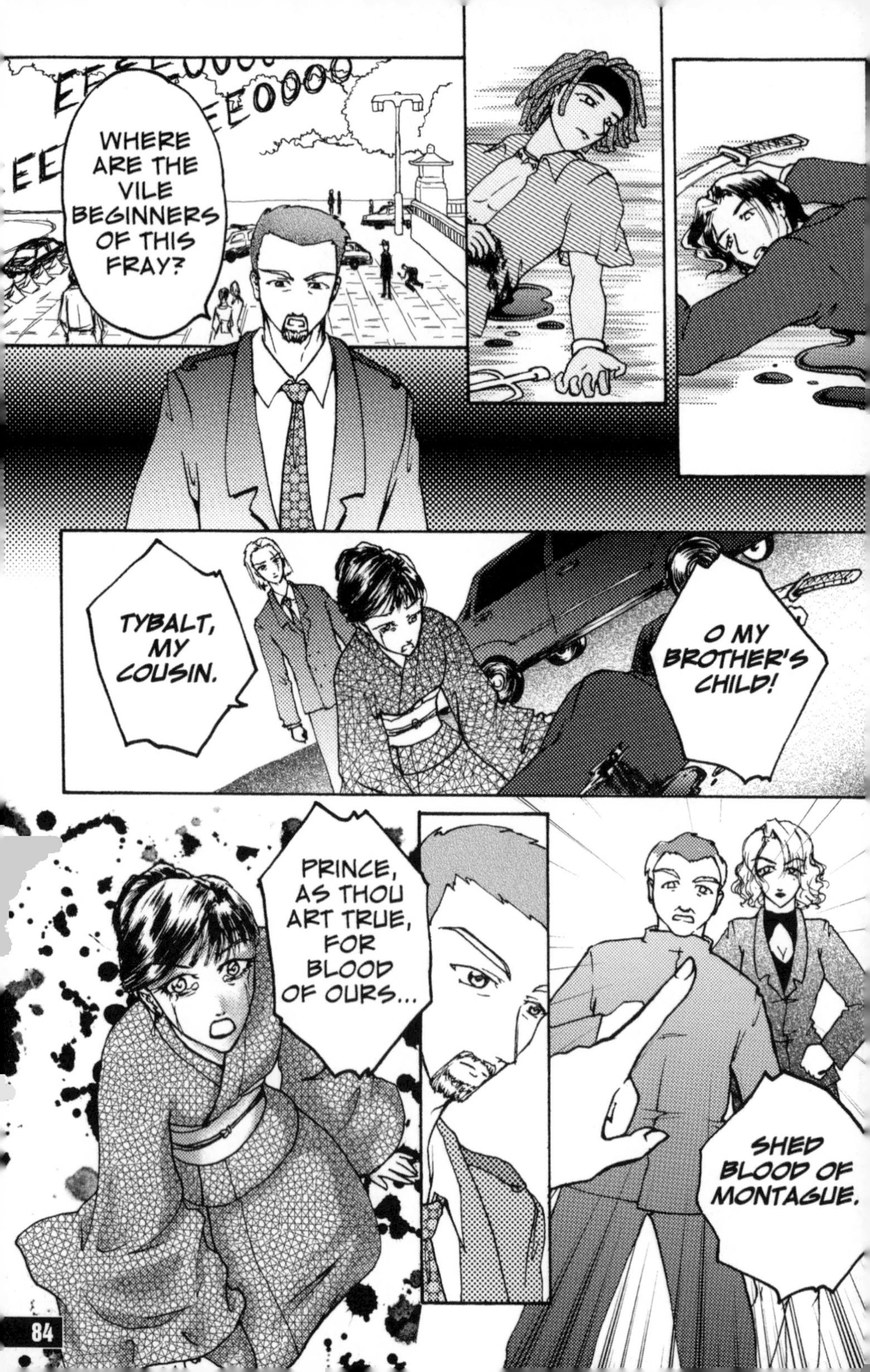
EEEEOOOO
EEEEOOOO
WHERE ARE THE VILE BEGINNERS OF THIS FRAY?
TYBALT, MY COUSIN.
O MY BROTHER'S CHILD!
PRINCE, AS THOU ART TRUE, FOR BLOOD OF OURS...
SHED BLOOD OF MONTAGUE.

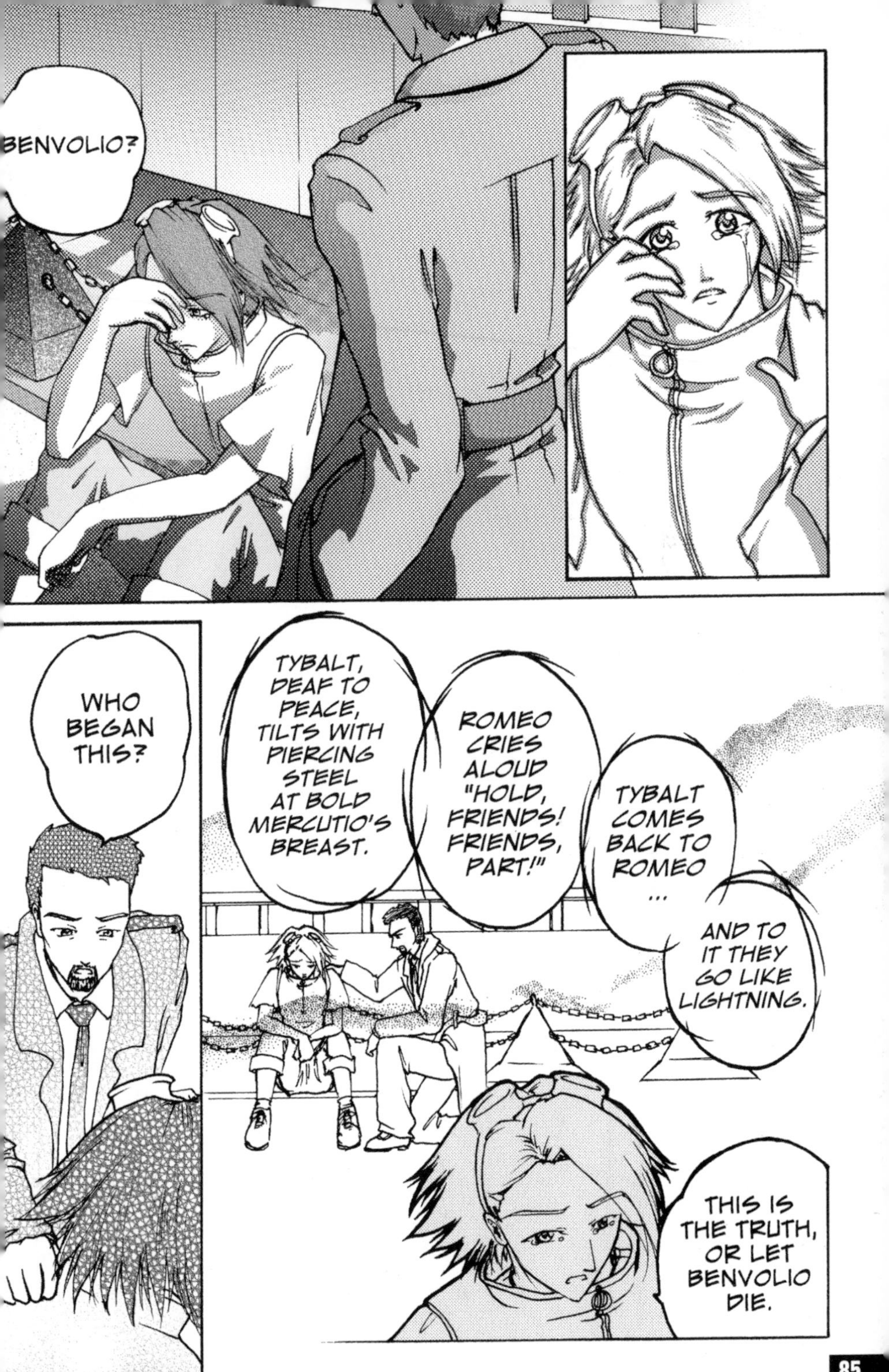

BENVOLIO?
WHO BEGAN THIS?
TYBALT, DEAF TO PEACE, TILTS WITH PIERCING STEEL AT BOLD MERCUTIO'S BREAST.
ROMEO CRIES ALOUD "HOLD, FRIENDS! FRIENDS, PART!"
TYBALT COMES BACK TO ROMEO ...
AND TO IT THEY GO LIKE LIGHTNING.
THIS IS THE TRUTH, OR LET BENVOLIO DIE.

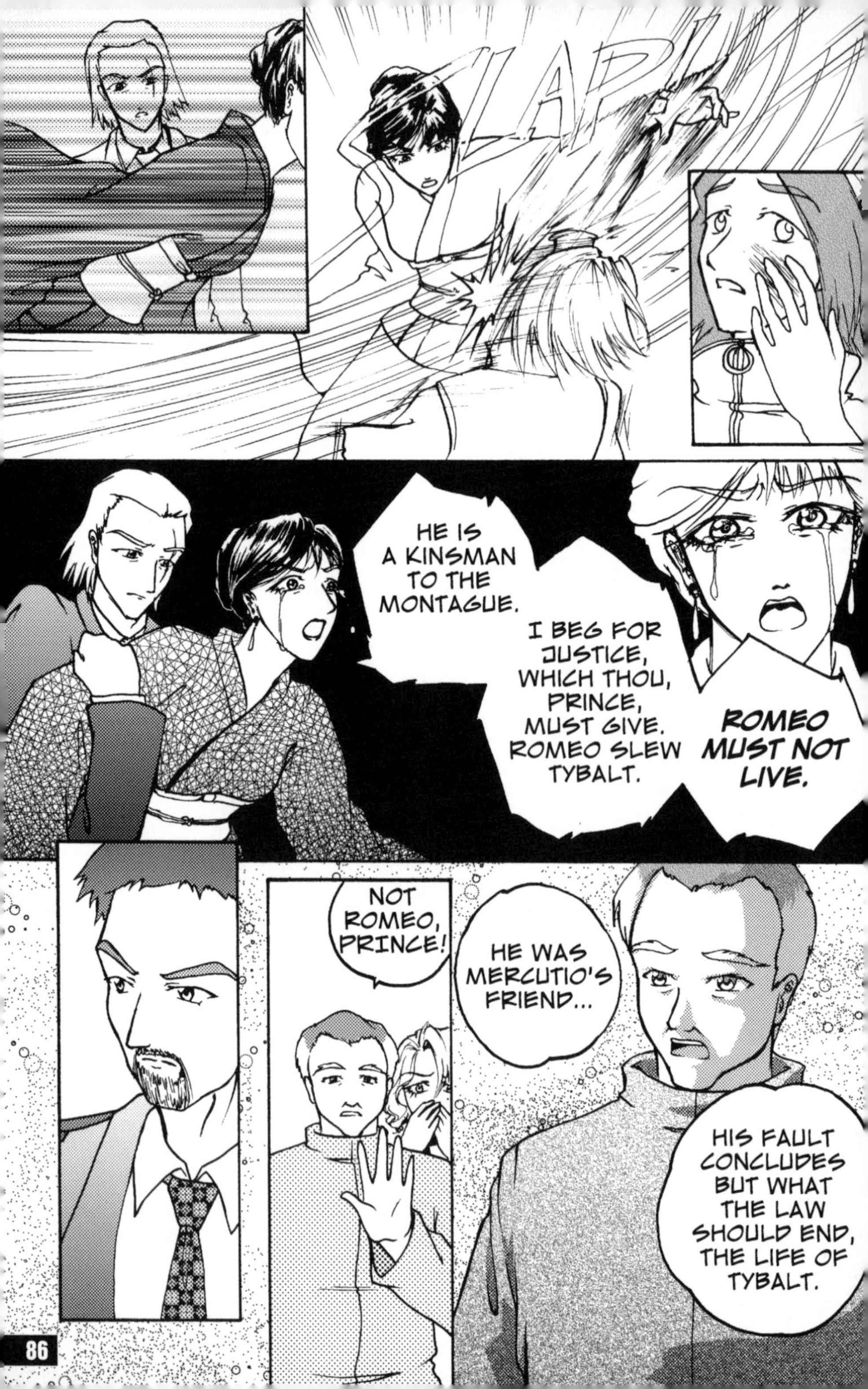
CLAP!
HE IS A KINSMAN TO THE MONTAGUE.
I BEG FOR JUSTICE, WHICH THOU, PRINCE, MUST GIVE. ROMEO SLEW TYBALT.
ROMEO MUST NOT LIVE.
NOT ROMEO, PRINCE!
HE WAS MERCUTIO'S FRIEND...
HIS FAULT CONCLUDES BUT WHAT THE LAW SHOULD END, THE LIFE OF TYBALT.

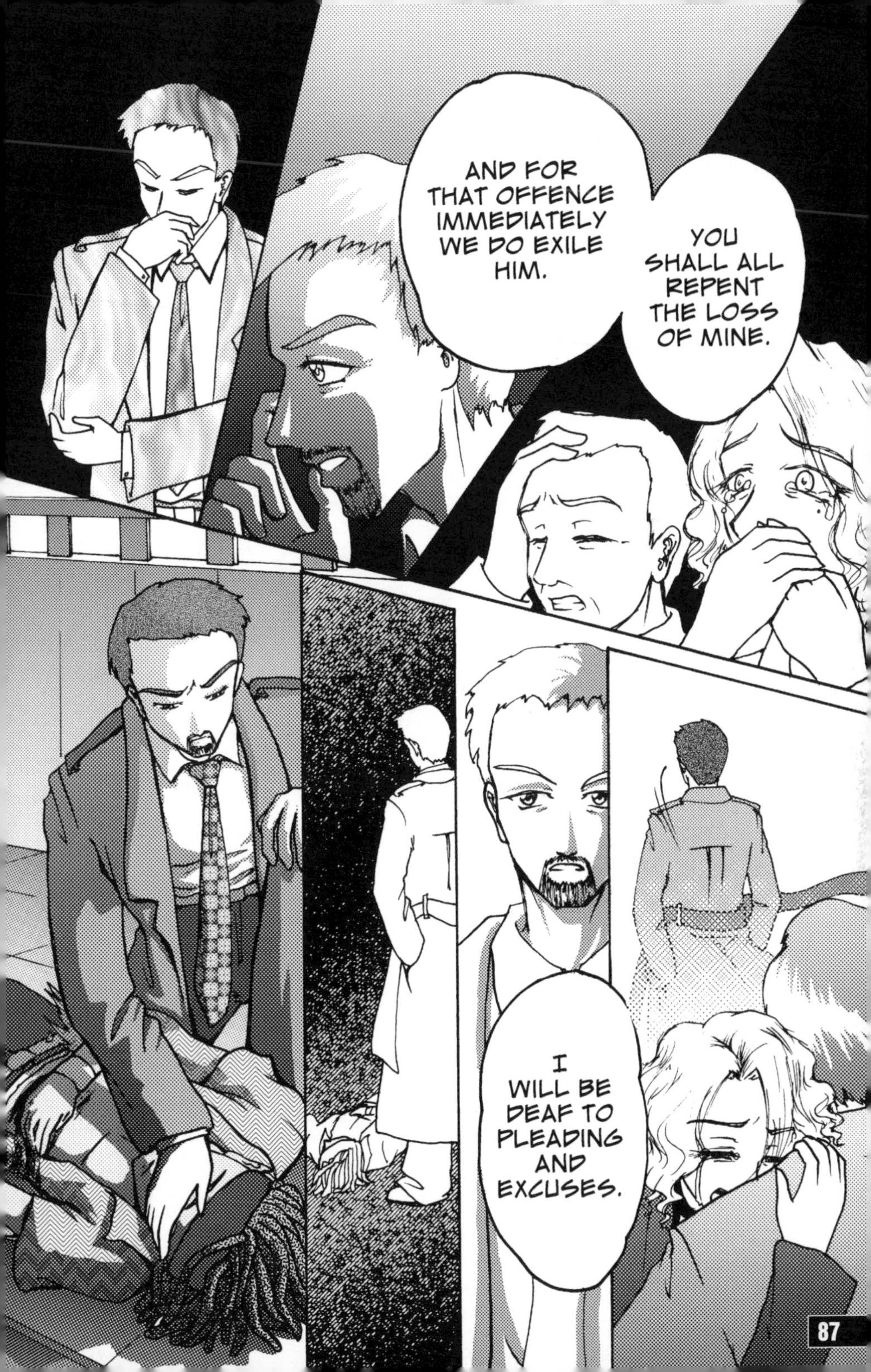
AND FOR THAT OFFENCE IMMEDIATELY WE DO EXILE HIM.
YOU SHALL ALL REPENT THE LOSS OF MINE.
I WILL BE DEAF TO PLEADING AND EXCUSES.

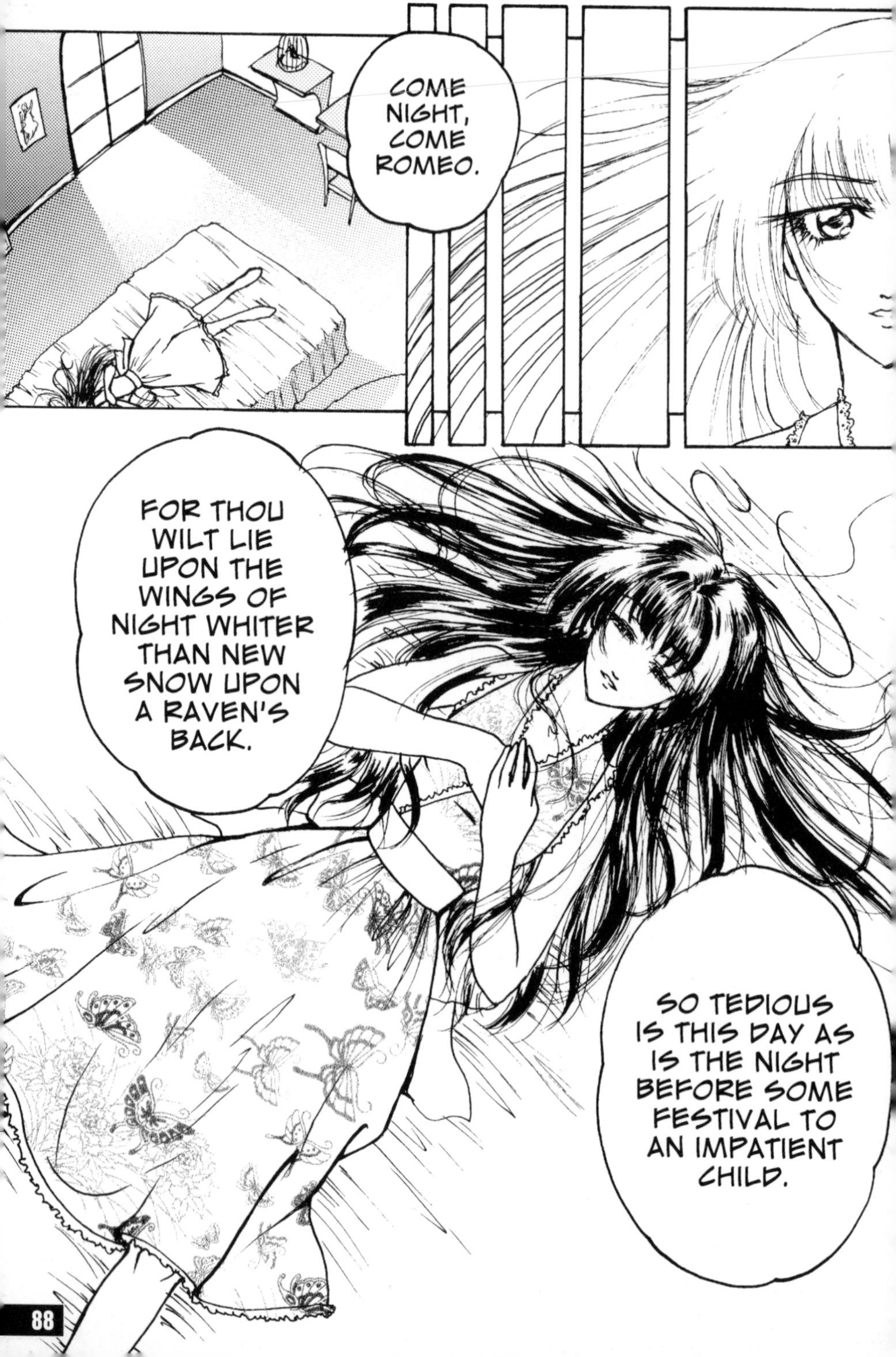
COME NIGHT, COME ROMEO.
FOR THOU WILT LIE UPON THE WINGS OF NIGHT WHITER THAN NEW SNOW UPON A RAVEN'S BACK.
SO TEDIOUS IS THIS DAY AS IS THE NIGHT BEFORE SOME FESTIVAL TO AN IMPATIENT CHILD.

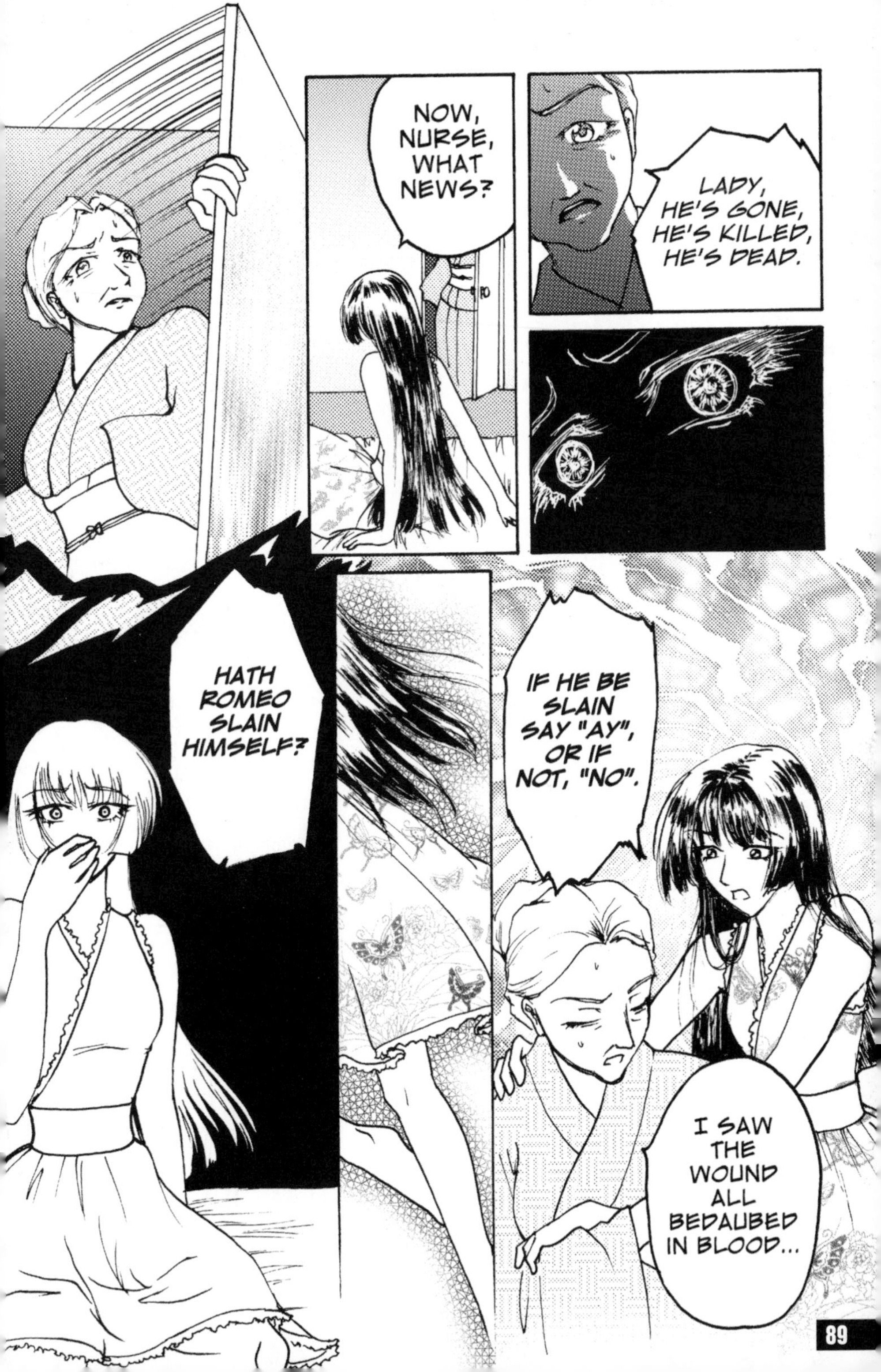
NOW, NURSE, WHAT NEWS?
LADY, HE'S GONE, HE'S KILLED, HE'S DEAD.
HATH ROMEO SLAIN HIMSELF?
IF HE BE SLAIN SAY "AY", OR IF NOT, "NO".
I SAW THE WOUND ALL BEDAUBED IN BLOOD...

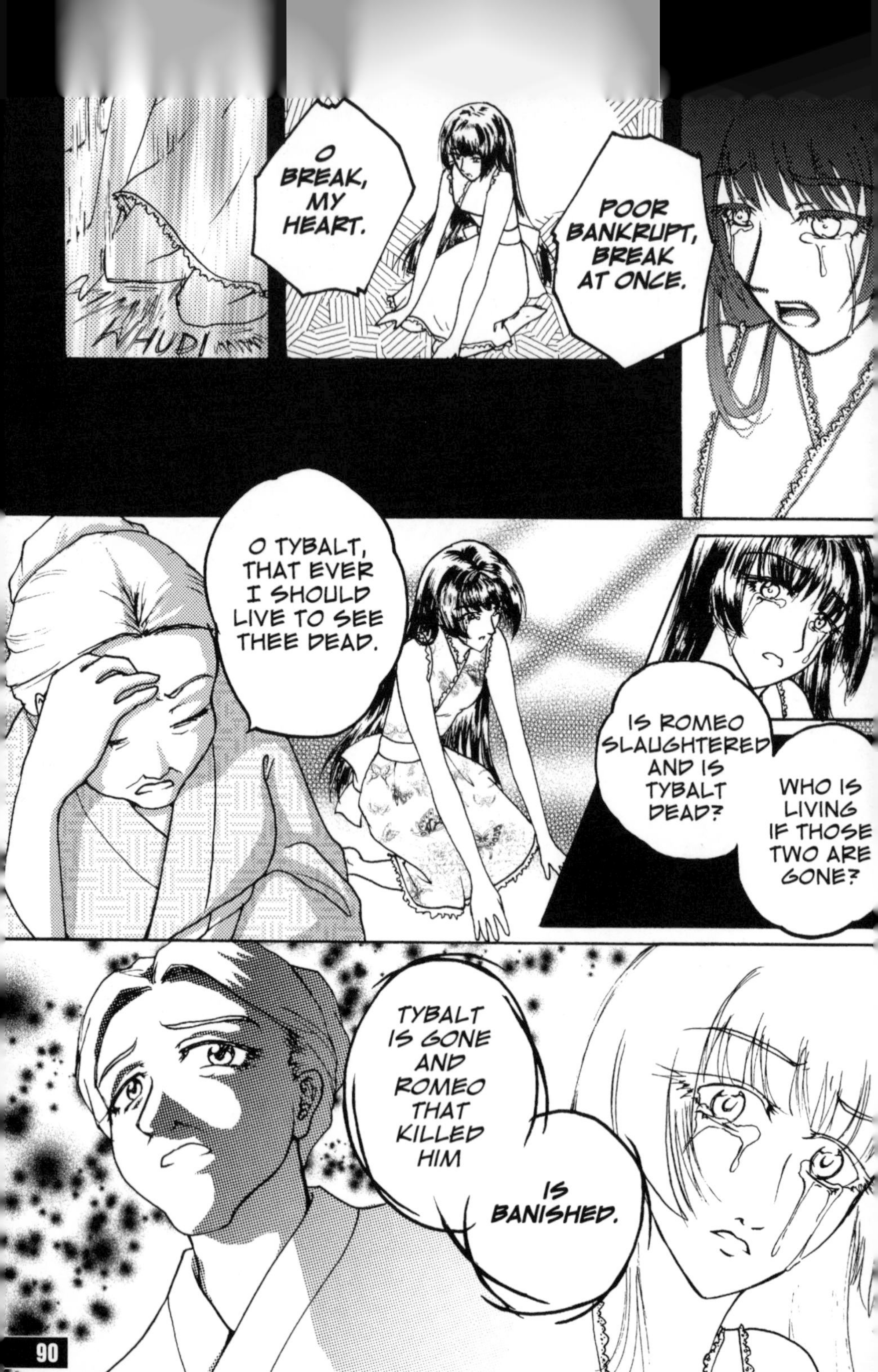
WHUD!
O BREAK, MY HEART.
POOR BANKRUPT, BREAK AT ONCE.
O TYBALT, THAT EVER I SHOULD LIVE TO SEE THEE DEAD.
IS ROMEO SLAUGHTERED AND IS TYBALT DEAD?
WHO IS LIVING IF THOSE TWO ARE GONE?
TYBALT IS GONE AND ROMEO THAT KILLED HIM
IS BANISHED.

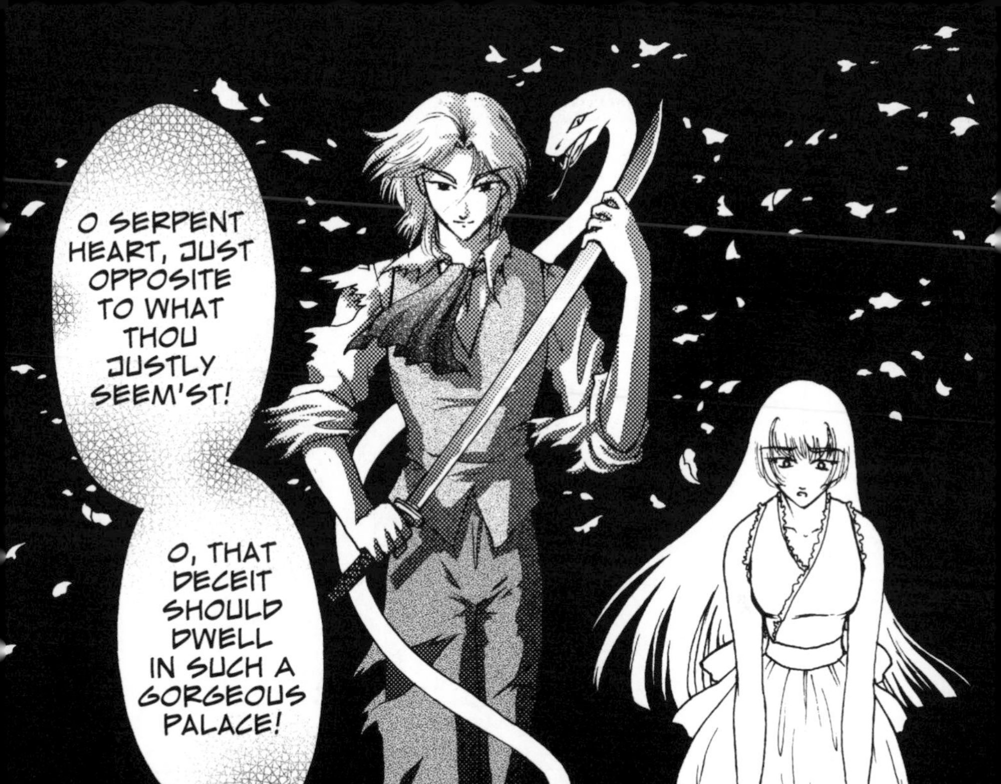
O SERPENT HEART, JUST OPPOSITE TO WHAT THOU JUSTLY SEEM'ST!
O, THAT DECEIT SHOULD DWELL IN SUCH A GORGEOUS PALACE!

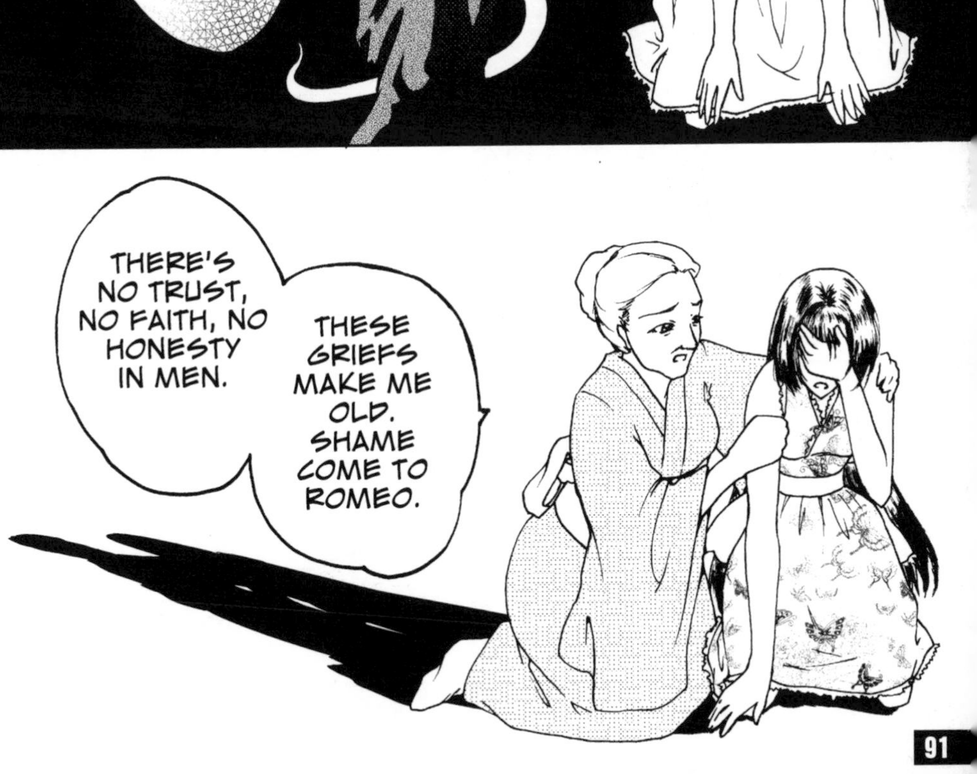
THERE'S NO TRUST, NO FAITH, NO HONESTY IN MEN.
THESE GRIEFS MAKE ME OLD. SHAME COME TO ROMEO.

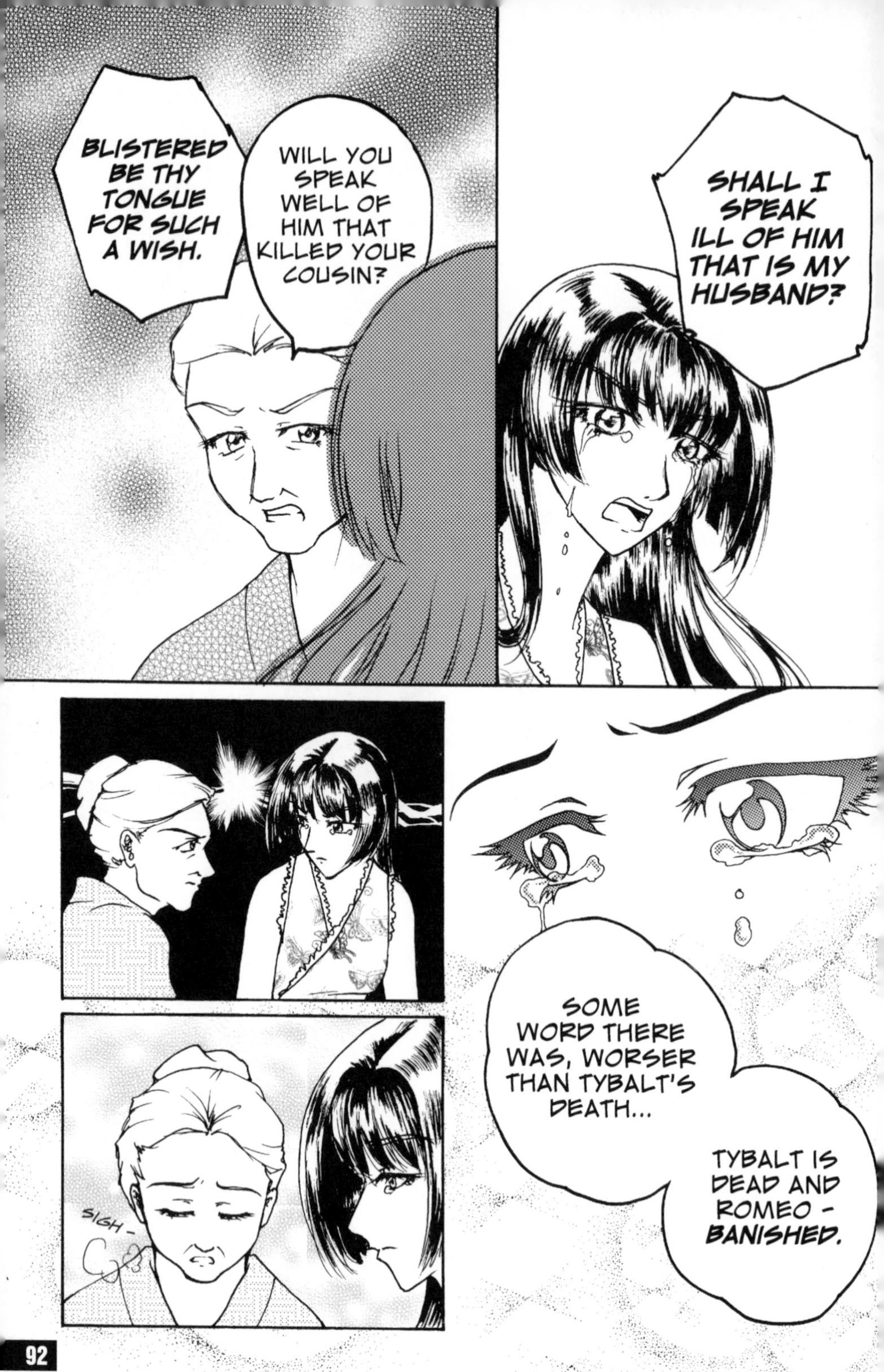
SHALL I SPEAK ILL OF HIM THAT IS MY HUSBAND?
WILL YOU SPEAK WELL OF HIM THAT KILLED YOUR COUSIN?
BLISTERED BE THY TONGUE FOR SUCH A WISH.
SIGH
SOME WORD THERE WAS, WORSER THAN TYBALT'S DEATH...
TYBALT IS DEAD AND ROMEO - BANISHED.

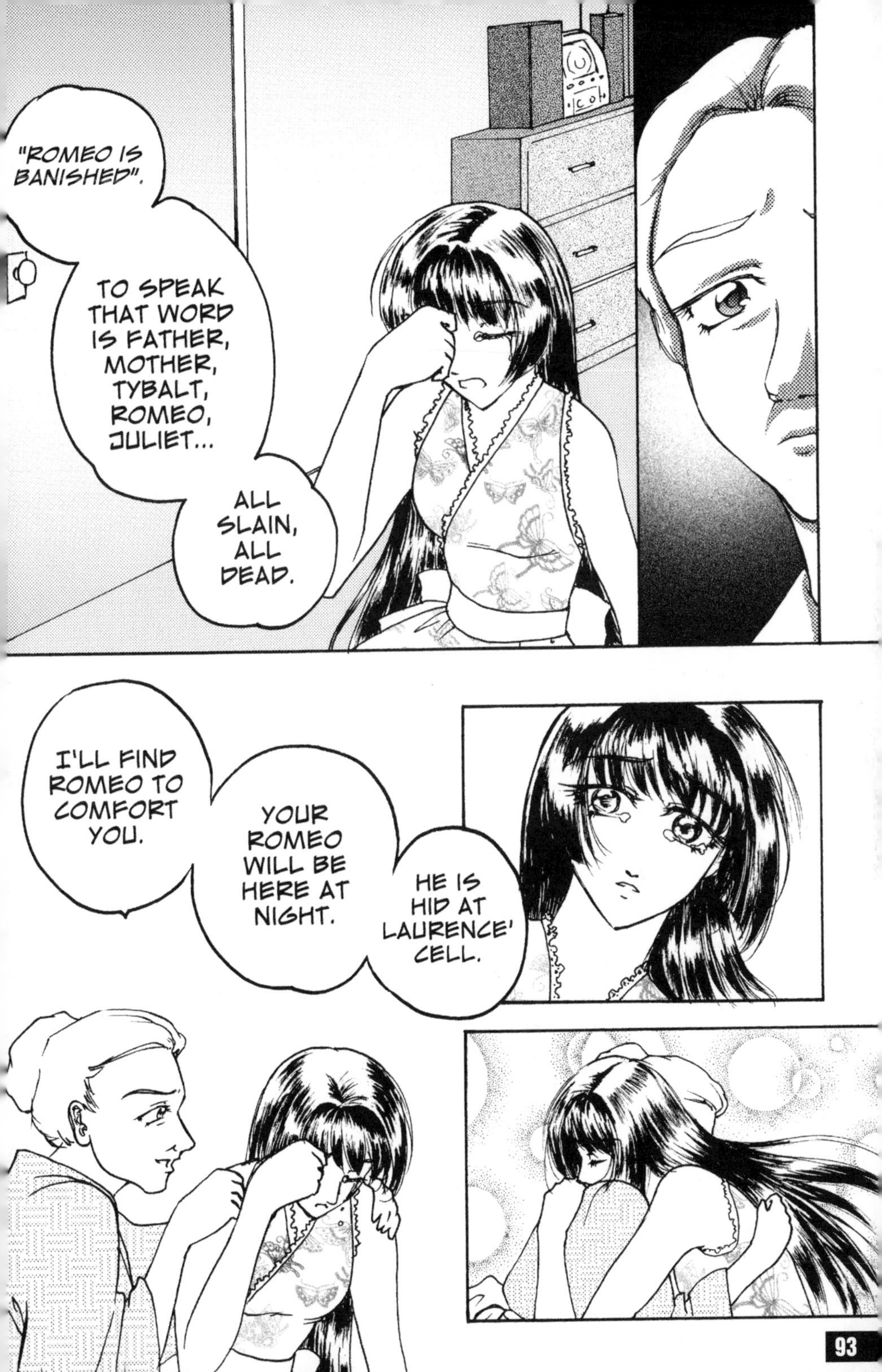
"ROMEO IS BANISHED".
TO SPEAK THAT WORD IS FATHER, MOTHER, TYBALT, ROMEO, JULIET...
ALL SLAIN, ALL DEAD.
I'LL FIND ROMEO TO COMFORT YOU.
YOUR ROMEO WILL BE HERE AT NIGHT.
HE IS HID AT LAURENCE' CELL.

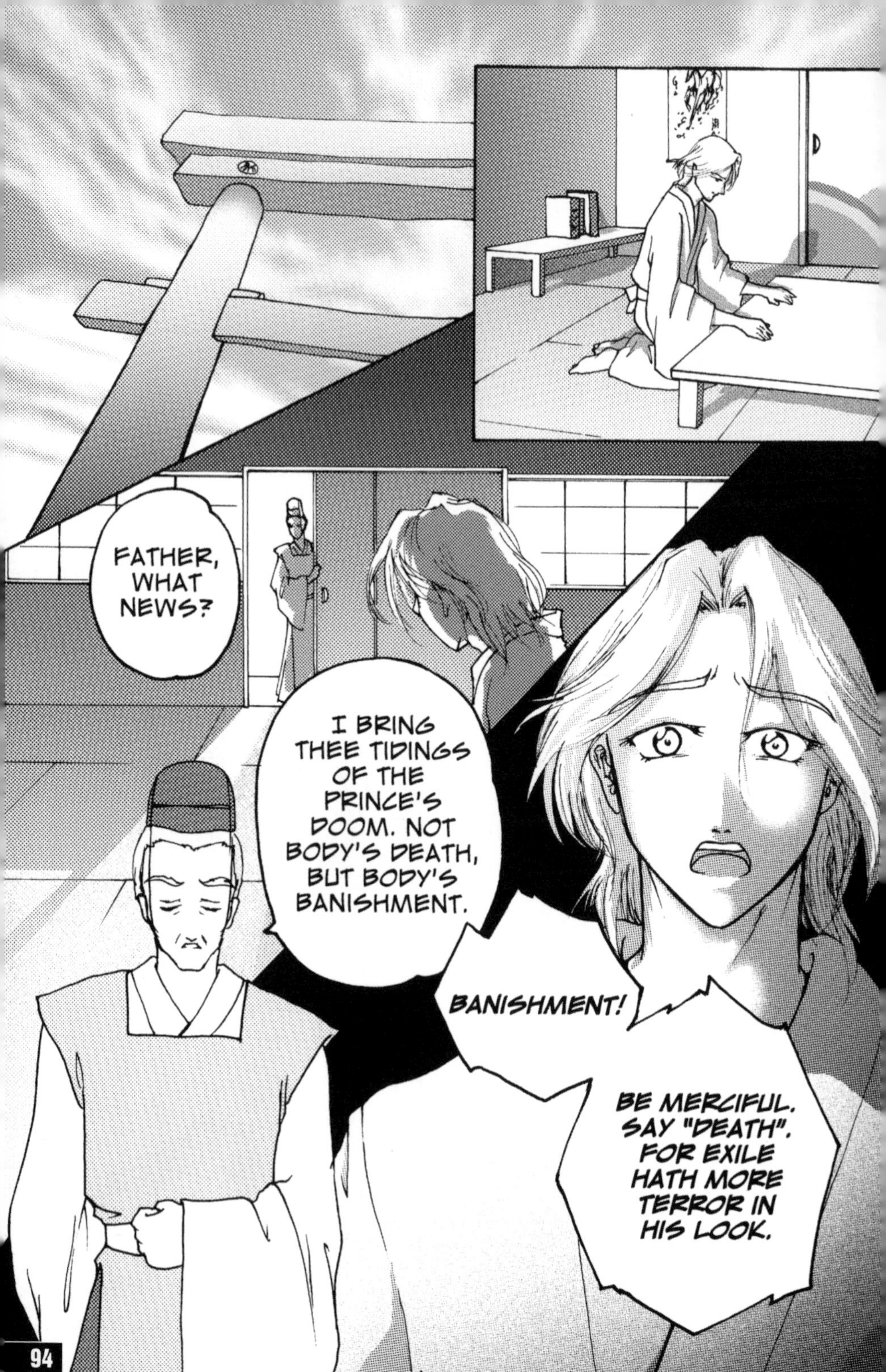
FATHER, WHAT NEWS?
I BRING THEE TIDINGS OF THE PRINCE'S DOOM. NOT BODY'S DEATH, BUT BODY'S BANISHMENT.
BANISHMENT!
BE MERCIFUL. SAY "DEATH". FOR EXILE HATH MORE TERROR IN HIS LOOK.

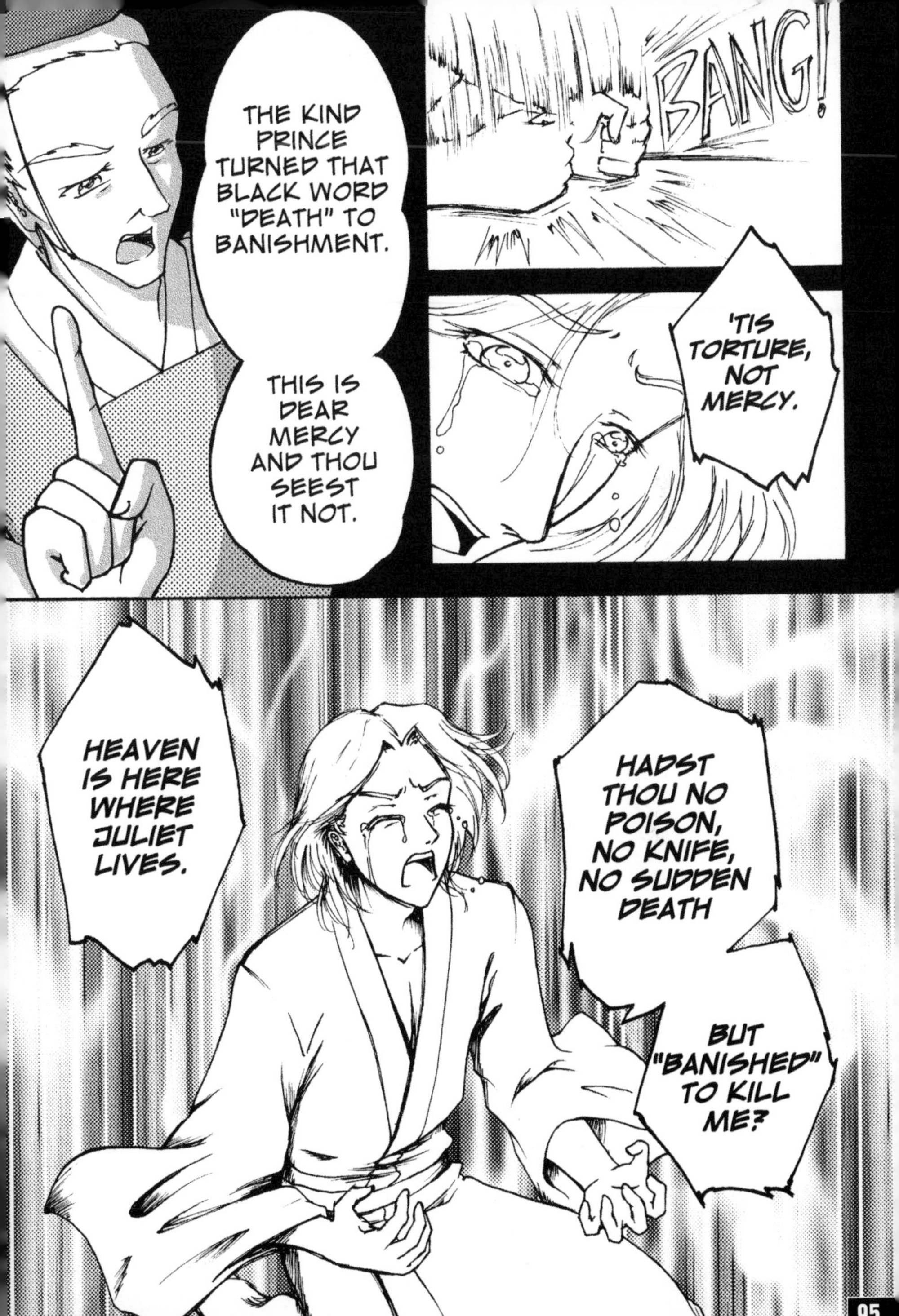
THE KIND PRINCE TURNED THAT BLACK WORD "DEATH" TO BANISHMENT.
THIS IS DEAR MERCY AND THOU SEEST IT NOT.
BANG!
'TIS TORTURE, NOT MERCY.
HEAVEN IS HERE WHERE JULIET LIVES.
HADST THOU NO POISON, NO KNIFE, NO SUDDEN DEATH
BUT "BANISHED" TO KILL ME?

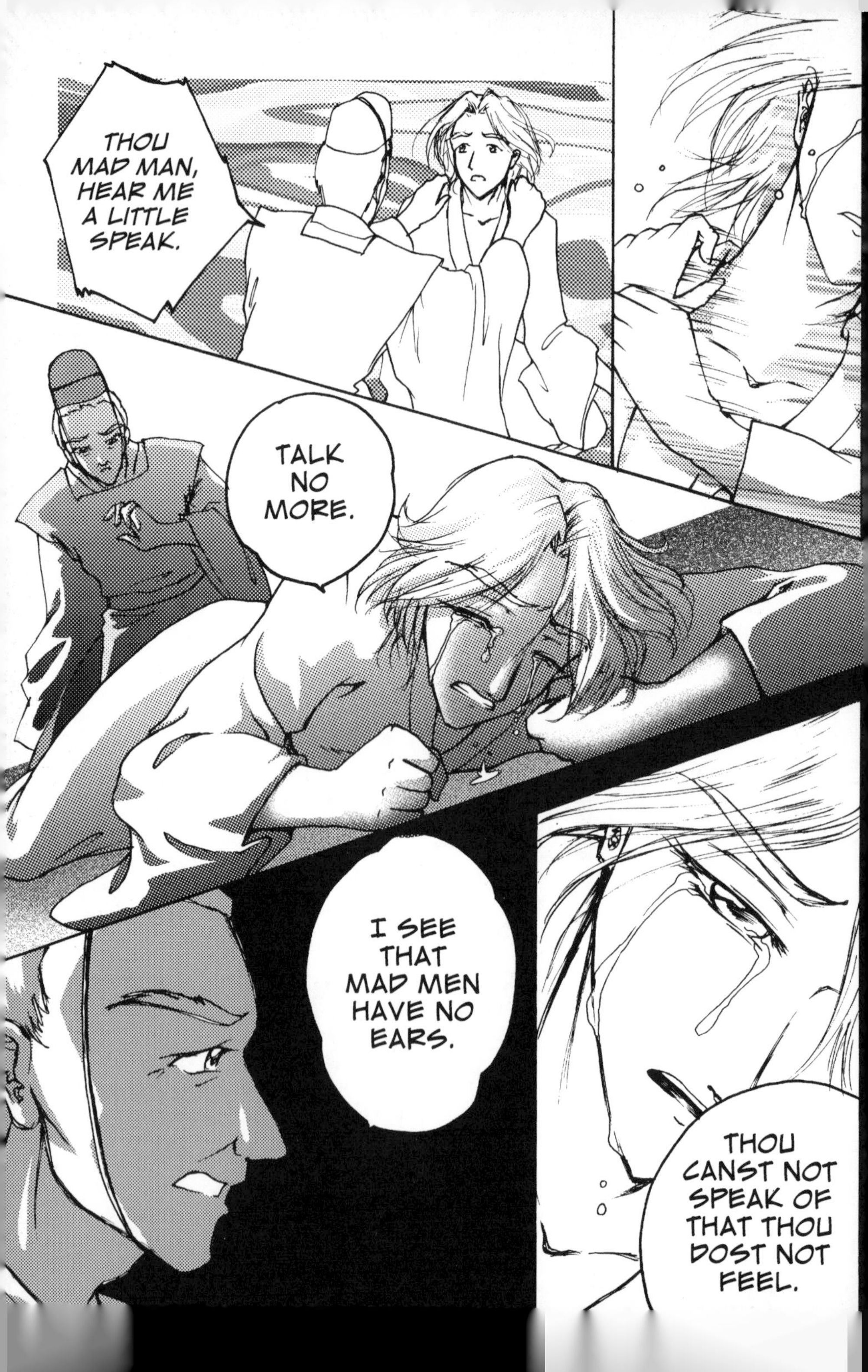
THOU MAD MAN, HEAR ME A LITTLE SPEAK.
TALK NO MORE.
I SEE THAT MAD MEN HAVE NO EARS.
THOU CANST NOT SPEAK OF THAT THOU DOST NOT FEEL.

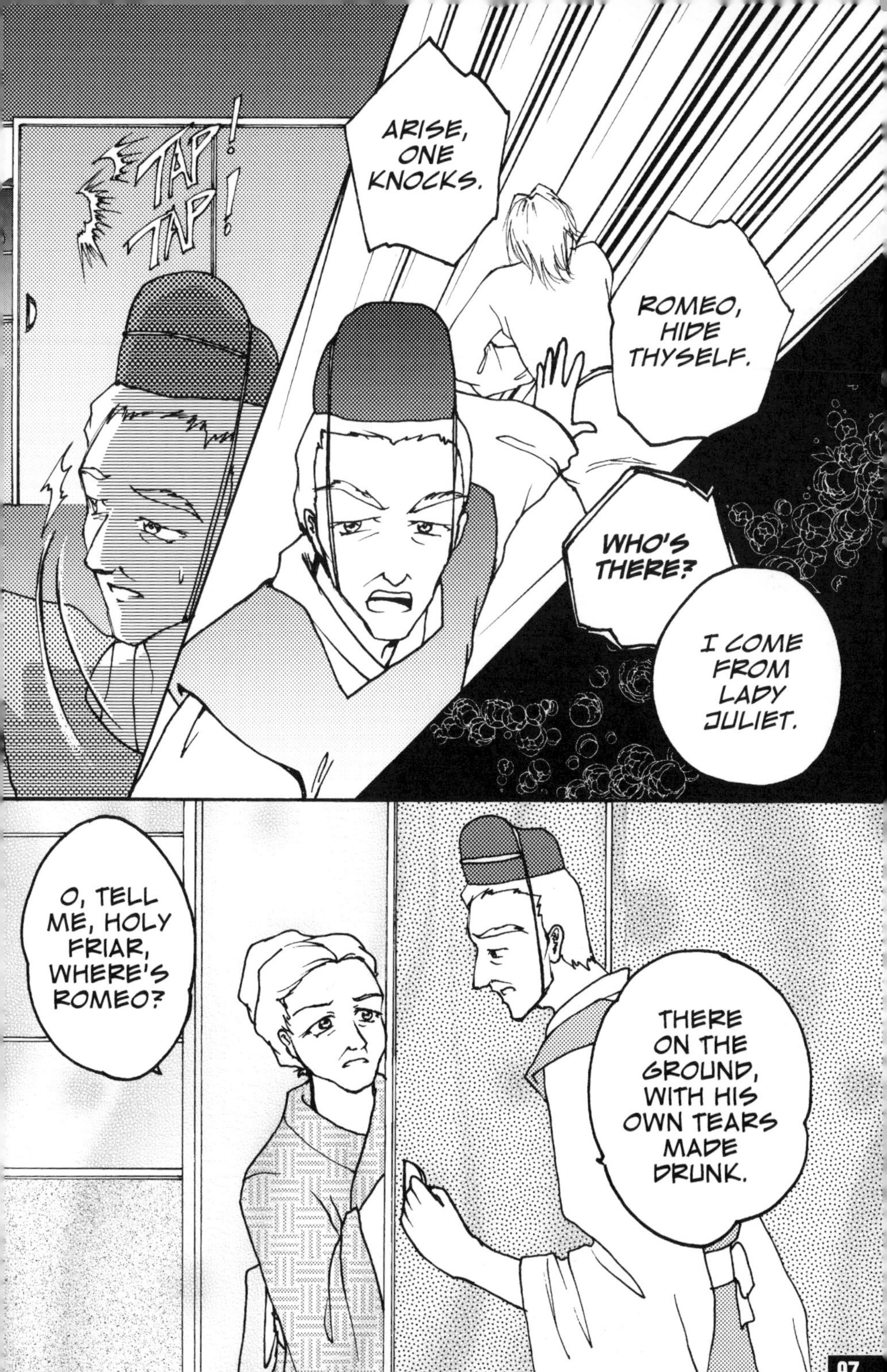
ARISE, ONE KNOCKS.
TAP! TAP!
ROMEO, HIDE THYSELF.
WHO'S THERE?
I COME FROM LADY JULIET.
O, TELL ME, HOLY FRIAR, WHERE'S ROMEO?
THERE ON THE GROUND, WITH HIS OWN TEARS MADE DRUNK.

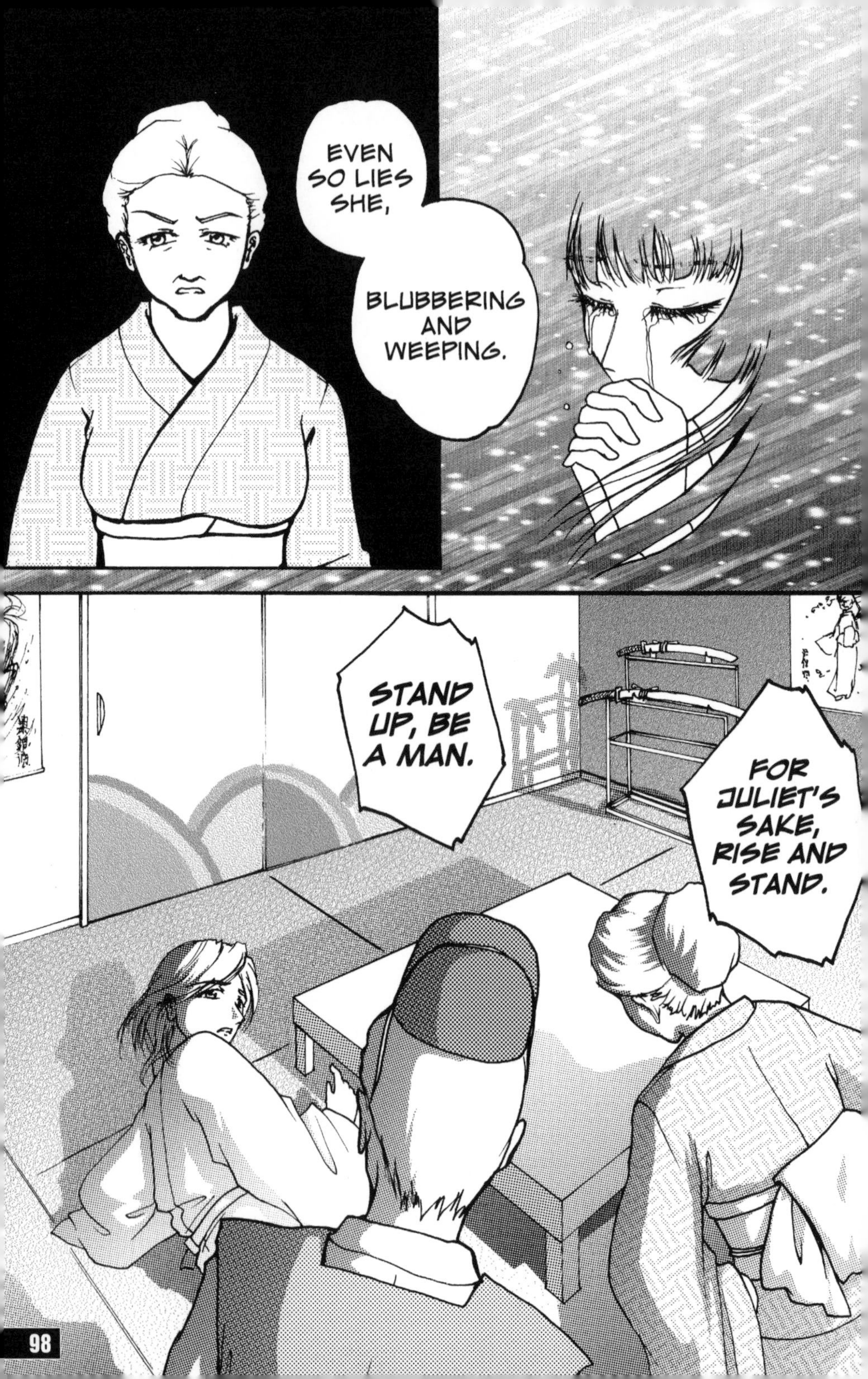
EVEN SO LIES SHE,
BLUBBERING AND WEEPING.
STAND UP, BE A MAN.
FOR JULIET'S SAKE, RISE AND STAND.

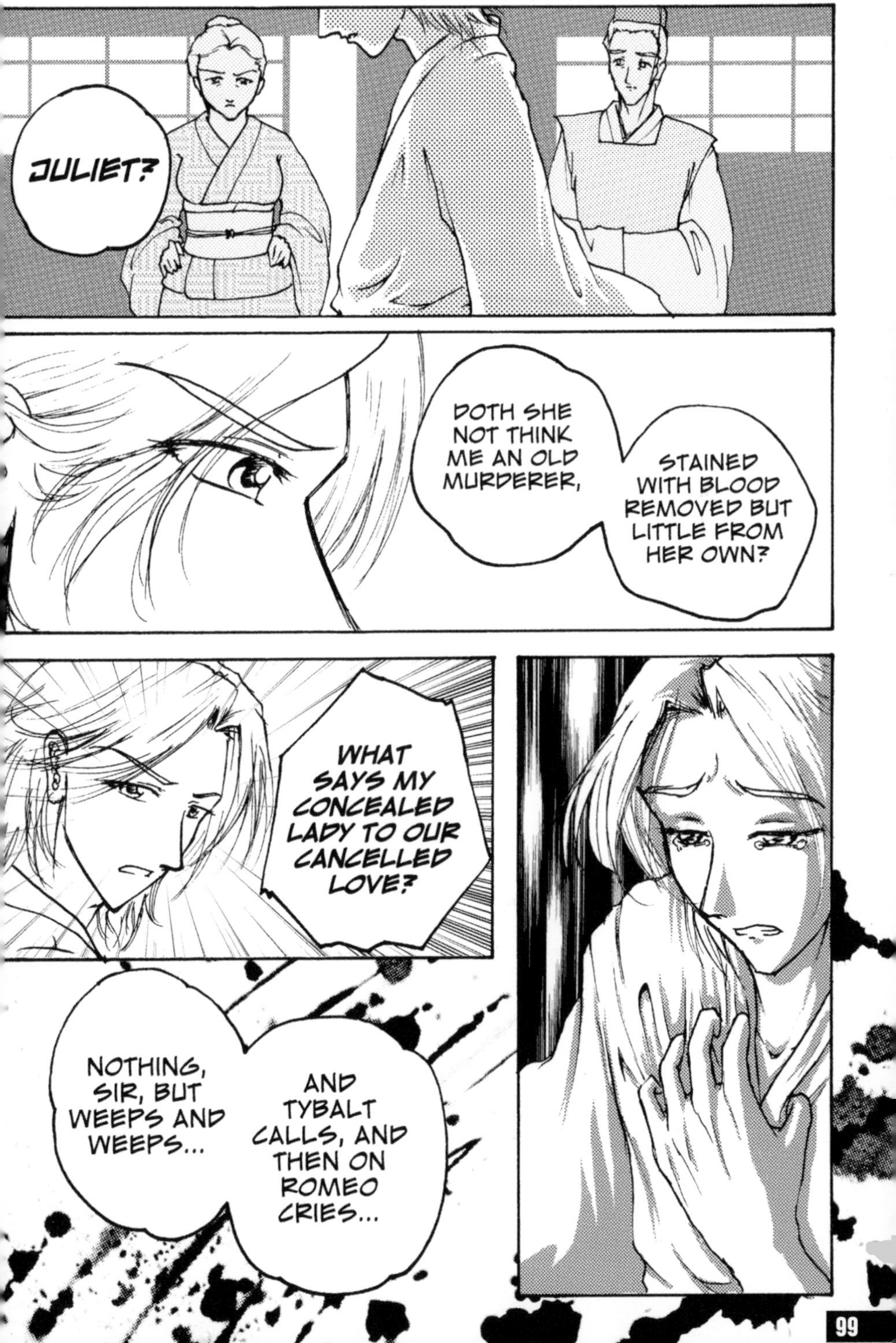
JULIET?
DOTH SHE NOT THINK ME AN OLD MURDERER,
STAINED WITH BLOOD REMOVED BUT LITTLE FROM HER OWN?
WHAT SAYS MY CONCEALED LADY TO OUR CANCELLED LOVE?
NOTHING, SIR, BUT WEEPS AND WEEPS...
AND TYBALT CALLS, AND THEN ON ROMEO CRIES...

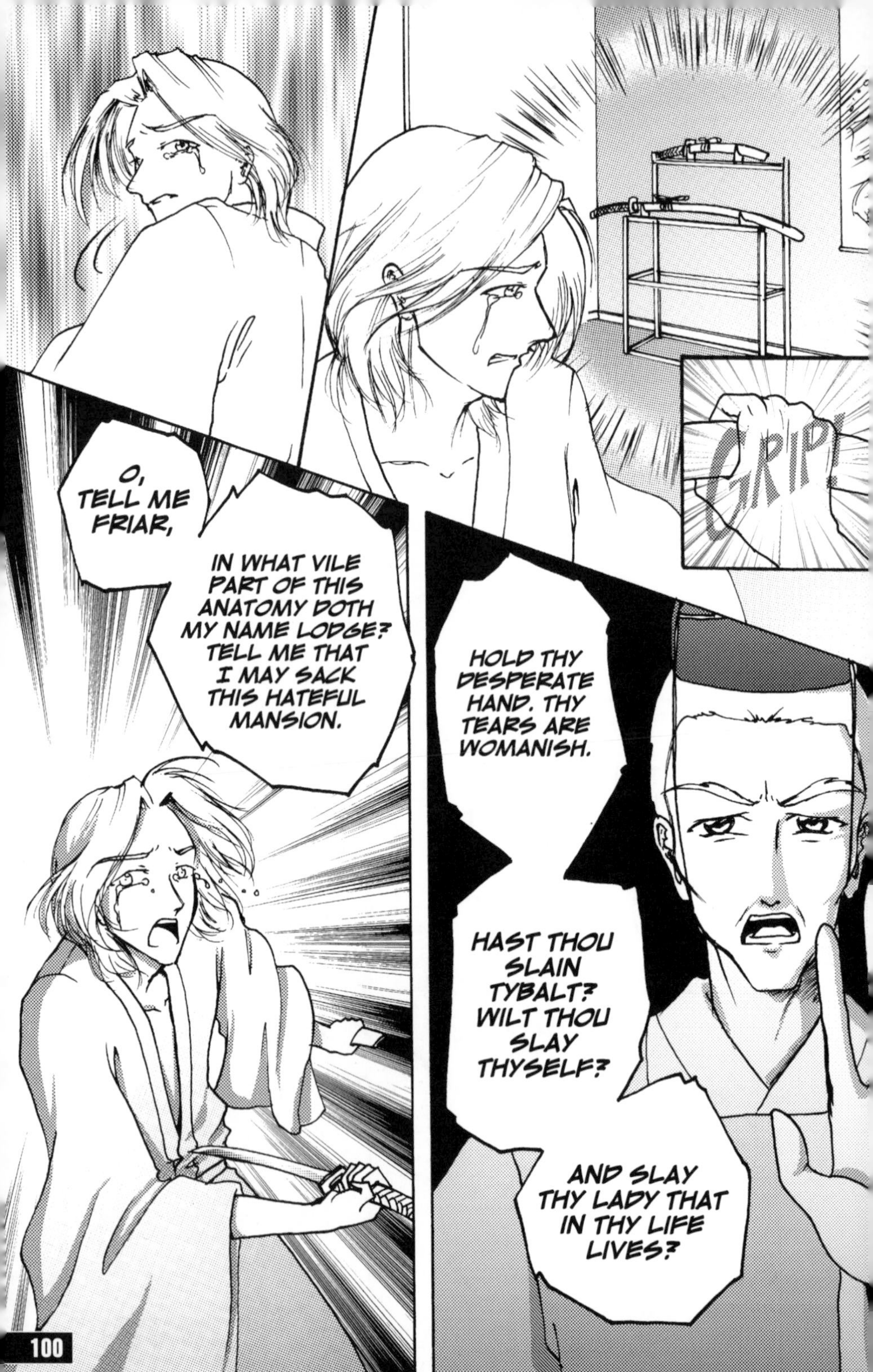
GRIP!
O, TELL ME FRIAR,
IN WHAT VILE PART OF THIS ANATOMY DOTH MY NAME LODGE? TELL ME THAT I MAY SACK THIS HATEFUL MANSION.
HOLD THY DESPERATE HAND. THY TEARS ARE WOMANISH.
HAST THOU SLAIN TYBALT? WILT THOU SLAY THYSELF?
AND SLAY THY LADY THAT IN THY LIFE LIVES?

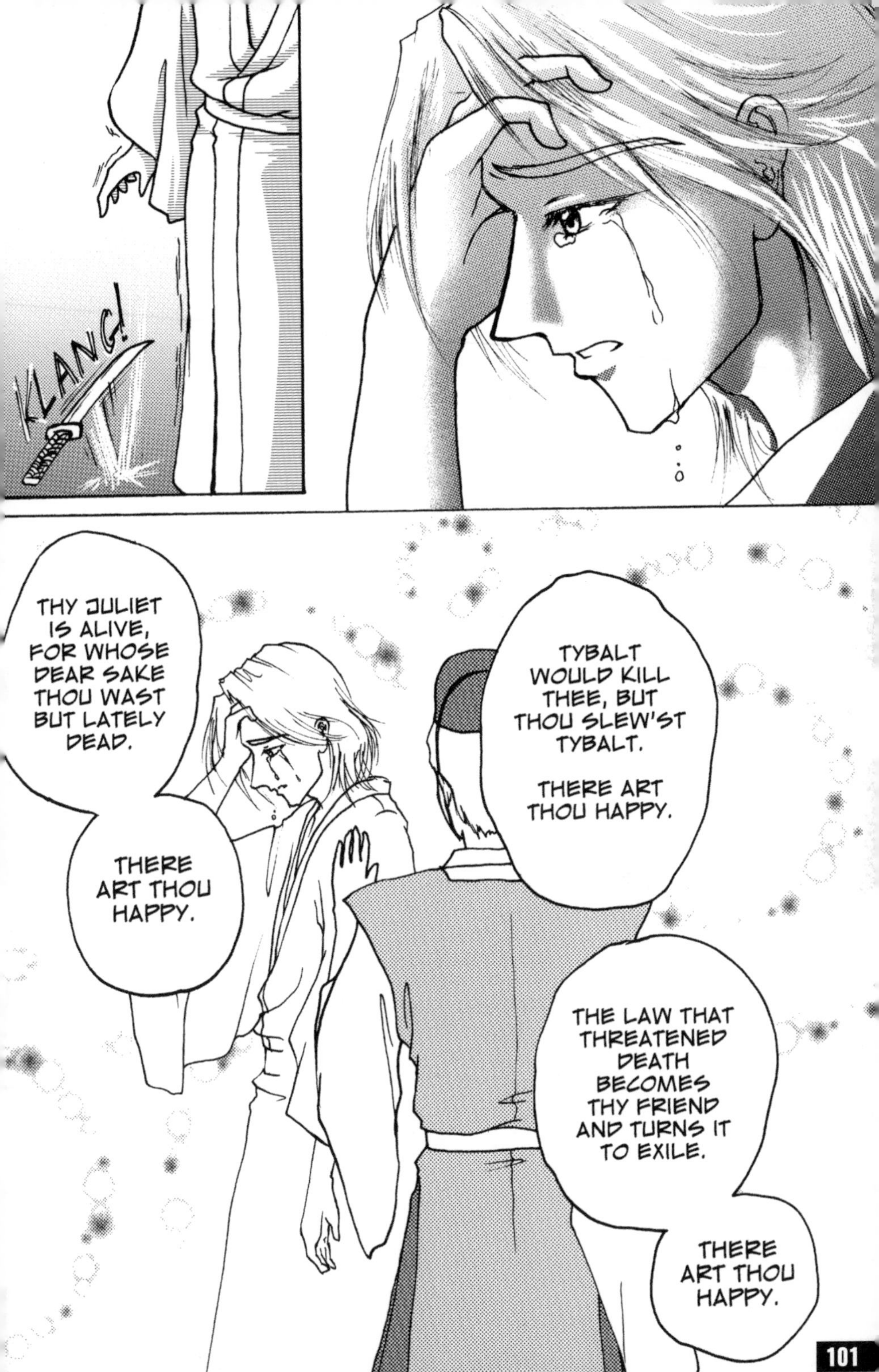
KLANG!
THY JULIET IS ALIVE, FOR WHOSE DEAR SAKE THOU WAST BUT LATELY DEAD.
THERE ART THOU HAPPY.
TYBALT WOULD KILL THEE, BUT THOU SLEW'ST TYBALT.
THERE ART THOU HAPPY.
THE LAW THAT THREATENED DEATH BECOMES THY FRIEND AND TURNS IT TO EXILE.
THERE ART THOU HAPPY.

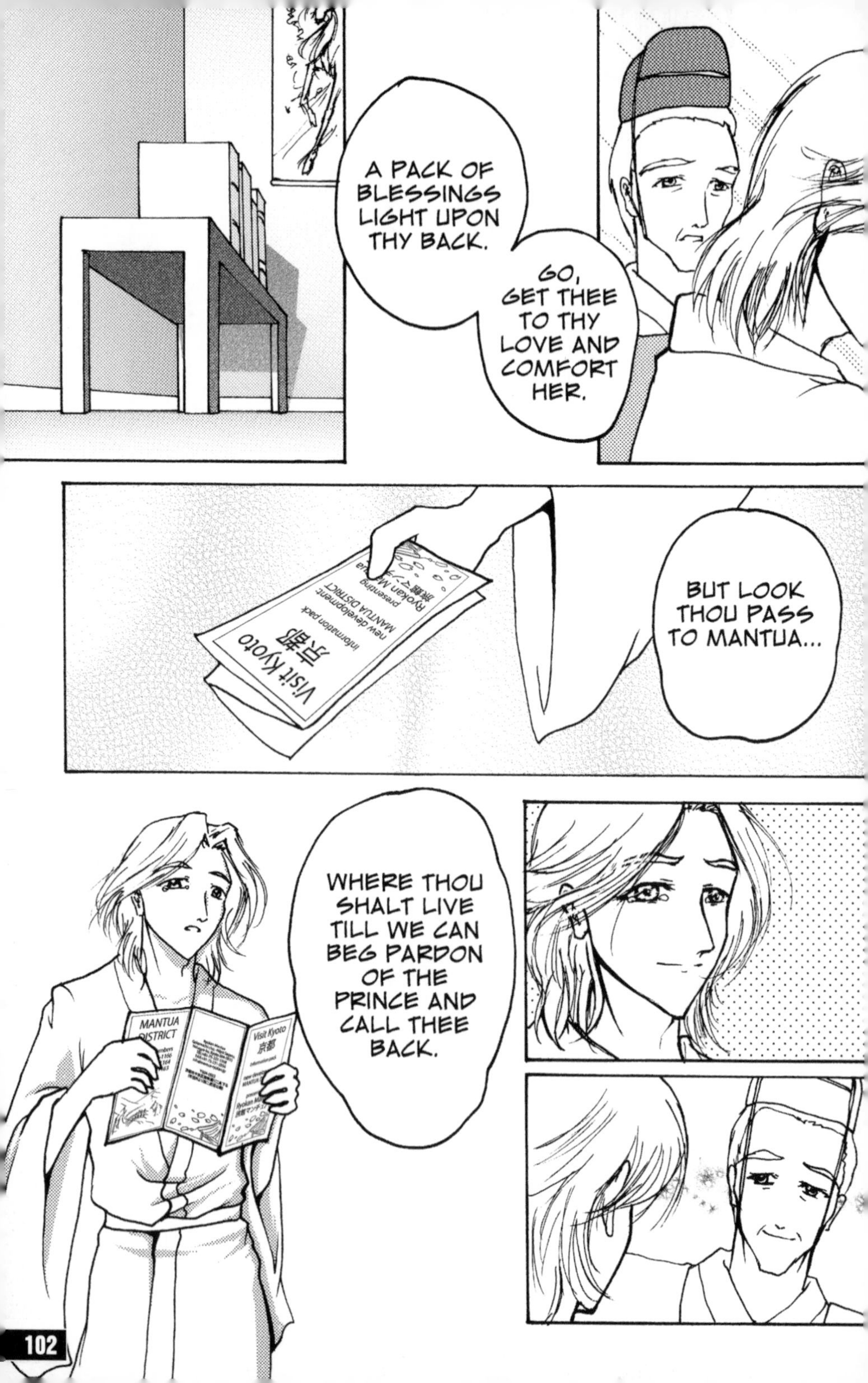
A PACK OF BLESSINGS LIGHT UPON THY BACK.
GO, GET THEE TO THY LOVE AND COMFORT HER.
Visit Kyoto
京都
information pack
new development
MANTUA DISTRICT
presenting
BUT LOOK THOU PASS TO MANTUA...
MANTUA DISTRICT
WHERE THOU SHALT LIVE TILL WE CAN BEG PARDON OF THE PRINCE AND CALL THEE BACK.

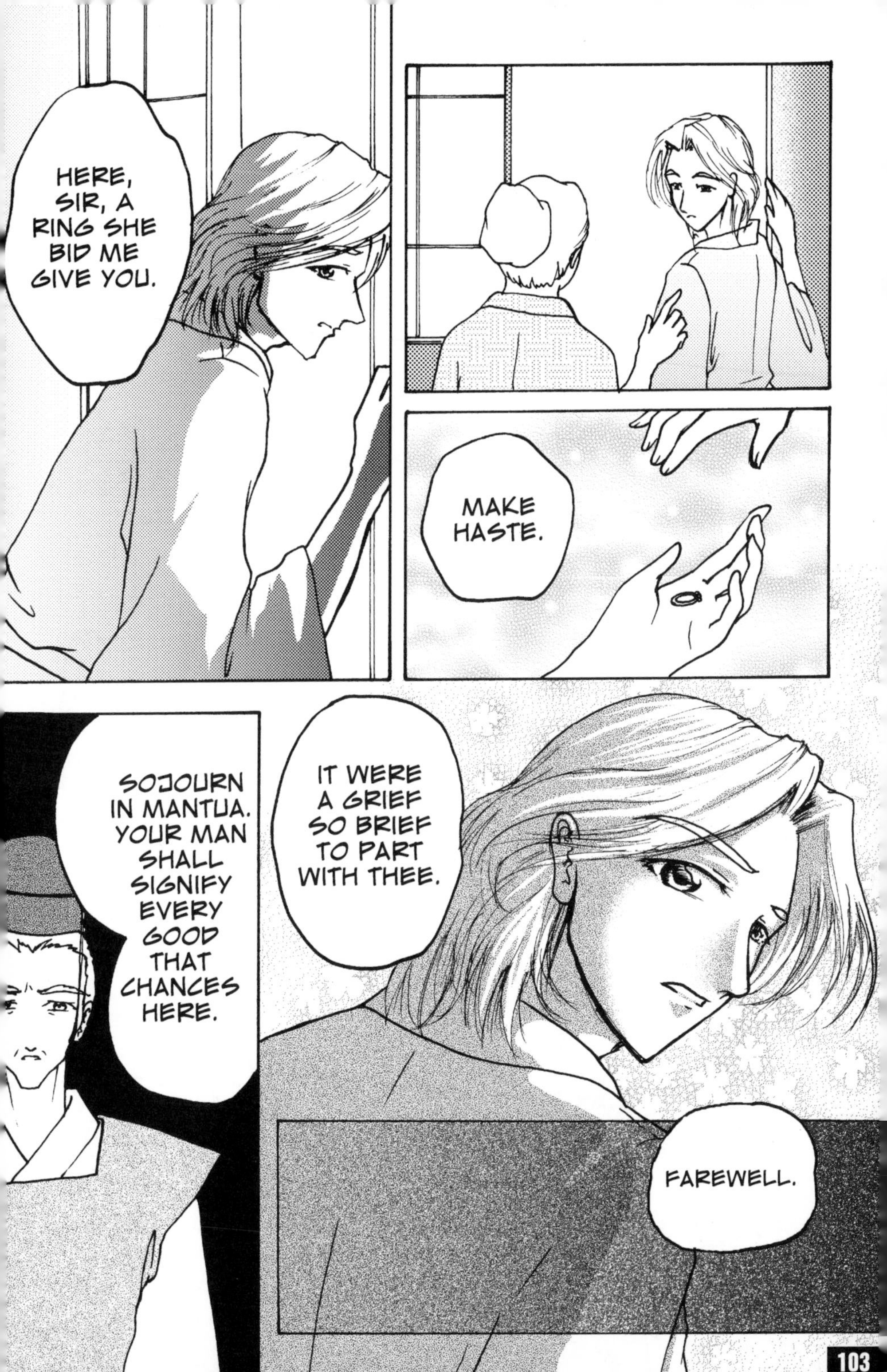
HERE, SIR, A RING SHE BID ME GIVE YOU.
MAKE HASTE.
SOJOURN IN MANTUA. YOUR MAN SHALL SIGNIFY EVERY GOOD THAT CHANCES HERE.
IT WERE A GRIEF SO BRIEF TO PART WITH THEE.
FAREWELL.

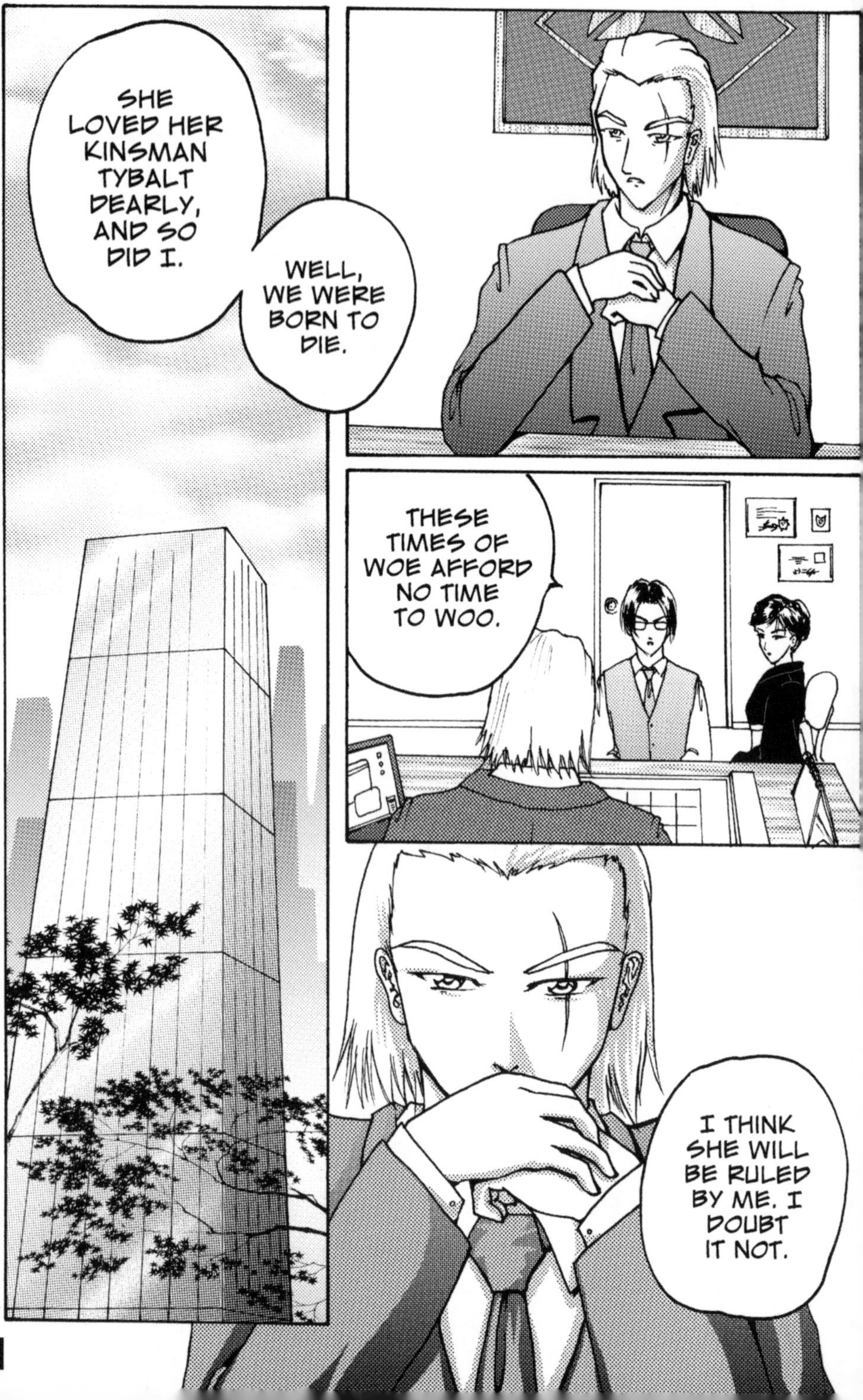
SHE LOVED HER KINSMAN TYBALT DEARLY, AND SO DID I.
WELL, WE WERE BORN TO DIE.
THESE TIMES OF WOE AFFORD NO TIME TO WOO.
I THINK SHE WILL BE RULED BY ME. I DOUBT IT NOT.

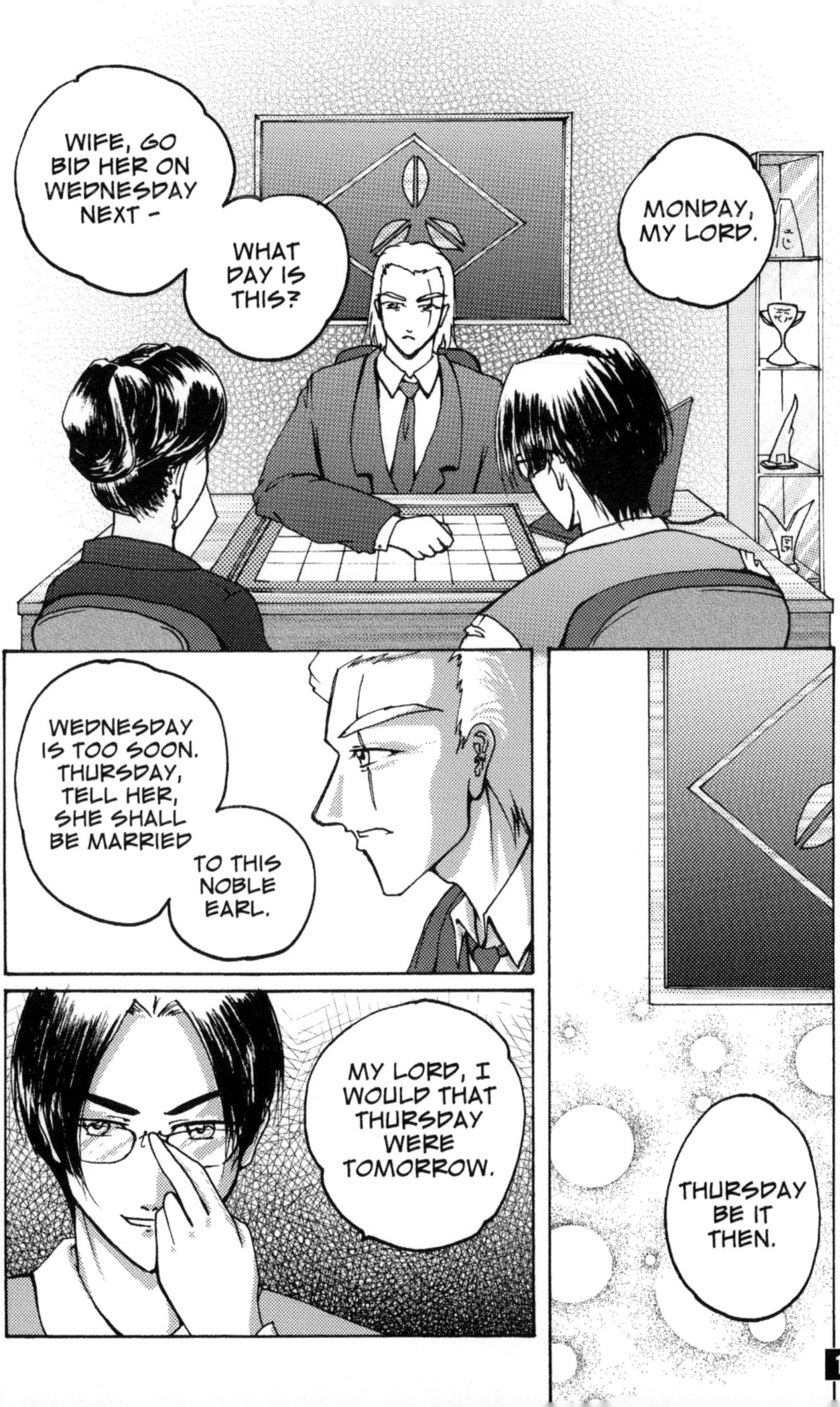

WIFE, GO BID HER ON WEDNESDAY NEXT -
WHAT DAY IS THIS?
MONDAY, MY LORD.
WEDNESDAY IS TOO SOON. THURSDAY, TELL HER, SHE SHALL BE MARRIED
TO THIS NOBLE EARL.
THURSDAY BE IT THEN.
MY LORD, I WOULD THAT THURSDAY WERE TOMORROW.

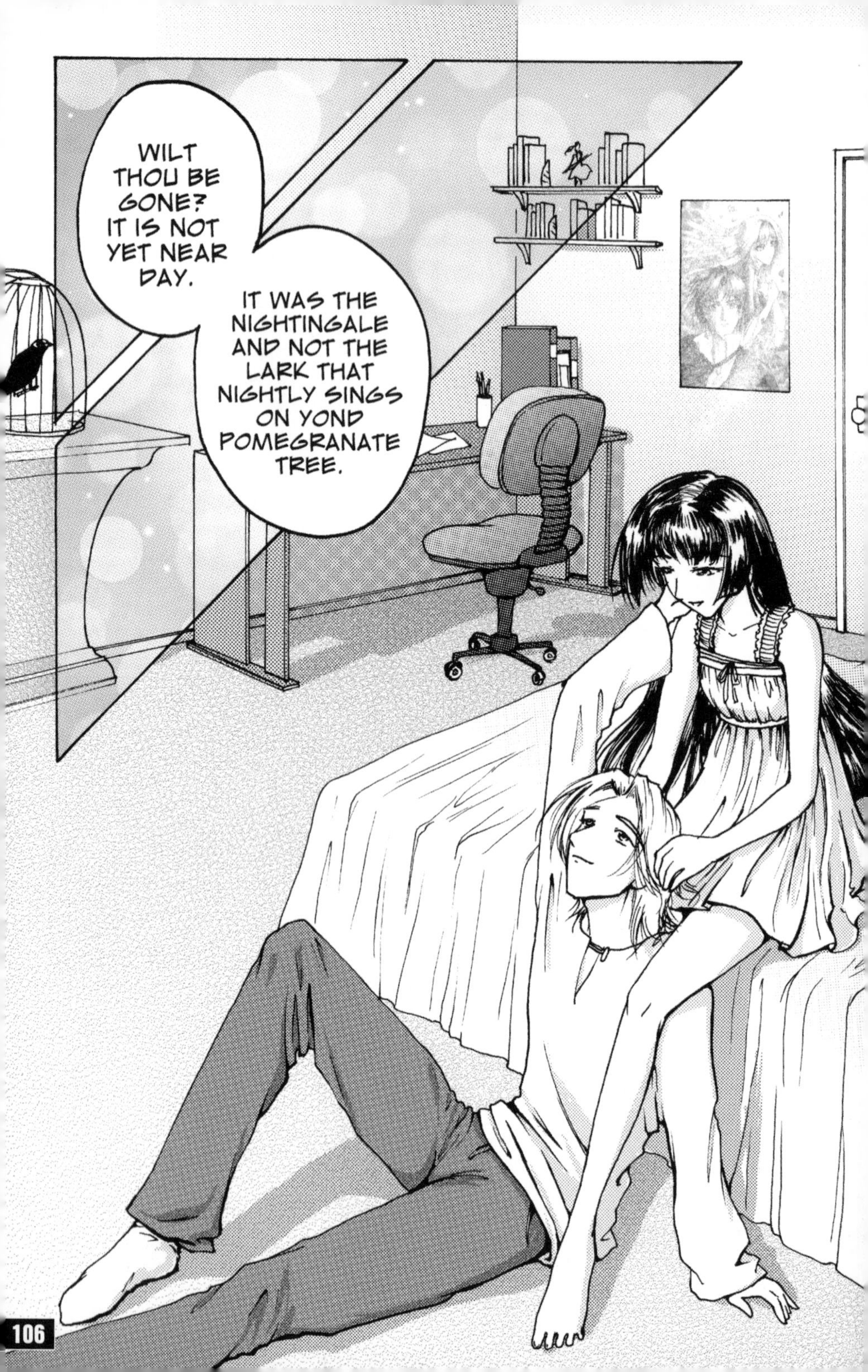
WILT THOU BE GONE? IT IS NOT YET NEAR DAY.
IT WAS THE NIGHTINGALE AND NOT THE LARK THAT NIGHTLY SINGS ON YOND POMEGRANATE TREE.

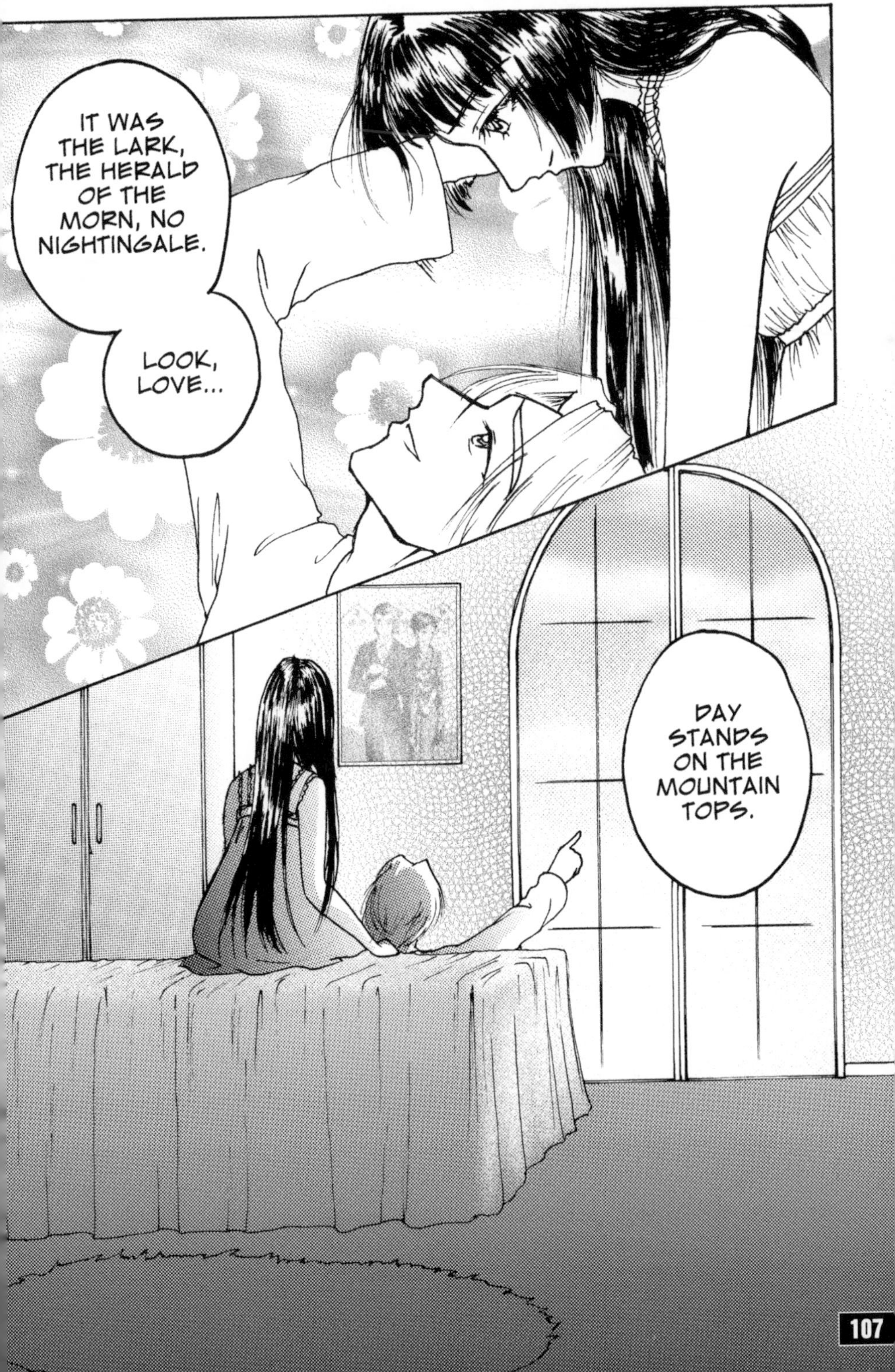
IT WAS THE LARK, THE HERALD OF THE MORN, NO NIGHTINGALE.
LOOK, LOVE...
DAY STANDS ON THE MOUNTAIN TOPS.

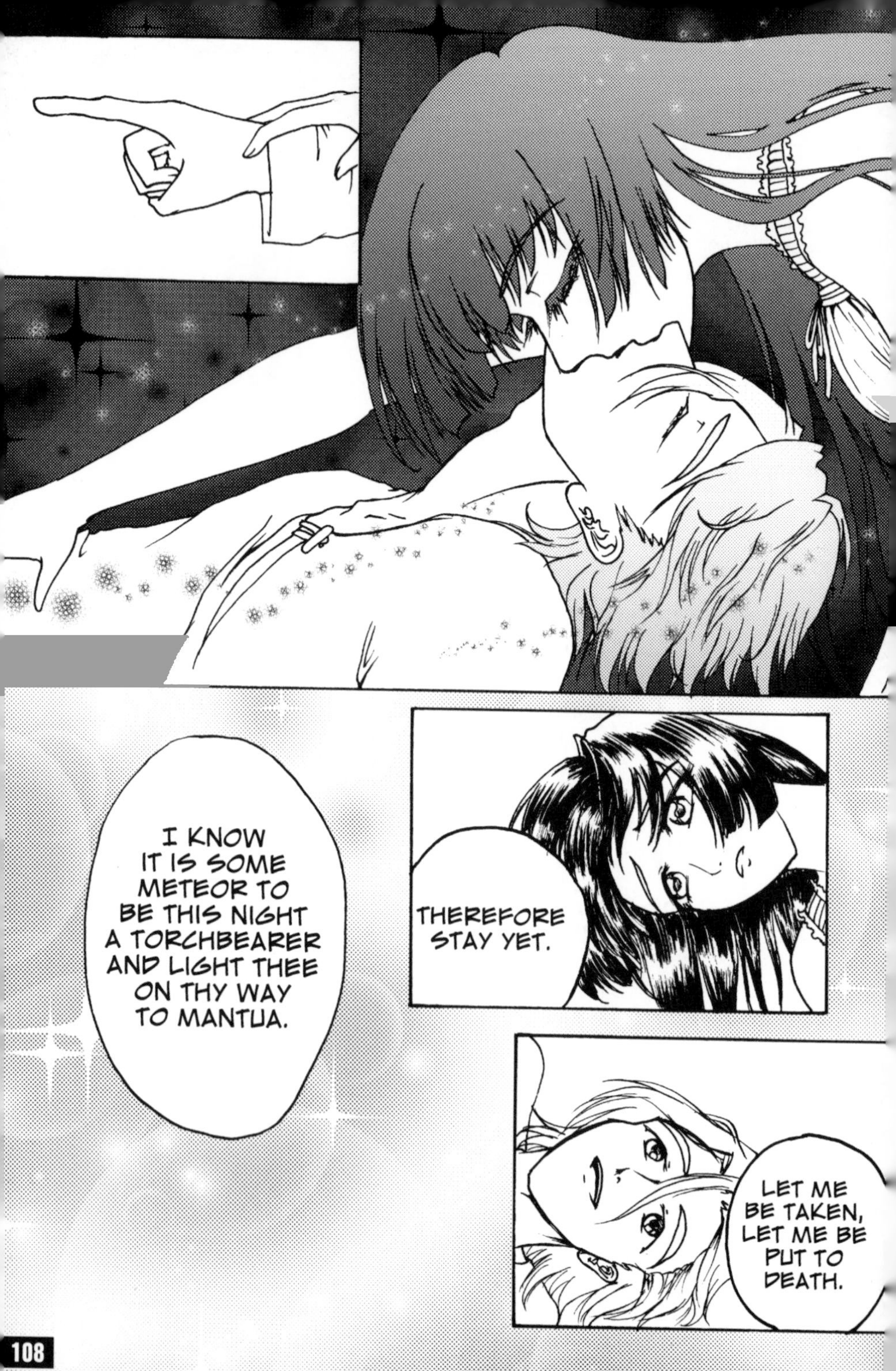
I KNOW IT IS SOME METEOR TO BE THIS NIGHT A TORCHBEARER AND LIGHT THEE ON THY WAY TO MANTUA.
THEREFORE STAY YET.
LET ME BE TAKEN, LET ME BE PUT TO DEATH.

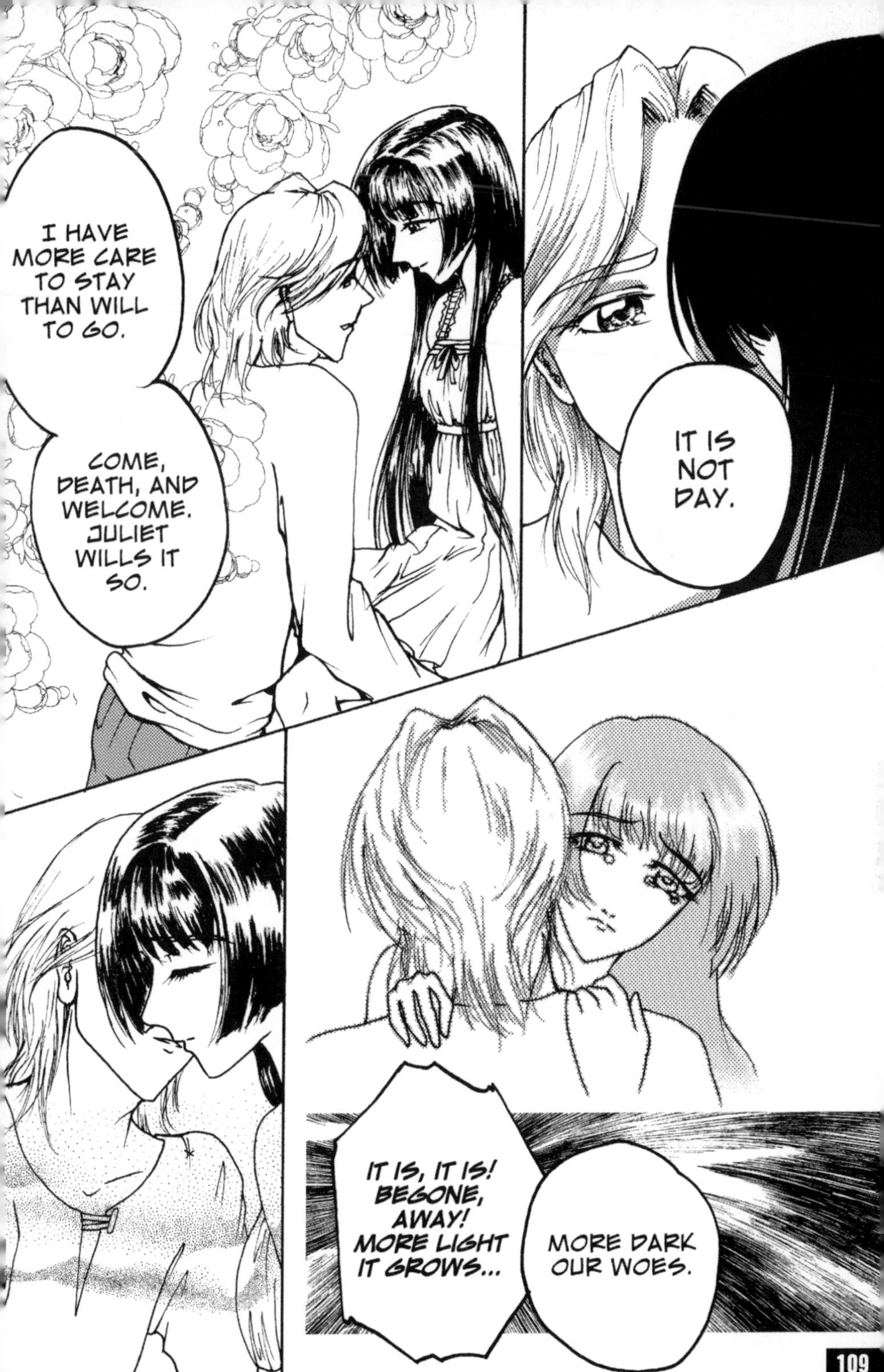
I HAVE MORE CARE TO STAY THAN WILL TO GO.
COME, DEATH, AND WELCOME. JULIET WILLS IT SO.
IT IS NOT DAY.
IT IS, IT IS! BEGONE, AWAY! MORE LIGHT IT GROWS...
MORE DARK OUR WOES.

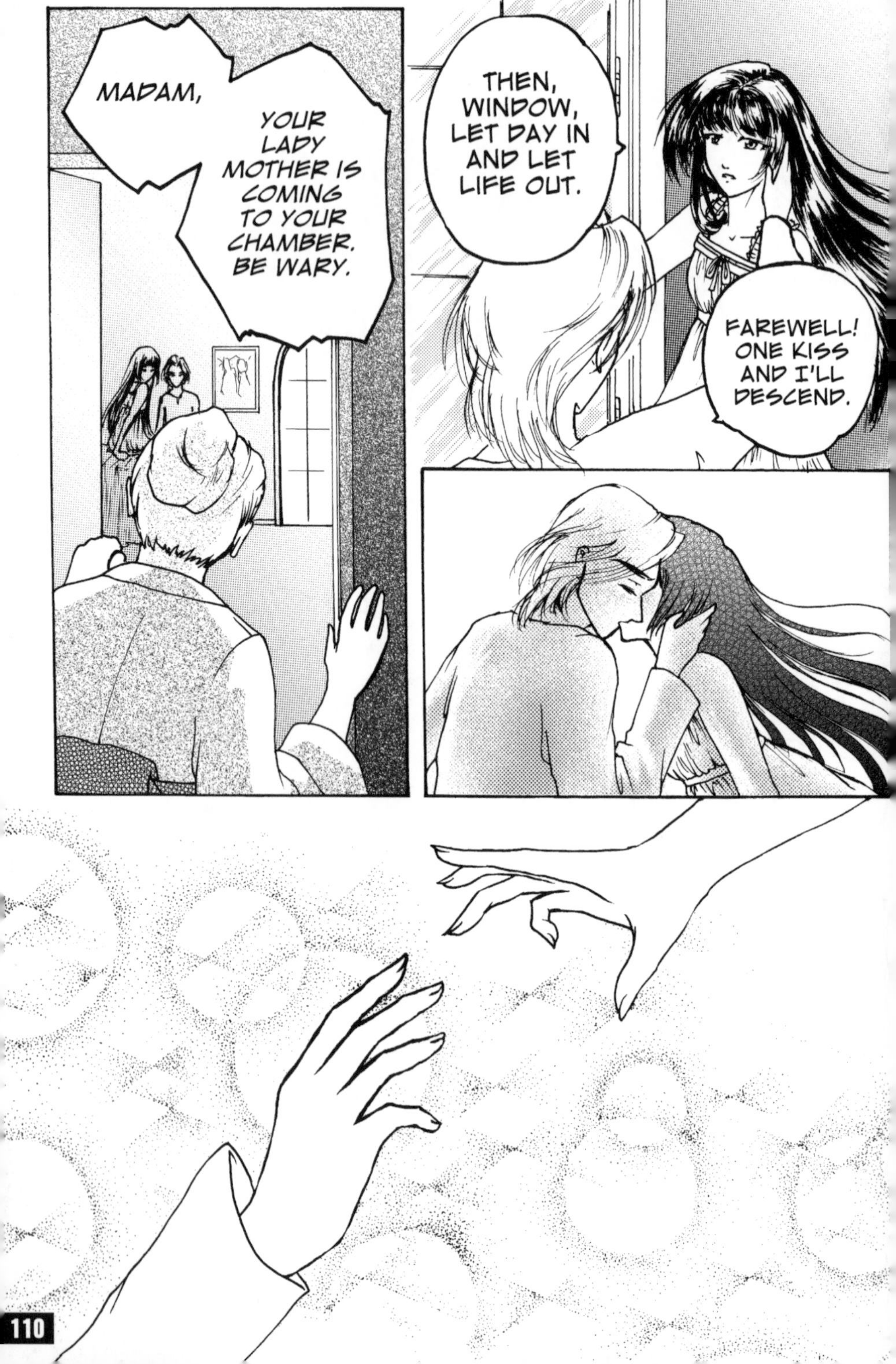
MADAM,
YOUR LADY MOTHER IS COMING TO YOUR CHAMBER. BE WARY.
THEN, WINDOW, LET DAY IN AND LET LIFE OUT.
FAREWELL! ONE KISS AND I'LL DESCEND.

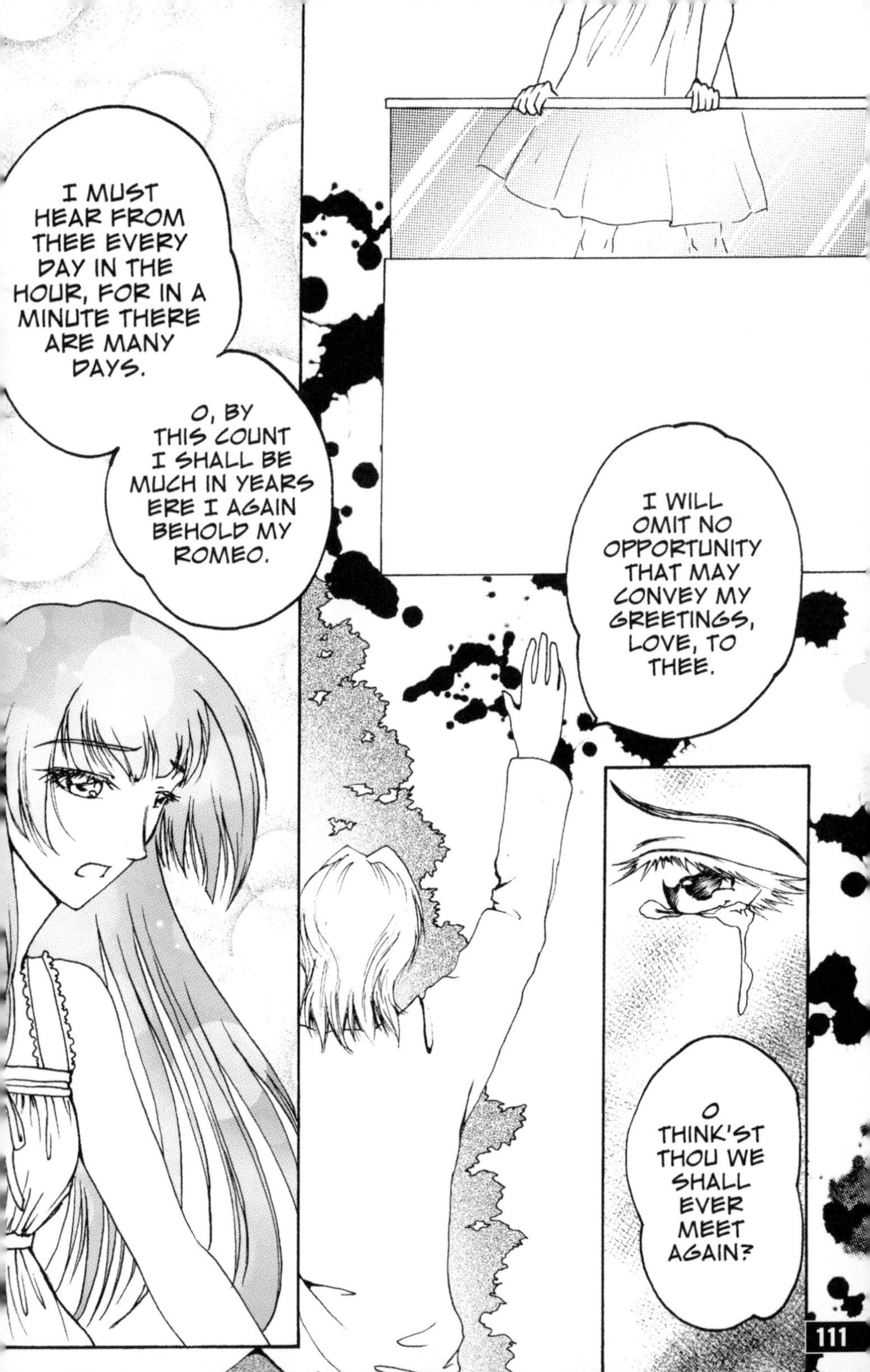
I MUST HEAR FROM THEE EVERY DAY IN THE HOUR, FOR IN A MINUTE THERE ARE MANY DAYS.
O, BY THIS COUNT I SHALL BE MUCH IN YEARS ERE I AGAIN BEHOLD MY ROMEO.
I WILL OMIT NO OPPORTUNITY THAT MAY CONVEY MY GREETINGS, LOVE, TO THEE.
O THINK'ST THOU WE SHALL EVER MEET AGAIN?

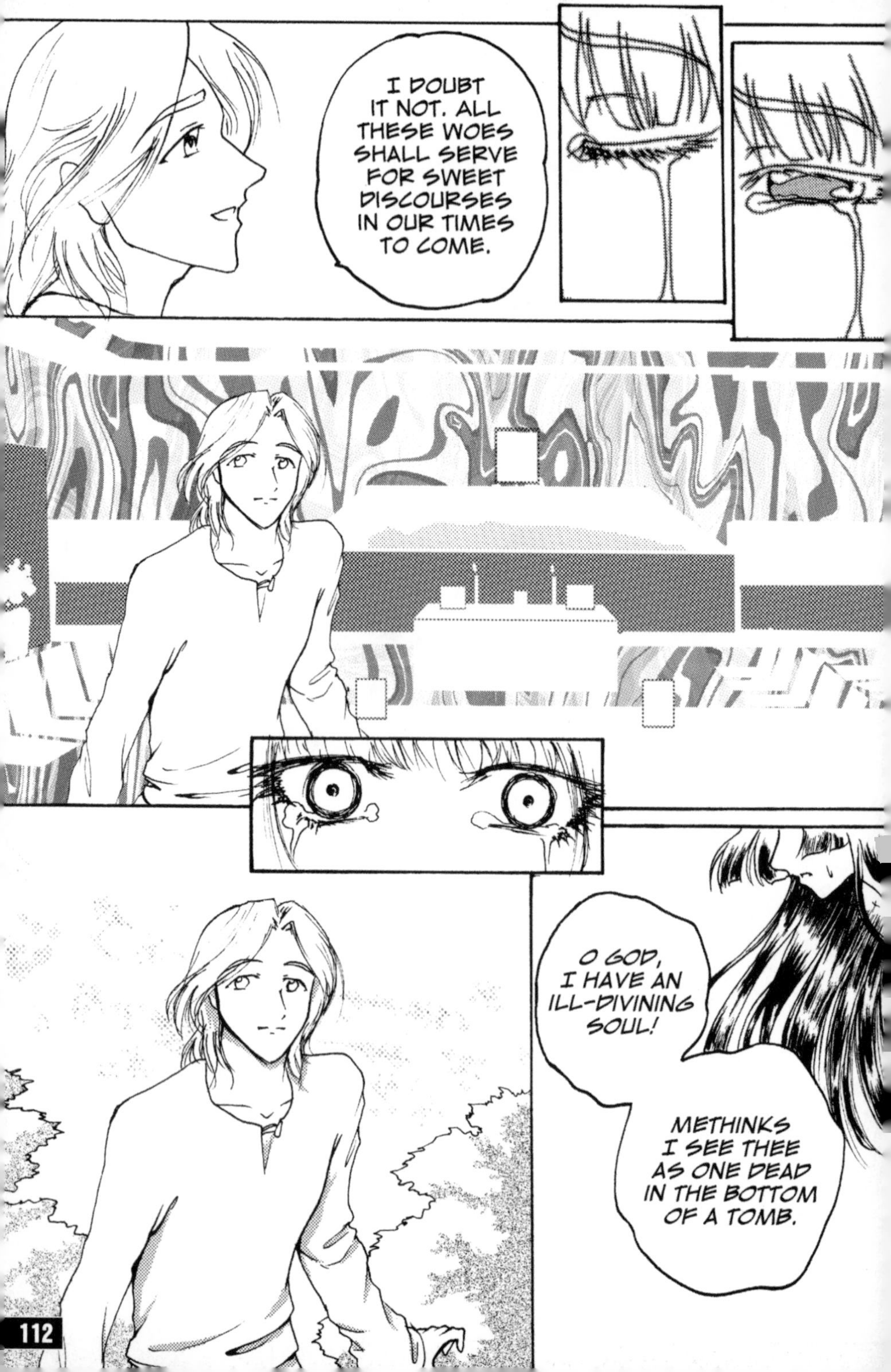
I DOUBT IT NOT. ALL THESE WOES SHALL SERVE FOR SWEET DISCOURSES IN OUR TIMES TO COME.
O GOD, I HAVE AN ILL-DIVINING SOUL!
METHINKS I SEE THEE AS ONE DEAD IN THE BOTTOM OF A TOMB.

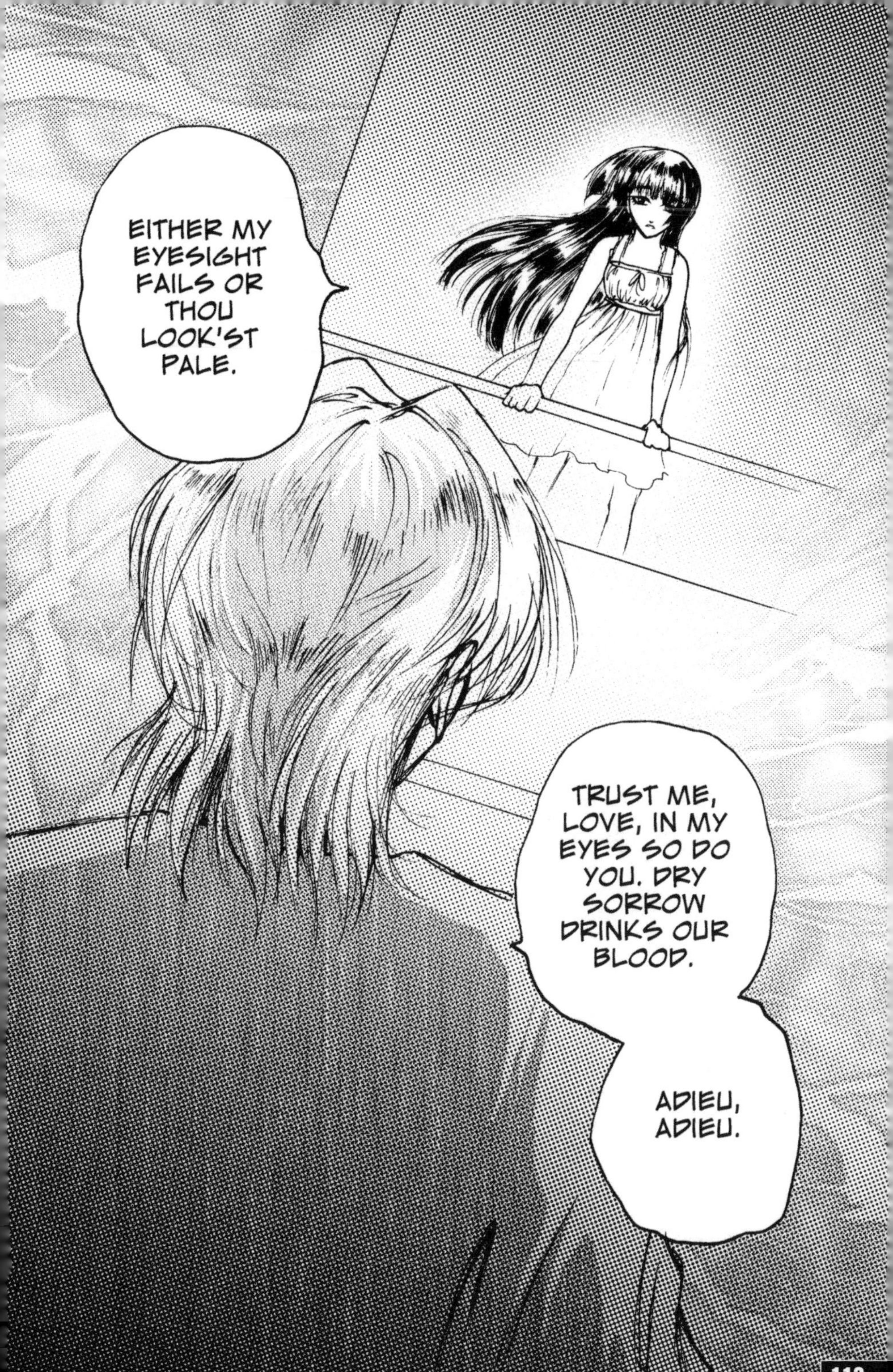
EITHER MY EYESIGHT FAILS OR THOU LOOK'ST PALE.
TRUST ME, LOVE, IN MY EYES SO DO YOU. DRY SORROW DRINKS OUR BLOOD.
ADIEU, ADIEU.

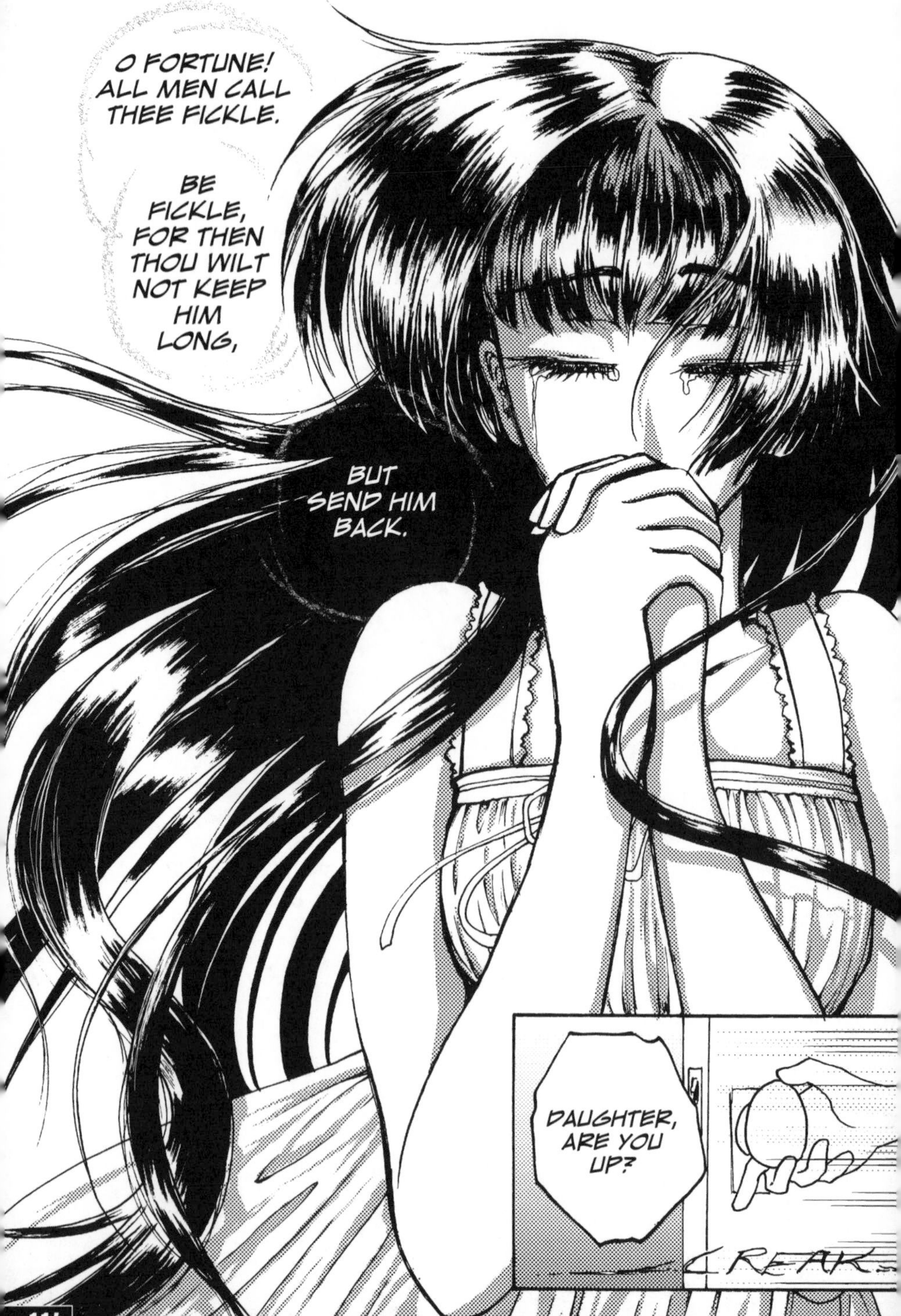
O FORTUNE! ALL MEN CALL THEE FICKLE.
BE FICKLE, FOR THEN THOU WILT NOT KEEP HIM LONG,
BUT SEND HIM BACK.
DAUGHTER, ARE YOU UP?
CREAK...

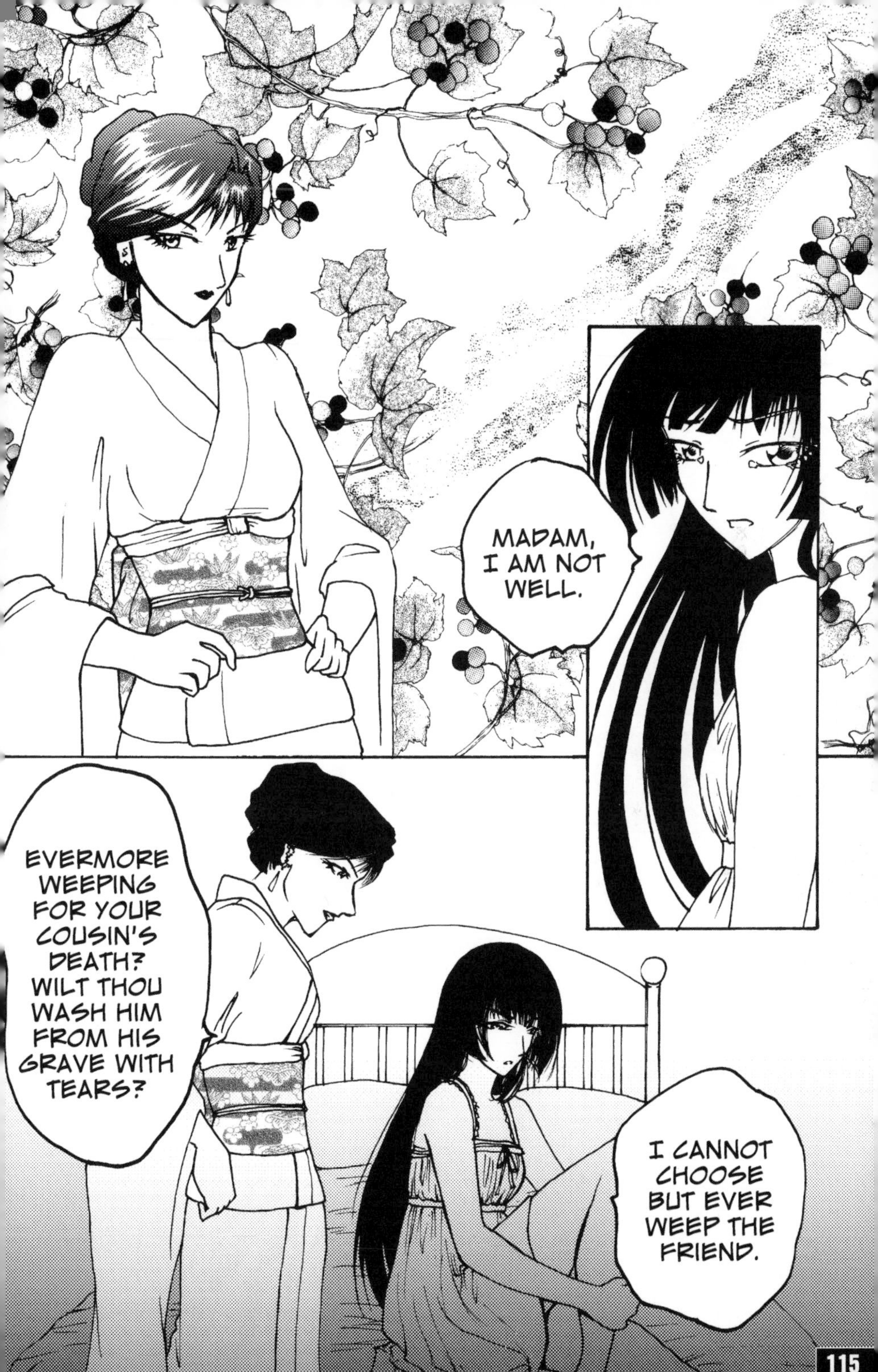
MADAM, I AM NOT WELL.
EVERMORE WEEPING FOR YOUR COUSIN'S DEATH? WILT THOU WASH HIM FROM HIS GRAVE WITH TEARS?
I CANNOT CHOOSE BUT EVER WEEP THE FRIEND.

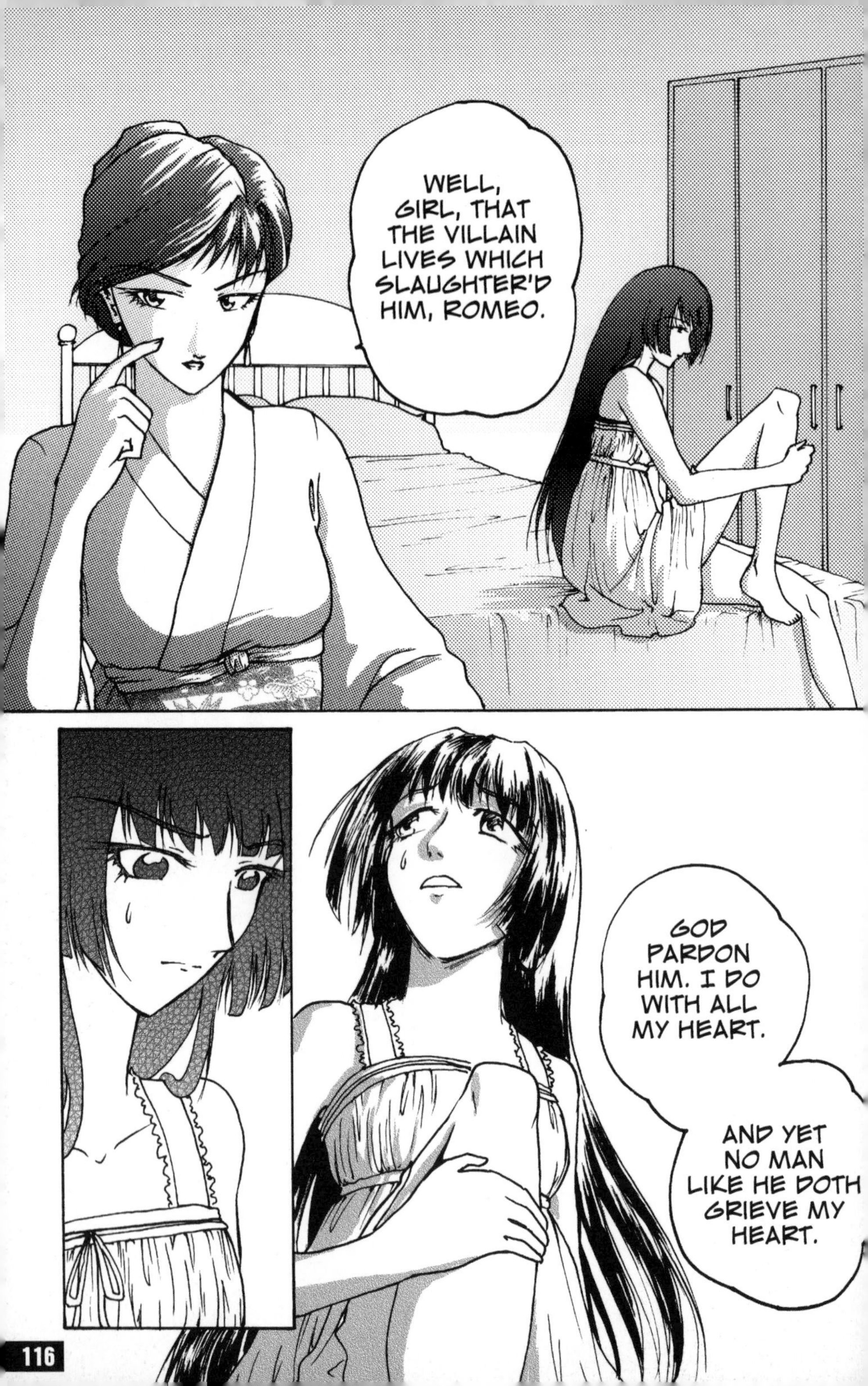
WELL, GIRL, THAT THE VILLAIN LIVES WHICH SLAUGHTER'D HIM, ROMEO.
GOD PARDON HIM. I DO WITH ALL MY HEART.
AND YET NO MAN LIKE HE DOTH GRIEVE MY HEART.

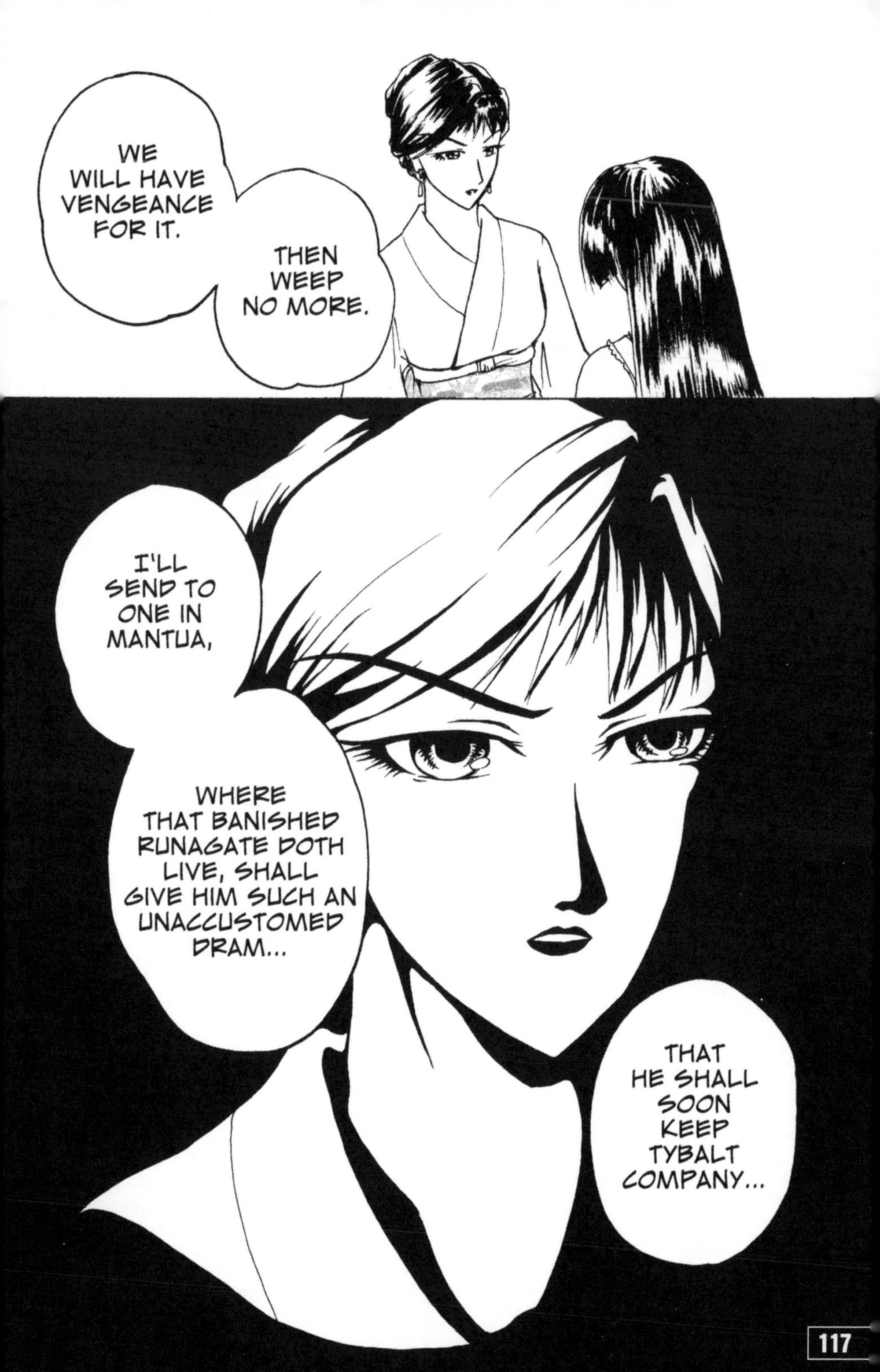
WE WILL HAVE VENGEANCE FOR IT.
THEN WEEP NO MORE.
I'LL SEND TO ONE IN MANTUA,
WHERE THAT BANISHED RUNAGATE DOTH LIVE, SHALL GIVE HIM SUCH AN UNACCUSTOMED DRAM...
THAT HE SHALL SOON KEEP TYBALT COMPANY...

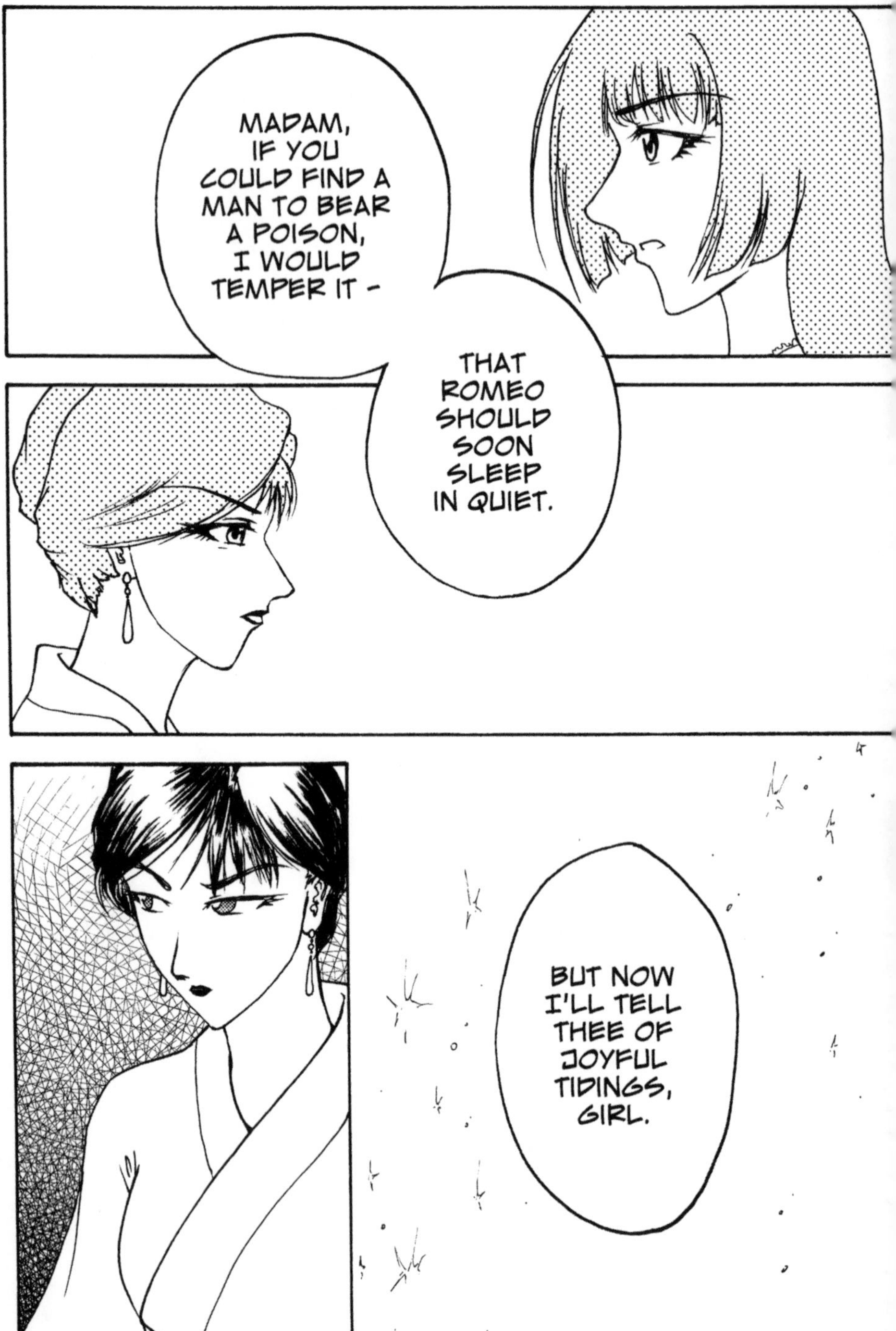
MADAM, IF YOU COULD FIND A MAN TO BEAR A POISON, I WOULD TEMPER IT -
THAT ROMEO SHOULD SOON SLEEP IN QUIET.
BUT NOW I'LL TELL THEE OF JOYFUL TIDINGS, GIRL.

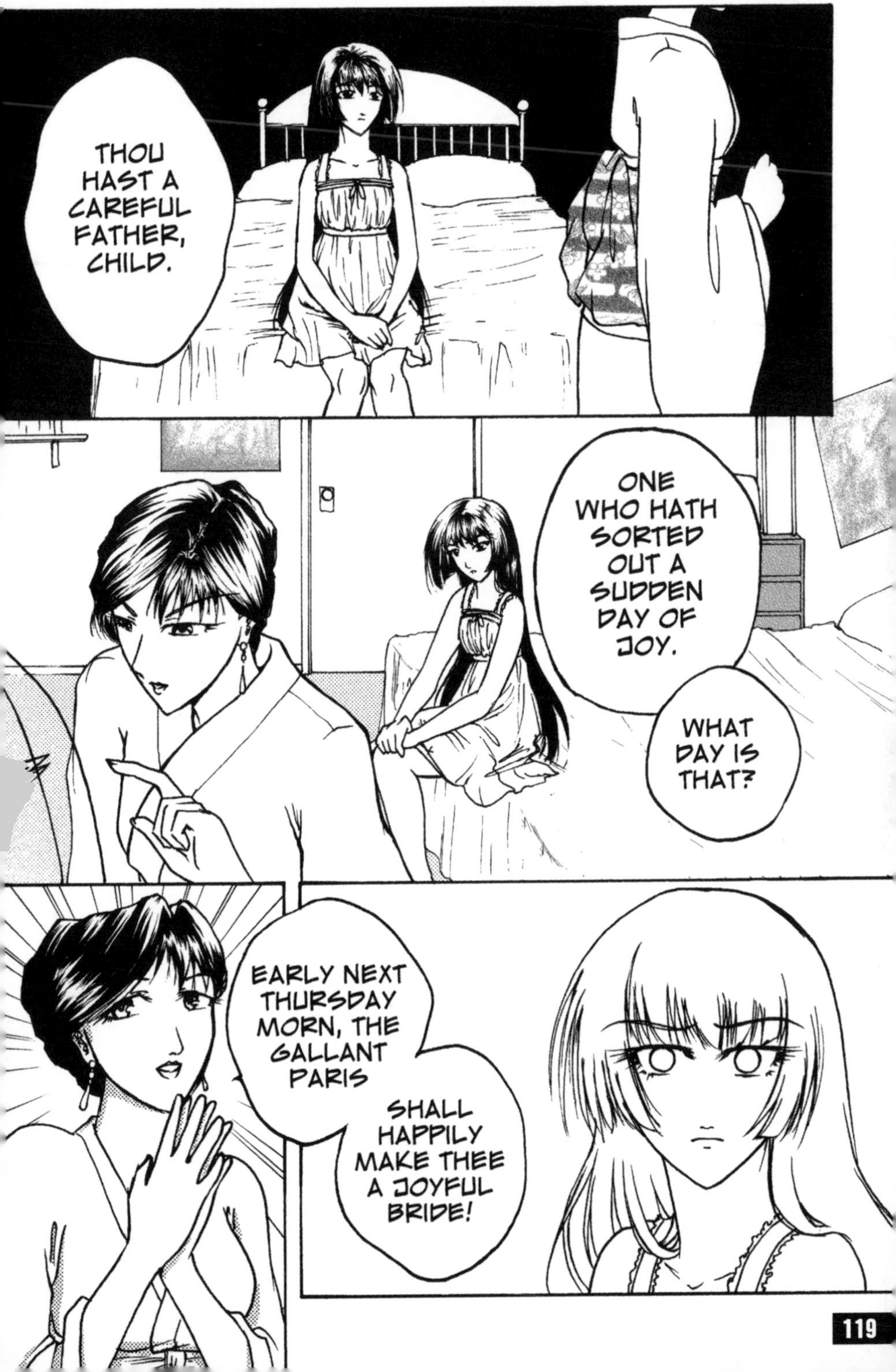
THOU HAST A CAREFUL FATHER, CHILD.
ONE WHO HATH SORTED OUT A SUDDEN DAY OF JOY.
WHAT DAY IS THAT?
EARLY NEXT THURSDAY MORN, THE GALLANT PARIS
SHALL HAPPILY MAKE THEE A JOYFUL BRIDE!

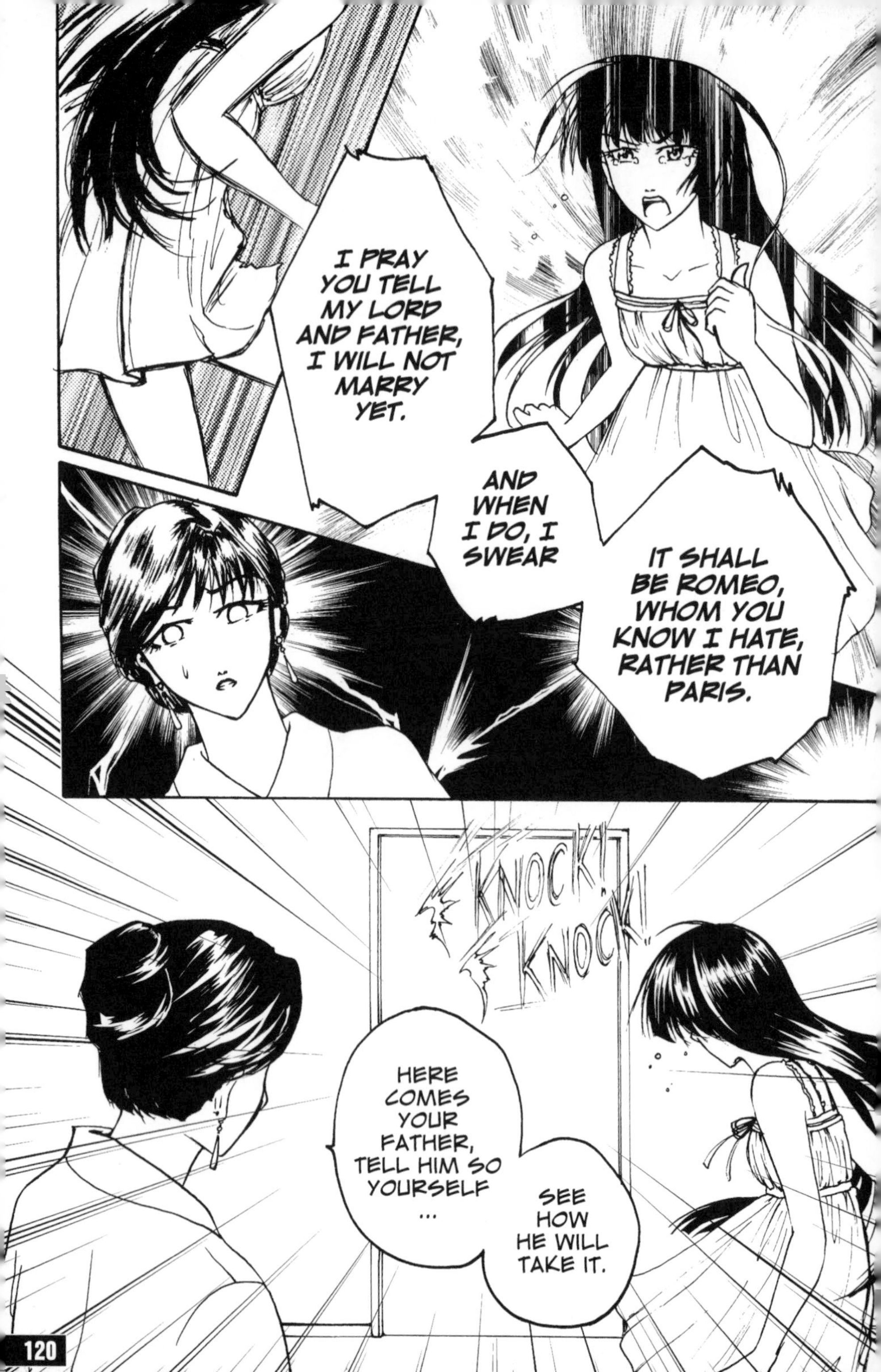
I PRAY YOU TELL MY LORD AND FATHER, I WILL NOT MARRY YET.
AND WHEN I DO, I SWEAR
IT SHALL BE ROMEO, WHOM YOU KNOW I HATE, RATHER THAN PARIS.
KNOCK! KNOCK!
HERE COMES YOUR FATHER, TELL HIM SO YOURSELF ...
SEE HOW HE WILL TAKE IT.

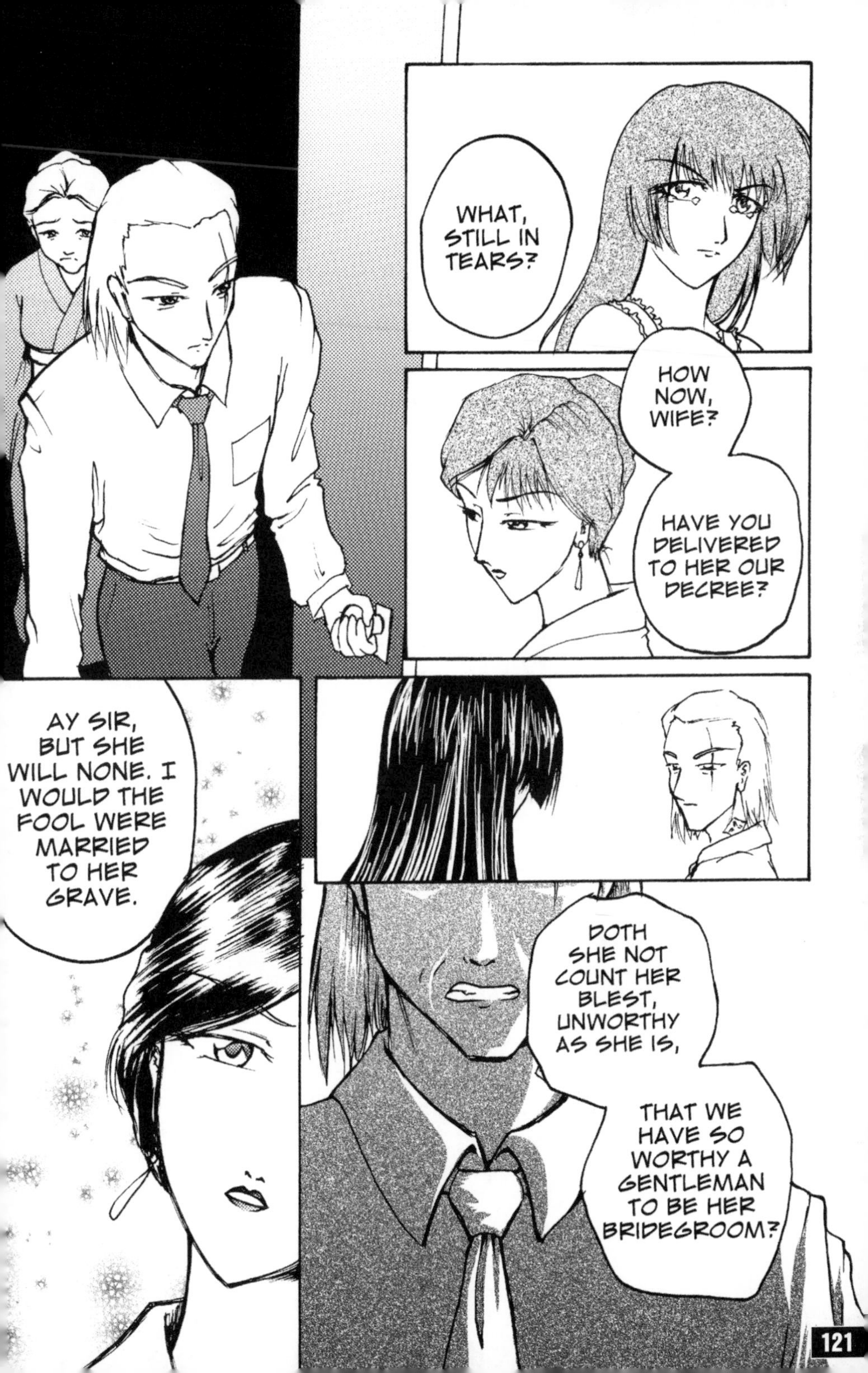
WHAT, STILL IN TEARS?
HOW NOW, WIFE?
HAVE YOU DELIVERED TO HER OUR DECREE?
AY SIR, BUT SHE WILL NONE. I WOULD THE FOOL WERE MARRIED TO HER GRAVE.
DOTH SHE NOT COUNT HER BLEST, UNWORTHY AS SHE IS,
THAT WE HAVE SO WORTHY A GENTLEMAN TO BE HER BRIDEGROOM?

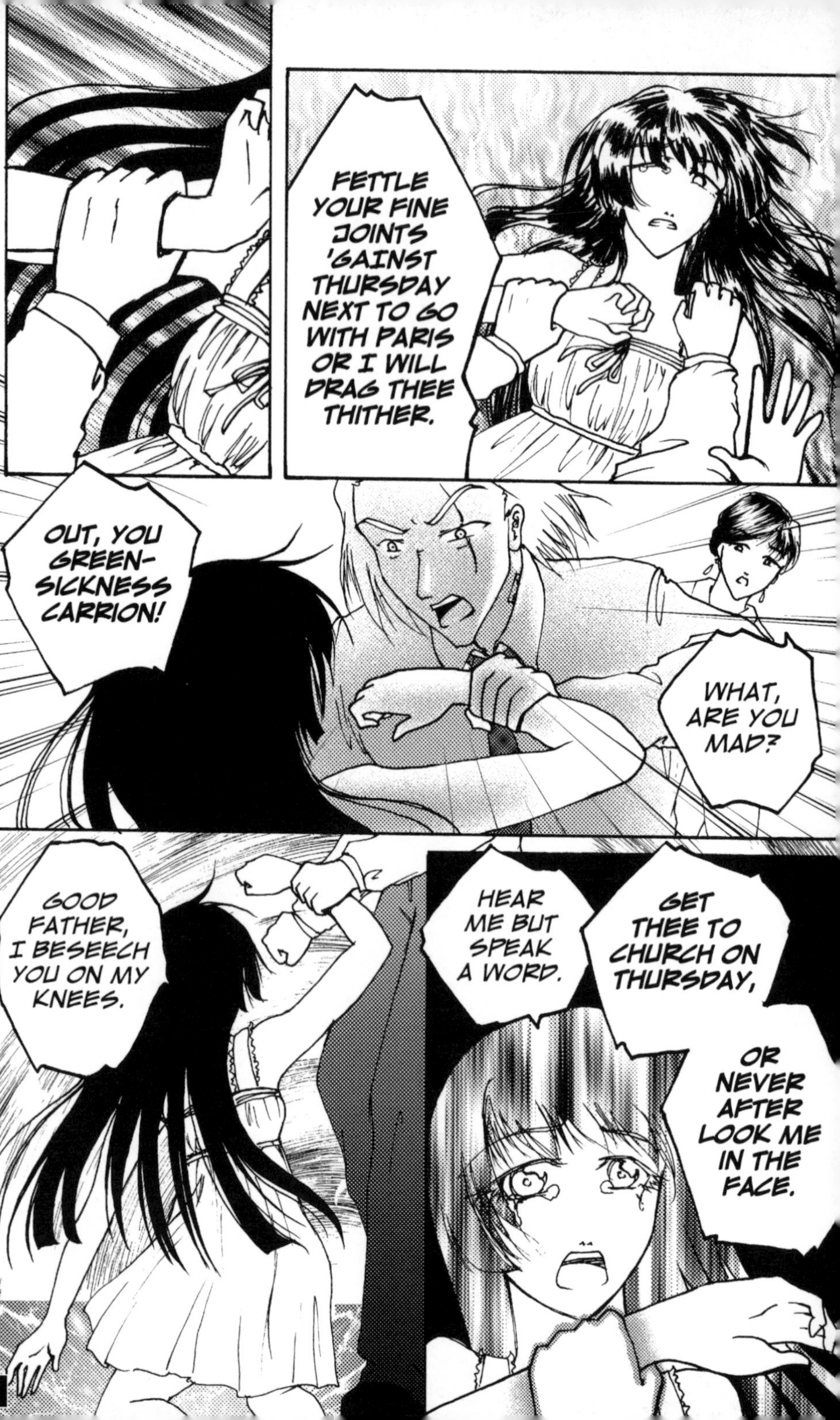
FETTLE YOUR FINE JOINTS 'GAINST THURSDAY NEXT TO GO WITH PARIS OR I WILL DRAG THEE THITHER.
OUT, YOU GREEN-SICKNESS CARRION!
WHAT, ARE YOU MAD?
GOOD FATHER, I BESEECH YOU ON MY KNEES.
HEAR ME BUT SPEAK A WORD.
GET THEE TO CHURCH ON THURSDAY,
OR NEVER AFTER LOOK ME IN THE FACE.

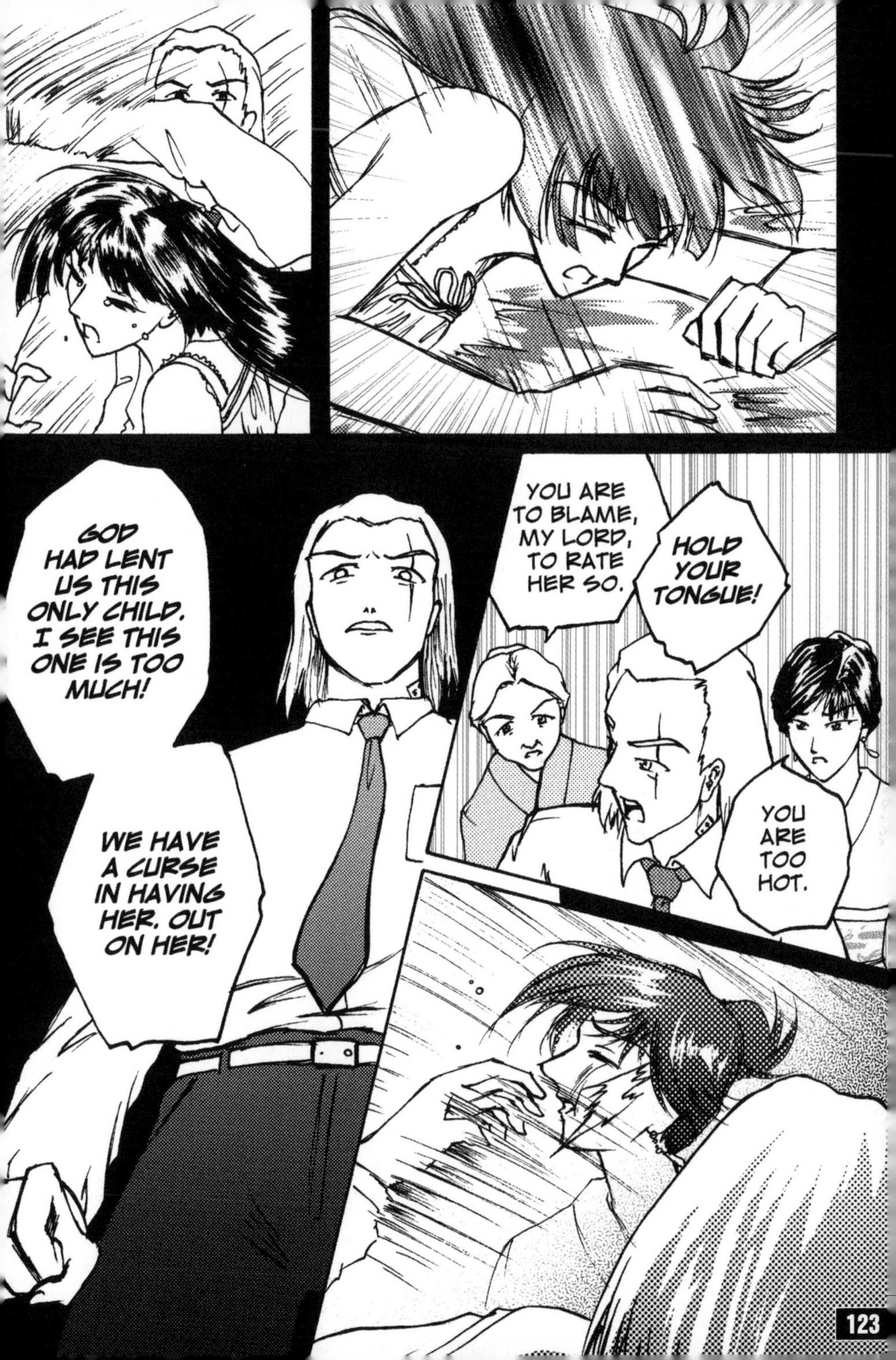
GOD HAD LENT US THIS ONLY CHILD. I SEE THIS ONE IS TOO MUCH!
WE HAVE A CURSE IN HAVING HER. OUT ON HER!
YOU ARE TO BLAME, MY LORD, TO RATE HER SO.
HOLD YOUR TONGUE!
YOU ARE TOO HOT.

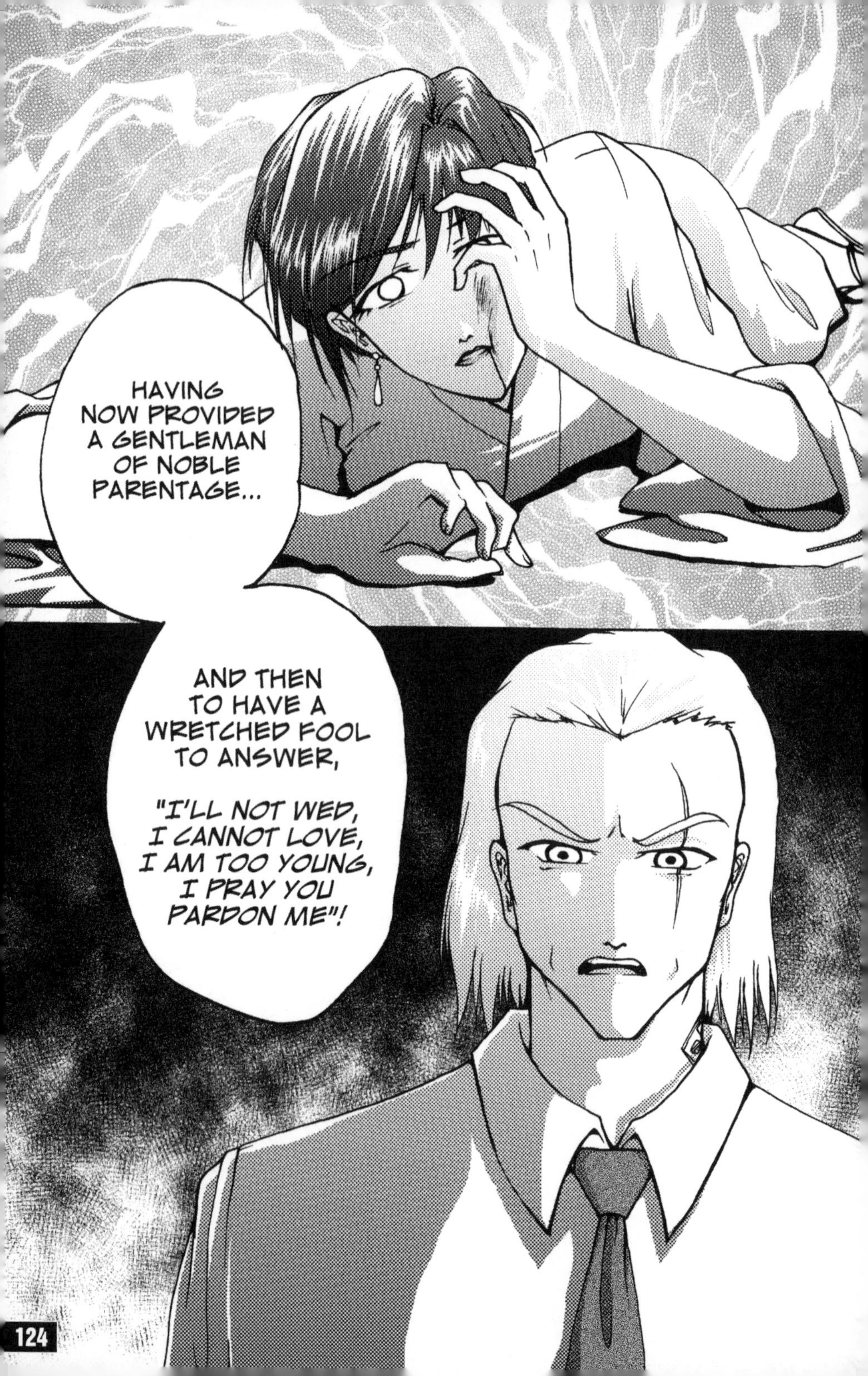
HAVING NOW PROVIDED A GENTLEMAN OF NOBLE PARENTAGE...
AND THEN TO HAVE A WRETCHED FOOL TO ANSWER,
"I'LL NOT WED, I CANNOT LOVE, I AM TOO YOUNG, I PRAY YOU PARDON ME"!

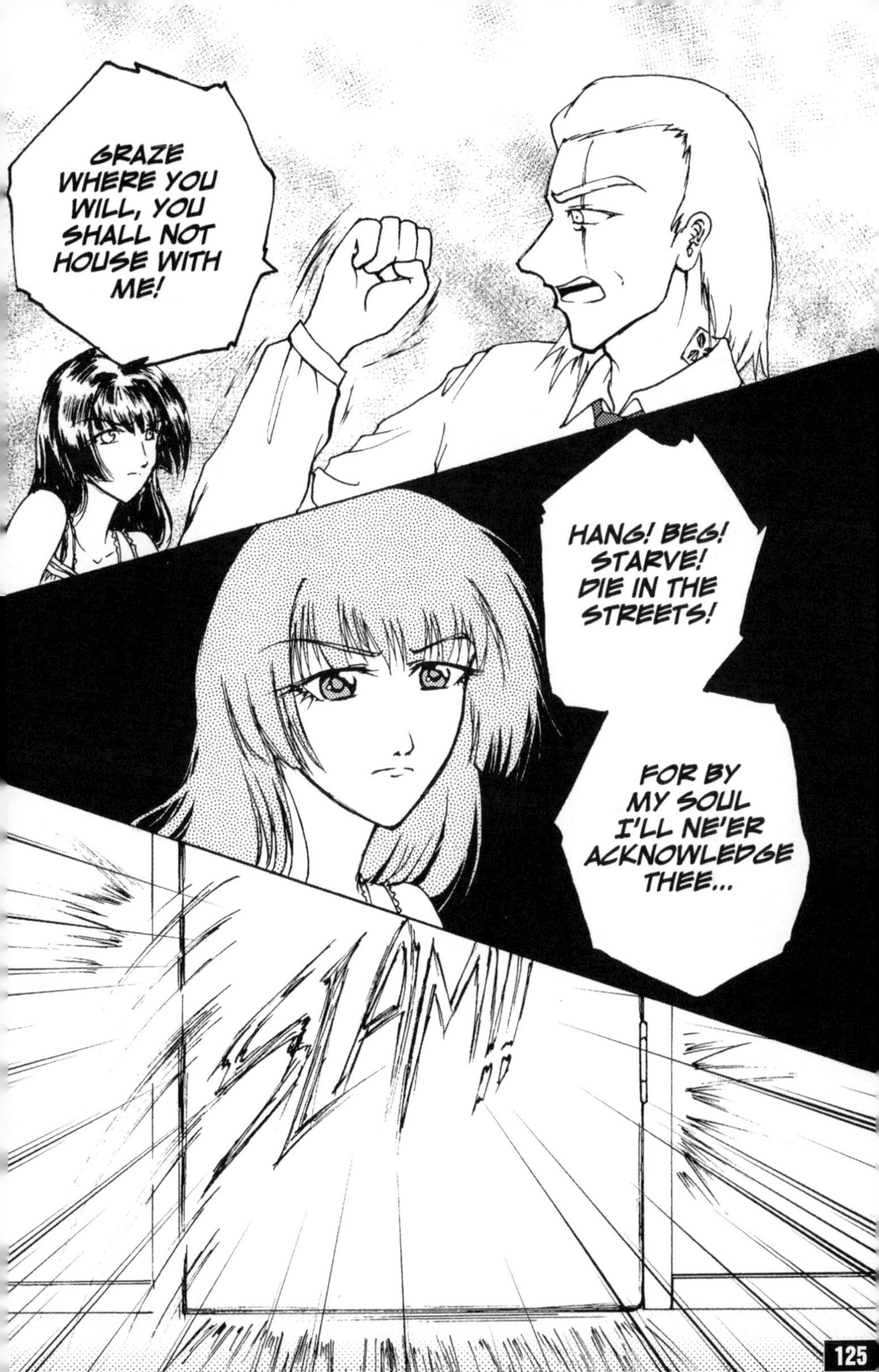
GRAZE WHERE YOU WILL, YOU SHALL NOT HOUSE WITH ME!
HANG! BEG! STARVE! DIE IN THE STREETS!
FOR BY MY SOUL I'LL NE'ER ACKNOWLEDGE THEE...
SLAM!!

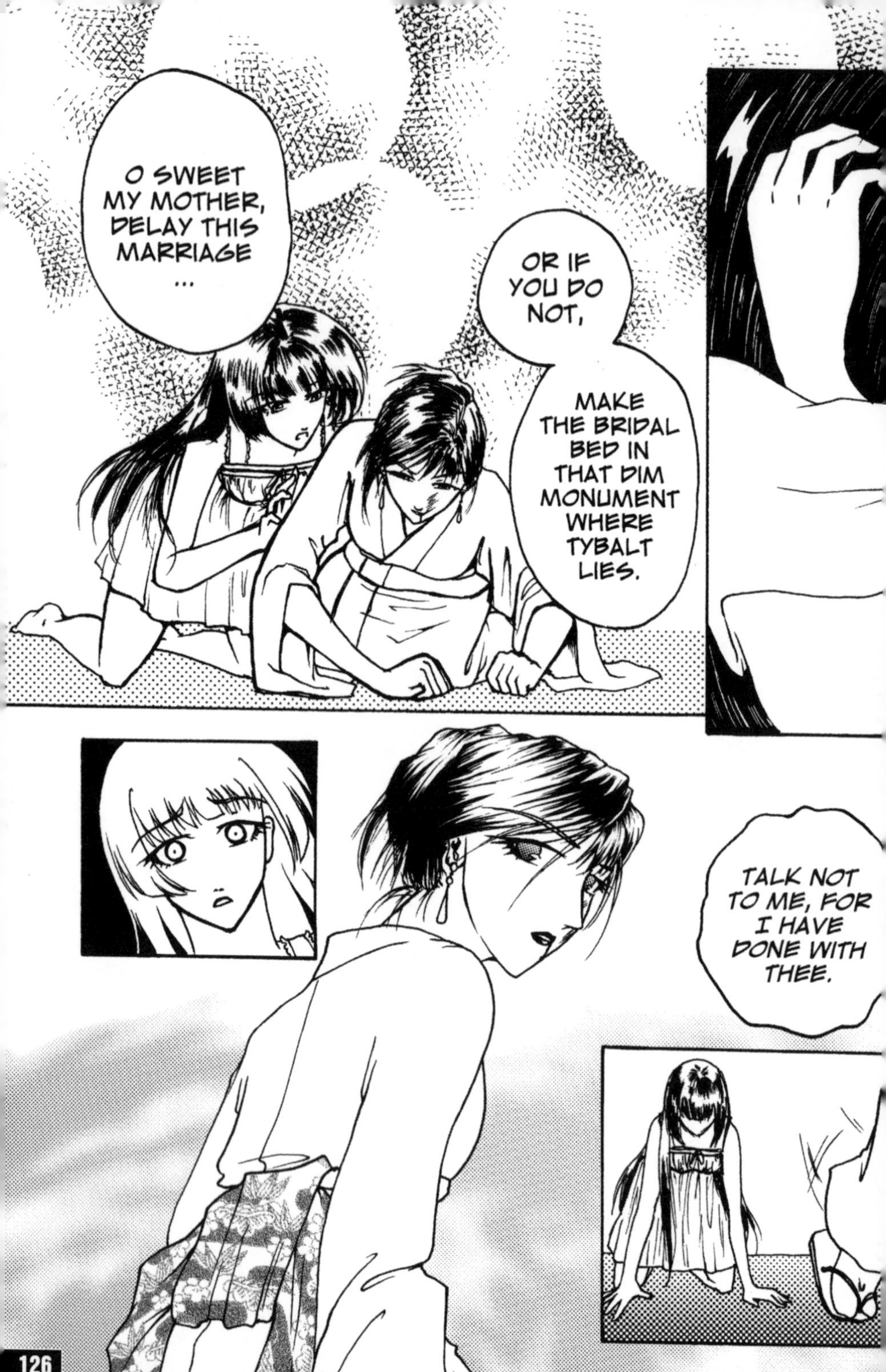
O SWEET MY MOTHER, DELAY THIS MARRIAGE ...
OR IF YOU DO NOT,
MAKE THE BRIDAL BED IN THAT DIM MONUMENT WHERE TYBALT LIES.
TALK NOT TO ME, FOR I HAVE DONE WITH THEE.

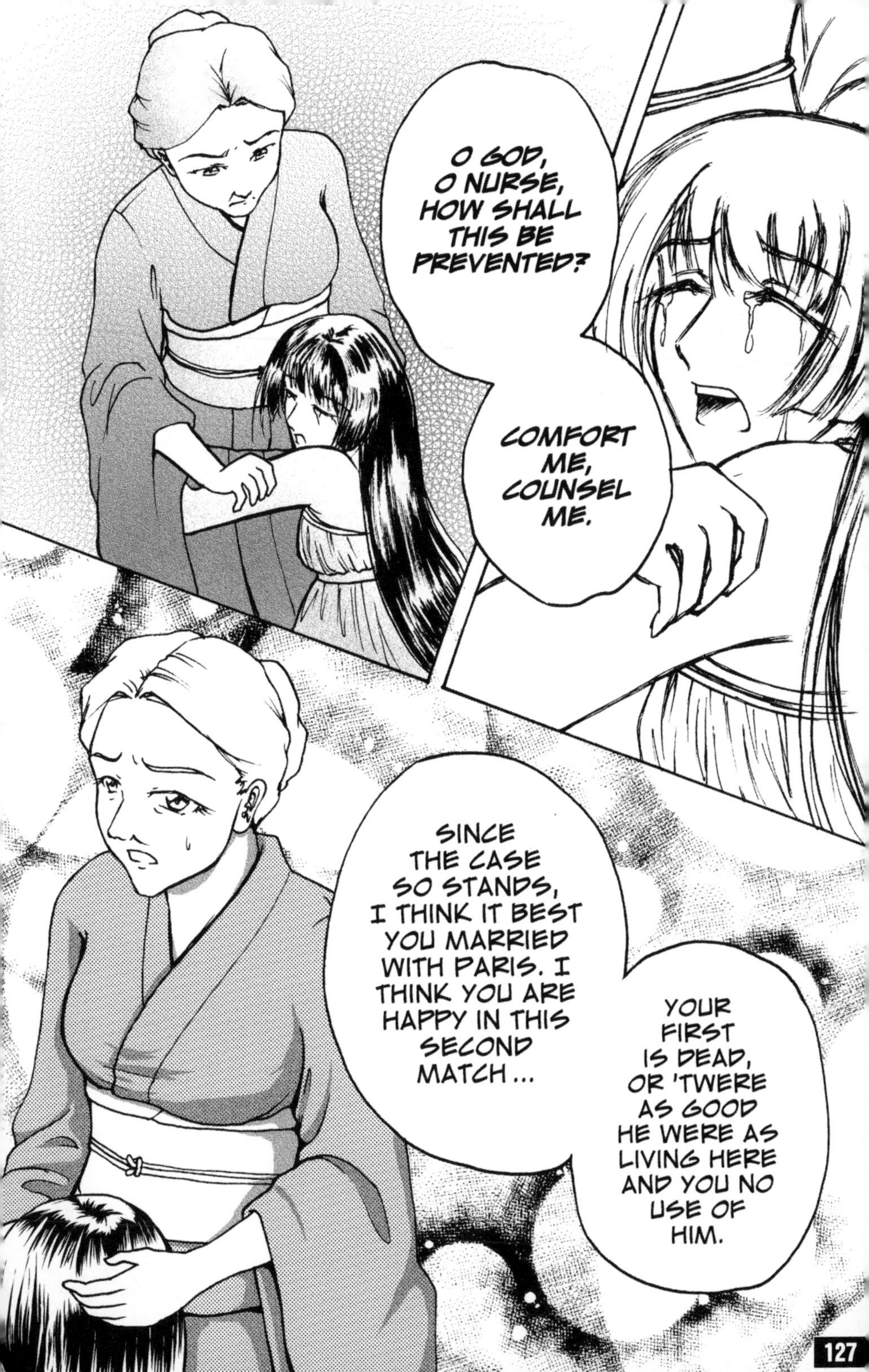
O GOD, O NURSE, HOW SHALL THIS BE PREVENTED?
COMFORT ME, COUNSEL ME.
SINCE THE CASE SO STANDS, I THINK IT BEST YOU MARRIED WITH PARIS. I THINK YOU ARE HAPPY IN THIS SECOND MATCH ...
YOUR FIRST IS DEAD, OR 'TWERE AS GOOD HE WERE AS LIVING HERE AND YOU NO USE OF HIM.

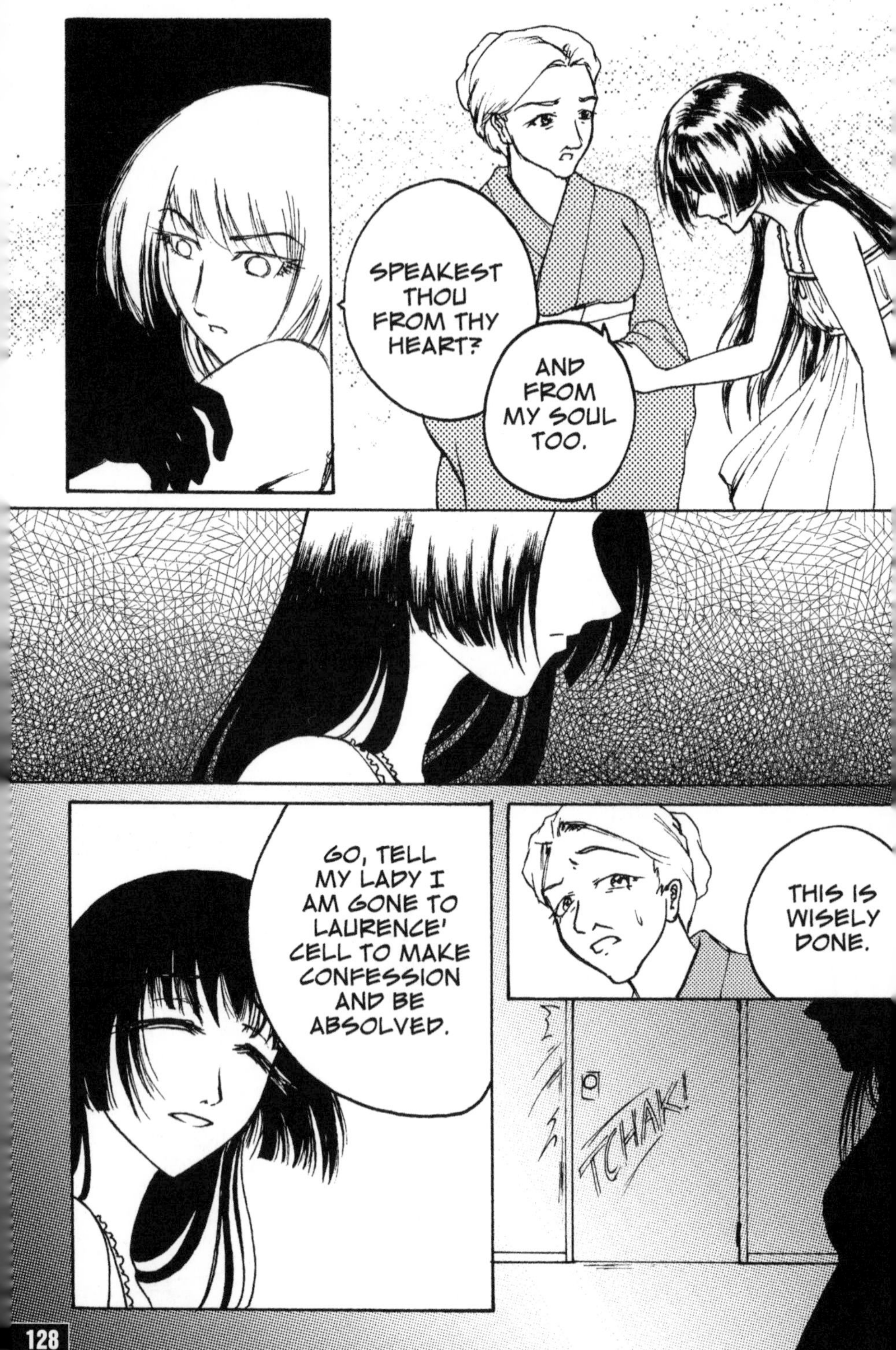
SPEAKEST THOU FROM THY HEART?
AND FROM MY SOUL TOO.
GO, TELL MY LADY I AM GONE TO LAURENCE' CELL TO MAKE CONFESSION AND BE ABSOLVED.
THIS IS WISELY DONE.
TCHAK!

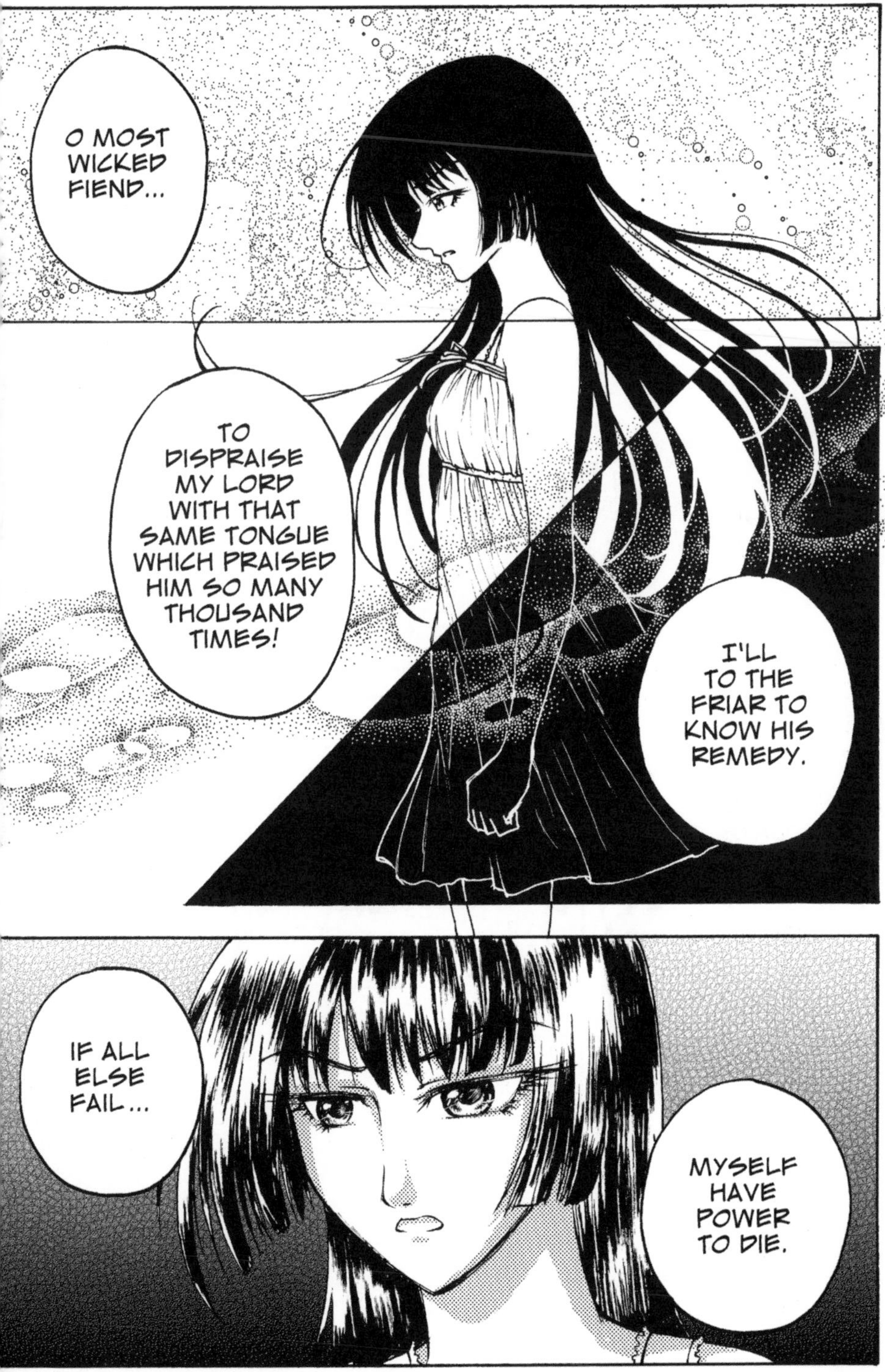
O MOST WICKED FIEND...
TO DISPRAISE MY LORD WITH THAT SAME TONGUE WHICH PRAISED HIM SO MANY THOUSAND TIMES!
I'LL TO THE FRIAR TO KNOW HIS REMEDY.
IF ALL ELSE FAIL...
MYSELF HAVE POWER TO DIE.

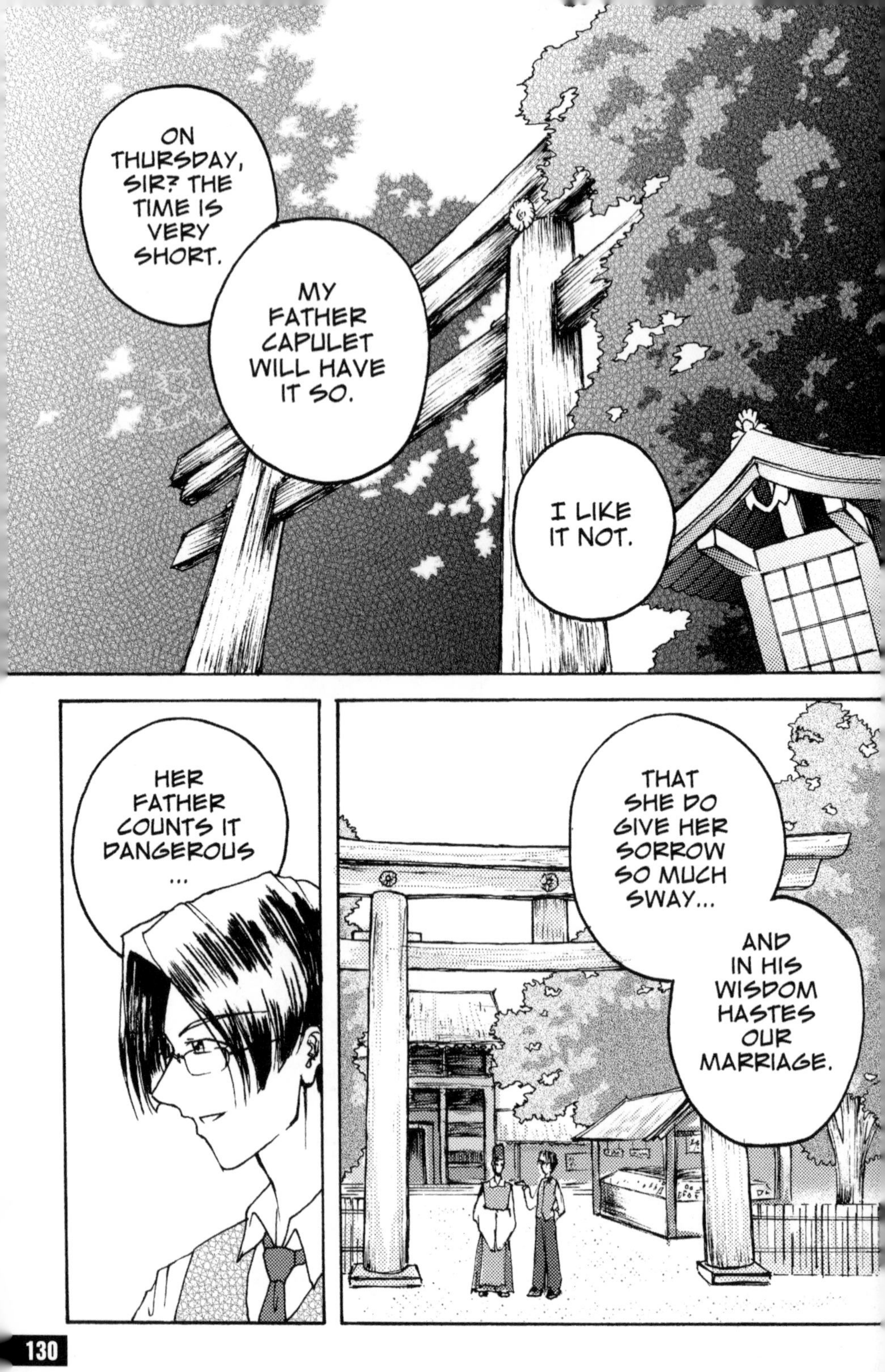
ON THURSDAY, SIR? THE TIME IS VERY SHORT.
MY FATHER CAPULET WILL HAVE IT SO.
I LIKE IT NOT.
THAT SHE DO GIVE HER SORROW SO MUCH SWAY...
AND IN HIS WISDOM HASTES OUR MARRIAGE.
HER FATHER COUNTS IT DANGEROUS ...

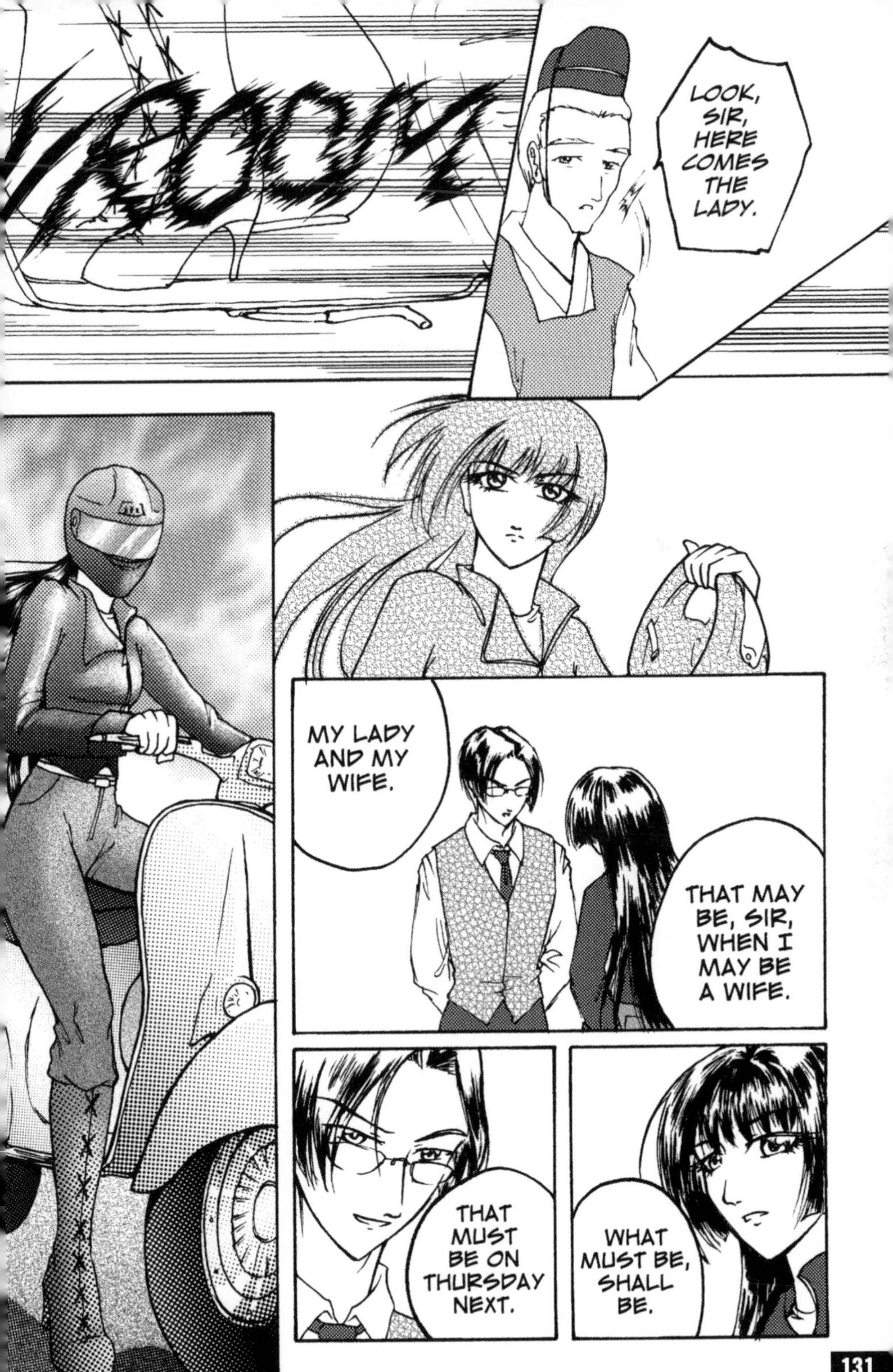
VROOM
LOOK, SIR, HERE COMES THE LADY.
MY LADY AND MY WIFE.
THAT MAY BE, SIR, WHEN I MAY BE A WIFE.
THAT MUST BE ON THURSDAY NEXT.
WHAT MUST BE, SHALL BE.

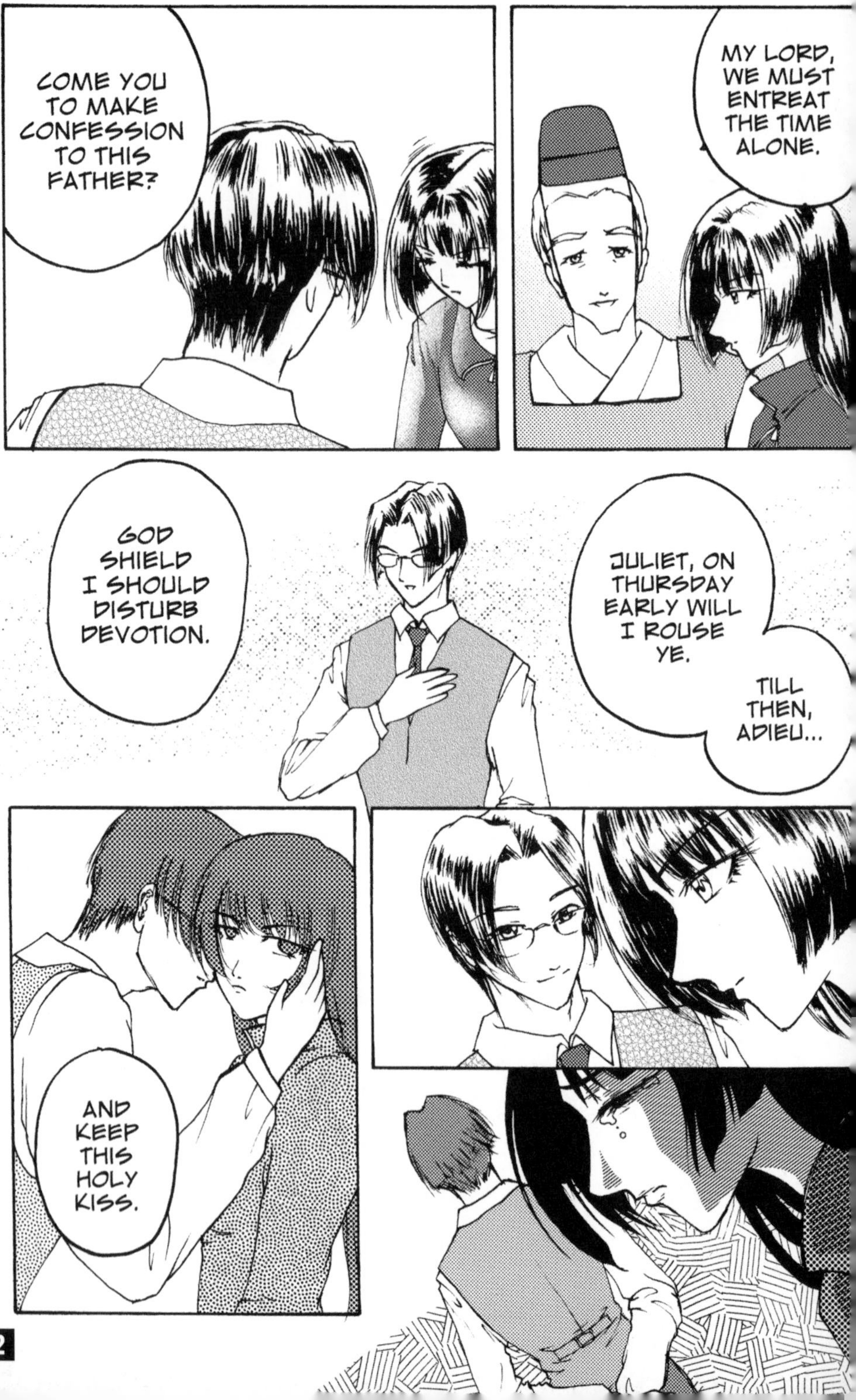
COME YOU TO MAKE CONFESSION TO THIS FATHER?
MY LORD, WE MUST ENTREAT THE TIME ALONE.
GOD SHIELD I SHOULD DISTURB DEVOTION.
JULIET, ON THURSDAY EARLY WILL I ROUSE YE.
TILL THEN, ADIEU...
AND KEEP THIS HOLY KISS.

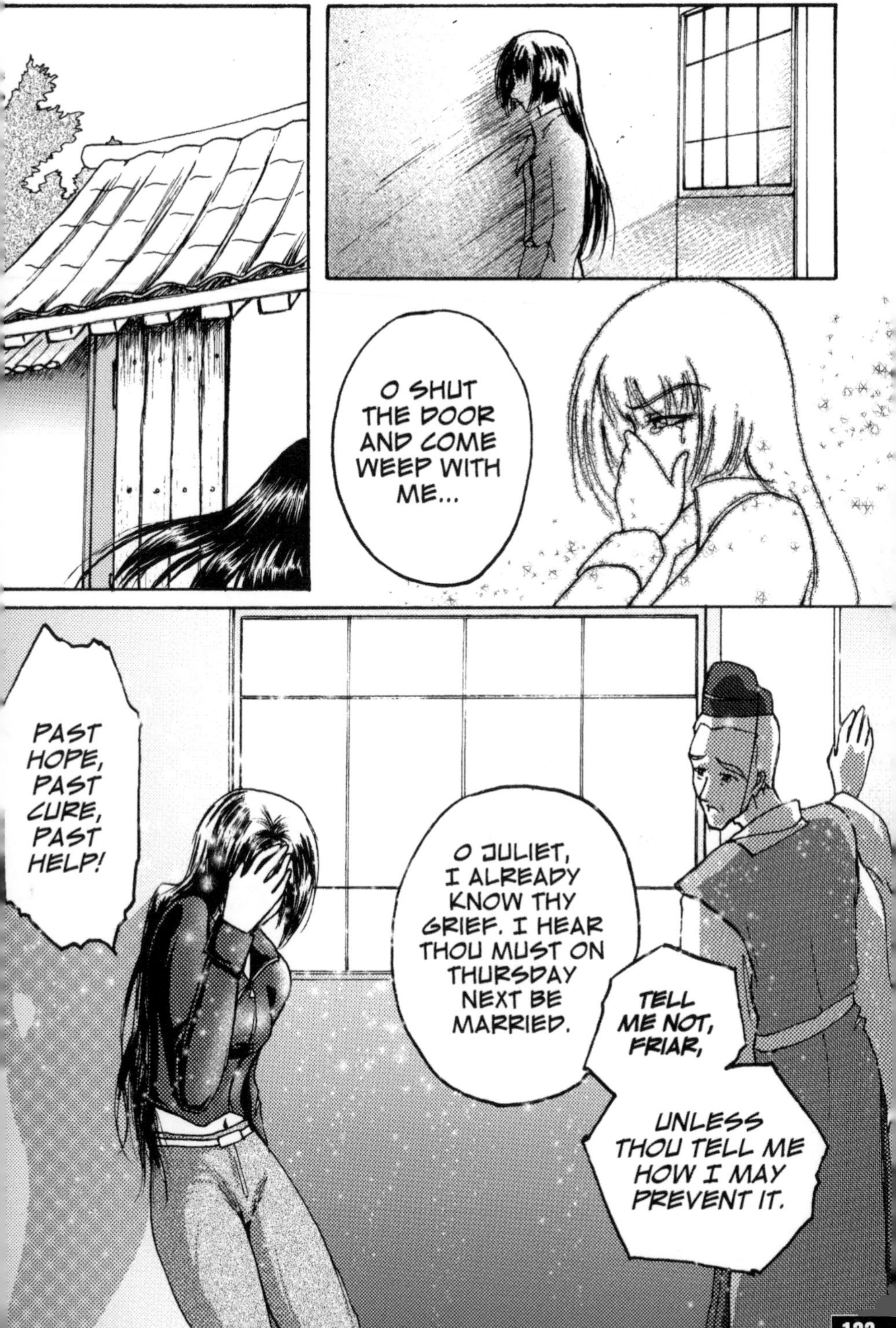
O SHUT THE DOOR AND COME WEEP WITH ME...
PAST HOPE, PAST CURE, PAST HELP!
O JULIET, I ALREADY KNOW THY GRIEF. I HEAR THOU MUST ON THURSDAY NEXT BE MARRIED.
TELL ME NOT, FRIAR,
UNLESS THOU TELL ME HOW I MAY PREVENT IT.

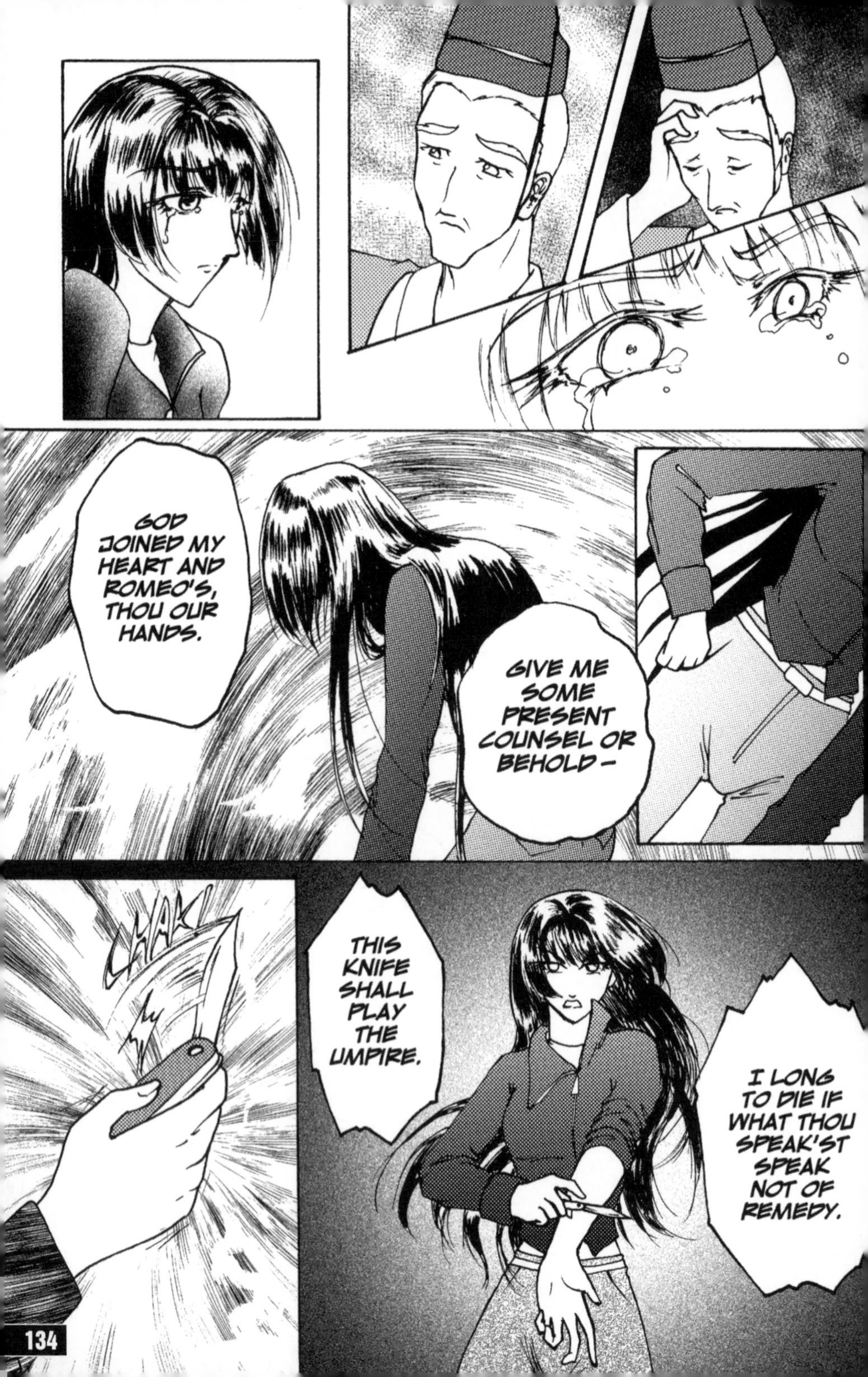
GOD JOINED MY HEART AND ROMEO'S, THOU OUR HANDS.
GIVE ME SOME PRESENT COUNSEL OR BEHOLD -
CHAK!
THIS KNIFE SHALL PLAY THE UMPIRE.
I LONG TO DIE IF WHAT THOU SPEAK'ST SPEAK NOT OF REMEDY.

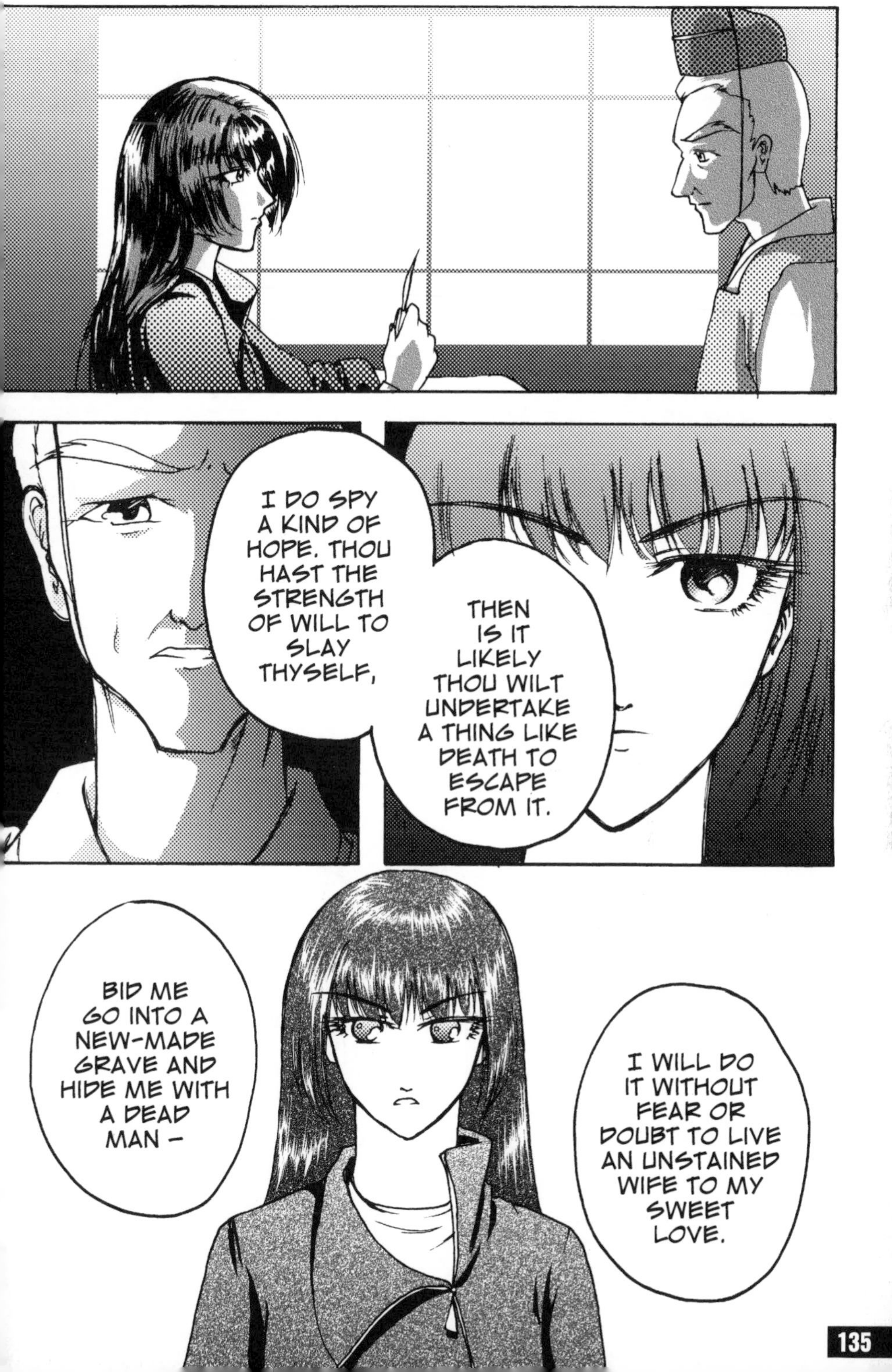
I DO SPY A KIND OF HOPE. THOU HAST THE STRENGTH OF WILL TO SLAY THYSELF,
THEN IS IT LIKELY THOU WILT UNDERTAKE A THING LIKE DEATH TO ESCAPE FROM IT.
BID ME GO INTO A NEW-MADE GRAVE AND HIDE ME WITH A DEAD MAN –
I WILL DO IT WITHOUT FEAR OR DOUBT TO LIVE AN UNSTAINED WIFE TO MY SWEET LOVE.

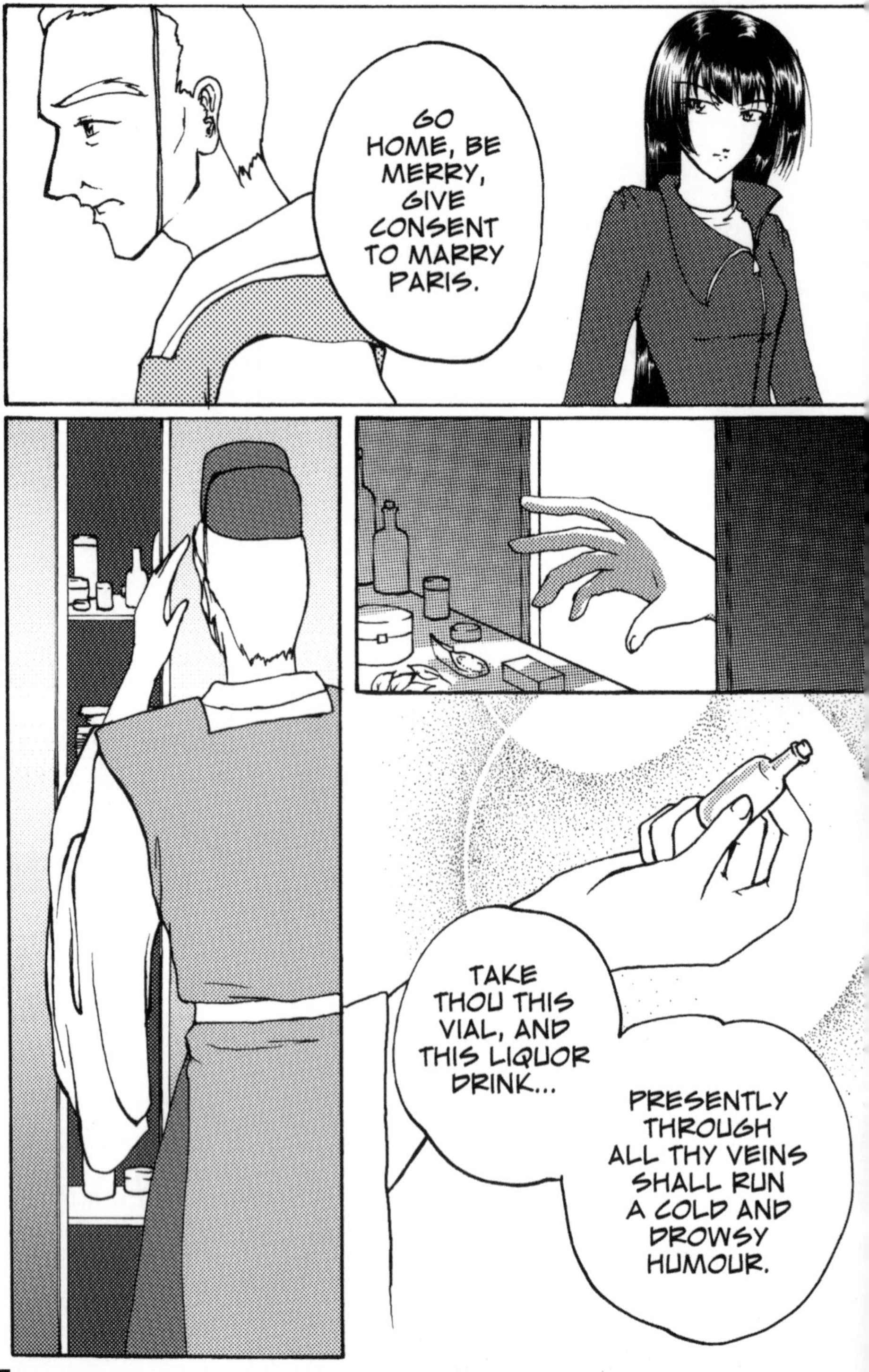
GO HOME, BE MERRY, GIVE CONSENT TO MARRY PARIS.
TAKE THOU THIS VIAL, AND THIS LIQUOR DRINK...
PRESENTLY THROUGH ALL THY VEINS SHALL RUN A COLD AND DROWSY HUMOUR.

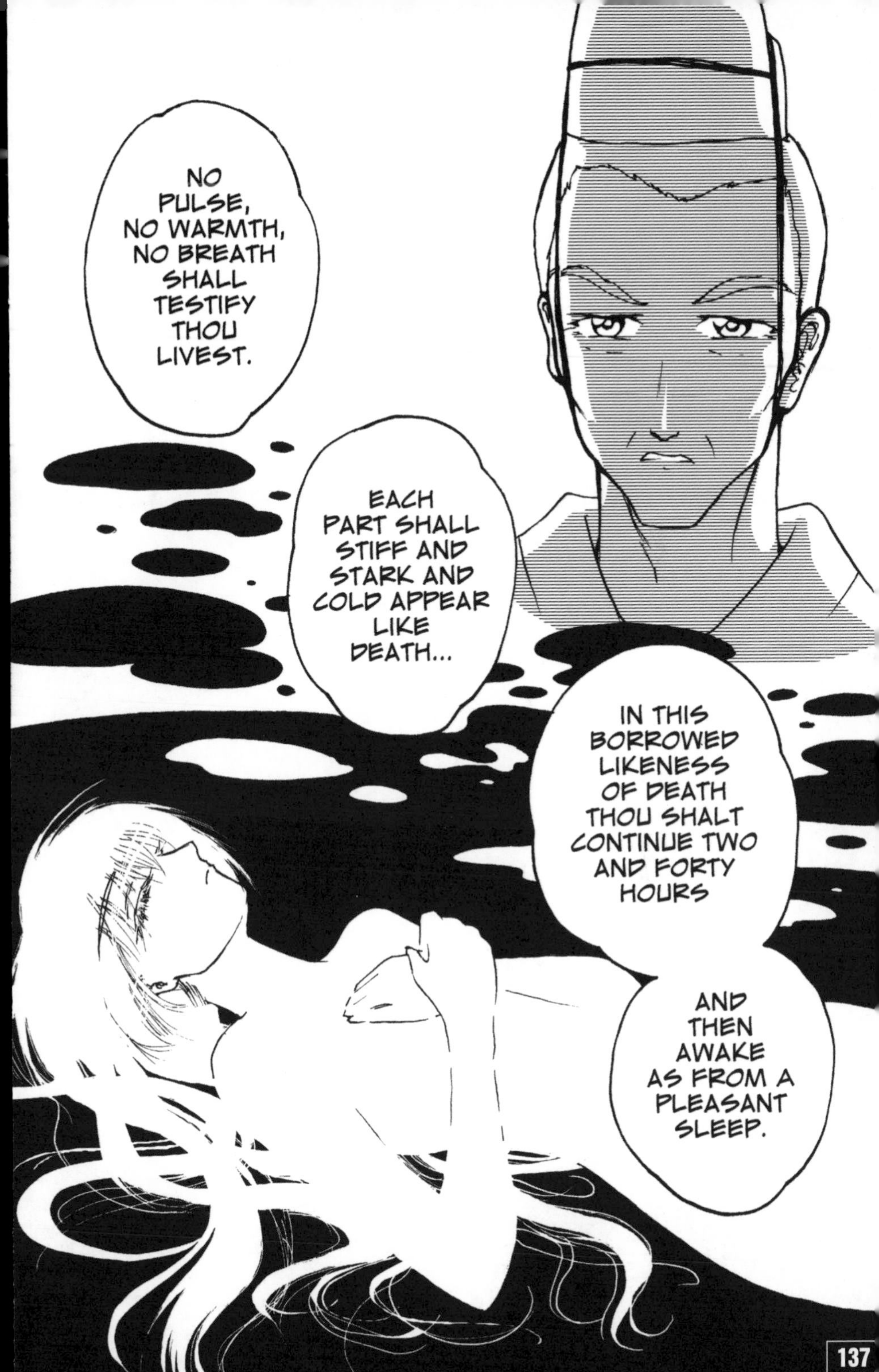
NO PULSE, NO WARMTH, NO BREATH SHALL TESTIFY THOU LIVEST.
EACH PART SHALL STIFF AND STARK AND COLD APPEAR LIKE DEATH...
IN THIS BORROWED LIKENESS OF DEATH THOU SHALT CONTINUE TWO AND FORTY HOURS
AND THEN AWAKE AS FROM A PLEASANT SLEEP.

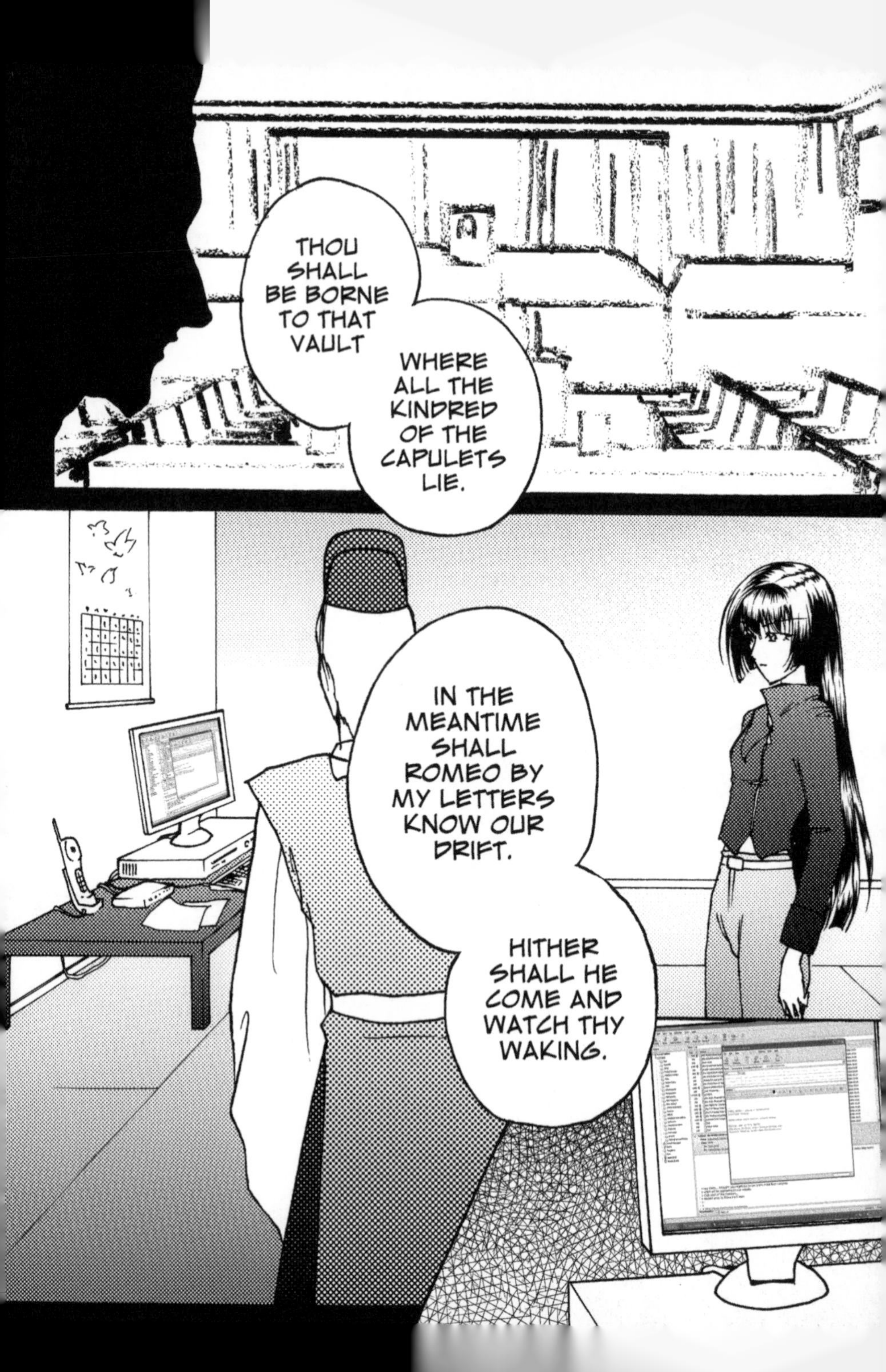
THOU SHALL BE BORNE TO THAT VAULT
WHERE ALL THE KINDRED OF THE CAPULETS LIE.
IN THE MEANTIME SHALL ROMEO BY MY LETTERS KNOW OUR DRIFT.
HITHER SHALL HE COME AND WATCH THY WAKING.

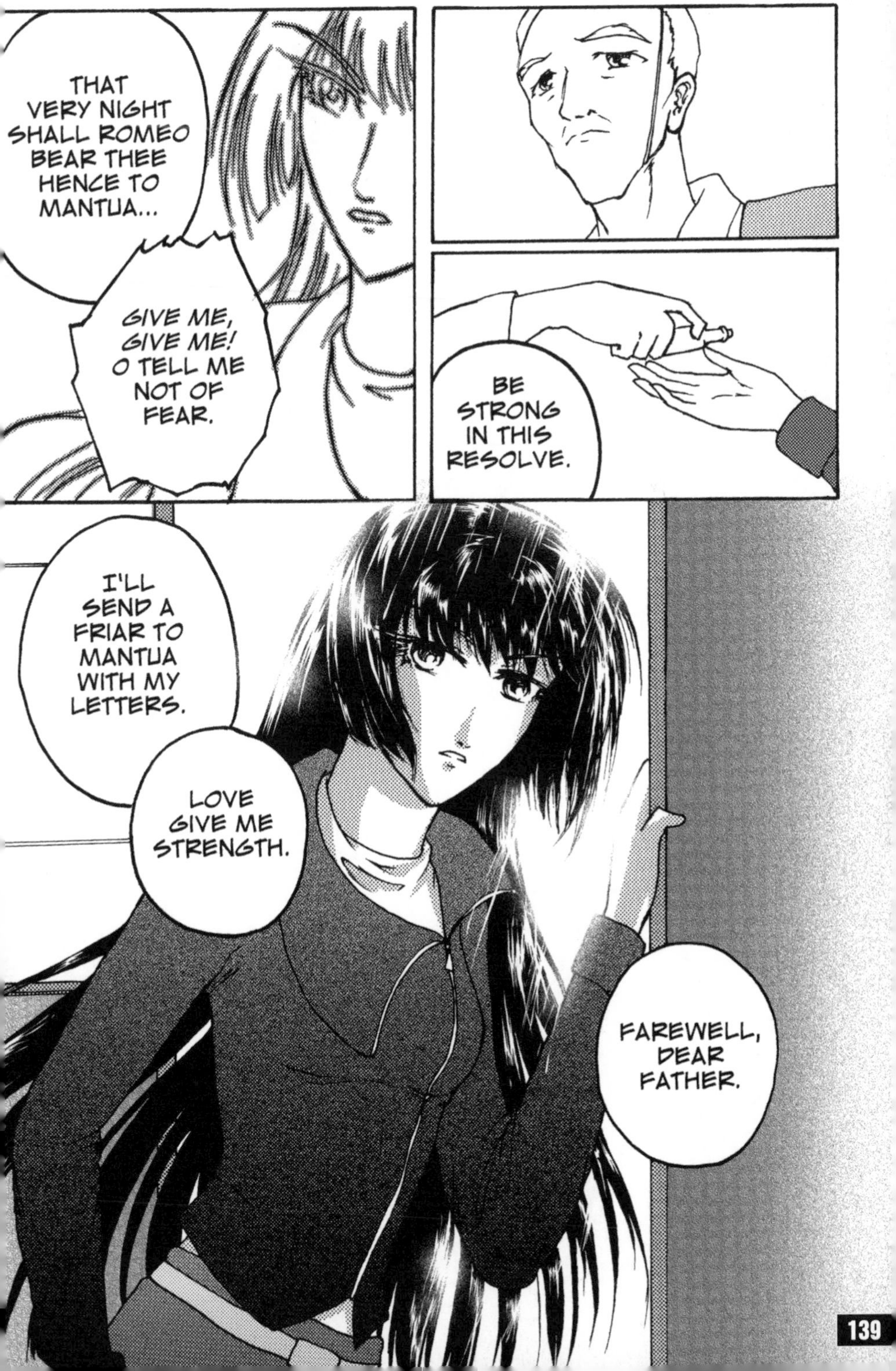
THAT VERY NIGHT SHALL ROMEO BEAR THEE HENCE TO MANTUA...
GIVE ME, GIVE ME! O TELL ME NOT OF FEAR.
BE STRONG IN THIS RESOLVE.
I'LL SEND A FRIAR TO MANTUA WITH MY LETTERS.
LOVE GIVE ME STRENGTH.
FAREWELL, DEAR FATHER.

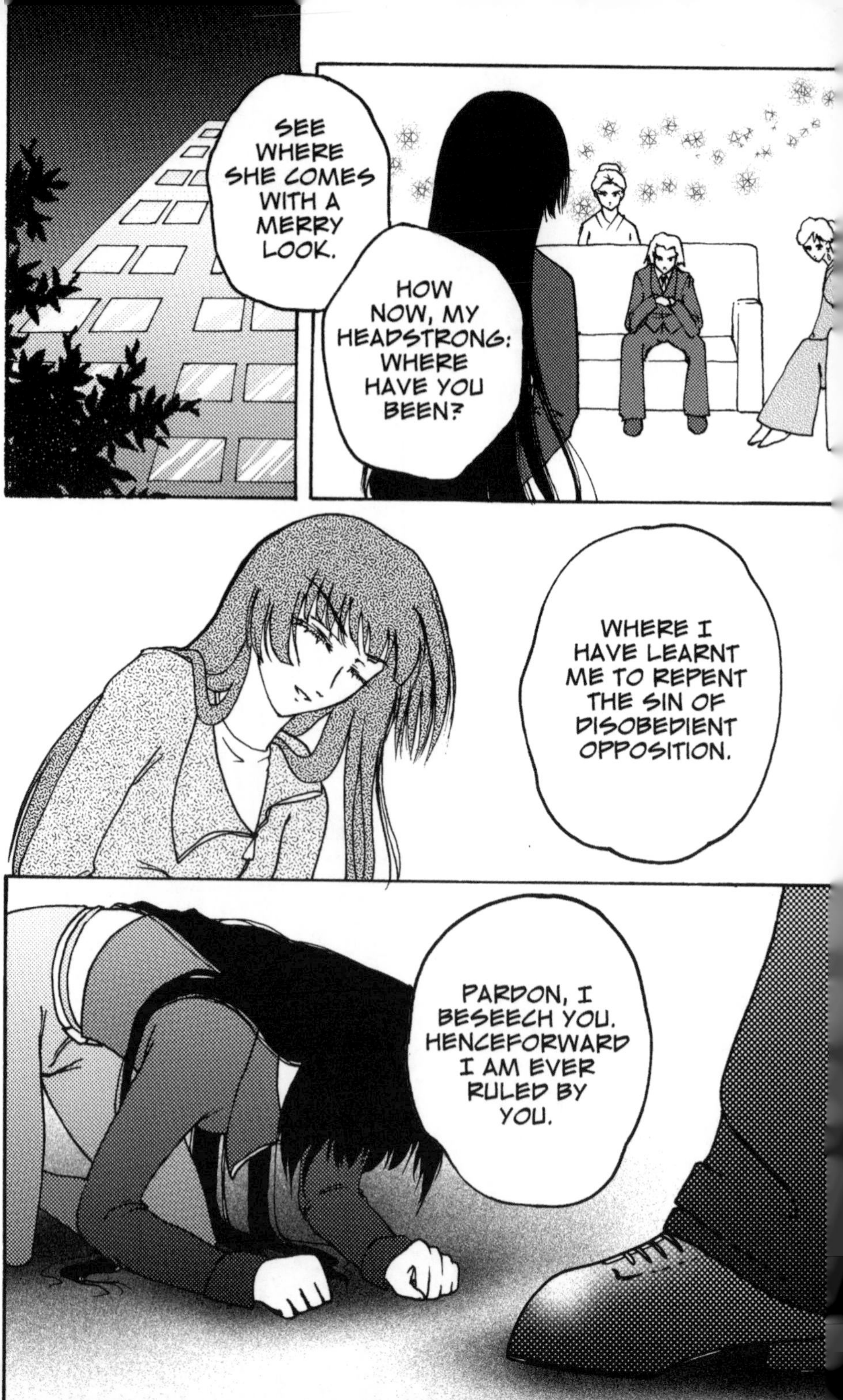
SEE WHERE SHE COMES WITH A MERRY LOOK.
HOW NOW, MY HEADSTRONG: WHERE HAVE YOU BEEN?
WHERE I HAVE LEARNT ME TO REPENT THE SIN OF DISOBEDIENT OPPOSITION.
PARDON, I BESEECH YOU. HENCEFORWARD I AM EVER RULED BY YOU.

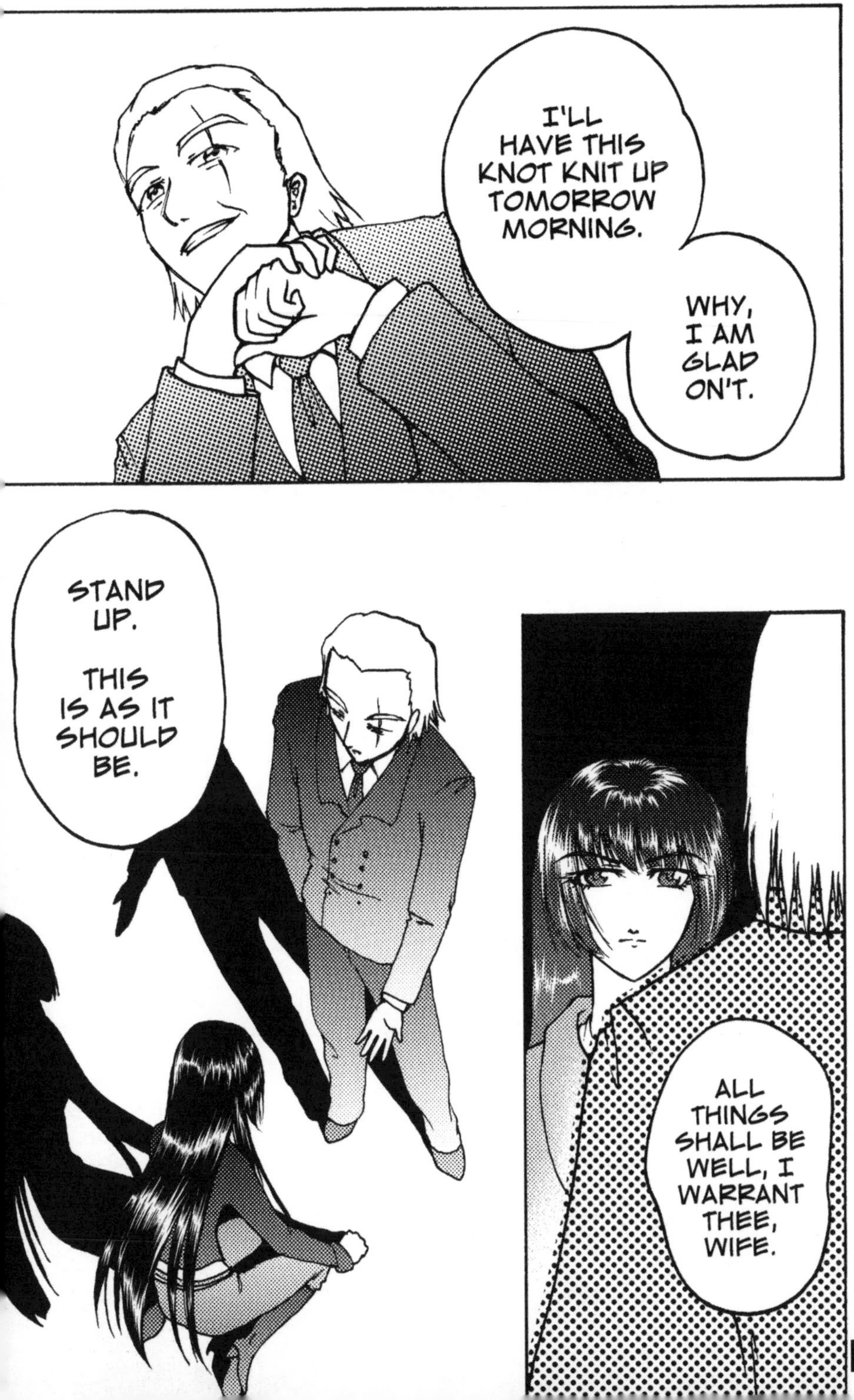
I'LL HAVE THIS KNOT KNIT UP TOMORROW MORNING.
WHY, I AM GLAD ON'T.
STAND UP.
THIS IS AS IT SHOULD BE.
ALL THINGS SHALL BE WELL, I WARRANT THEE, WIFE.

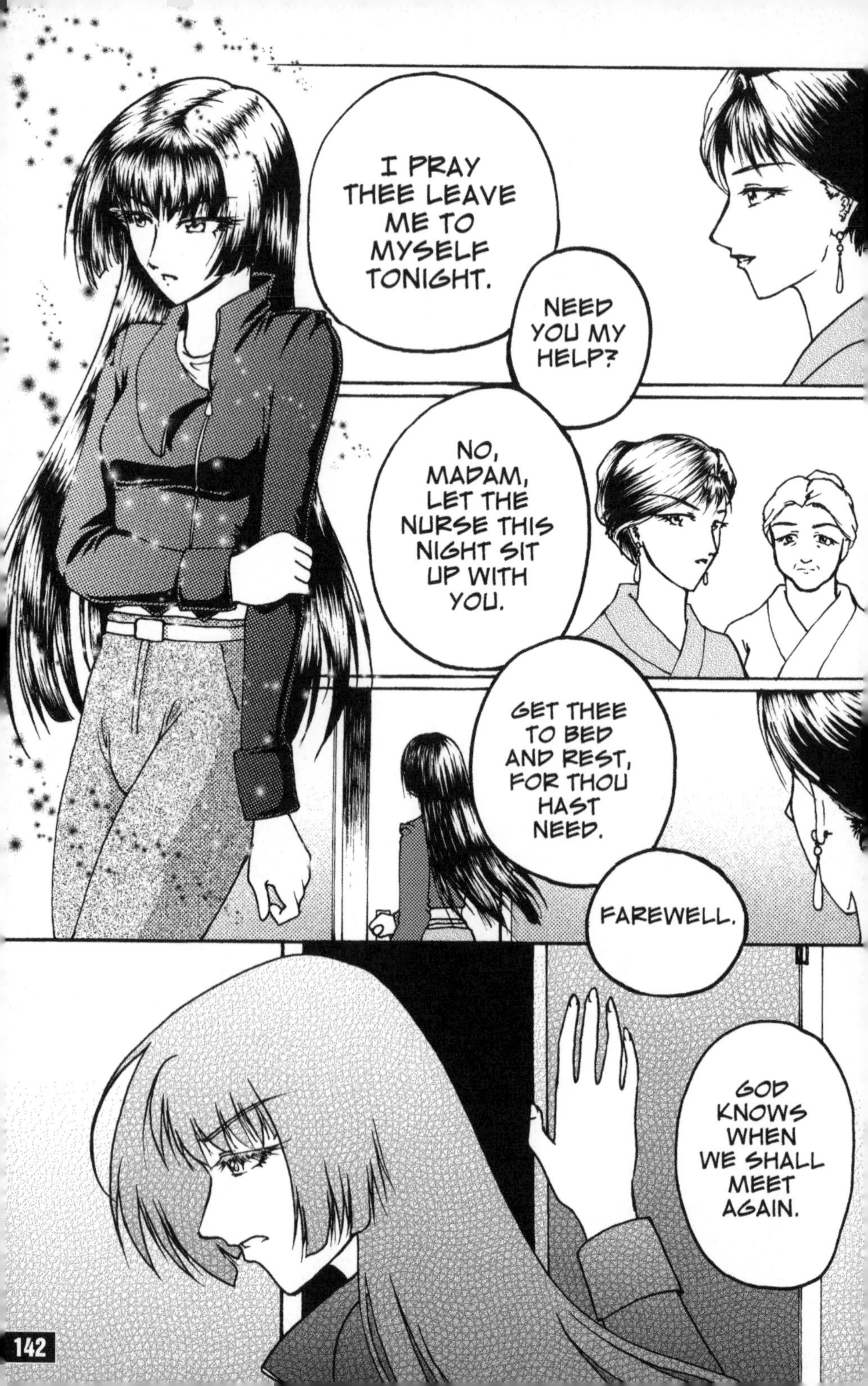
I PRAY THEE LEAVE ME TO MYSELF TONIGHT.
NEED YOU MY HELP?
NO, MADAM, LET THE NURSE THIS NIGHT SIT UP WITH YOU.
GET THEE TO BED AND REST, FOR THOU HAST NEED.
FAREWELL.
GOD KNOWS WHEN WE SHALL MEET AGAIN.

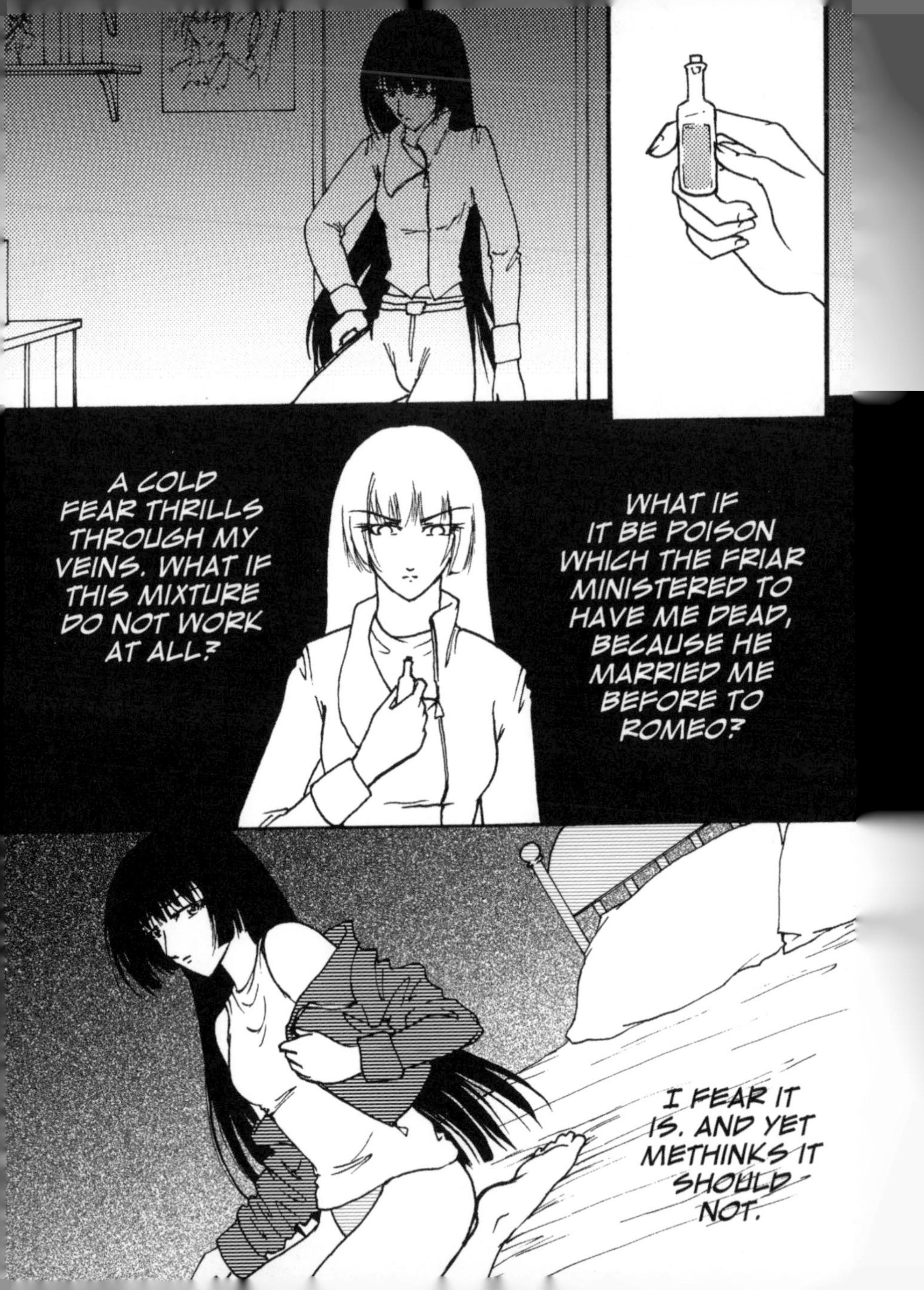
A COLD FEAR THRILLS THROUGH MY VEINS. WHAT IF THIS MIXTURE DO NOT WORK AT ALL?
WHAT IF IT BE POISON WHICH THE FRIAR MINISTERED TO HAVE ME DEAD, BECAUSE HE MARRIED ME BEFORE TO ROMEO?
I FEAR IT IS. AND YET METHINKS IT SHOULD NOT.

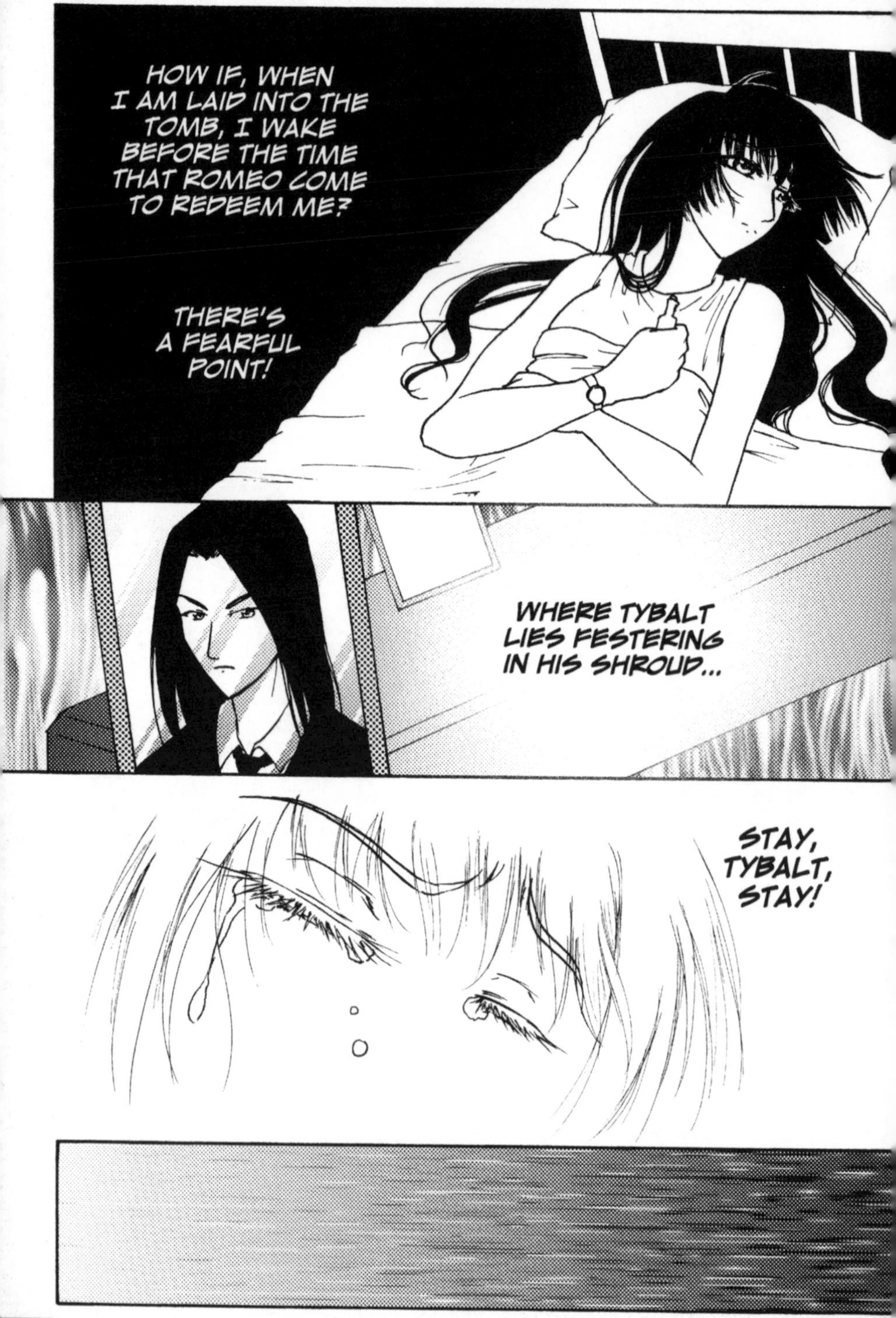
HOW IF, WHEN I AM LAID INTO THE TOMB, I WAKE BEFORE THE TIME THAT ROMEO COME TO REDEEM ME?
THERE'S A FEARFUL POINT!
WHERE TYBALT LIES FESTERING IN HIS SHROUD...
STAY, TYBALT, STAY!

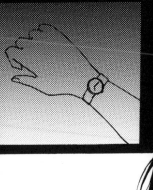

ROMEO,
ROMEO,
I DRINK
TO THEE!

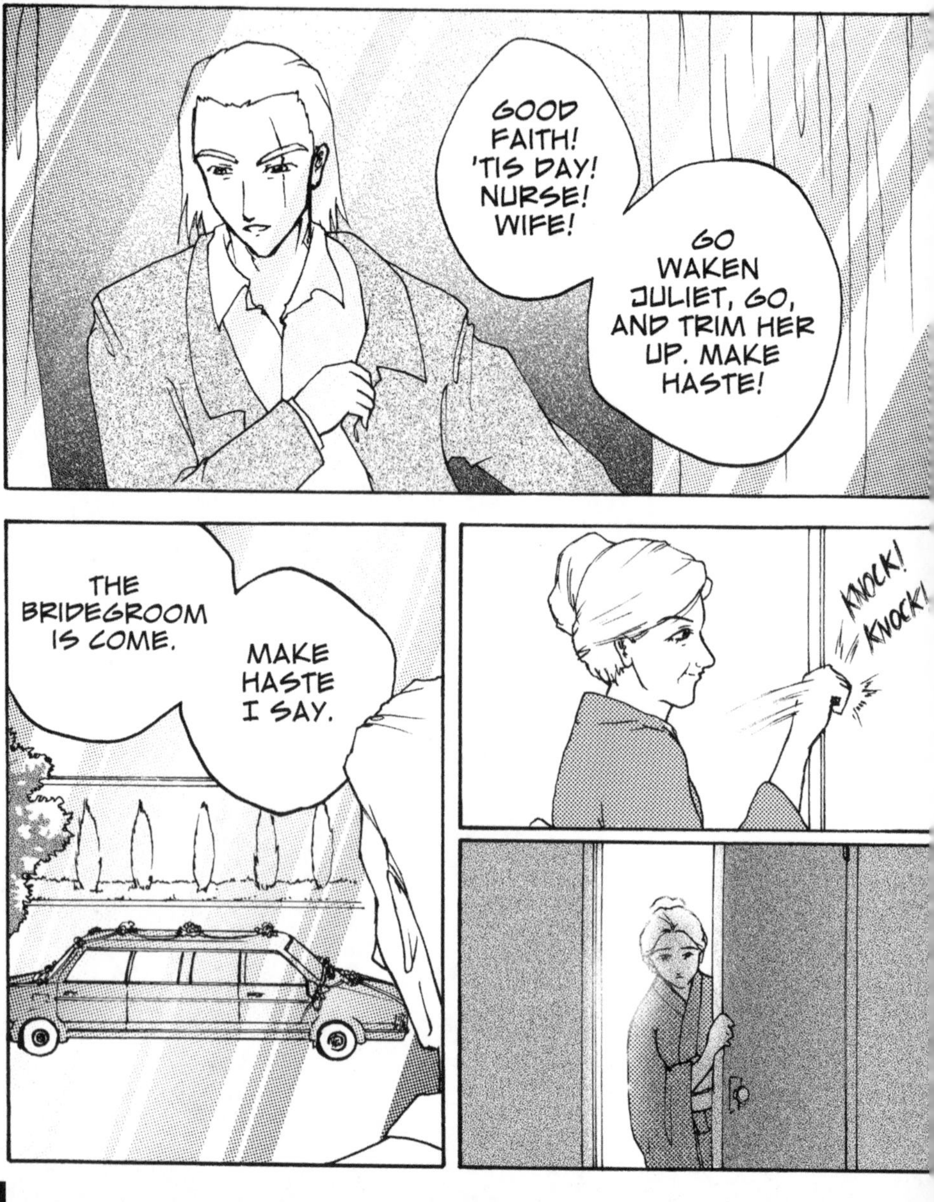
GOOD FAITH! 'TIS DAY! NURSE! WIFE!
GO WAKEN JULIET, GO, AND TRIM HER UP. MAKE HASTE!
THE BRIDEGROOM IS COME.
MAKE HASTE I SAY.
KNOCK! KNOCK!

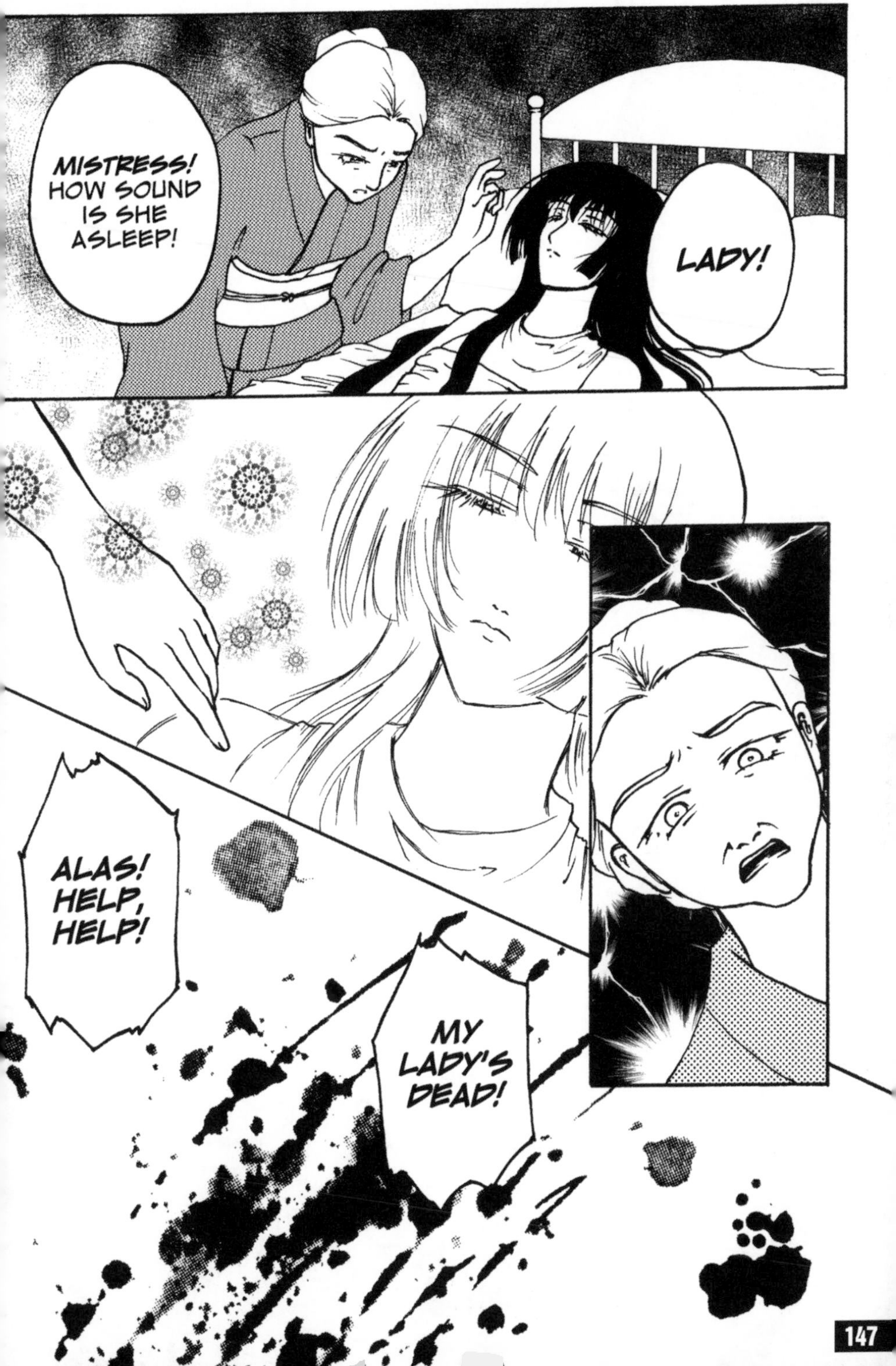
MISTRESS! HOW SOUND IS SHE ASLEEP!
LADY!
ALAS! HELP, HELP!
MY LADY'S DEAD!

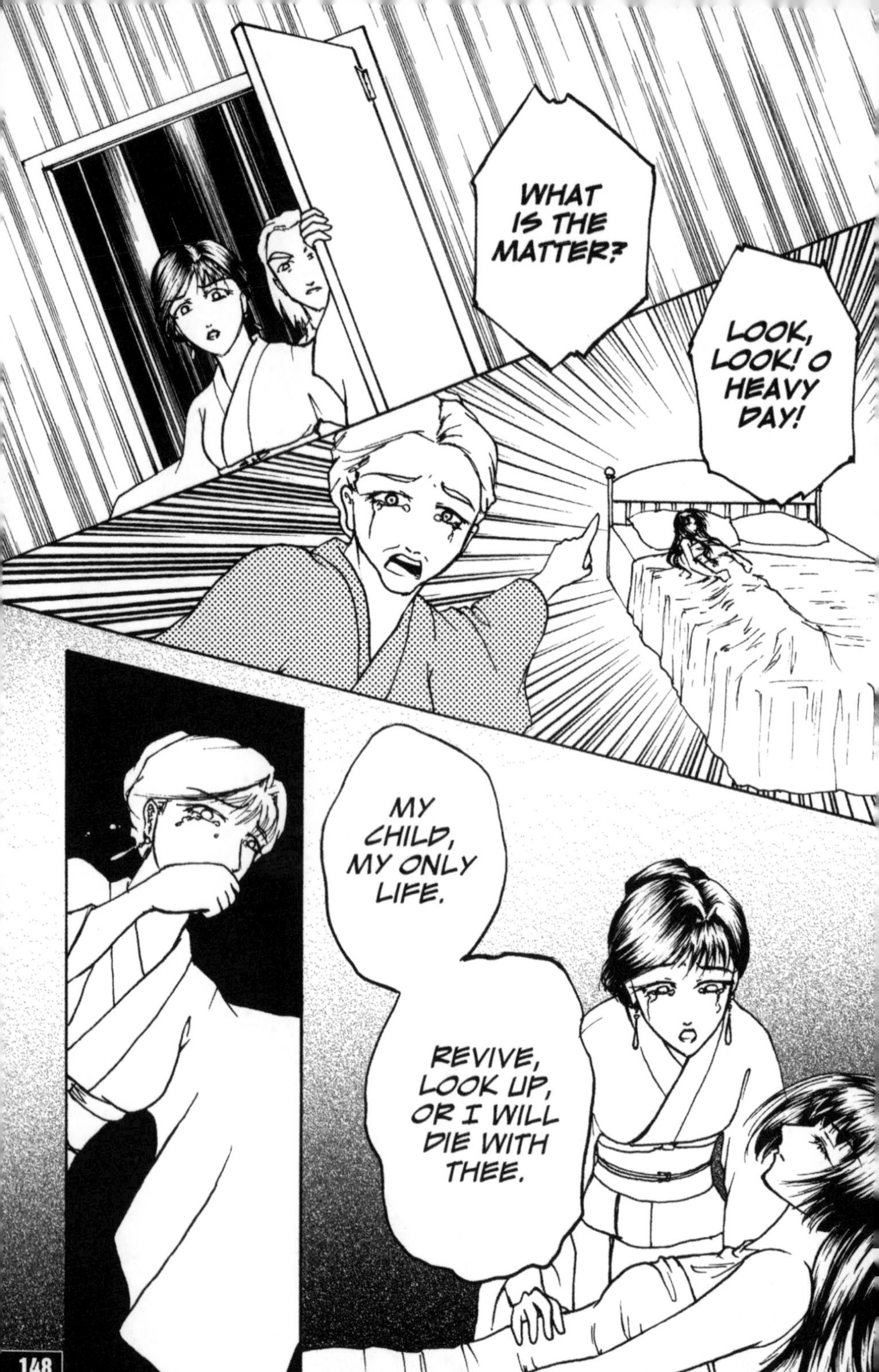
WHAT IS THE MATTER?
LOOK, LOOK! O HEAVY DAY!
MY CHILD, MY ONLY LIFE.
REVIVE, LOOK UP, OR I WILL DIE WITH THEE.

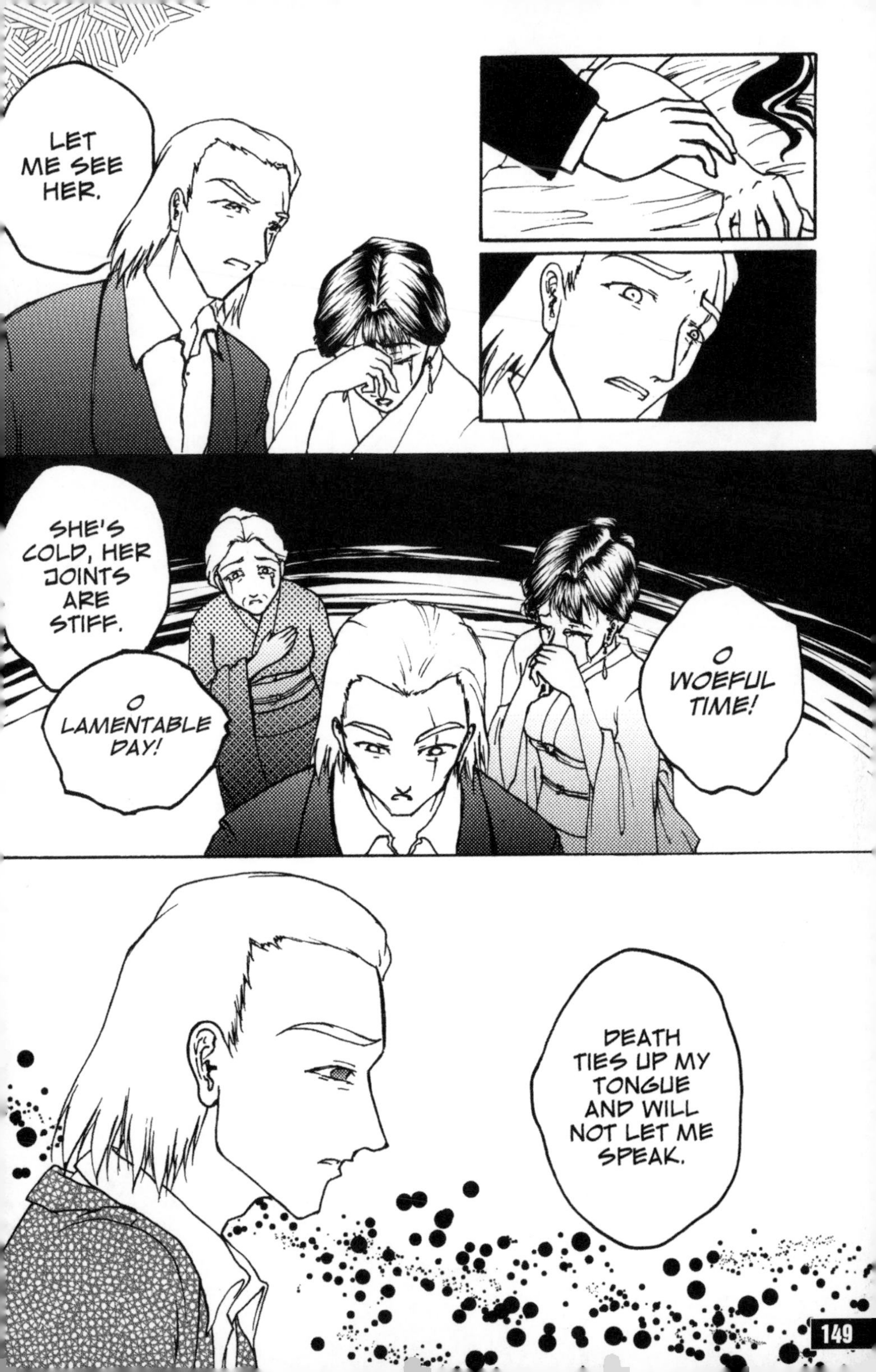
LET ME SEE HER.
SHE'S COLD, HER JOINTS ARE STIFF.
O LAMENTABLE DAY!
O WOEFUL TIME!
DEATH TIES UP MY TONGUE AND WILL NOT LET ME SPEAK.

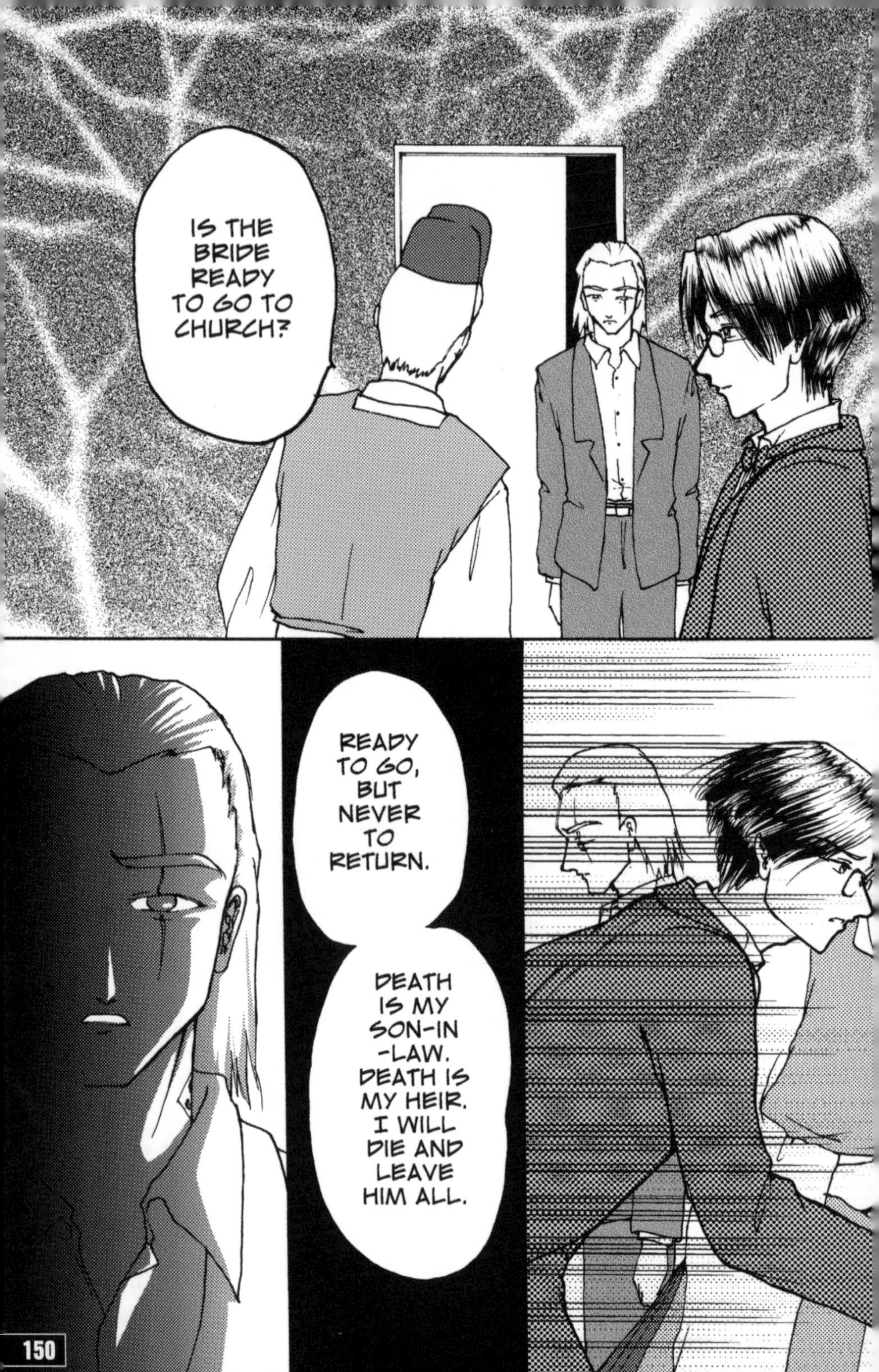
IS THE BRIDE READY TO GO TO CHURCH?
READY TO GO, BUT NEVER TO RETURN.
DEATH IS MY SON-IN-LAW. DEATH IS MY HEIR. I WILL DIE AND LEAVE HIM ALL.

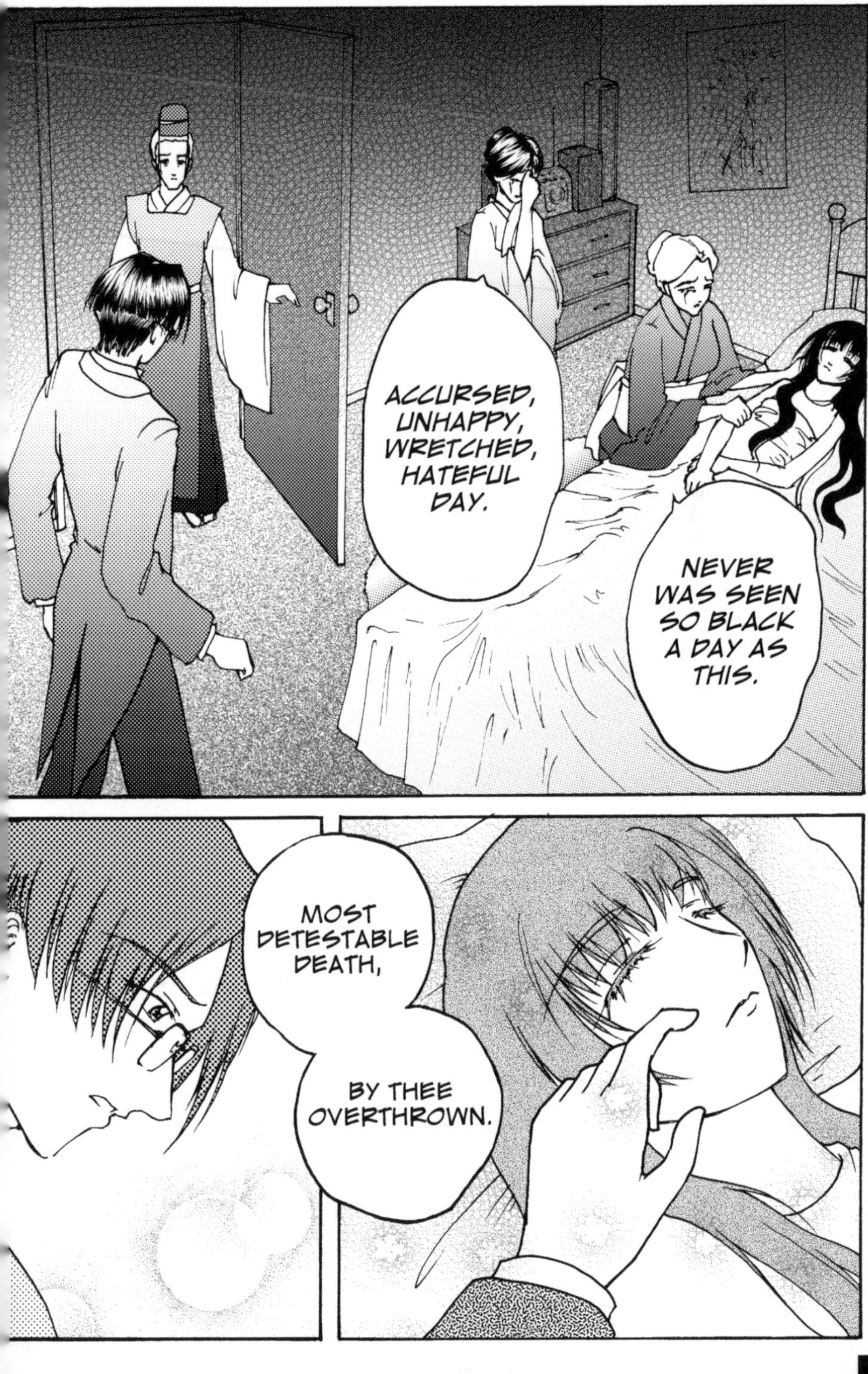
ACCURSED, UNHAPPY, WRETCHED, HATEFUL DAY.
NEVER WAS SEEN SO BLACK A DAY AS THIS.
MOST DETESTABLE DEATH,
BY THEE OVERTHROWN.

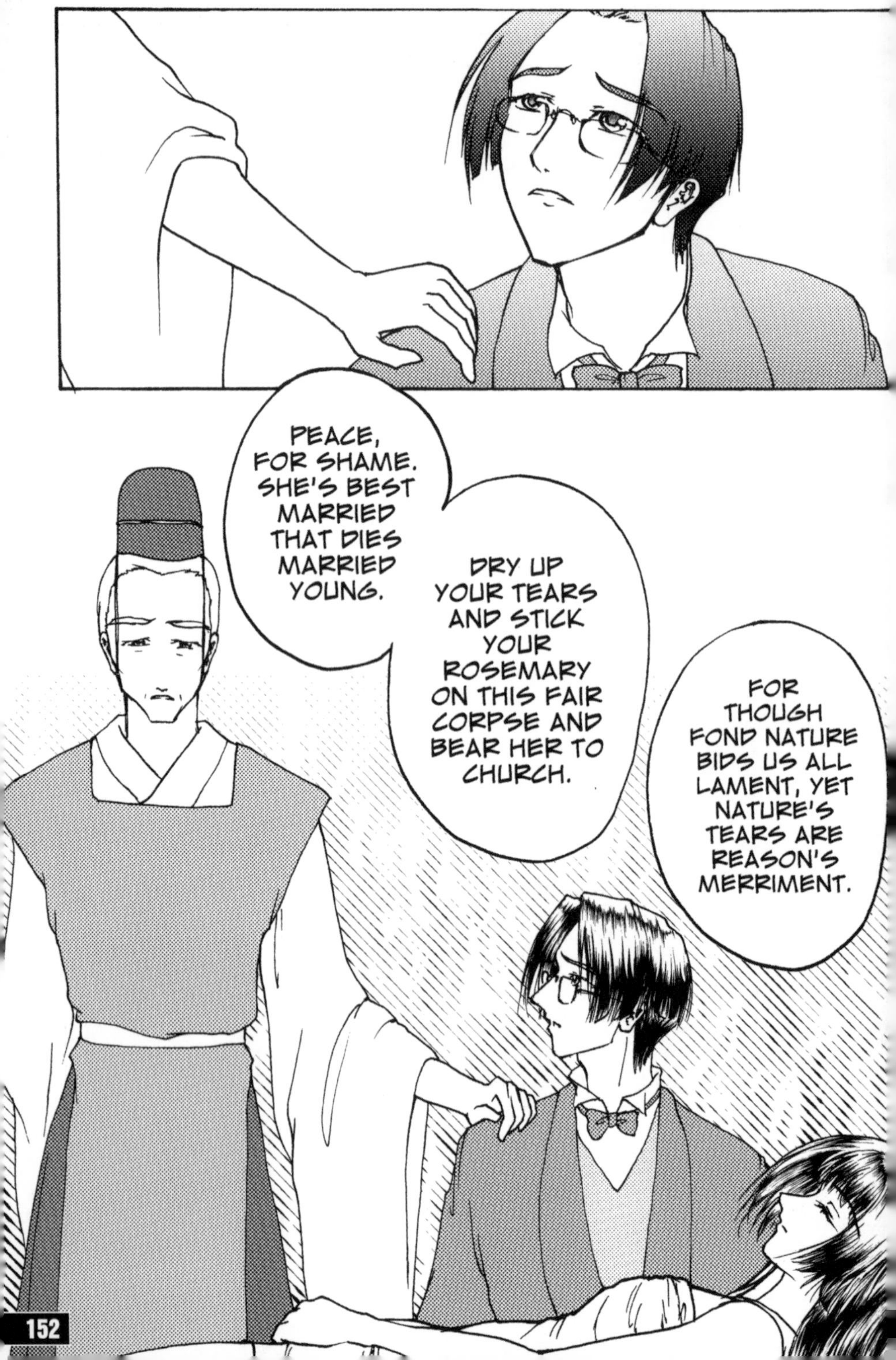
PEACE, FOR SHAME. SHE'S BEST MARRIED THAT DIES MARRIED YOUNG.
DRY UP YOUR TEARS AND STICK YOUR ROSEMARY ON THIS FAIR CORPSE AND BEAR HER TO CHURCH.
FOR THOUGH FOND NATURE BIDS US ALL LAMENT, YET NATURE'S TEARS ARE REASON'S MERRIMENT.

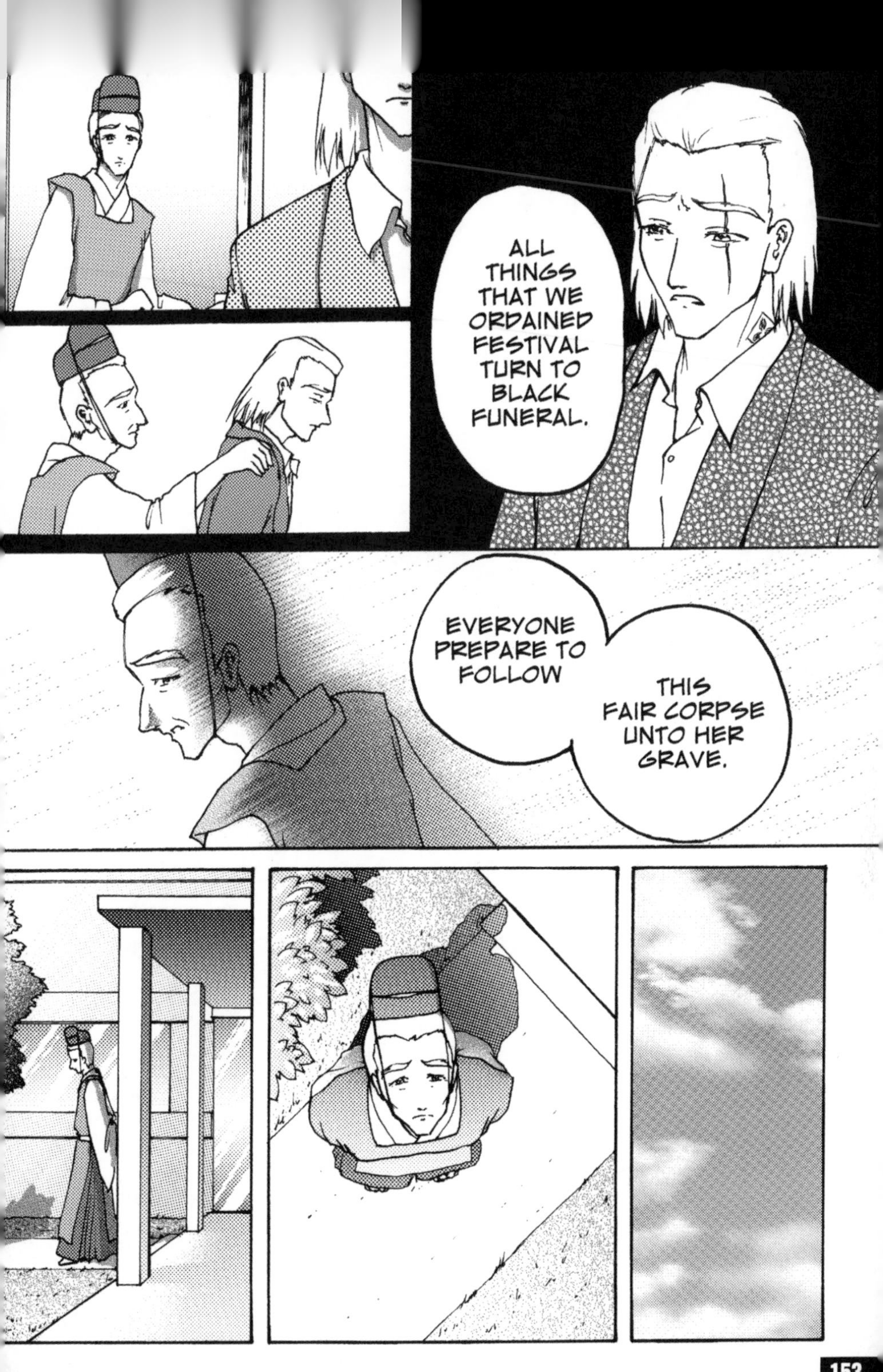
ALL THINGS THAT WE ORDAINED FESTIVAL TURN TO BLACK FUNERAL.
EVERYONE PREPARE TO FOLLOW
THIS FAIR CORPSE UNTO HER GRAVE.

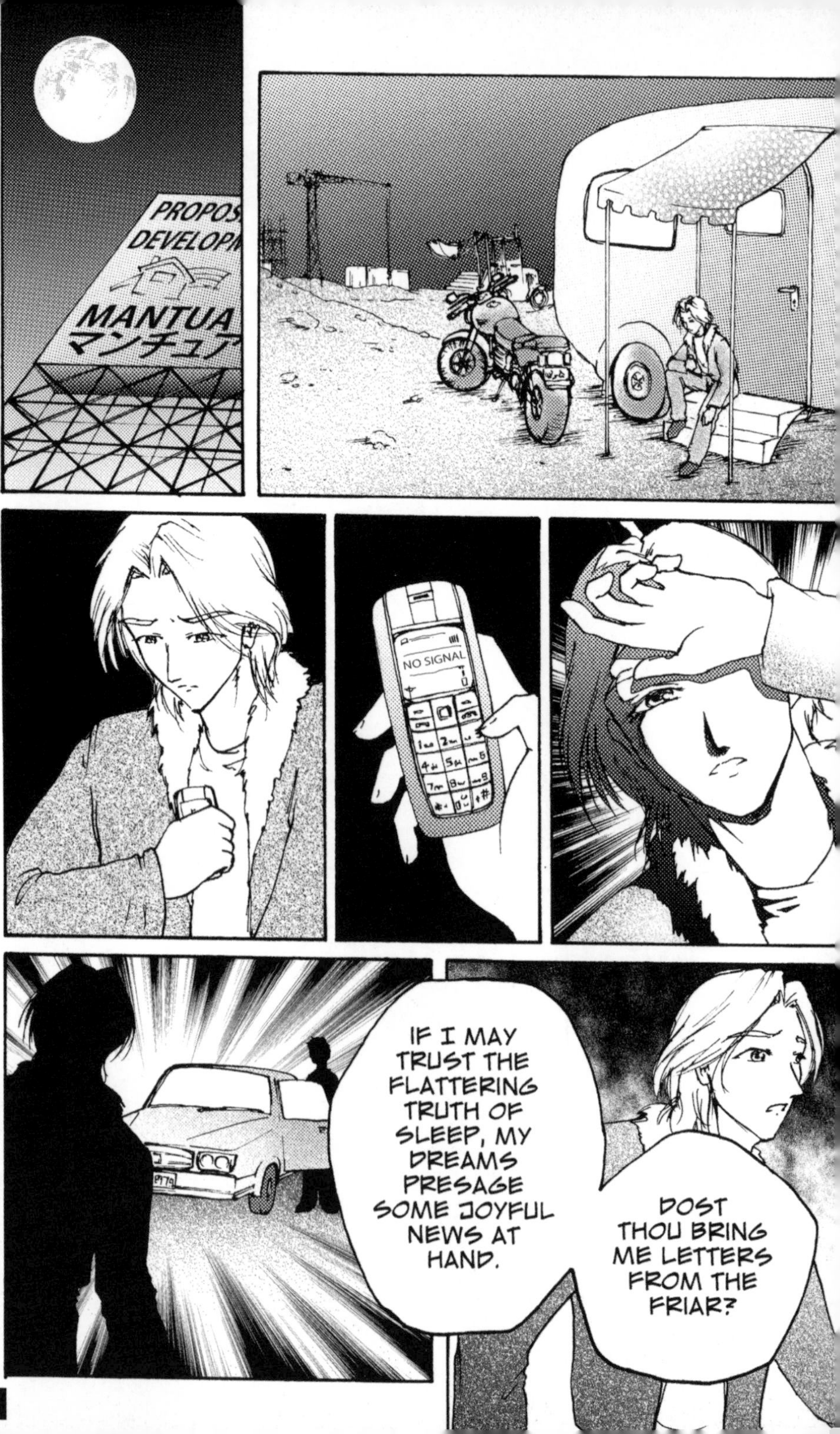
PROPOS
DEVELOPM
MANTUA
マンチュア
NO SIGNAL
IF I MAY TRUST THE FLATTERING TRUTH OF SLEEP, MY DREAMS PRESAGE SOME JOYFUL NEWS AT HAND.
DOST THOU BRING ME LETTERS FROM THE FRIAR?

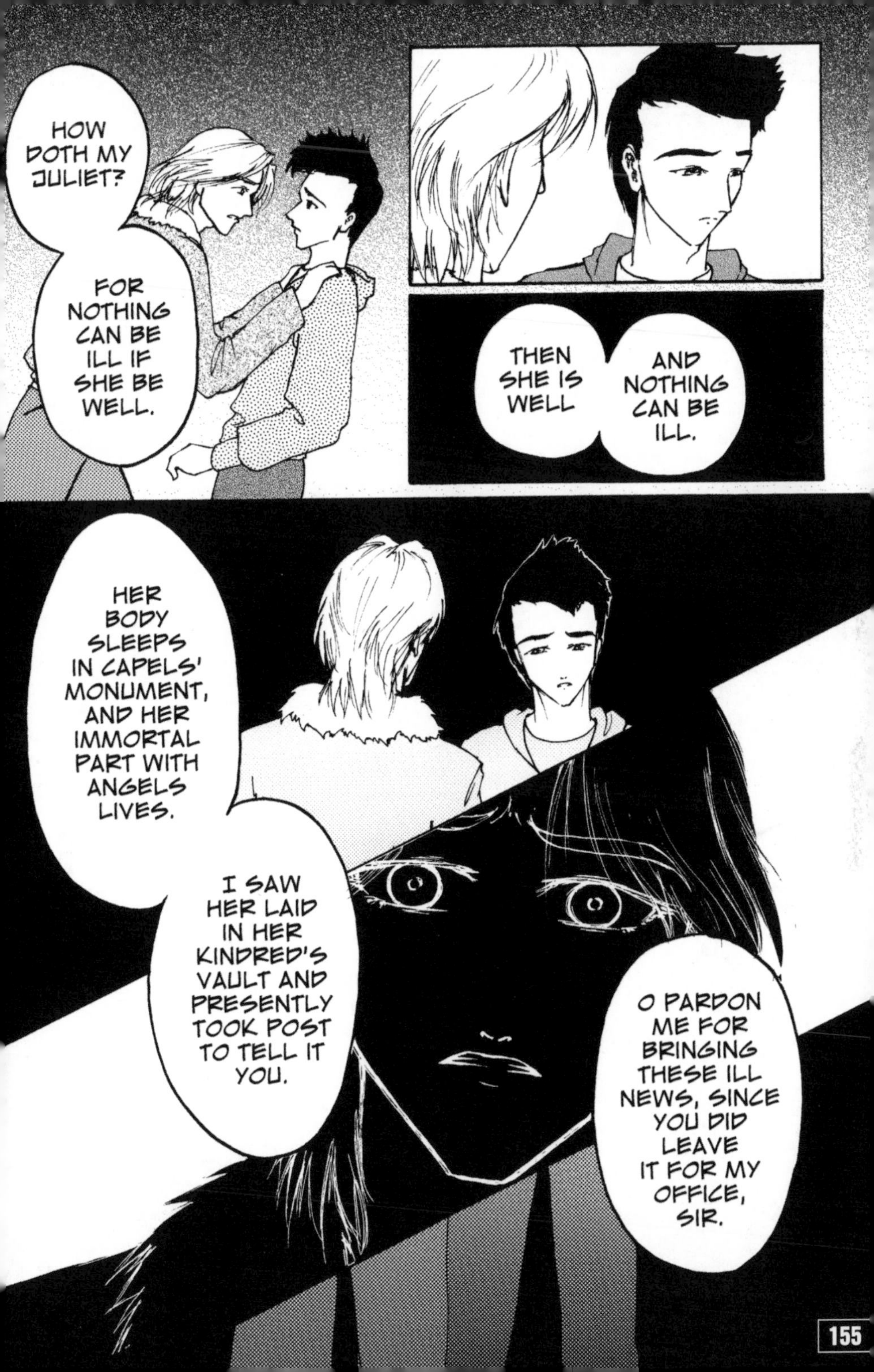
HOW DOTH MY JULIET?
FOR NOTHING CAN BE ILL IF SHE BE WELL.
THEN SHE IS WELL
AND NOTHING CAN BE ILL.
HER BODY SLEEPS IN CAPELS' MONUMENT, AND HER IMMORTAL PART WITH ANGELS LIVES.
I SAW HER LAID IN HER KINDRED'S VAULT AND PRESENTLY TOOK POST TO TELL IT YOU.
O PARDON ME FOR BRINGING THESE ILL NEWS, SINCE YOU DID LEAVE IT FOR MY OFFICE, SIR.

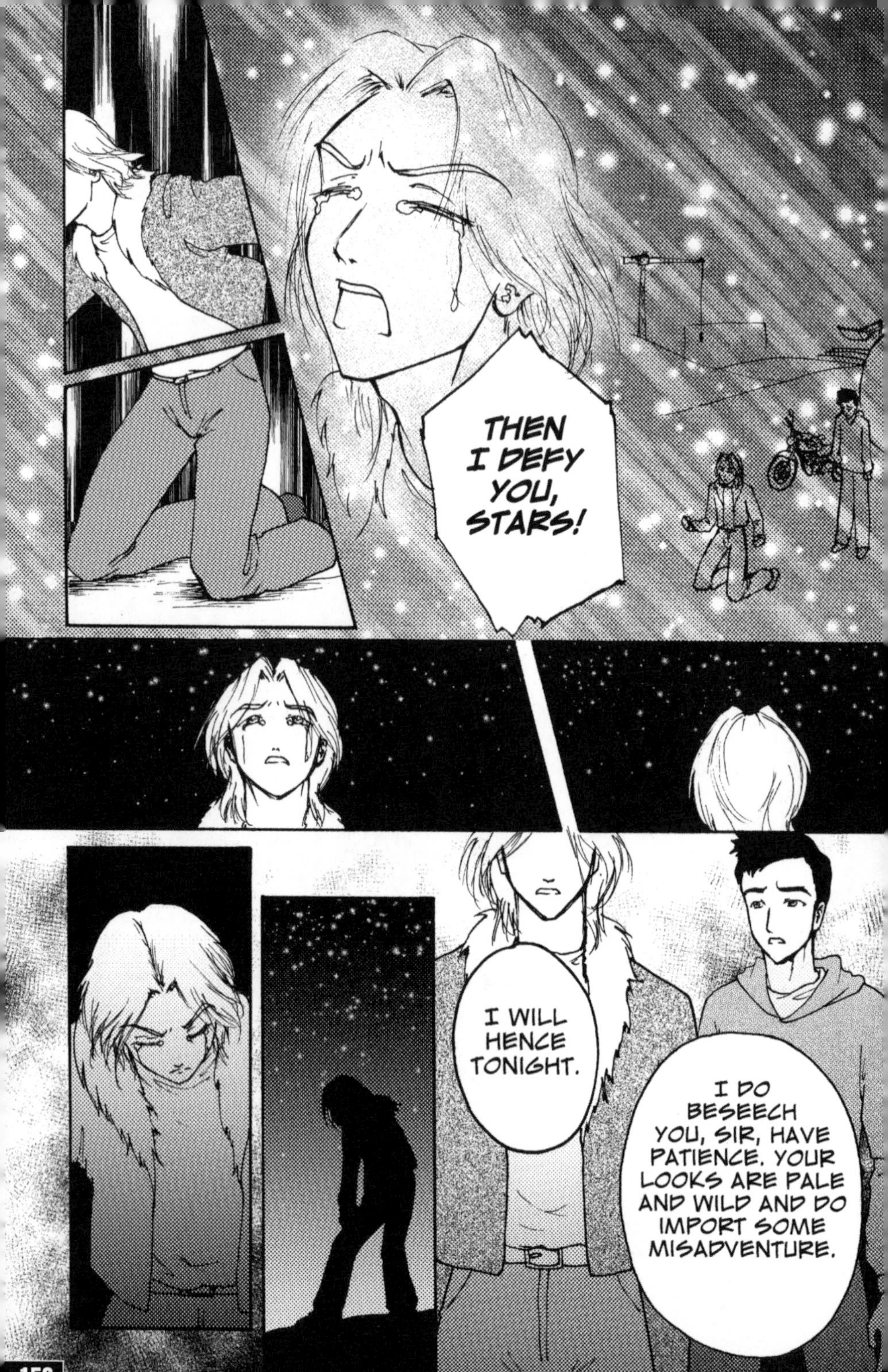
THEN I DEFY YOU, STARS!
I WILL HENCE TONIGHT.
I DO BESEECH YOU, SIR, HAVE PATIENCE. YOUR LOOKS ARE PALE AND WILD AND DO IMPORT SOME MISADVENTURE.

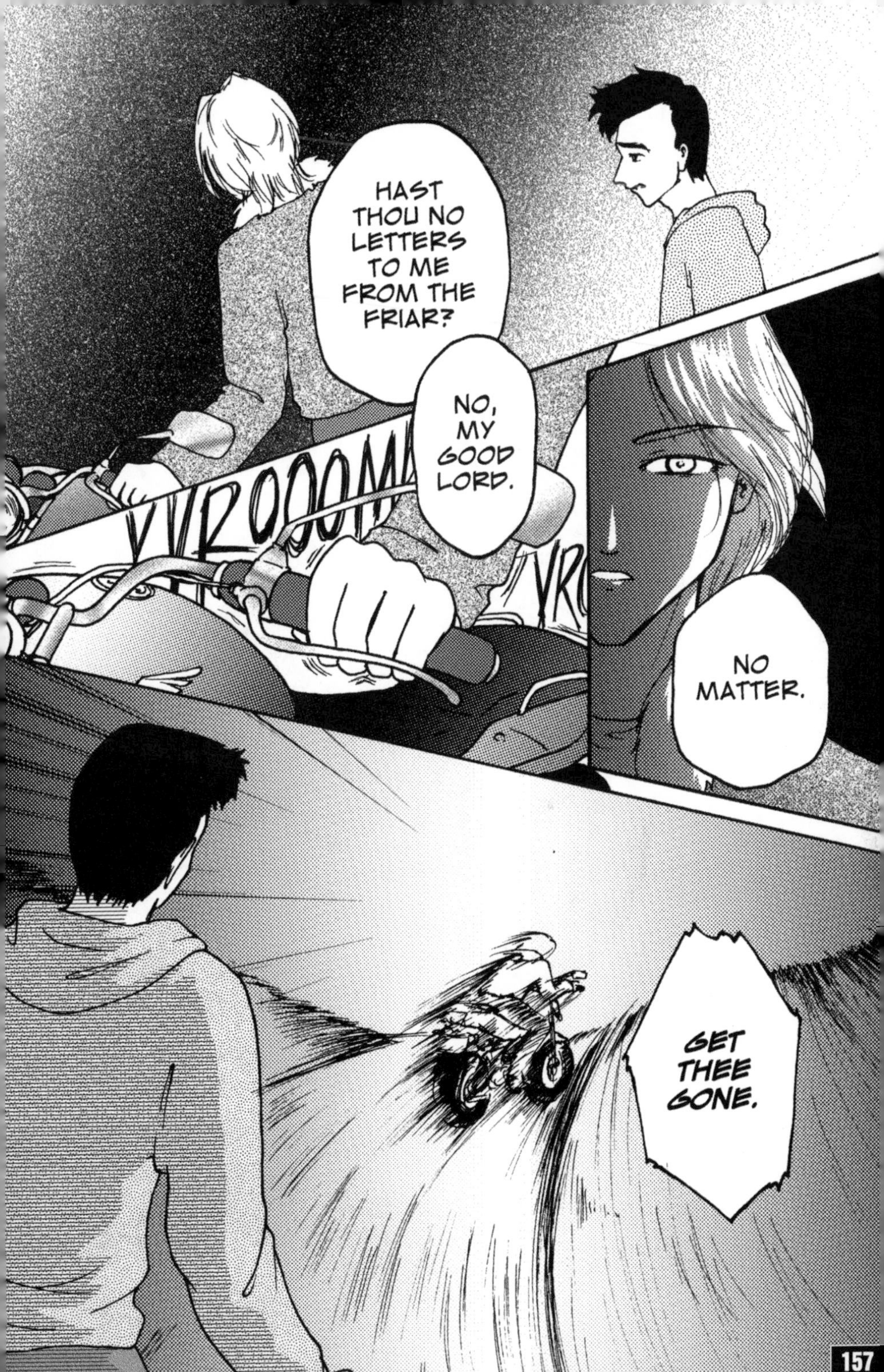
HAST THOU NO LETTERS TO ME FROM THE FRIAR?
NO, MY GOOD LORD.
VVROOOOM
VRO
NO MATTER.
GET THEE GONE.

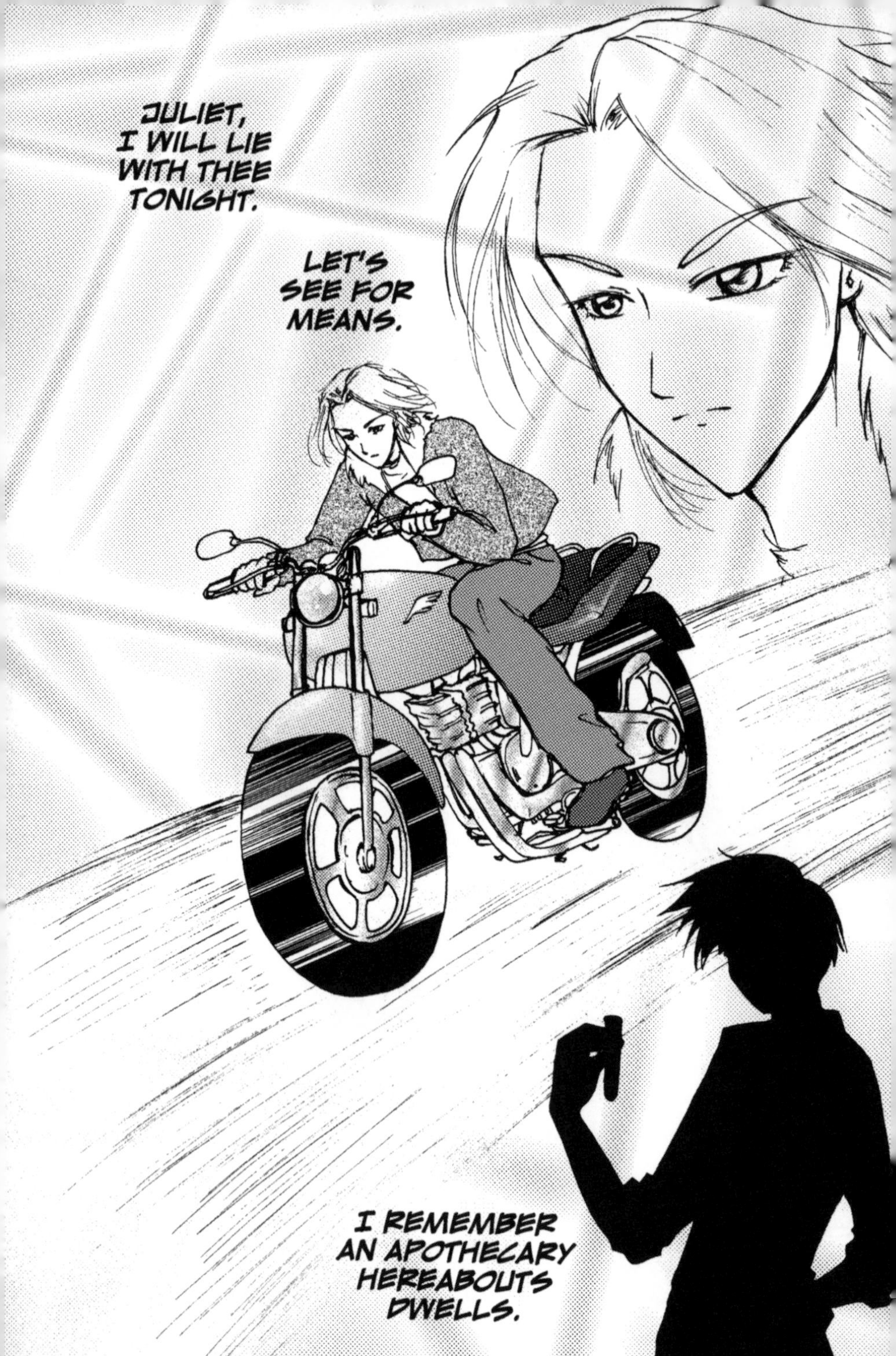
JULIET, I WILL LIE WITH THEE TONIGHT.
LET'S SEE FOR MEANS.
I REMEMBER AN APOTHECARY HEREABOUTS DWELLS.

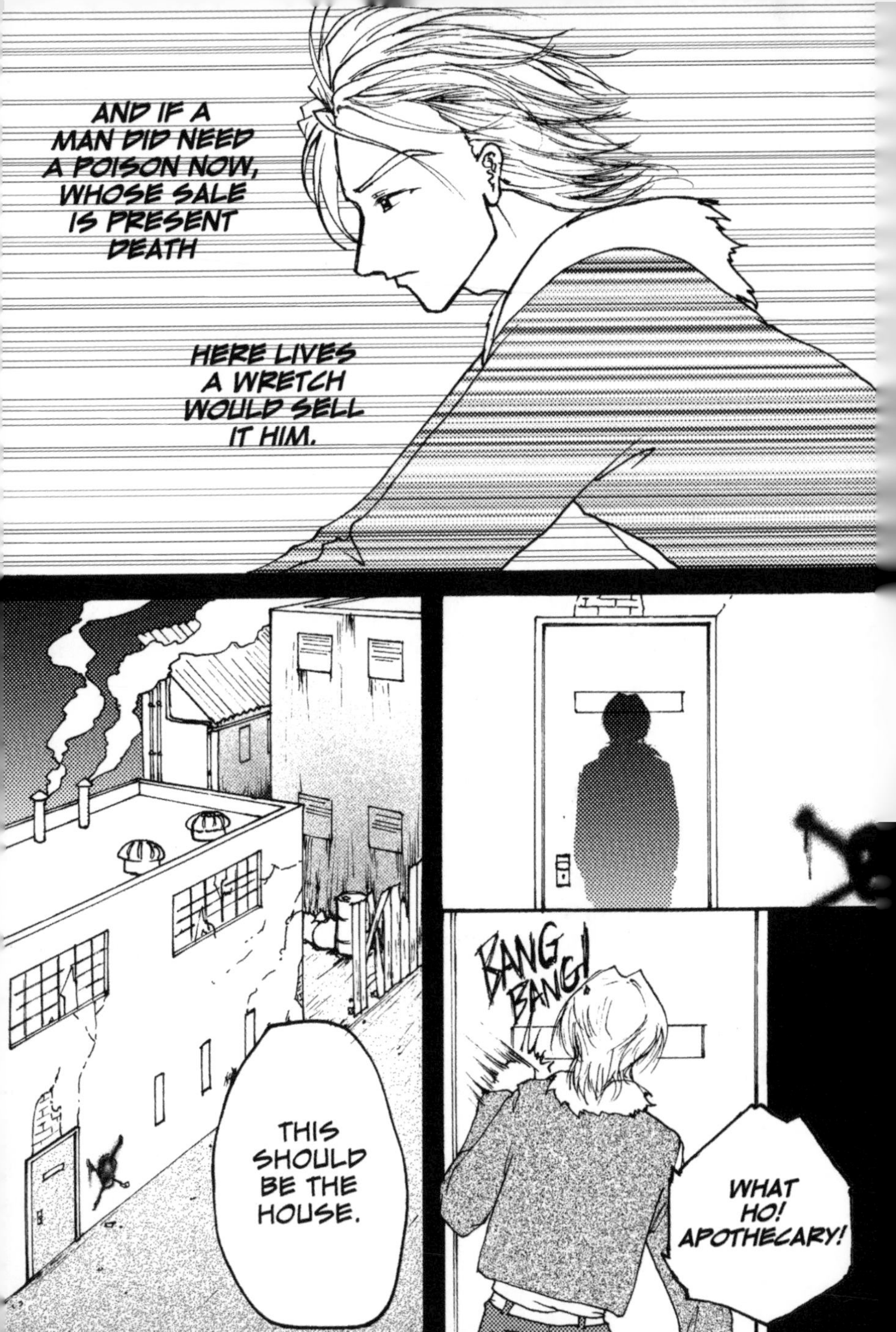
AND IF A MAN DID NEED A POISON NOW, WHOSE SALE IS PRESENT DEATH
HERE LIVES A WRETCH WOULD SELL IT HIM.
THIS SHOULD BE THE HOUSE.
BANG BANG!
WHAT HO! APOTHECARY!

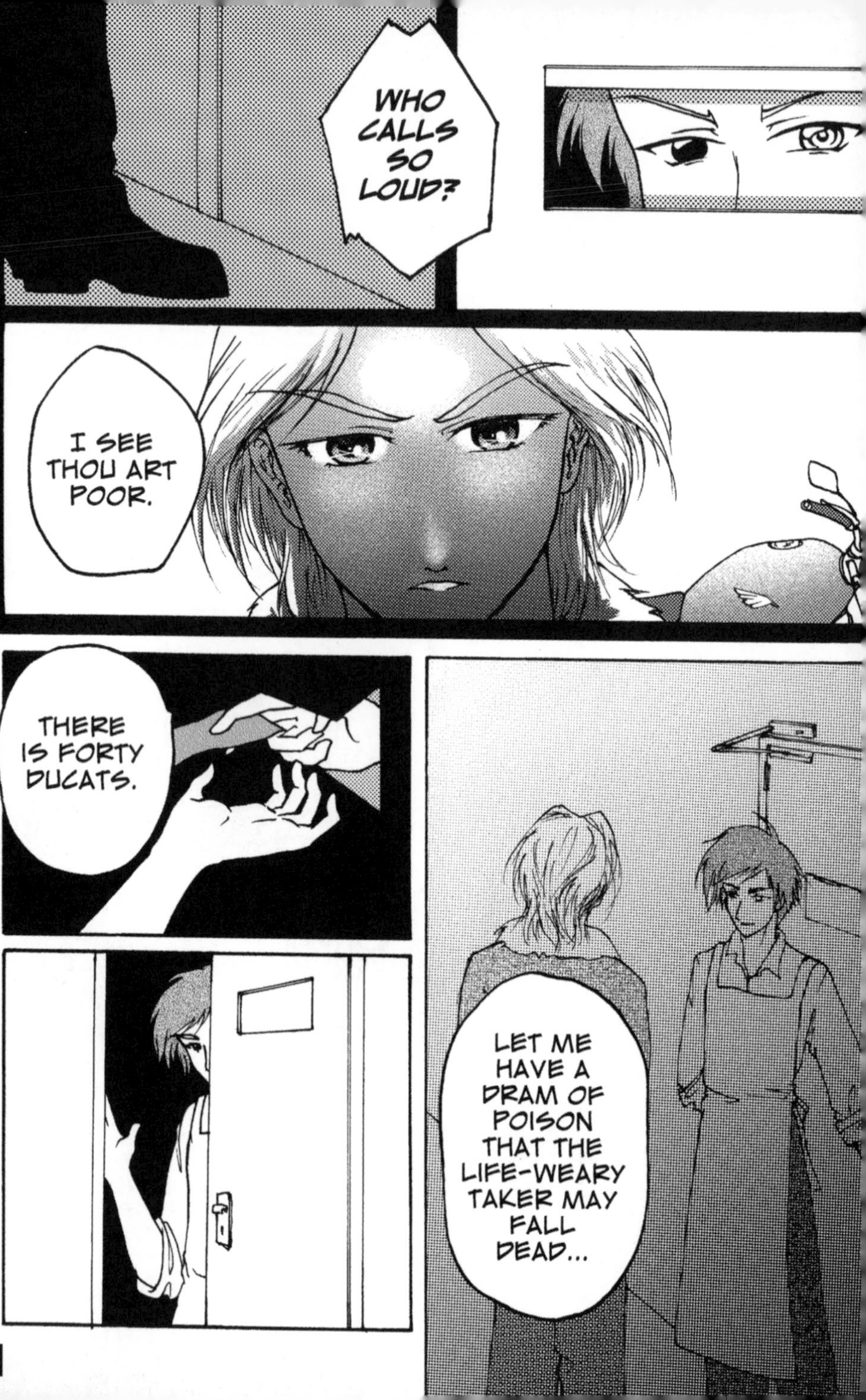
WHO CALLS SO LOUD?
I SEE THOU ART POOR.
THERE IS FORTY DUCATS.
LET ME HAVE A DRAM OF POISON THAT THE LIFE-WEARY TAKER MAY FALL DEAD...

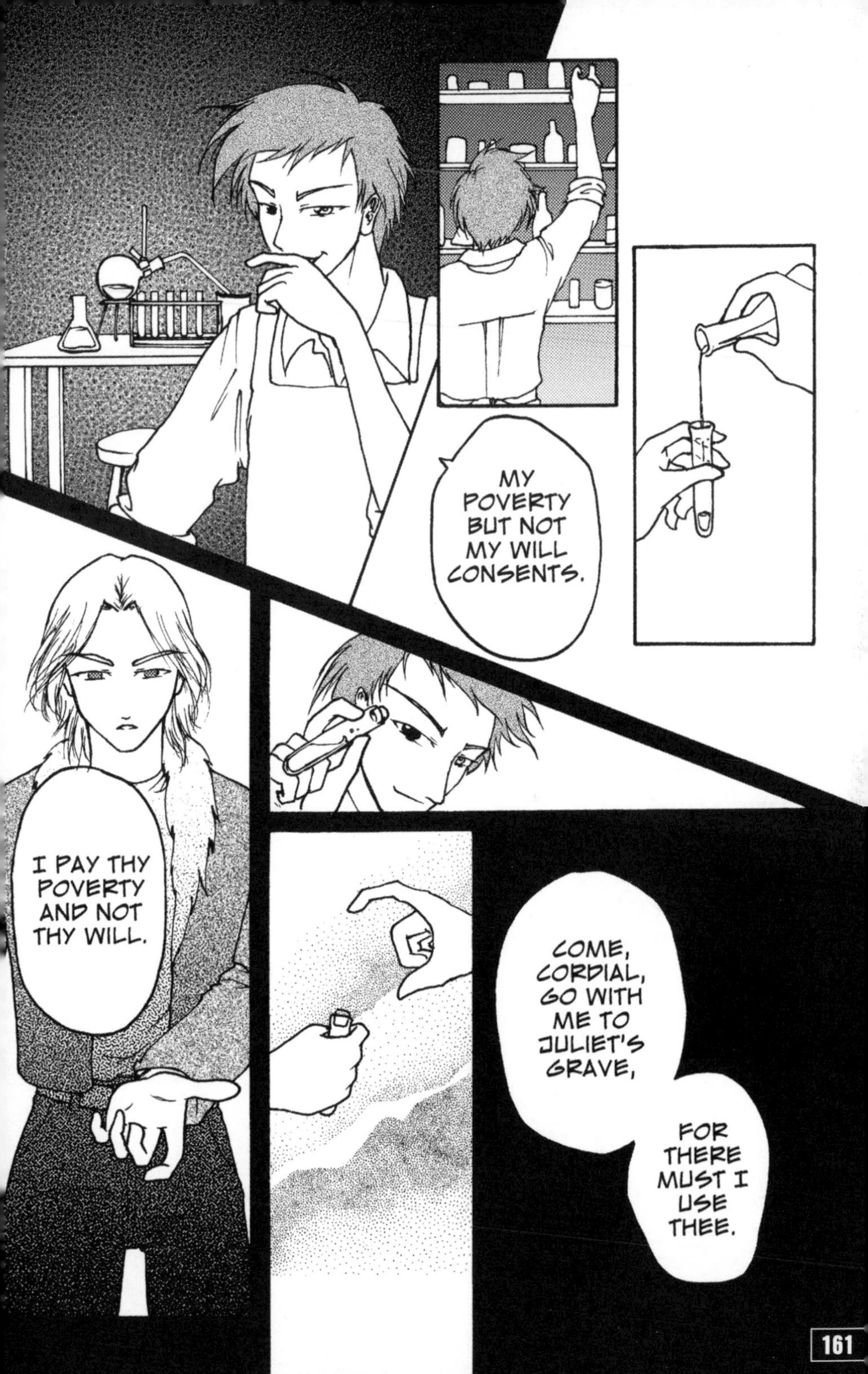

MY POVERTY BUT NOT MY WILL CONSENTS.
I PAY THY POVERTY AND NOT THY WILL.
COME, CORDIAL, GO WITH ME TO JULIET'S GRAVE,
FOR THERE MUST I USE THEE.

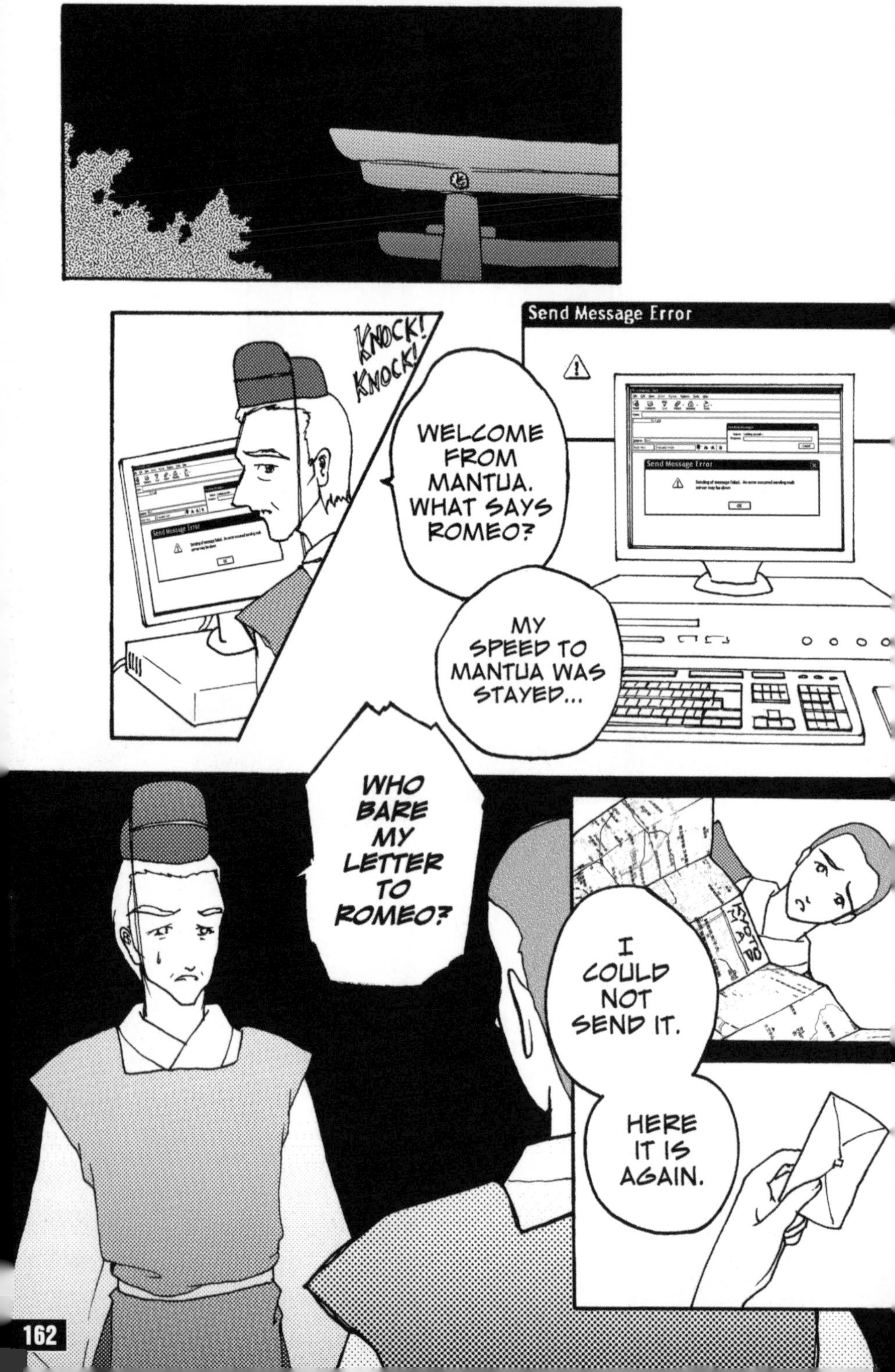
KNOCK! KNOCK!
Send Message Error
WELCOME FROM MANTUA. WHAT SAYS ROMEO?
MY SPEED TO MANTUA WAS STAYED...
WHO BARE MY LETTER TO ROMEO?
I COULD NOT SEND IT.
HERE IT IS AGAIN.

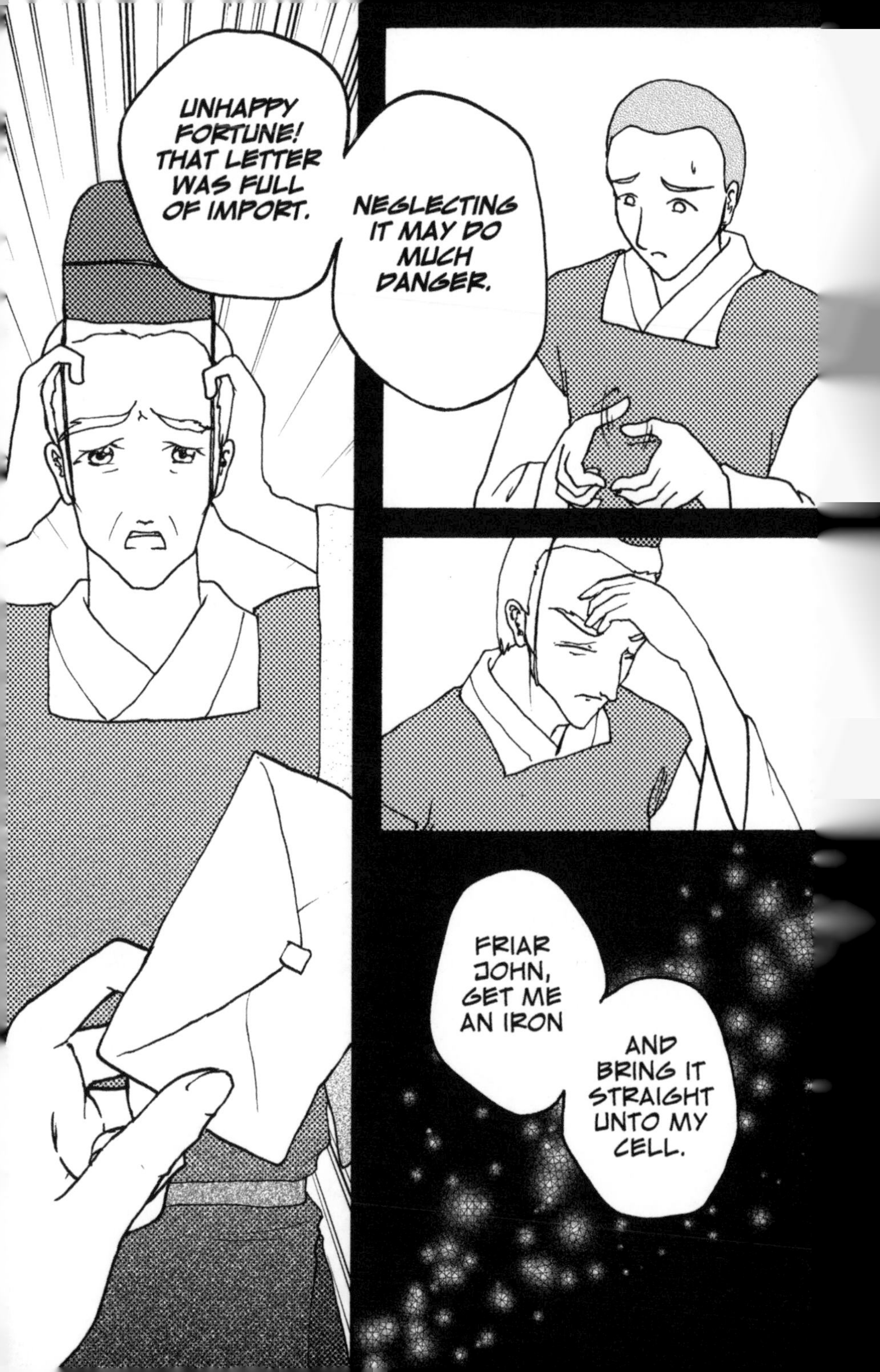
UNHAPPY FORTUNE! THAT LETTER WAS FULL OF IMPORT.
NEGLECTING IT MAY DO MUCH DANGER.
FRIAR JOHN, GET ME AN IRON
AND BRING IT STRAIGHT UNTO MY CELL.

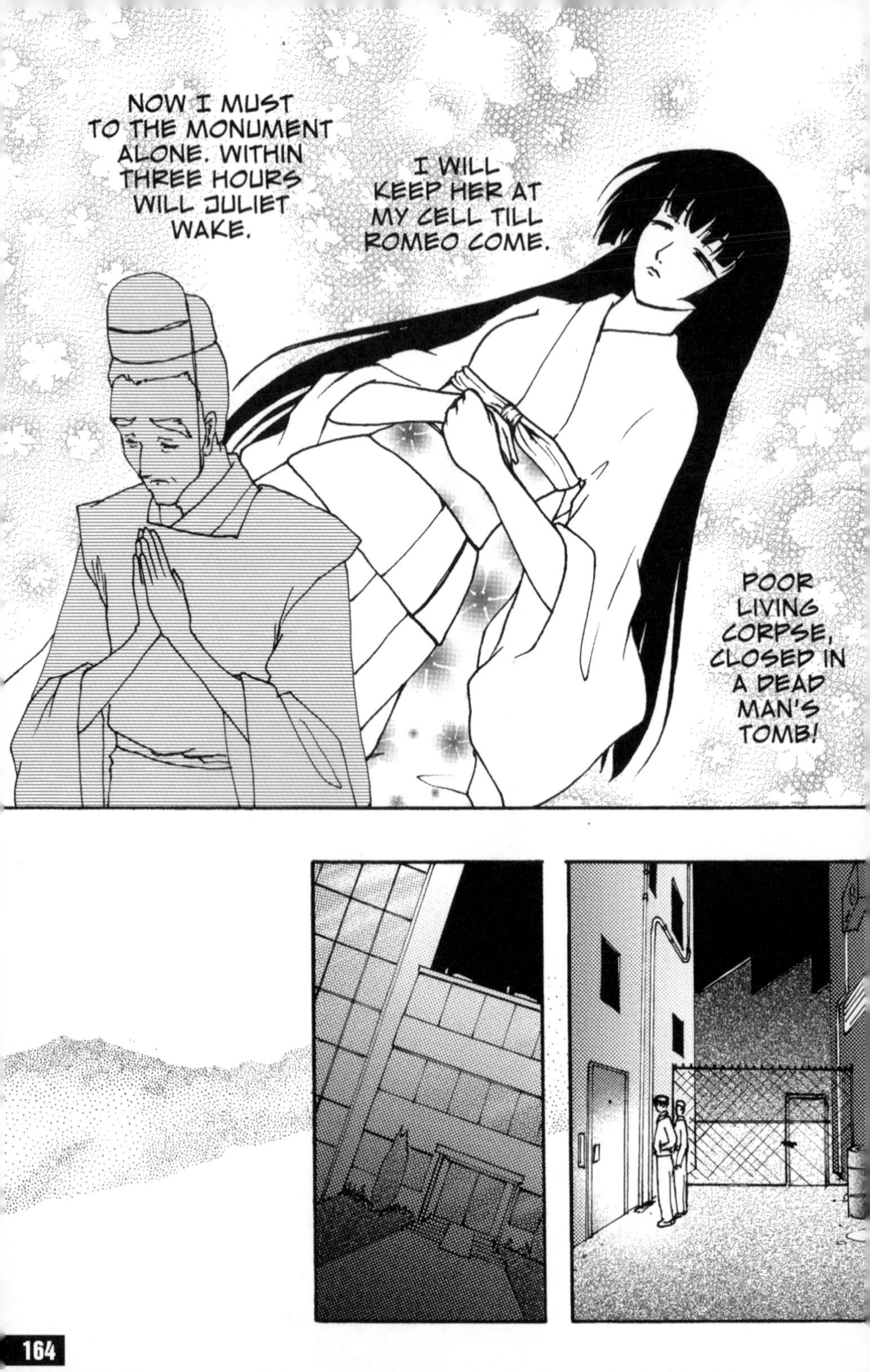
NOW I MUST TO THE MONUMENT ALONE. WITHIN THREE HOURS WILL JULIET WAKE.
I WILL KEEP HER AT MY CELL TILL ROMEO COME.
POOR LIVING CORPSE, CLOSED IN A DEAD MAN'S TOMB!

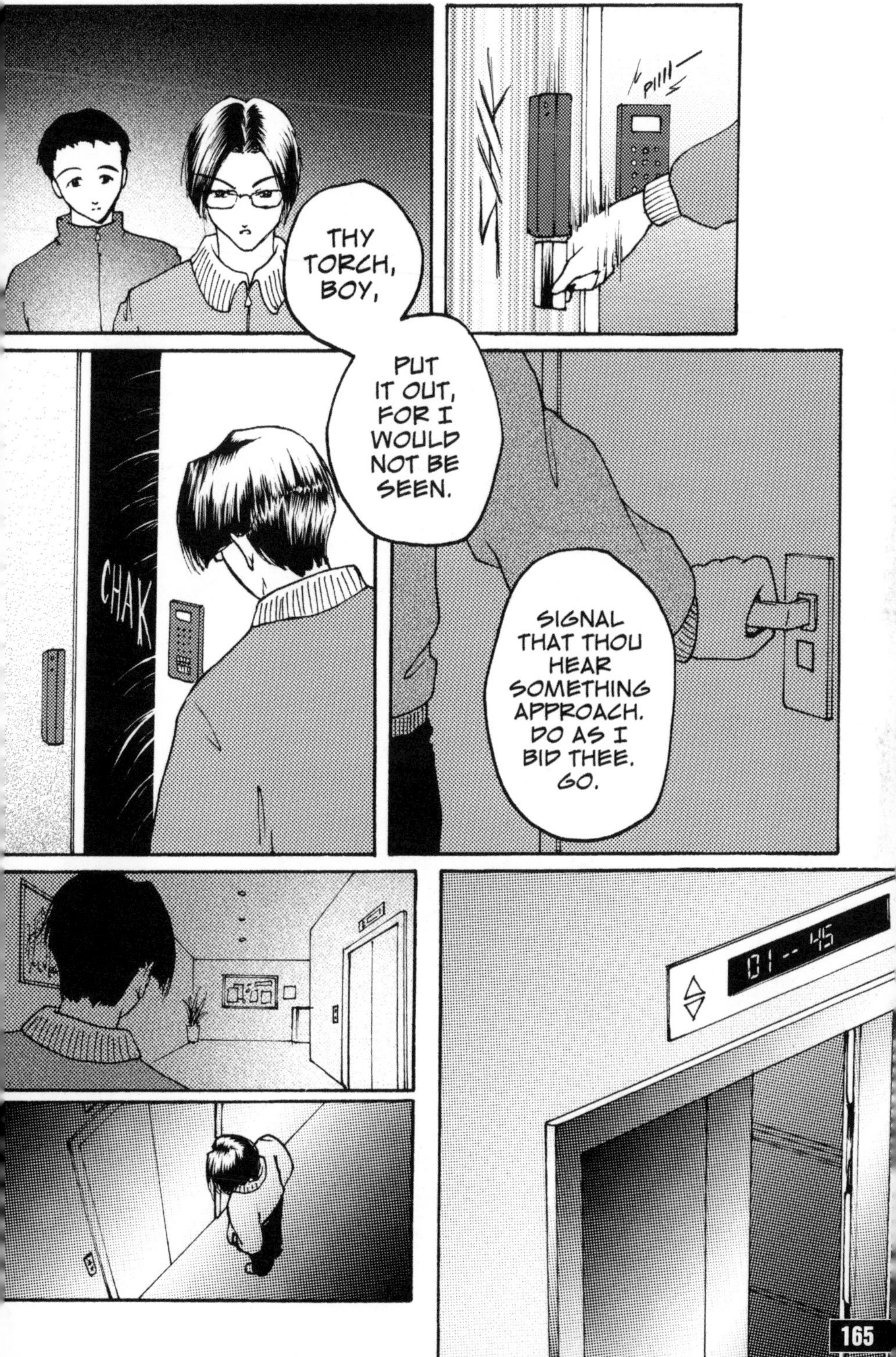
PIIII—
THY TORCH, BOY,
PUT IT OUT, FOR I WOULD NOT BE SEEN.
CHAK
SIGNAL THAT THOU HEAR SOMETHING APPROACH. DO AS I BID THEE. GO.
01 -- 45

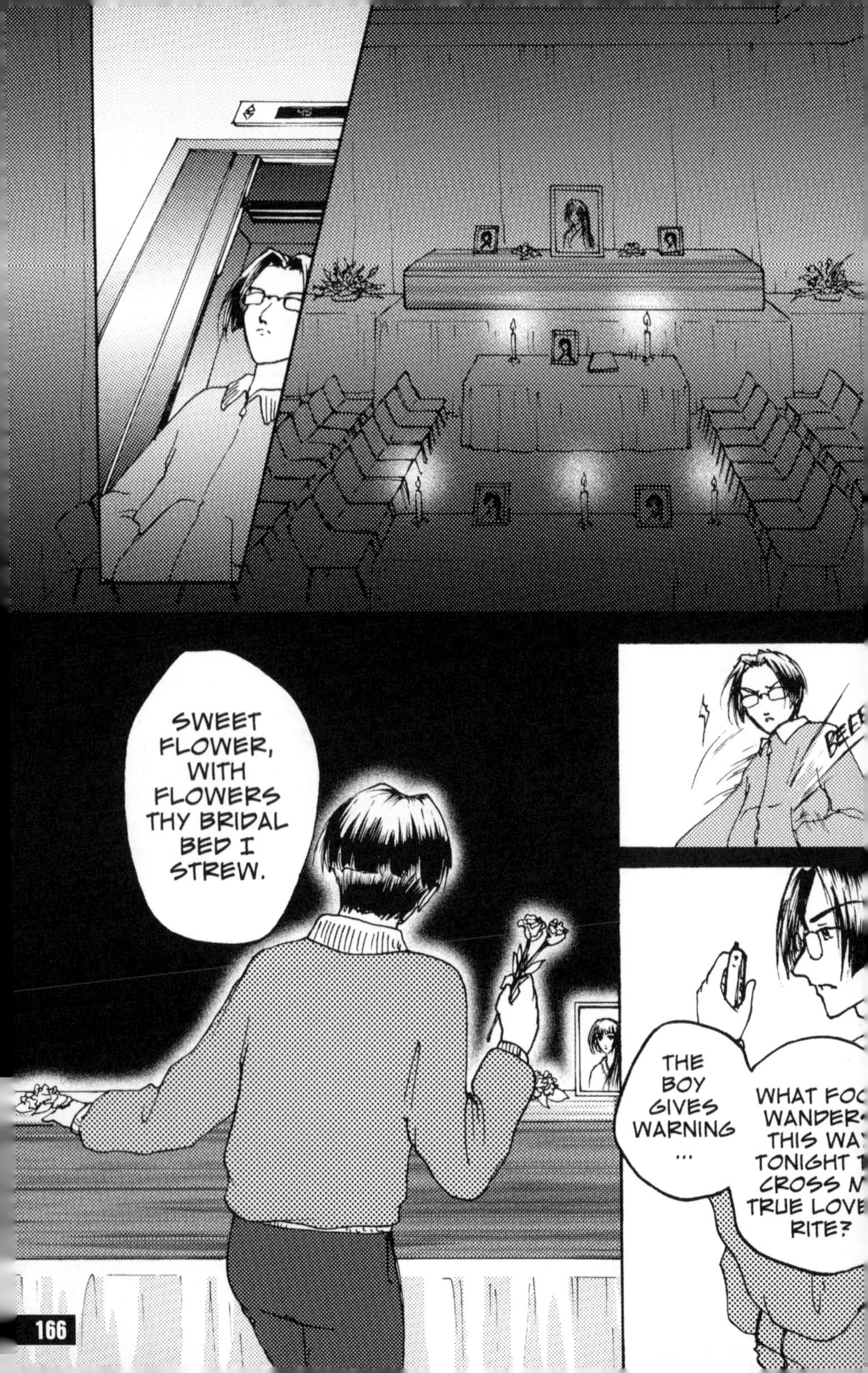
SWEET FLOWER, WITH FLOWERS THY BRIDAL BED I STREW.
THE BOY GIVES WARNING ...
WHAT FOO WANDER THIS WA TONIGHT CROSS M TRUE LOVE RITE?

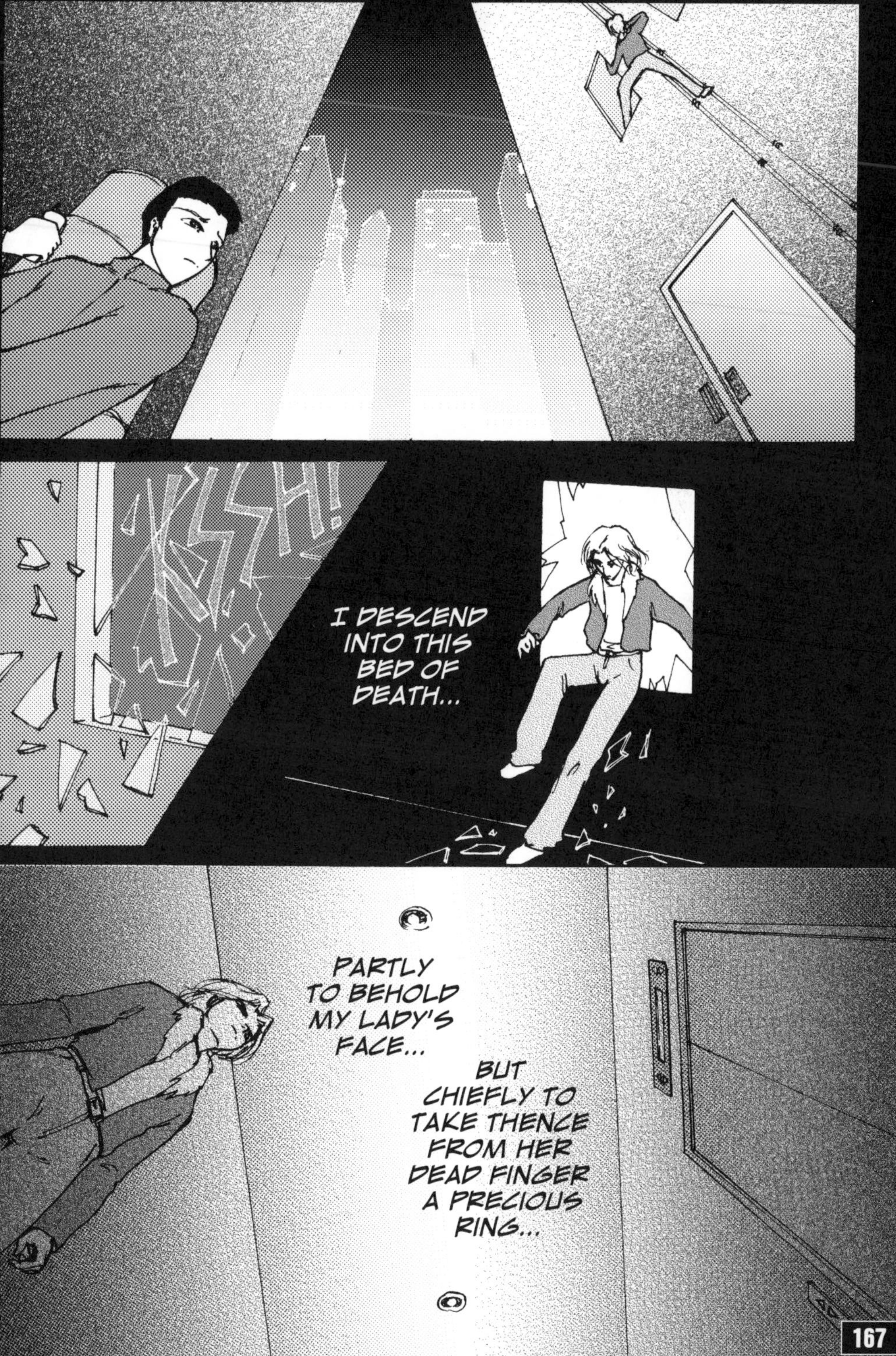
KSSH!
I DESCEND INTO THIS BED OF DEATH...
PARTLY TO BEHOLD MY LADY'S FACE...
BUT CHIEFLY TO TAKE THENCE FROM HER DEAD FINGER A PRECIOUS RING...

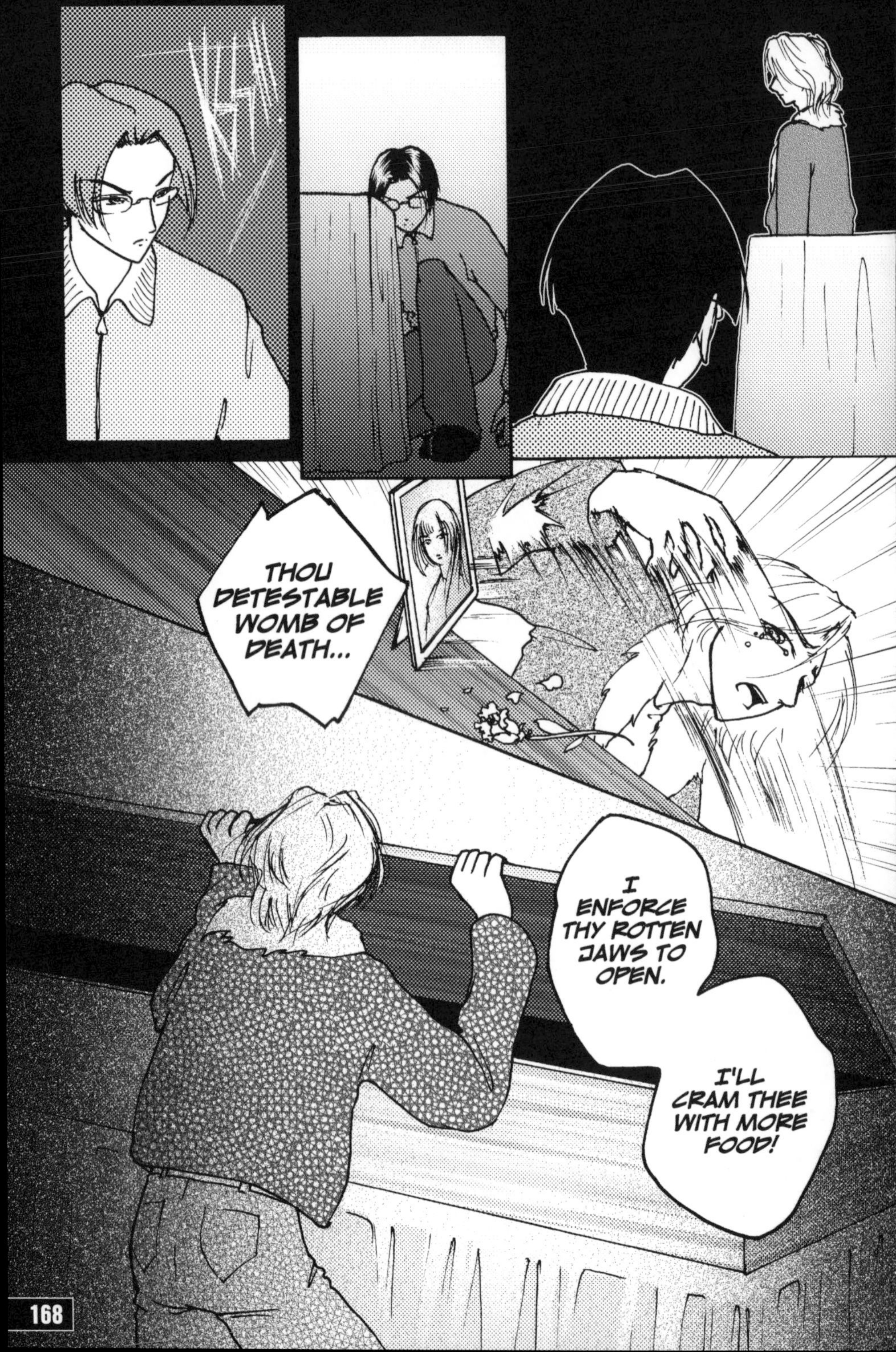

KSH!!
THOU DETESTABLE WOMB OF DEATH...
I ENFORCE THY ROTTEN JAWS TO OPEN.
I'LL CRAM THEE WITH MORE FOOD!

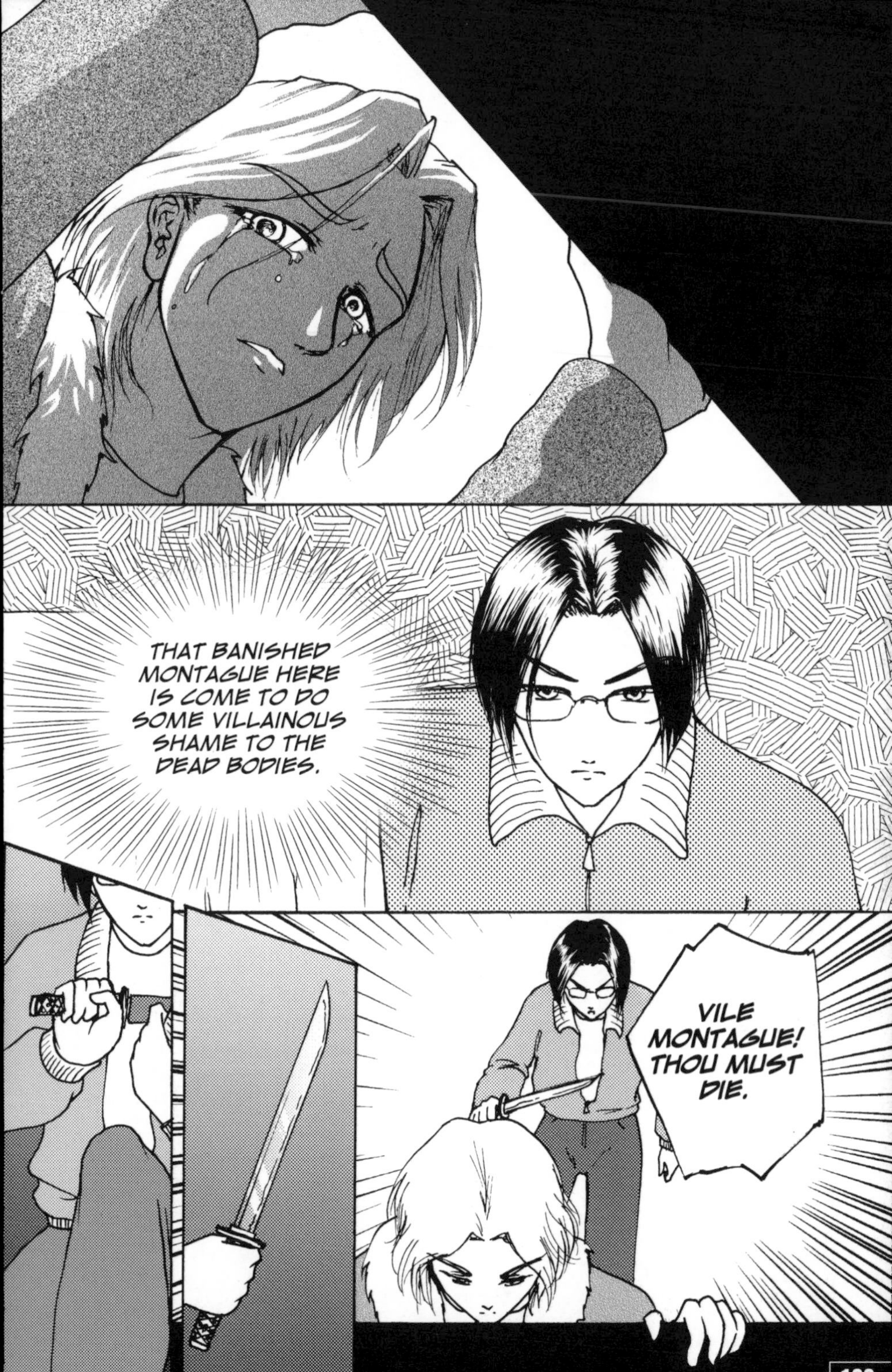
THAT BANISHED MONTAGUE HERE IS COME TO DO SOME VILLAINOUS SHAME TO THE DEAD BODIES.
VILE MONTAGUE! THOU MUST DIE.

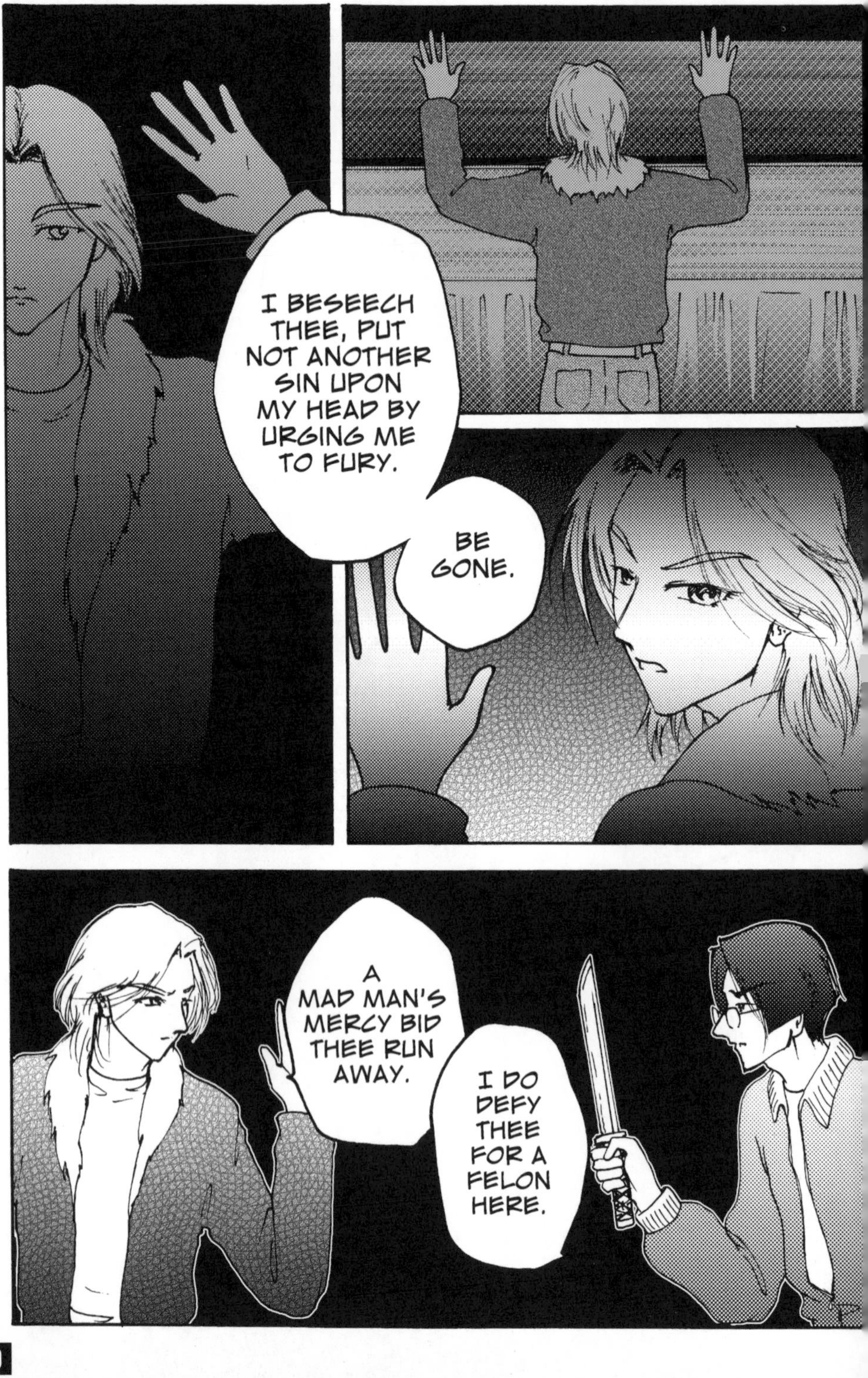
I BESEECH THEE, PUT NOT ANOTHER SIN UPON MY HEAD BY URGING ME TO FURY.
BE GONE.
A MAD MAN'S MERCY BID THEE RUN AWAY.
I DO DEFY THEE FOR A FELON HERE.

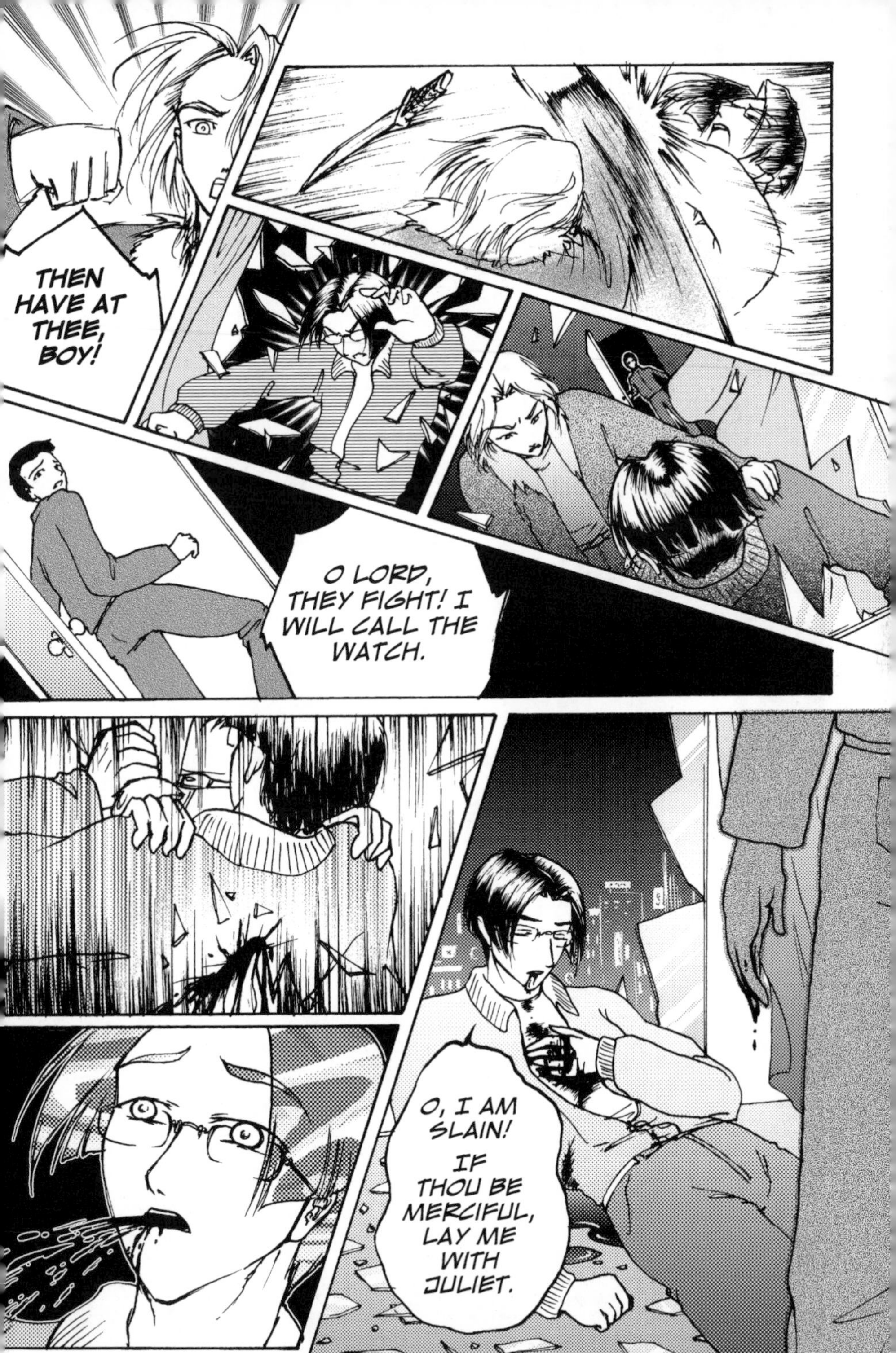
THEN HAVE AT THEE, BOY!
O LORD, THEY FIGHT! I WILL CALL THE WATCH.
O, I AM SLAIN!
IF THOU BE MERCIFUL, LAY ME WITH JULIET.

LET ME PERUSE THIS FACE.

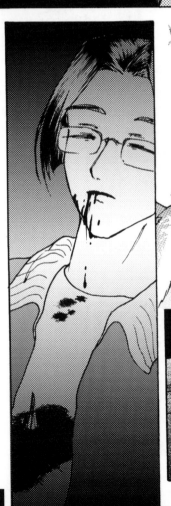

MERCUTIO'S KINSMAN, NOBLE PARIS!

HE SHOULD HAVE MARRIED JULIET. SAID HE NOT SO?

OR DID I DREAM IT SO?

OR AM I MAD TO THINK IT WAS SO?

O, GIVE ME THY HAND...

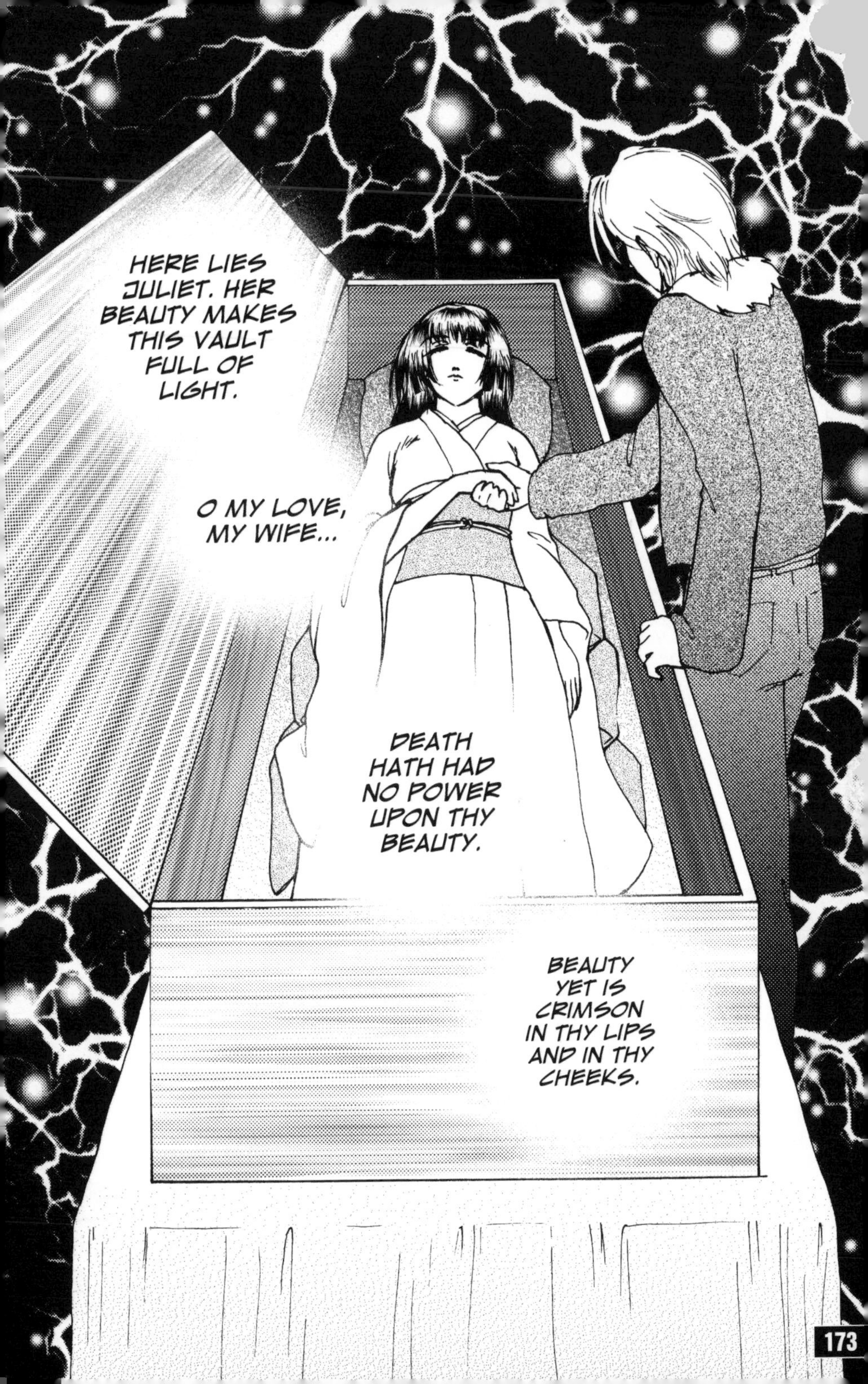
HERE LIES JULIET. HER BEAUTY MAKES THIS VAULT FULL OF LIGHT.
O MY LOVE, MY WIFE...
DEATH HATH HAD NO POWER UPON THY BEAUTY.
BEAUTY YET IS CRIMSON IN THY LIPS AND IN THY CHEEKS.

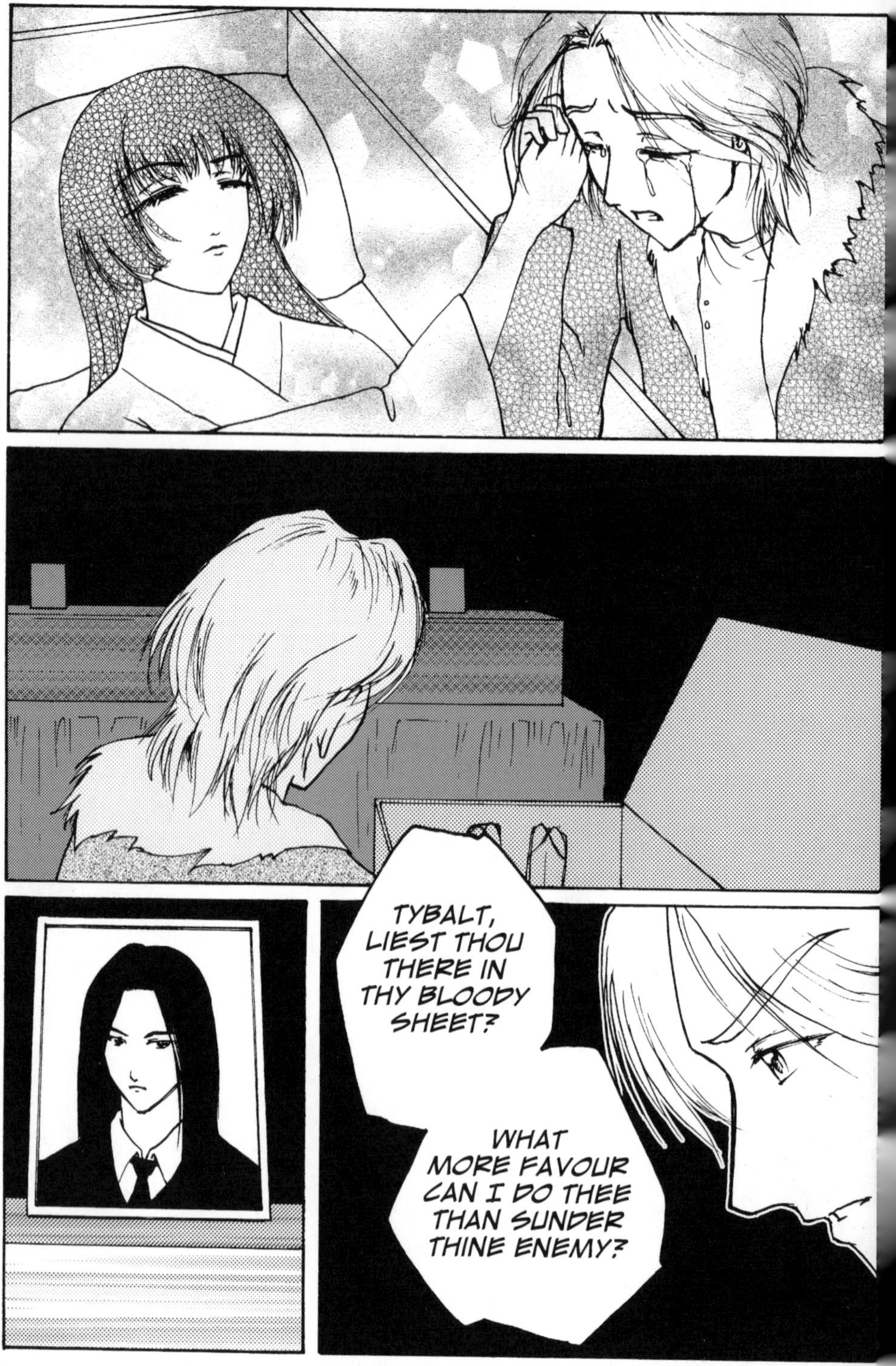
TYBALT, LIEST THOU THERE IN THY BLOODY SHEET?
WHAT MORE FAVOUR CAN I DO THEE THAN SUNDER THINE ENEMY?

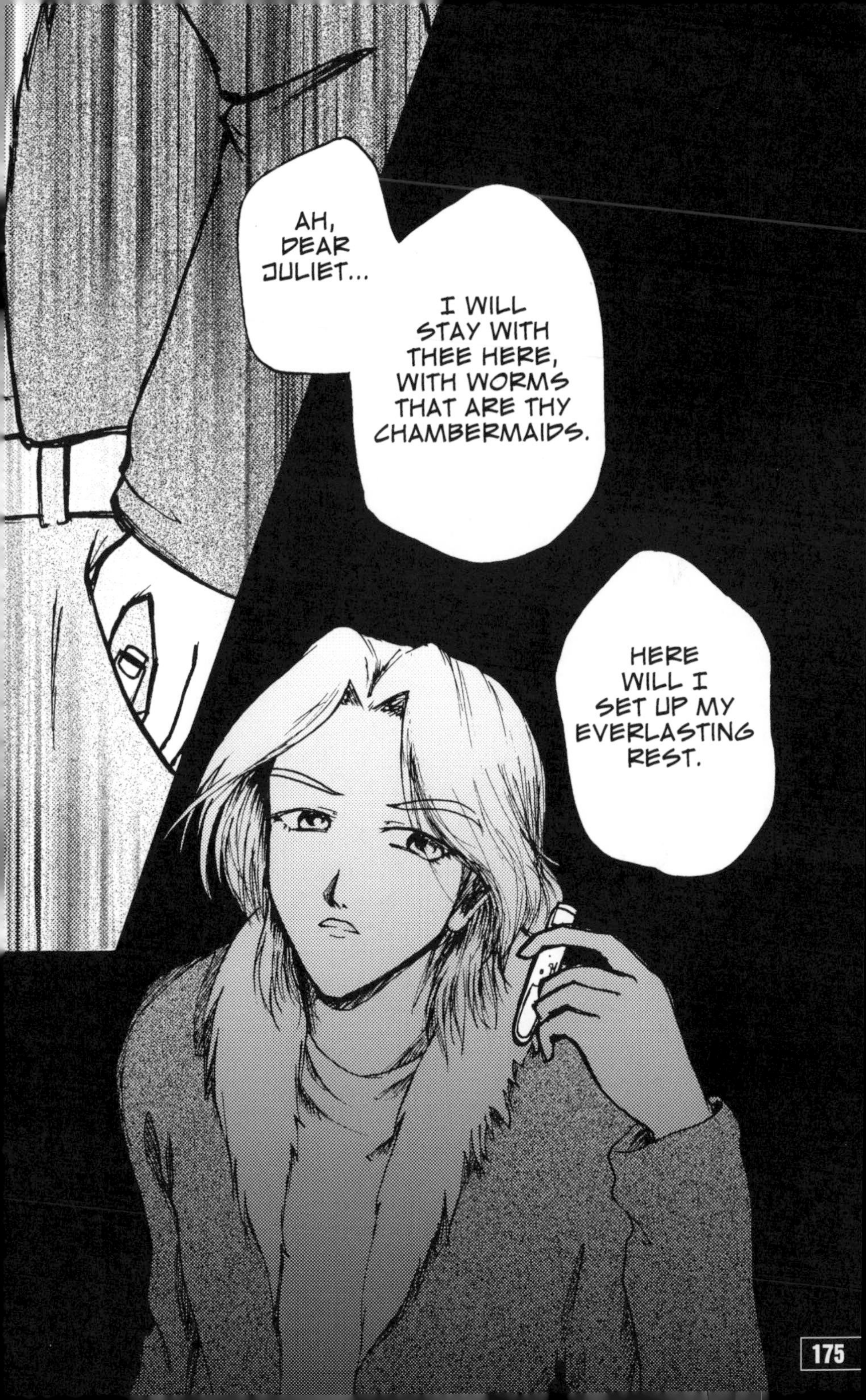
AH, DEAR JULIET...
I WILL STAY WITH THEE HERE, WITH WORMS THAT ARE THY CHAMBERMAIDS.
HERE WILL I SET UP MY EVERLASTING REST.

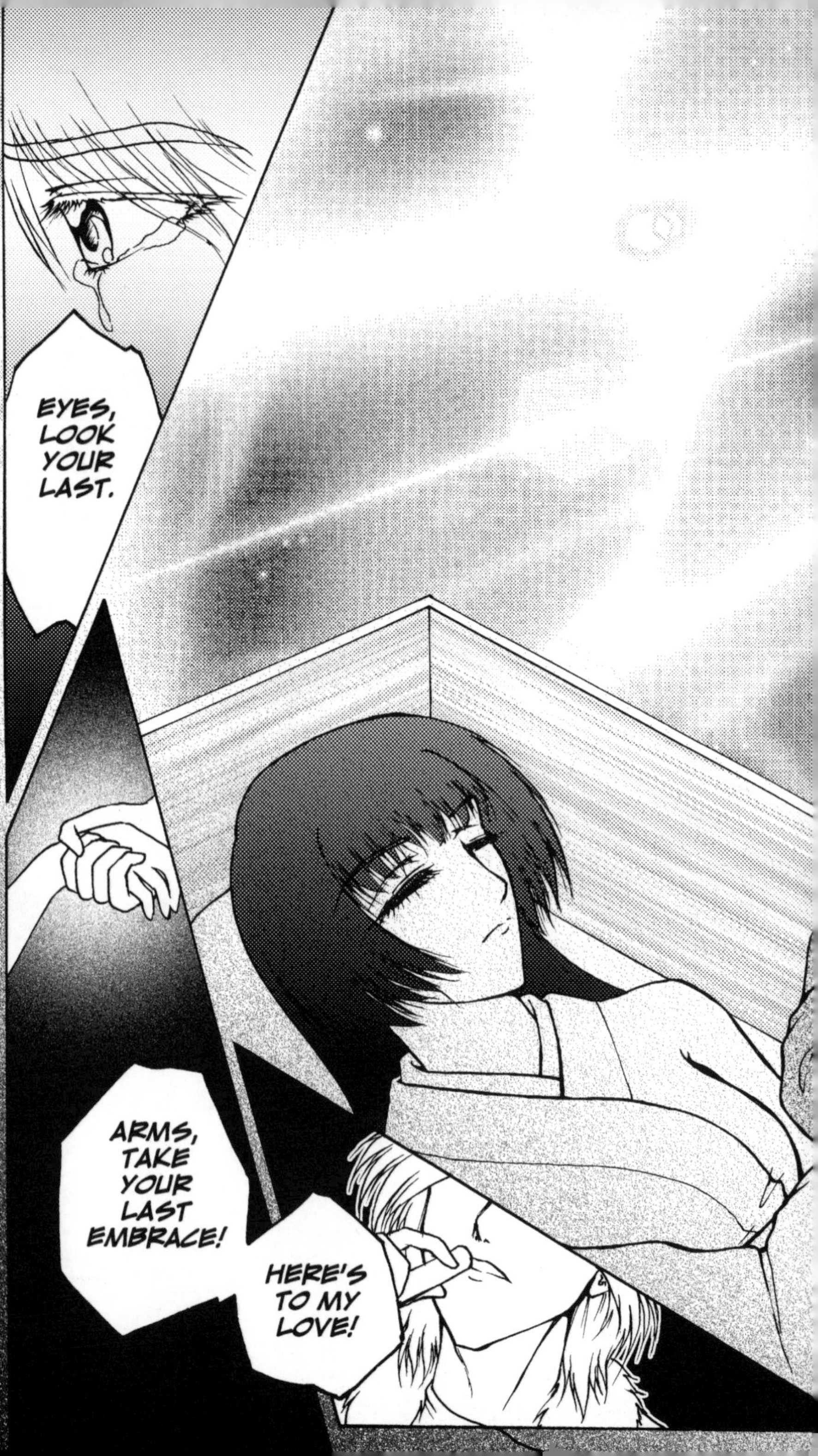
EYES, LOOK YOUR LAST.
ARMS, TAKE YOUR LAST EMBRACE!
HERE'S TO MY LOVE!

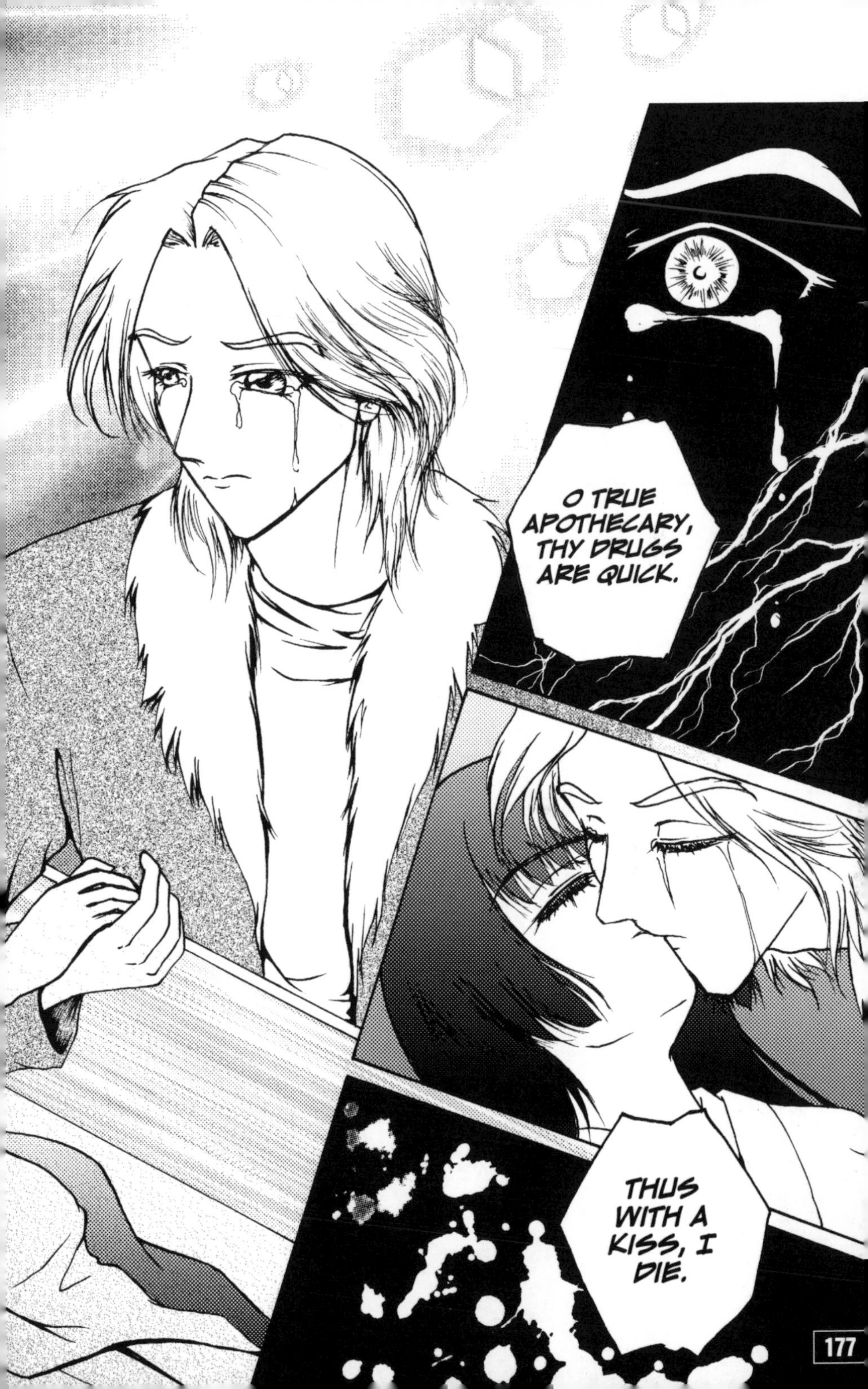
O TRUE APOTHECARY, THY DRUGS ARE QUICK.
THUS WITH A KISS, I DIE.

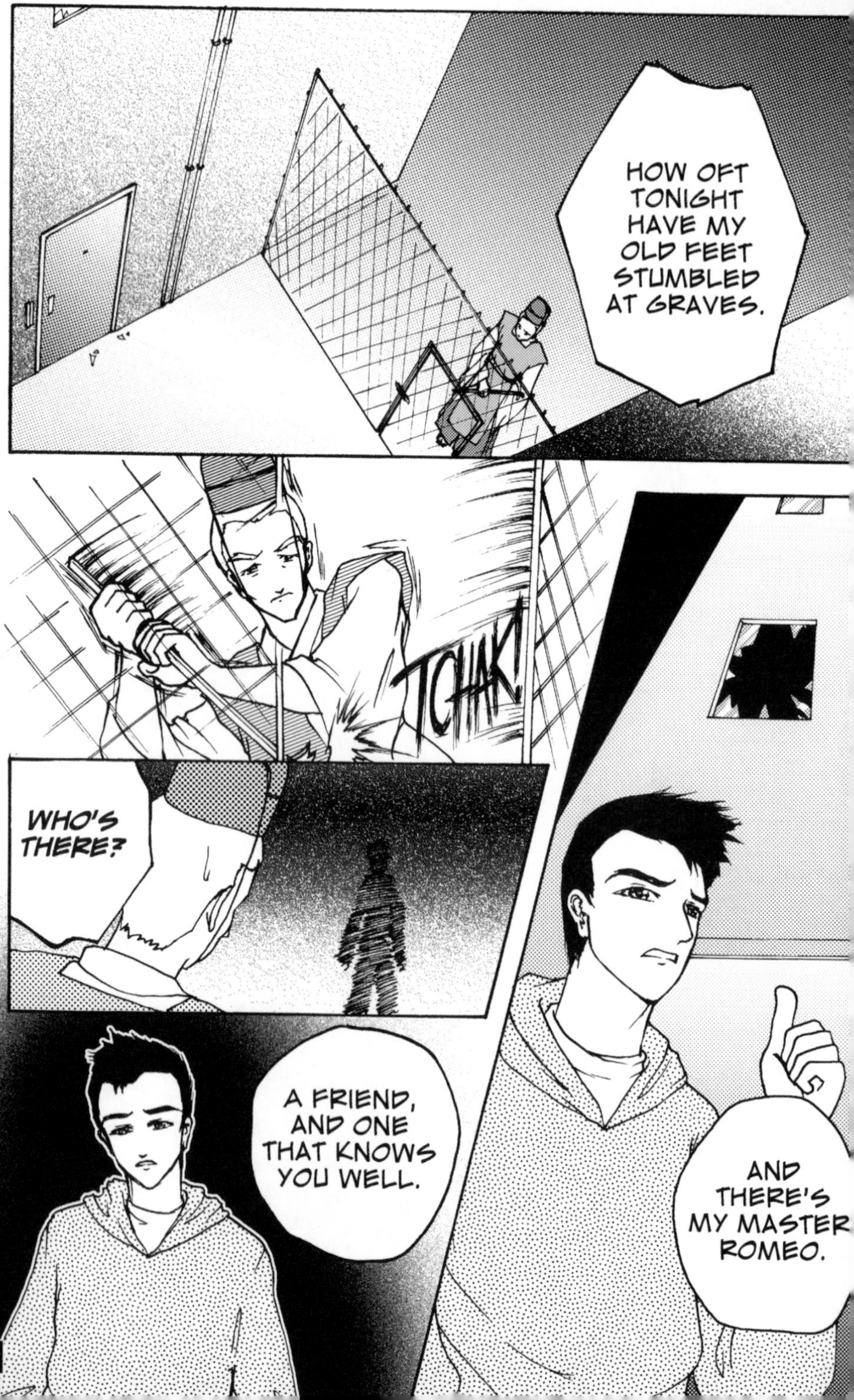
HOW OFT TONIGHT HAVE MY OLD FEET STUMBLED AT GRAVES.
TCHAK!
WHO'S THERE?
A FRIEND, AND ONE THAT KNOWS YOU WELL.
AND THERE'S MY MASTER ROMEO.

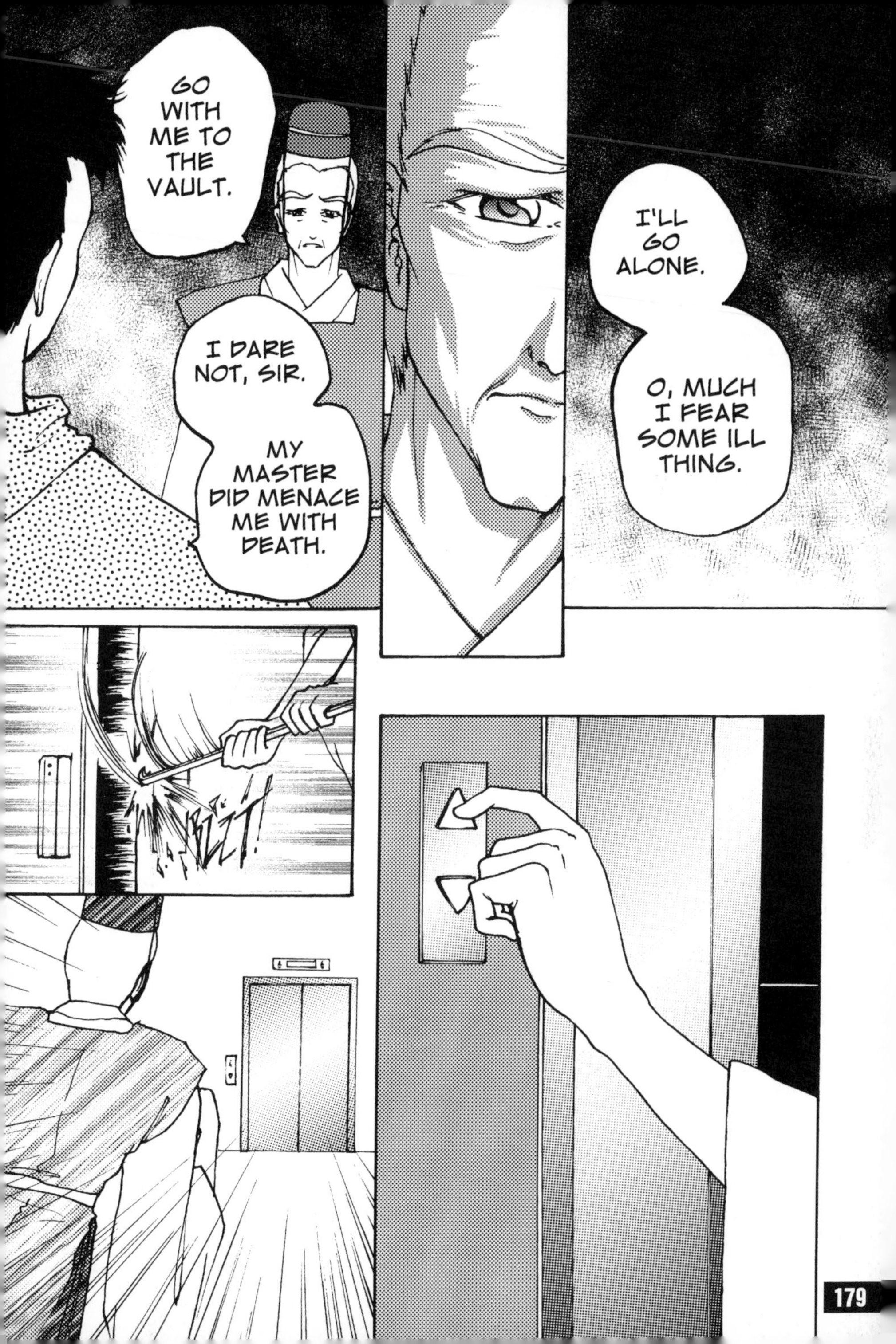
GO WITH ME TO THE VAULT.
I DARE NOT, SIR.
MY MASTER DID MENACE ME WITH DEATH.
I'LL GO ALONE.
O, MUCH I FEAR SOME ILL THING.

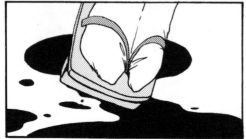

WHAT BLOOD IS THIS?

ROMEO! O, PALE!

WHAT, PARIS TOO? AND STEEPED IN BLOOD?

THE LADY STIRS.

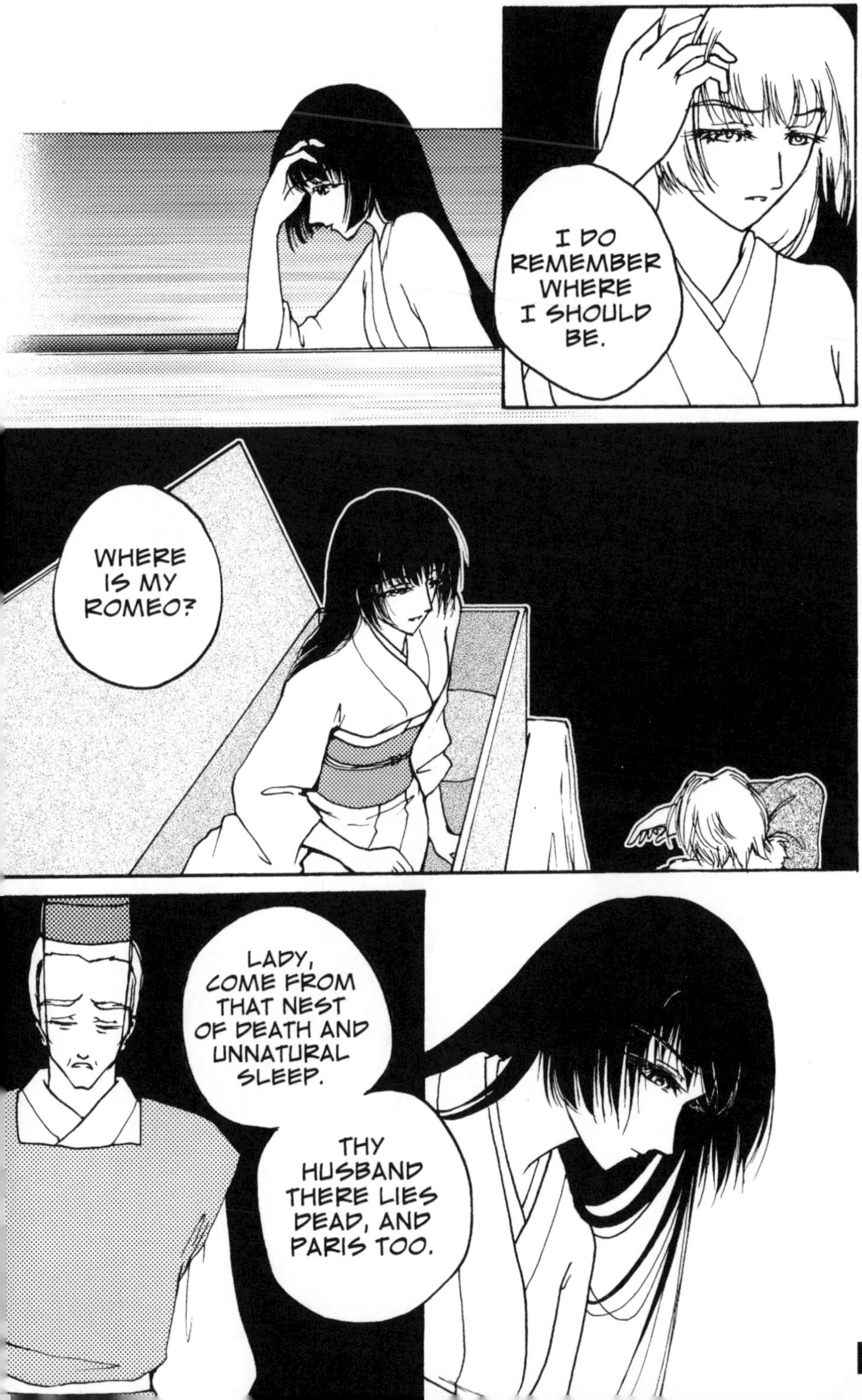
I DO REMEMBER WHERE I SHOULD BE.
WHERE IS MY ROMEO?
LADY, COME FROM THAT NEST OF DEATH AND UNNATURAL SLEEP.
THY HUSBAND THERE LIES DEAD, AND PARIS TOO.

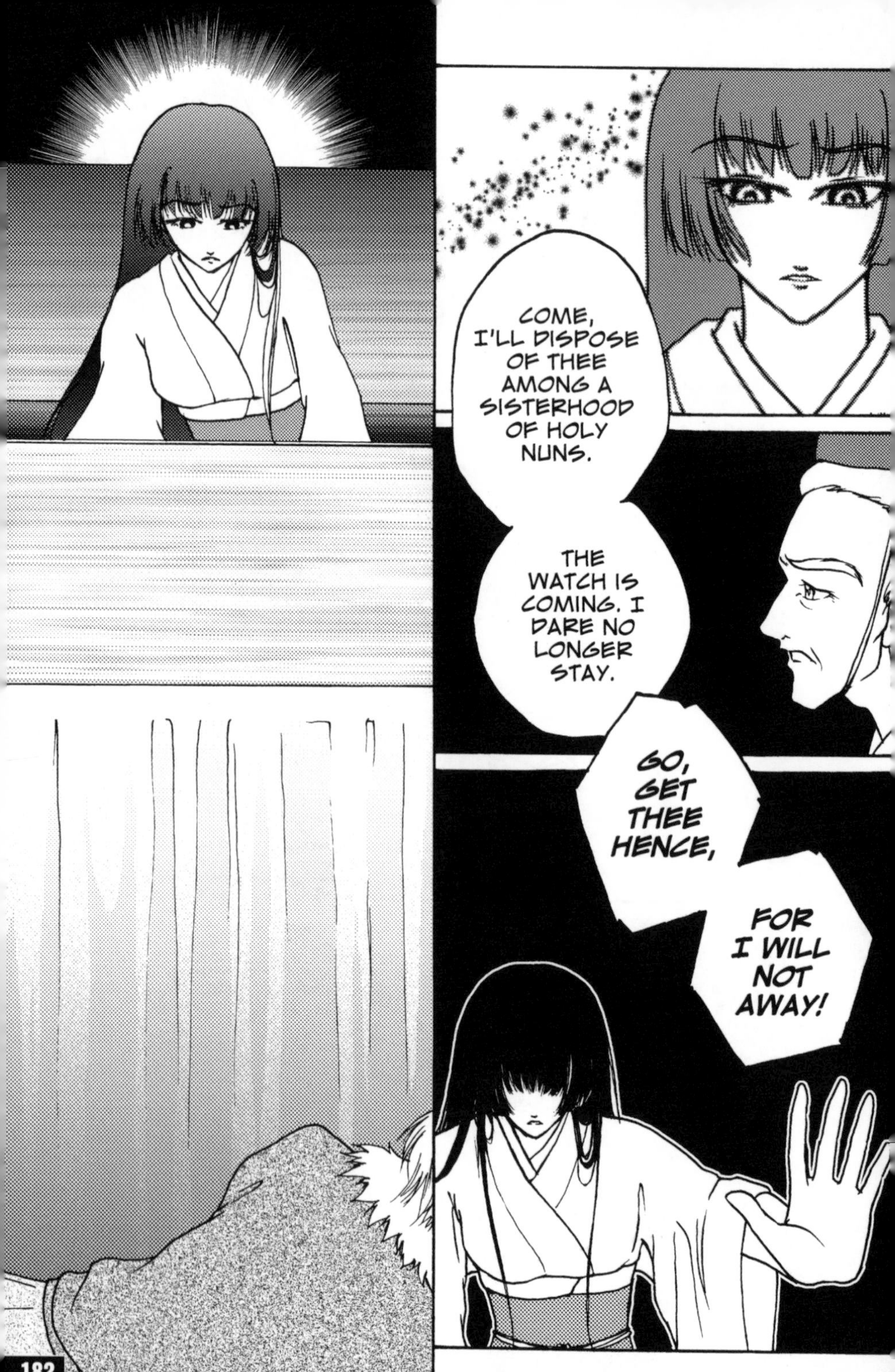
COME, I'LL DISPOSE OF THEE AMONG A SISTERHOOD OF HOLY NUNS.
THE WATCH IS COMING. I DARE NO LONGER STAY.
GO, GET THEE HENCE,
FOR I WILL NOT AWAY!

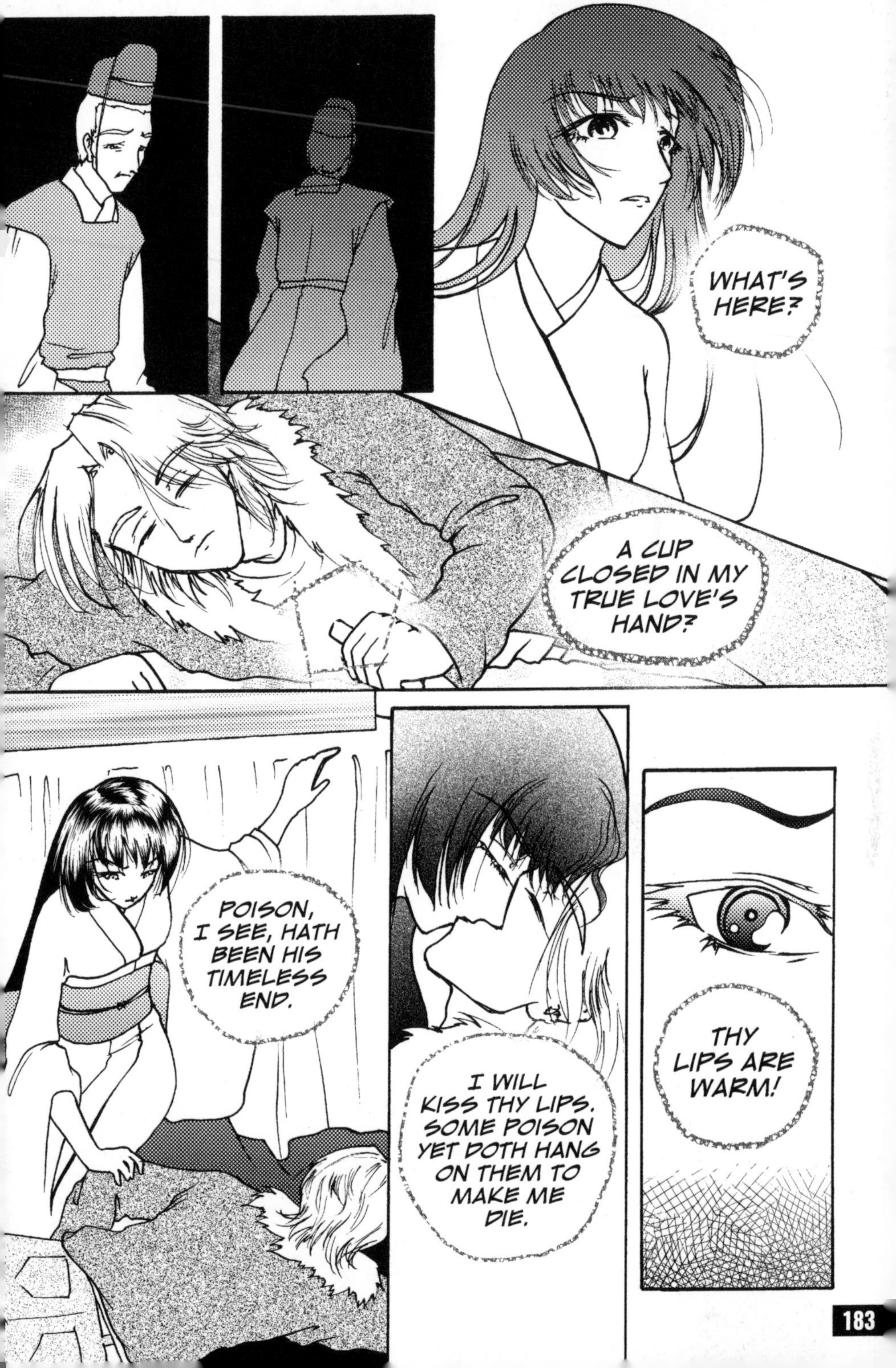
WHAT'S HERE?
A CUP CLOSED IN MY TRUE LOVE'S HAND?
POISON, I SEE, HATH BEEN HIS TIMELESS END.
I WILL KISS THY LIPS. SOME POISON YET DOTH HANG ON THEM TO MAKE ME DIE.
THY LIPS ARE WARM!

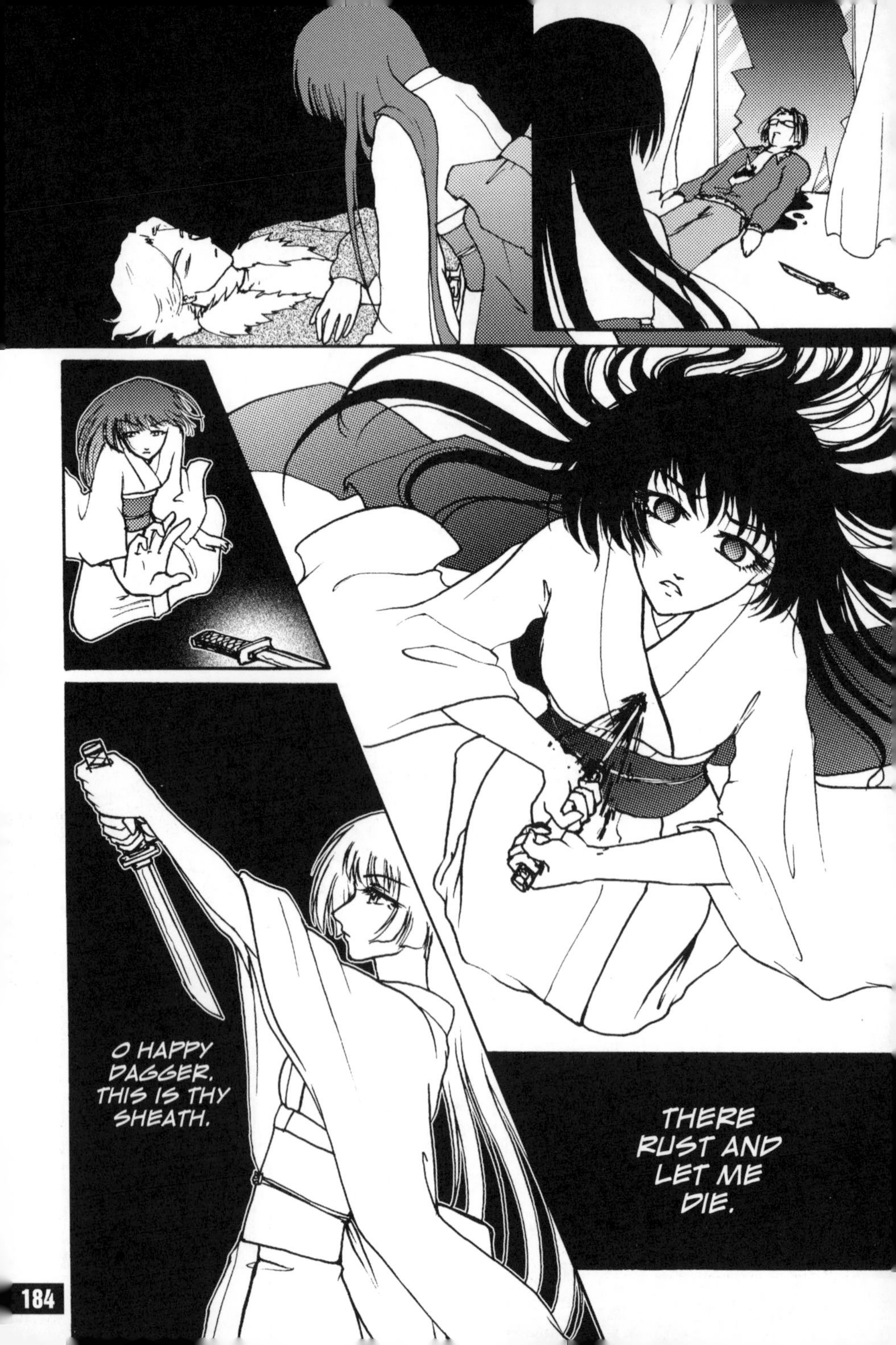
O HAPPY DAGGER. THIS IS THY SHEATH.
THERE RUST AND LET ME DIE.

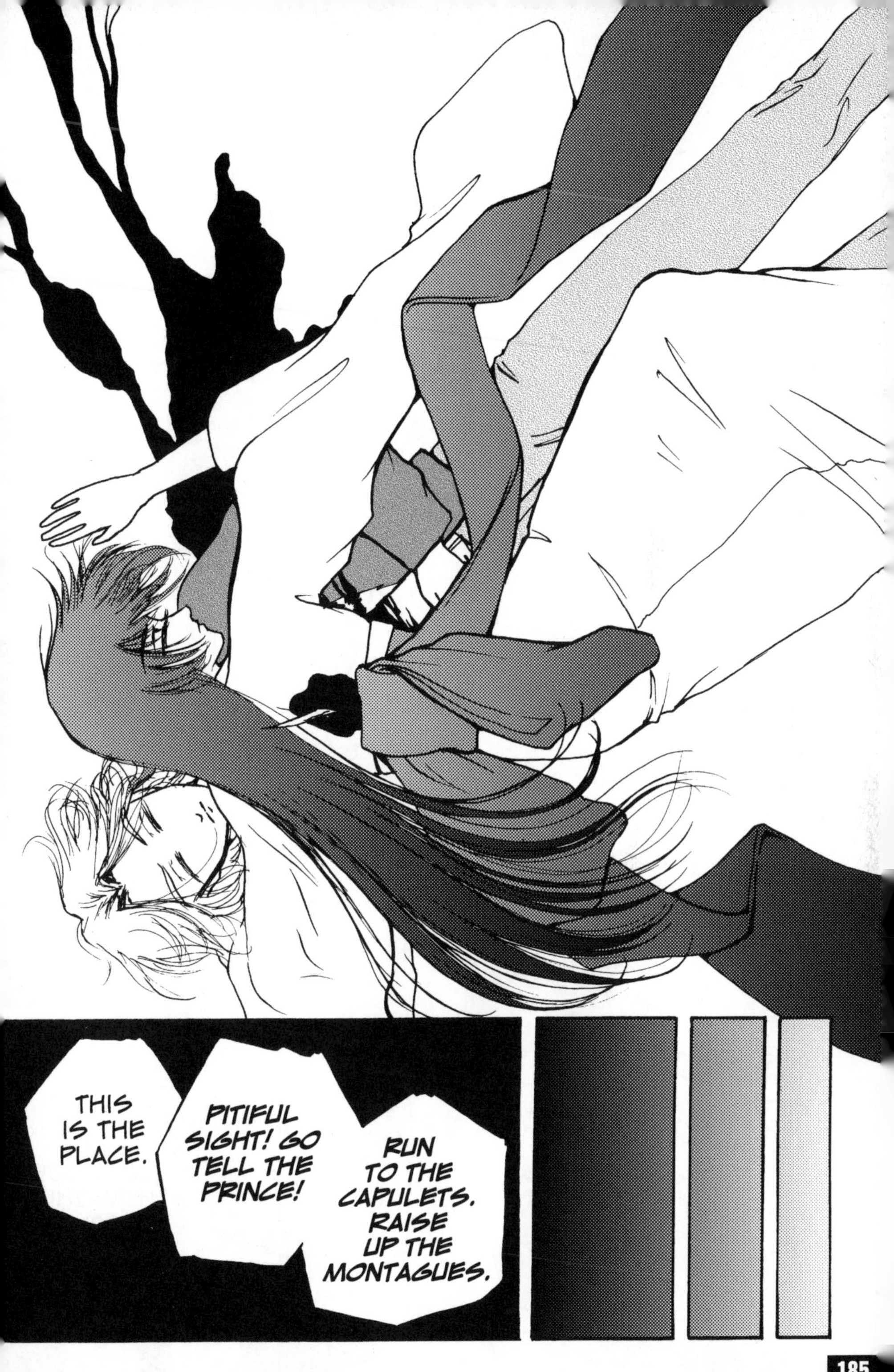
THIS IS THE PLACE.
PITIFUL SIGHT! GO TELL THE PRINCE!
RUN TO THE CAPULETS. RAISE UP THE MONTAGUES.

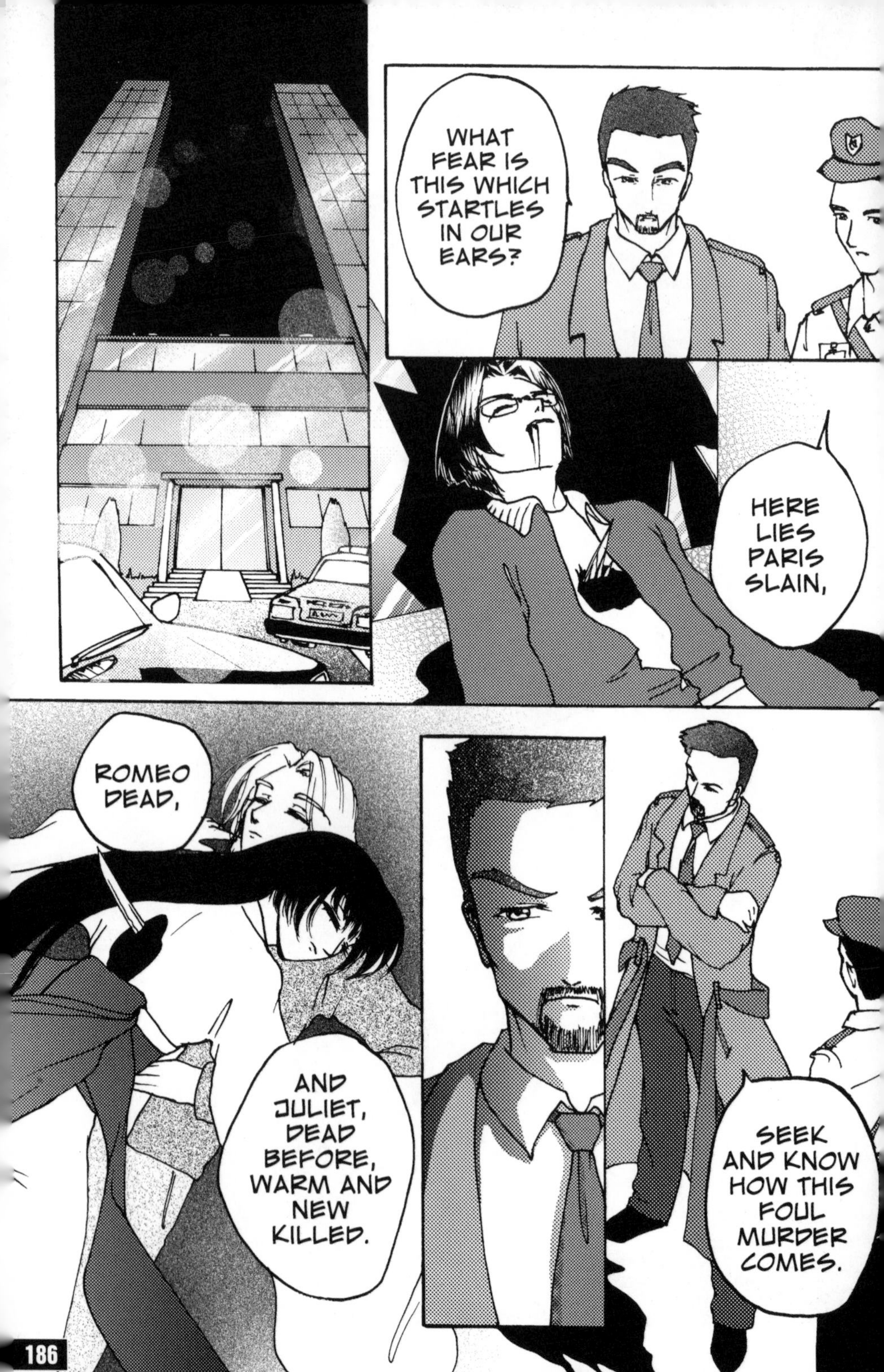
WHAT FEAR IS THIS WHICH STARTLES IN OUR EARS?
HERE LIES PARIS SLAIN,
ROMEO DEAD,
AND JULIET, DEAD BEFORE, WARM AND NEW KILLED.
SEEK AND KNOW HOW THIS FOUL MURDER COMES.

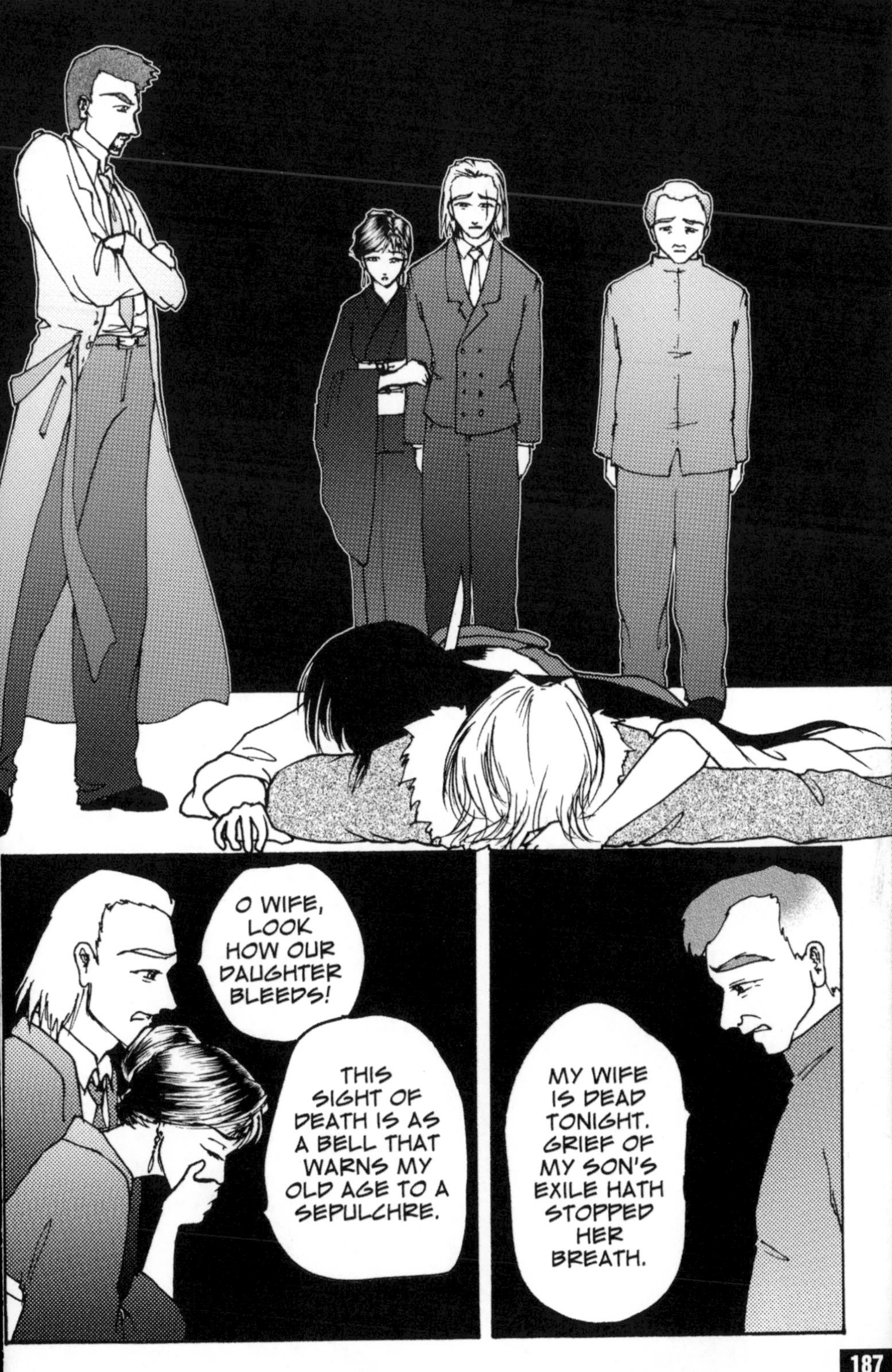
O WIFE, LOOK HOW OUR DAUGHTER BLEEDS!
THIS SIGHT OF DEATH IS AS A BELL THAT WARNS MY OLD AGE TO A SEPULCHRE.
MY WIFE IS DEAD TONIGHT. GRIEF OF MY SON'S EXILE HATH STOPPED HER BREATH.

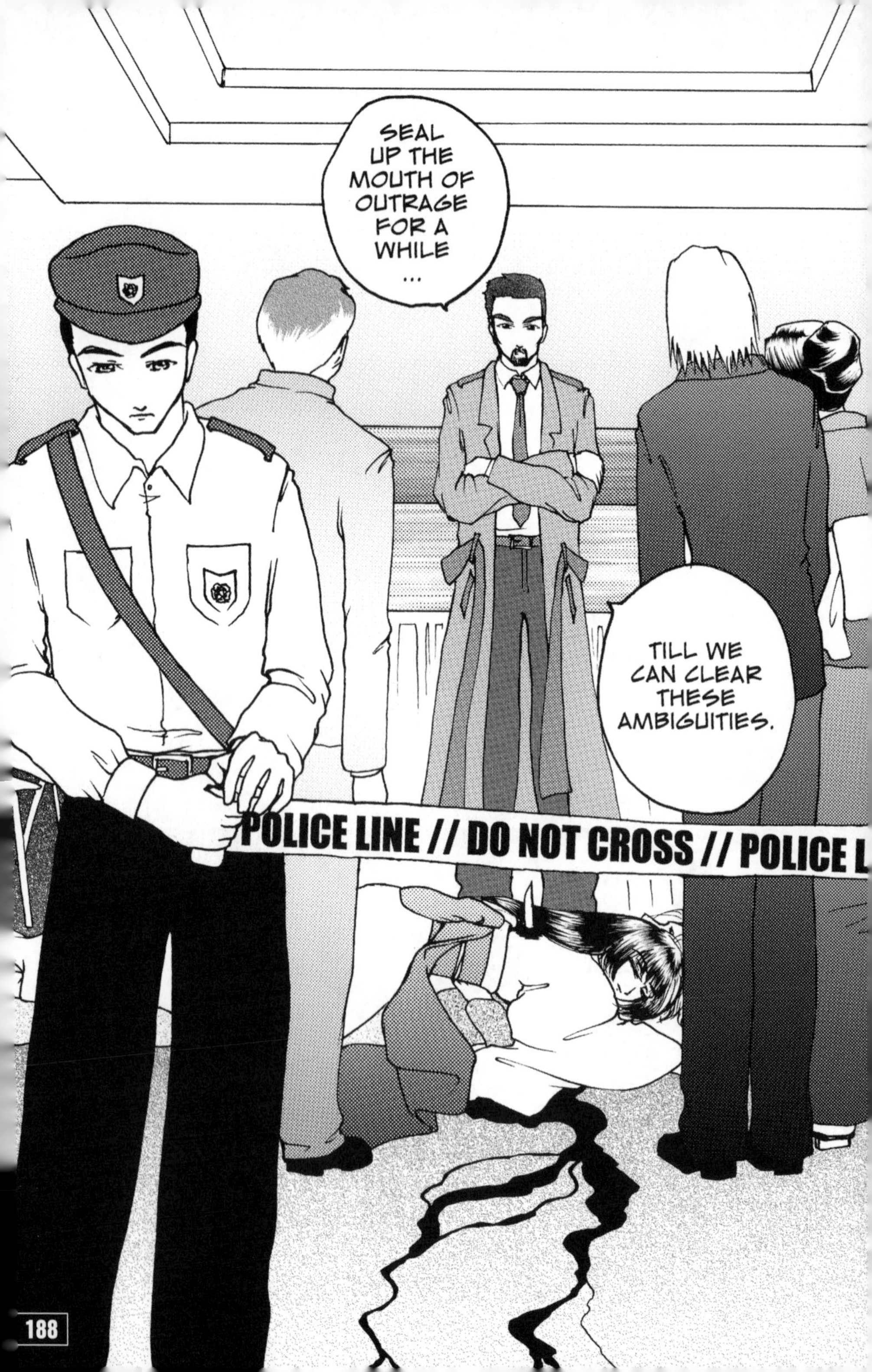
SEAL UP THE MOUTH OF OUTRAGE FOR A WHILE ...
TILL WE CAN CLEAR THESE AMBIGUITIES.
POLICE LINE // DO NOT CROSS // POLICE L

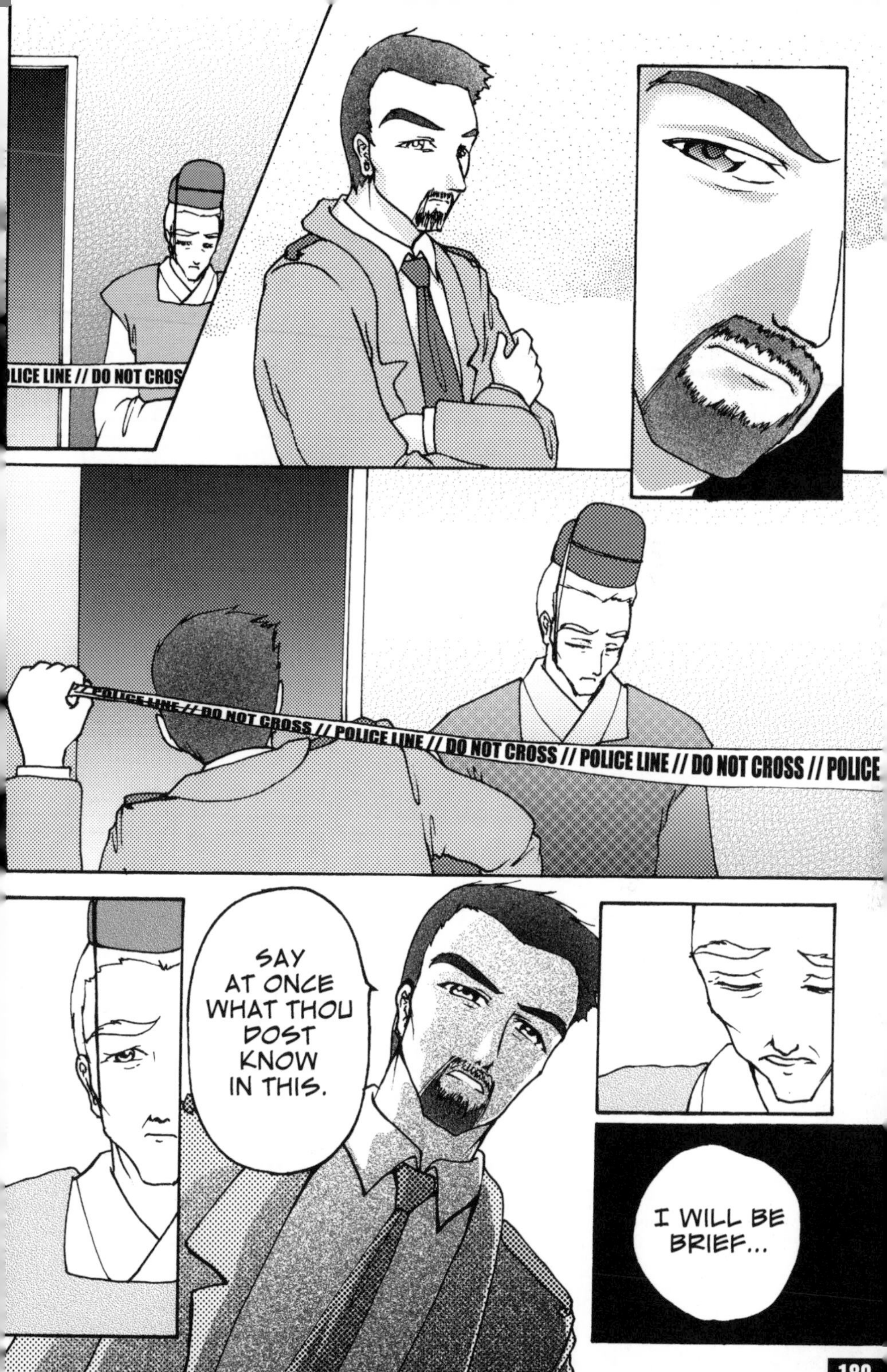
POLICE LINE // DO NOT CROS
POLICE LINE // DO NOT CROSS // POLICE LINE // DO NOT CROSS // POLICE LINE // DO NOT CROSS // POLICE
SAY AT ONCE WHAT THOU DOST KNOW IN THIS.
I WILL BE BRIEF...

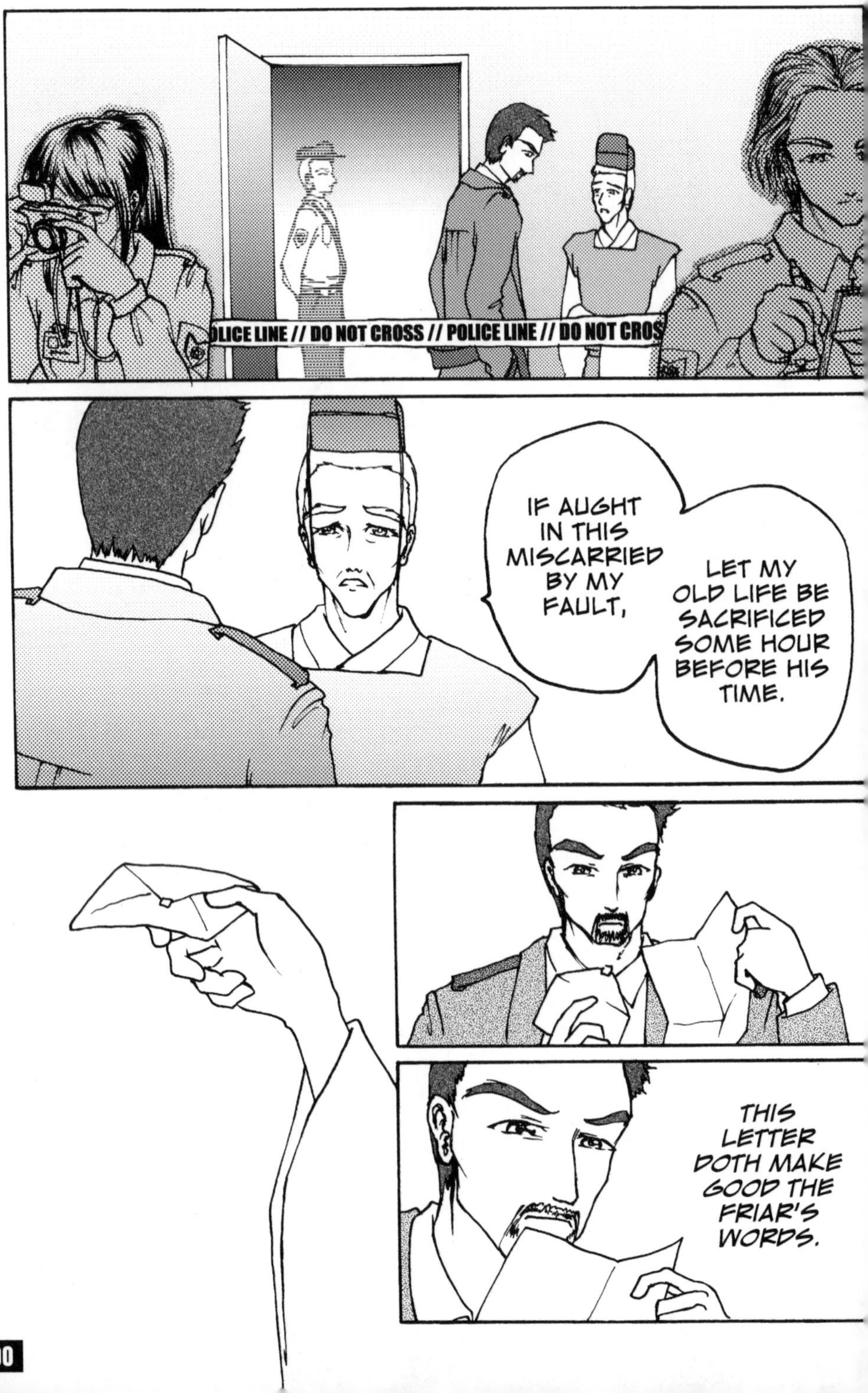
POLICE LINE // DO NOT CROSS // POLICE LINE // DO NOT CROS
IF AUGHT IN THIS MISCARRIED BY MY FAULT,
LET MY OLD LIFE BE SACRIFICED SOME HOUR BEFORE HIS TIME.
THIS LETTER DOTH MAKE GOOD THE FRIAR'S WORDS.

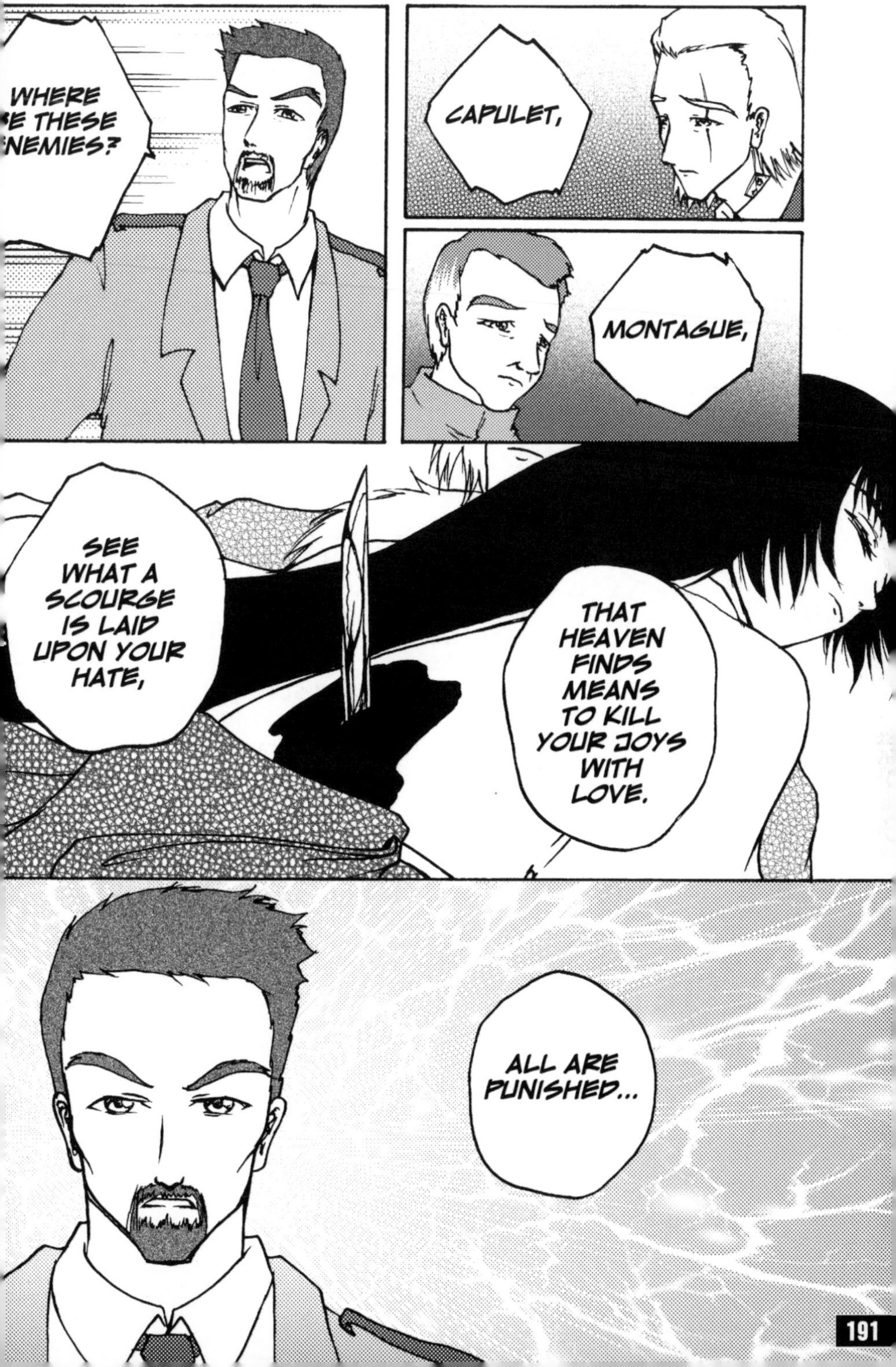
WHERE E THESE NEMIES?
CAPULET,
MONTAGUE,
SEE WHAT A SCOURGE IS LAID UPON YOUR HATE,
THAT HEAVEN FINDS MEANS TO KILL YOUR JOYS WITH LOVE.
ALL ARE PUNISHED...

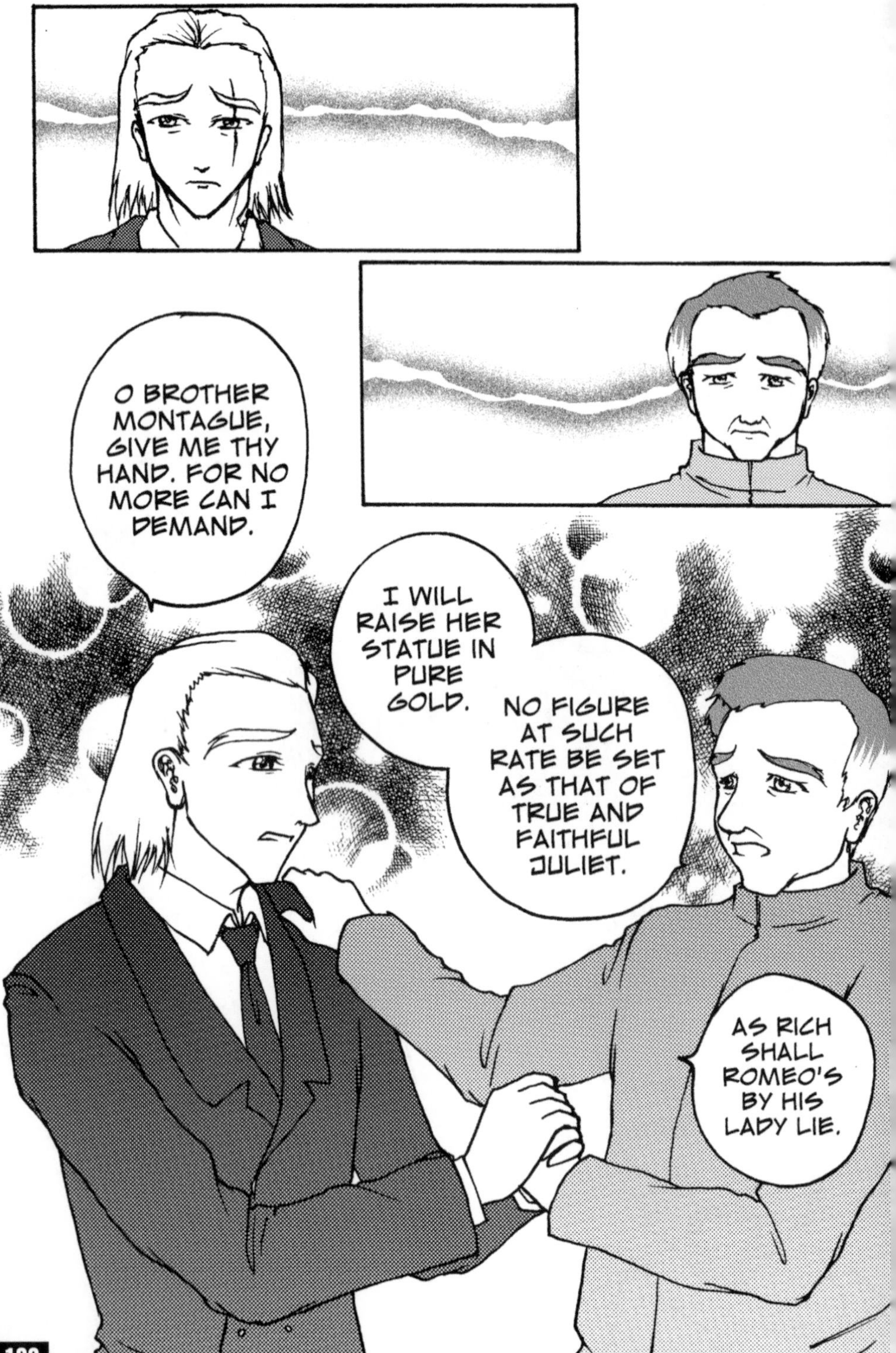
O BROTHER MONTAGUE, GIVE ME THY HAND. FOR NO MORE CAN I DEMAND.
I WILL RAISE HER STATUE IN PURE GOLD.
NO FIGURE AT SUCH RATE BE SET AS THAT OF TRUE AND FAITHFUL JULIET.
AS RICH SHALL ROMEO'S BY HIS LADY LIE.

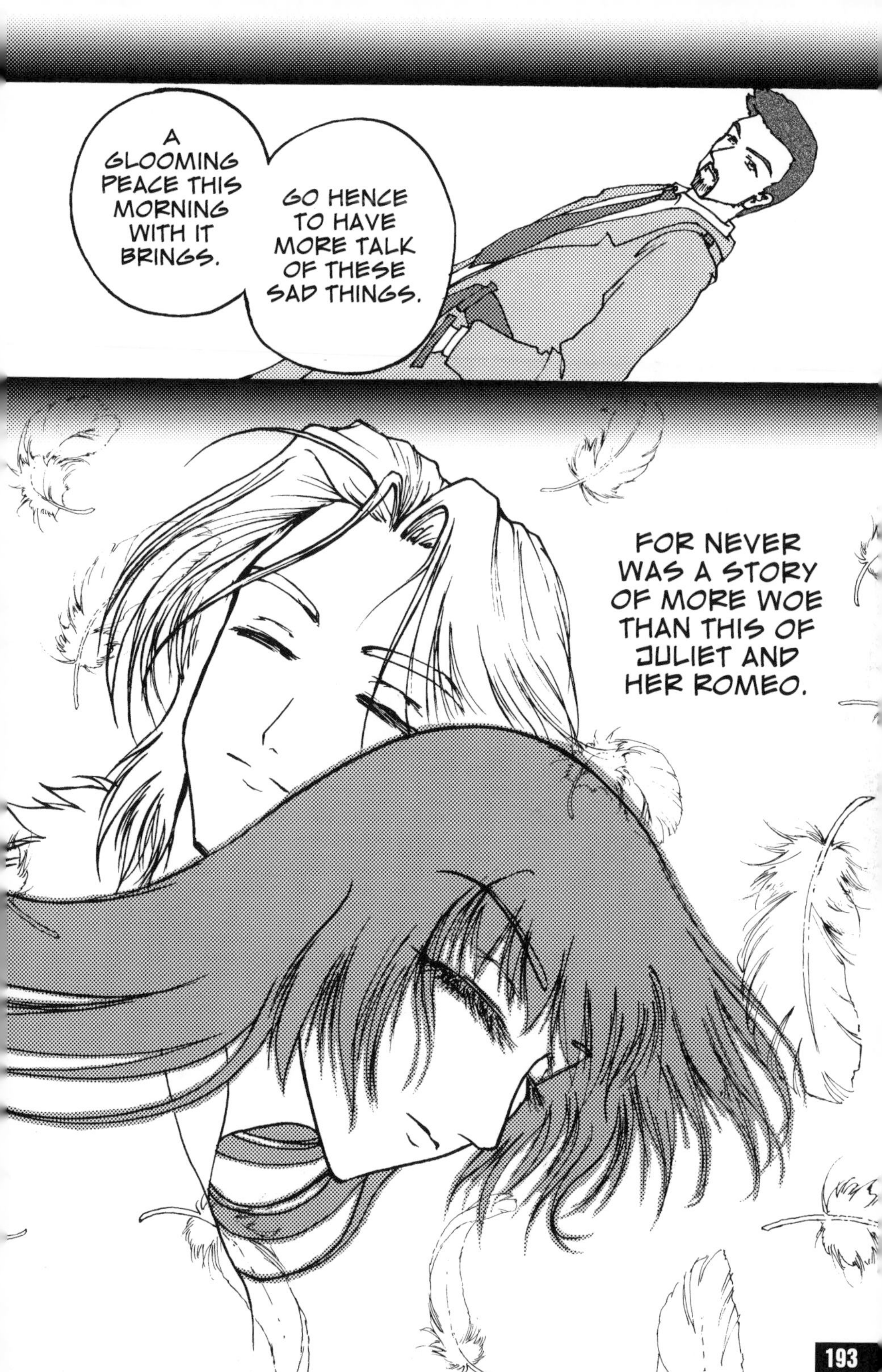
A GLOOMING PEACE THIS MORNING WITH IT BRINGS.
GO HENCE TO HAVE MORE TALK OF THESE SAD THINGS.
FOR NEVER WAS A STORY OF MORE WOE THAN THIS OF JULIET AND HER ROMEO.

PLOT SUMMARY OF ROMEO AND JULIET

The play begins with a street fight between two rival families, the Montagues and the Capulets. Benvolio, Romeo's friend, intervenes but is confronted by the fiery Tybalt who hates all Montagues. The Prince stops the brawl and orders both sides to cease feuding under pain of death. Romeo, brooding on his love for Rosaline, is absent from this fight. Benvolio advises him to end his melancholy by finding another woman.

Lord Capulet encourages the courtship of his daughter Juliet by the nobleman Paris and invites him to a celebration that night. Romeo and Benvolio hear of this party from Capulet's servant and decide to attend.

Lady Capulet tries to persuade Juliet to marry Paris. Juliet's old nurse adds comic commentary. Romeo, his friends Benvolio and the madcap Mercutio, gatecrash the Capulet party – and Romeo falls instantly in love with Juliet. He is recognized by the quarrelsome Tybalt. Later that same night, Romeo climbs into the Capulet garden and overhears Juliet confessing her love for him. They defy their hostile families by vowing to marry secretly the next day.

Romeo obtains Friar Laurence's consent to marry them and Juliet's nurse acts as go-between.

Tybalt encounters Benvolio and Mercutio and provokes a swordfight with Mercutio. Romeo arrives and tries to stop them but Mercutio is killed. Romeo, forced to take revenge, kills Tybalt and has to flee. The Prince imposes a penalty of exile on Romeo.

Juliet's nurse brings news of Tybalt's death and Romeo's banishment. Juliet despairs. Her father meanwhile arranges for her immediate marriage to Paris. Juliet tries to resist her parents' wishes but even her nurse advises her to forget Romeo. Juliet seeks Friar Laurence's help. He gives her a sleeping potion which will make her appear dead. He will summon Romeo from exile to arrive as she awakens in the tomb and they can escape together. But the plan goes badly wrong. Romeo hears of Juliet's death but does not get the Friar's message explaining the trick. He buys poison and plans to join Juliet in death.

Romeo, at Juliet's tomb, is confronted by Paris. They duel and Romeo kills him. Romeo takes the poison and dies as Juliet awakens. She refuses to leave with Friar Laurence but instead stabs herself with a dagger.

The Prince, the Capulets and Montagues are summoned to the scene of the two dead lovers.

A BRIEF LIFE OF WILLIAM SHAKESPEARE

He learned his craft the hard way. He soon won fame as a playwright with often-staged popular hits.

He and his colleagues formed a stage company, the Lord Chamberlain's Men, which built the famous Globe Theatre. It opened in 1599 but was destroyed by fire in 1613 during a performance of *Henry VIII* which used gunpowder special effects. It was rebuilt in brick the following year.

Shakespeare was a financially successful writer who invested his money wisely in property. In 1597, he bought an enormous house in Stratford, and in 1608 became a shareholder in London's Blackfriars Theatre. He also redeemed the family's honour by acquiring a personal coat of arms.

Shakespeare's birthday is traditionally said to be the 23rd of April – St George's Day, patron saint of England. A good start for England's greatest writer. But that date and even his name are uncertain. He signed his own name in different ways. "Shakespeare" is now the accepted one out of dozens of different versions.

He was born at Stratford-upon-Avon in 1564, and baptized on 26th April. His mother, Mary Arden, was the daughter of a prosperous farmer. His father John Shakespeare, a glove-maker, was a respected civic figure – and probably also a Catholic. In 1570, just as Will began school, his father was accused of illegal dealings. The family fell into debt and disrepute.

Will attended a local school for eight years. He did not go to university. The next ten years are a blank filled by suppositions. Was he briefly a Latin teacher, a soldier, a sea-faring explorer? Was he prosecuted and whipped for poaching deer?

We do know that in 1582 he married Anne Hathaway, eight years his senior, and three months pregnant. Two more children – twins – were born three years later but, by around 1590, Will had left Stratford to pursue a theatre career in London. Shakespeare's apprenticeship began as an actor and "pen for hire".

Shakespeare wrote over 40 works, including poems, "lost" plays and collaborations, in a career spanning nearly 25 years. He retired to Stratford in 1613, where he died on 23rd April 1616, aged 52, apparently of a fever after a "merry meeting" of drinks with friends. Shakespeare did in fact die on St George's Day! He was buried "full 17 foot deep" in Holy Trinity Church, Stratford, and left an epitaph cursing anyone who dared disturb his bones.

There have been preposterous theories disputing Shakespeare's authorship. Some claim that Sir Francis Bacon (1561–1626), philosopher and Lord Chancellor, was the real author of Shakespeare's plays. Others propose Edward de Vere, Earl of Oxford (1550–1604), or, even more weirdly, Queen Elizabeth I. The implication is that the "real" Shakespeare had to be a university graduate or an aristocrat. Nothing less would do for the world's greatest writer.

Shakespeare is mysteriously hidden behind his work. His life will not tell us what inspired his genius.

MANGA SHAKESPEARE ®

EDITORIAL

Richard Appignanesi: Series Editor

Richard Appignanesi was a founder and co-director of the Writers & Readers Publishing Cooperative and Icon Books where he originated the internationally acclaimed Introducing series. His own best-selling titles written for the series include *Freud*, *Postmodernism* and *Existentialism*. He is also the author of the fiction trilogy *Italia Perversa* and the novel *Yukio Mishima's Report to the Emperor*. He is currently associate editor of the art and culture journal *Third Text* and reviews editor of the journal *Futures*. His latest book *What do Existentialists Believe?* was released in 2006.

Nick de Somogyi: Textual Consultant

Nick de Somogyi works as a freelance writer and researcher, as a genealogist at the College of Arms, and as a contributing editor to *New Theatre Quarterly*. He is the founding editor of the Globe Quartos series, and was the visiting curator at Shakespeare's Globe, 2003–6. His publications include *Shakespeare's Theatre of War* (1998), *Jokermen and Thieves: Bob Dylan and the Ballad Tradition* (1986), and, as editor, *The Little Book of War Poems* (1999), and (from 2001) the *Shakespeare Folios* series for Nick Hern Books. His other work has included contributions to the Open University (1995) and Carlton Television (2000), BBC Radio 3 and Radio 4, and the National Portrait Gallery (2006).

ARTIST

Sonia Leong

Sonia's awards include Winner in Tokyopop's UK Rising Stars of Manga competition (2005/06) and Winner in NEO Magazine's 2005 Manga Competition. Responsible for Wacom-Europe's Manga Catgirl mascot and the comic artwork in the British movie, *Popcorn* (2007), Sonia was Lead Artist for the book *Draw Manga* by Sweatdrop Studios. She illustrates the *Manga Life* series of self-help comics by Infinite Ideas and is the artist for *Aya Takeo*, a full-colour comic published weekly online since April 2007. She also contributed to Image Comic's anthology *Comic Book Tattoo* inspired by the musician Tori Amos.

PUBLISHER

SelfMadeHero is a UK-based manga and graphic novel imprint, reinventing some of the most important works of European and world literature In 2008 SelfMadeHero was named **UK Young Publisher of the Year** at the prestigious British Book Industry Awards.

OTHER SELFMADEHERO TITLES:

EYE CLASSICS: *Nevermore, The Picture of Dorian Gray, The Trial, The Master and Margarita, Crime and Punishment, Dr. Jekyll and Mr. Hyde.*

SELF MADE HERO

www.selfmadehero.co